An Introduction to Air Pollution

2nd Revised Edition

An Introduction to Air Pollution

2nd Revised Edition

R. K. Trivedy

P. K. Goel

Department of Pollution Studies
Y.C. College of Science
Karad - 415124, Vidyanagar,
Maharashtra, India.

BSP **BS Publications**
A unit of **BSP Books Pvt., Ltd.**

4-4-309, Giriraj Lane, Sultan Bazar,
Hyderabad - 500 095 - A.P.
Phone : 040 - 23445605, 23445688

Sixth Reprint 2017

Published by :

BSP BS Publications

A unit of **BSP Books Pvt., Ltd.**

4-4-309/316, Giriraj Lane, Sultan Bazar,
Hyderabad - 500 095.
Phone : 040 - 23445605, 23445688
e-mail : info@bspbooks.net
www.bspbooks.net

Printed at

Aditya Offset Process (I) Pvt. Ltd.
Hyderabad.

Price : Rs. 350.00

ISBN : 978-81-7800-083-1

Preface

We are glad to present here second revised edition of "An Introduction to Air Pollution". The book, first published in 1995 by Techno Science Publication, Jaipur, was well received by all that prompted us to go for a revised edition especially after supreme court directive for states to start 'Environmental Science' course in undergraduate colleges of all universities in India.

Air pollution has emerged in the past few decades as a most challenging problem before the mankind, although air pollution existed even in the prehistoric time, never in the history the problem took as menacing proportion as now. The urban population is choked with combined onslaught of smoke spewing industries and automobile, while the countryside with industrial areas are silently suffering with hardly any notice of their woes.

However, since then the progress has been relatively faster on this front. Several comprehensive legislations have come out and air monitoring by industries as well as by regulatory authorities is more frequent. There is also considerable Indian participation in Global programmes in this field.

All pollution is taught at length in environmental science, engineering, life sciences, and social science courses. The syllabii of these courses are as vast and varied as the dimentions of this global problem and consequently there is ever increasing need of information on sources, effects and control of air pollution.

The present book is an attempt in this direction and has been particularly written to fill up the visible gaps in the information required by various users in India. Having taught this subject for over two and a half decades, we were constantly conscious of a comprehensive book in this field.

The book has 20 chapters and an appendix dealing extensively on history of air pollution, primary and secondary air pollutants, industrial sources of air pollution, automobiles generated air pollution, natural air pollution, the effects of air pollution on plants and Man as well as on property and cultural heritage. The global effects like ozone depletion and green house effects are discussed incorporating most latest developments in the field. Air pollution meteorology is discussed in considerable detail.

Air pollution control has been treated extensively. Sampling and analysis of air pollutants, air quality monitoring, biomonitoring and air quality management comprise various chapters. Necessary legislations have been also covered. Environmental criteria for siting the industries and green belts are also discussed.

This book covers a major portion of syllabii of various universities in both academic and professional courses and shall be primarily useful to them. Besides, it will be a ready source of information for industries, pollution control authorities, NGOs and all those concerned with air pollution in any way.

We are thankful to M/S BS Publications, Hyderabad for agreeing to publish the second revised edition.

R.K. Trivedy

P.K. Goel

Contents

1 General

Introduction

Air pollution has always been with Man although different aspects have been important at different times. Air pollution is mentioned in ancient literature. Air pollution became a serious problem in London during the late thirteenth century when coal was indiscriminately used by people as a cheap source of fuel. Several laws were passed and regulations imposed on use of coal. Spanish explorers have noticed 'smog' in Los Angeles in 16th century. Air pollution began to be noticed as a serious problem after a series of episodes in twentieth century. These dramatic episodes have demonstrated that in extreme cases, community air pollution can result in considerable loss of life and serious illness. The Bhopal episode, where toxic methyl isocyanate killed more than 2500 and injured over 2 lakh people, established air pollution to be a very serious problem.

Rapid advancement in industry, particularly in Europe and America led to heavy and noticeable pollution of air. First serious note of it was taken when in Meuse Valley in December 1930 a heavy fog associated with a very stable air mass, trapped emissions from neighbouring industrial plants, the residents immediately complained of respiratory trouble and many died in the episode. However, no measurement of air pollution was recorded. It happened again in Donora (Pennsylvania) in October 1948 where more than half of 1200 inhabitants of the town complained of respiratory troubles and over 20 people died. Measurement of air pollution was done in this case. Sulphur dioxide and suspended particulate matter were found to be responsible. However, the worst air pollution disaster took place in London city, resulting in about 4000 deaths.

Greatest industrial disaster leading to toxic air pollution took place in Bhopal where extremely poisonous gas, methyl isocyanate, released from the Union Carbide's pesticide manufacturing plant on December 3/4 1984. Over 2500 people died (unofficial figure is much higher) and over 1,50,000 injured in this industrial accident.

The air is mixture of several gases comprising pirmarly of nitrogen, oxygen, carbon dioxide and certain inert gases. Nitrogen forms the main bulk of volume of the air with a concentration of nearly 78% together with oxygen (21%). Average composition of common gases in the atmosphere is given in Table 1.1.

Table 1.1 Composition of clean dry air.

Component	By Volume	By Weight	Total mass (g × 10^{20})
Nitrogen	78.084%	75.51%	33.648
Oxygen	20.946%	23.15%	11.841
Argon	0.934%	1.28%	0.6555
Carbon dioxide	0.033%	0.046%	0.02333
Neon	18.180 ppm	12.50 ppm	6.36×10^{-4}
Helium	5.240 ppm	0.72 ppm	3.70×10^{-5}
Krypton	1.190 ppm	2.90 ppm	1.46×10^{-4}
Xenon	0.087 ppm	0.36 ppm	1.80×10^{-5}
Nitrous oxide	0.500 ppm	1.50 ppm	7.70×10^{-5}
Methane	2.0 ppm	1.20 ppm	6.20×10^{-5}
Hydrogen	0.5 ppm	0.03 ppm	2.0×10^{-5}
Ozone	0.01 ppm		

Composition of air, though, has changed over a period of time with the age of the earth, it can be considered fairly stable and suitable to life in the present era. The oxygen was absent in the atmosphere during the early history of the earth, but presently it constitutes about 20.95% of the atmospheric gases. The life is so inseparable from the atmosphere that both have evolved side by side. The first life did not require oxygen but it slowly evolved into the oxygen requiring organisms in line with evolution of the atmosphere.

The atmosphere is not infinite but extends upto certain height above the surface of the earth forming various characteristic layers called troposphere, stratosphere, mesosphere and thermosphere. The troposphere is the lowermost layer containing 80% of the gases and extending upto 10-12 km above the earth's surface. The lower troposphere upto 2 km is of greater interest as far as air pollution is considered.

Average human requires about 12 kg of air each day which is nearly12-15 times higher than the food we take. This is why even the small concentration of pollutants in the air become more significant in comparison to the similar levels present in the food.

1.1 Definition

A number of authors have defined air pollution in various ways. The most commonly refered definition is of Perkins (1974).

"Air pollution means the presence in the outdoor atmosphere of one or more contaminants such as dust, fumes, gas, mist, odour, smoke or vapour in quantities or characteristics and of duration such as to be injurious to human, plant or animal life or to property or which unreasonably interferes with the comfortable enjoyment of life and property".

Some others definitions are :

- "Unfavorable alteration to the environment".
- "The presence in the atmosphere of a substance or substances added directly or indirectly by an act of Man" (Arora 1999).

According to Bureau of Indian Standards IS 4167 (1980) 'air pollution' is the presence in ambient atmosphere of substances generally resulting from the activities of Man in sufficient concentration present for a significant time and under circumstances such as to interfere with comfort, health or welfare of persons or with reasonable use of enjoyment of property.

The Air Act of Govt. of India (Amendment 1987) defines air pollution as "Air pollution means any solid, liquid or gaseous substances present in the atmosphere in such concentration that may tend to be injurious to human beings or other living creatures or plants or property or enjoyment".

The pollutants in the atmosphere occur mostly as a result of human activities, though, significant quantities are also introduced naturally by volcanoes, dust storms, decomposition of organic matter and salt sprays. High standards of living at a minimal cost, without regard to the environment, together with greater industrialization are leading to the increased concentration of atmospheric pollutants causing dangerous effects. The combustion of fuels is one of the most significant sources of air pollutants. Large quantities of air are used in combustion of fuels, for example, nearly 15 kg of air is consumed in burning of 1 kg of fuel in automobiles. During the high temperature combustion, substantial quantities of inert nitrogen gas (N_2) are converted into the gaseous pollutant, NO_2. The pollutants in the air can also be formed by photochemical reactions involving atmospheric gases and certain primary pollutants, especially those emitted from the automobiles. The formation of ozone, peroxy acetyl nitrate (PAN) and acid rain etc. are some of the important examples of secondary pollutants formed photochemically in the atmosphere. Air pollutants and their main sources are described in Table 1.2.

Worldwide production of atmospheric aerosols is given in Table 1.2.

Table 1.2 Worldwide production of atmospheric aerosols.

Sources	Estimated production rate	
	X 10^6 Tons/day	% of total
Natural		
1. Primary		
A. Dust rise by wind	0.02-1.0	9.3
B. Sea spray	2.70-3.0	28.0
C. Extra terrestial (meteoric dust)	5.0-500*	–
D. Volcanic dust	0.01	0.09
E. Forest fires (intermittent)	0.008-0.40	3.8
2. Secondary		
A. Vegetation (hydrocarbons-terpines)	0.5-3.0	28.0
B. Sulphur cycle (Oxidation of H_2S to SO_4)	0.1-1.0	9.3
C. Nitrogen cycle (Ammonia NOx, NO_3)	0.1-1.0	9.3
D. Volcanoes (Volatiles H_2S and SO_2)	0.0001	0.0009
Total Natural	10.12	93.0
Anthropogenic		
1. Primary combustion and Industrial	0.1-0.3	2.8
2. Secondary		
A. Hydrocarbons	0.0007-0.007	0.007
B. Oxidation of SO_2 and H_2S to SO_4	0.3	2.8
C. Oxidation of NOx to NO_3	0.06	0.56
D. Ammonia	0.003	0.028
Total anthropogenic	0.67	7.0
Grand Total (all sources)	**10.79**	

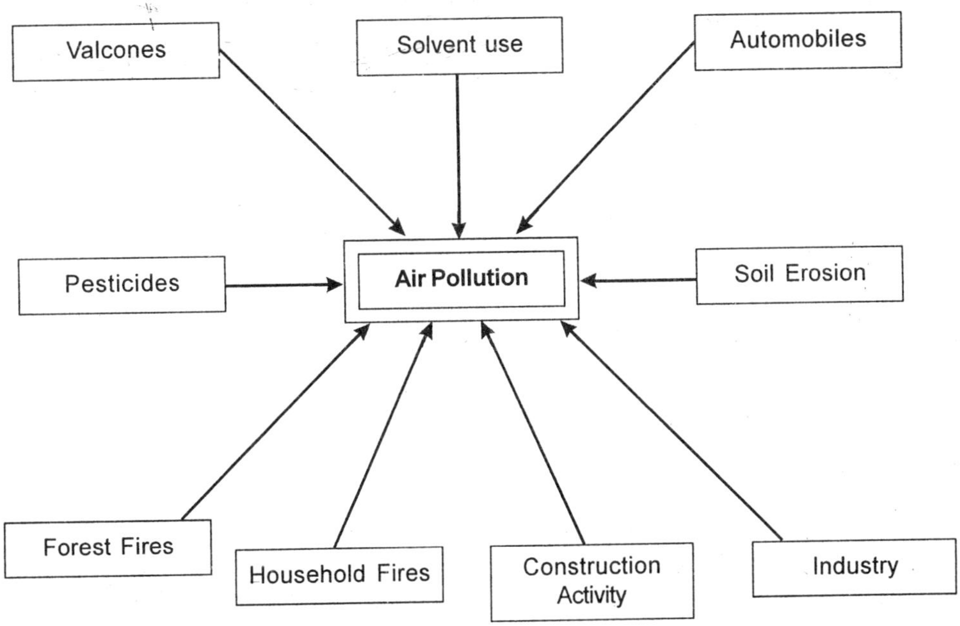

Figure 1.1 Major sources of air pollution

Major emission source categories for WHO criteria air pollution are given in Table 1.3, while the chief sources of air pollutants are provided in Table 1.4.

Table 1.3 Major emission sources categories for WHO criteria air pollution

Substances	Major emissions sources
Major Pollutants	
Particulate matter	Fuel combustion (95% in industrialized countries) Natural and Man made dust erosion Construction industry Mining operations Pottery, ceramics
Sulphur dioxide	Energy production especially in power plants Industrial combustion Industrial processes, especially sulphuric acid production Petroleum industry, oil refining
Nitrogen dioxide	Road traffic (50%) Power plants and industrial combustion Industrial processes especially nitric acid production Explosive industry
Carbon monoxide	Automobiles (90% in industrialized countries) Biomass burning
Ozone and other Photochemical oxidants	Not directly emitted but formed in the air Presence of nitrogen dioxide, volatile organic compound (VOC) and methane by silent elelctric discharge and by intense UV radiations.

Table 1.3 *Contd...*

Substances	Major emissions sources
Hydrogen sulphide	Decomposition of organic material Coke production Viscose rayon productions Waste water treatmen Wood pulp production with sulphate process Tanning industry
Hydrogen fluoride	Fertilizer industry, chemical industry, aluminium industry
Radon	Building materials Natural emissions from ground Well drilled tap water
Organic Substances	
Benezene	Gasoline powered motor vehicles without catalytic converters (80-85%) Chemical and petroleum industry Domestic heating Coke ovens
Carbon disulfide	Production of viscose rayon fibers Coal gasification
1,2-dichloroethane	Synthesis of vinyl chloride Production of ethylene diamines Use as solvent and fumigant
Formaldehyde	Catalytic cracking in petroleum refining industry Charcoal production Internal combustion engines Resin and formaldehyde production
Vinyl Chloride	PVC (Polyvinyl chloride) production
Volatile Organic Carbon (VOC)	Road traffic Use of solvents
Trace Metals	
Arsenic	Non-ferrous metal industry Stationary combustion sources Use as catalyst and reagant in inorganic chemical industry Pesticides use
Cadmium	Metal production, especially zinc processing Electroplating Production of plastics; pigments and batteries Fertilizers processing and application Natural sources, especially volcanoes.
Chromium	Production of chromium compounds Chromium production from chromite
Lead	Road traffic, maily gasoline-powered vehicles Non-ferrous metal industry Iron and steel industry Production of lead-acid batteries
Manganese	Use as additive in metallurgical processes Production of dry-cell batteries Chemical industry Glass leather and textiles industries Fertilizers use
Mercury	Coal combustion in stationary sources

Table 1.4 Air pollutants and their chief sources.

Pollutant	Sources
1. Particulates	
Dust	Grinding, abrasion, quarrying, erosion, automobiles, construction, industries.
SPM	Mining, wind erosion, spraying, grinding, power station, cement, steel industries, sugar industries, automobiles
2. Sulphur oxides (SO_x)	Power houses, smelters, fuel combustion, oil refineries, sulphuric acid plants, automobiles
3. Hydrogen sulphide	Petroleum industries, wastewater treatment, tanneries, oil refineries
4. Nitrogen oxides (NO_x)	Fuel burning, acid manufacturing, automobile exhaust
5. Carbon monoxide	Metabolic activity, fuel combustion
6. Carbon monoxide	Fuel burning, automobile exhaust, mines
7. Ozone	Photochemical reactions
8. Lead	Automobile exhaust
9. Organic solvents	Vapourization from fuels, solvent use, paint, pesticides, cooking, cosmetics
10. Mercury	Pesticides, paints, laboratories
11. Fluorides (HF)	Glass and ceramics, cement factories, aluminium industry, fertilizer industry

Air pollution is a mixture of gases, solids and liquids in the form of gas, vapour, odour, smoke, dust, mist, soot and grime etc. The traditional definition of air pollution takes into consideration of the pollutants which are chemical entities excluding physical factors like heat, noise or harmful radiations which travel through air. However, noise has been included under air pollution in some cases, like the amended Air Pollution Act 1987 of India.

An air contaminant in the air can be present in such quantities that may or may not be harmful. Under the normal circumstances, the air is considered to be polluted, when the quantities of pollutants are at such levels that can cause some harm. However, the balance of life on the earth is so delicate and not fully understood, that even the so called harmless quantities may affect the environment in a number of ways.

As composition of the gases in the air remains almost constant, any rise in its components can be considered as a kind of air pollution which may have widespread ecological implications on global scale. Special mention can be made here of the large quantities of carbon dioxide released into the air by combustion of coal and other carbonaceous fuels. These excessive quantities, though, may not be harmful to life, but can alter the earth's heat balance by "green house effect" in such a way as to result in the global warming, the consequences of which may be catastrophic.

Almost all kind of life, ranging from microorganisms to higher organisms, has been found to be affected by air pollution. However, the effects considered to be most significant are those on the human health and vegetation. The effects on humans can be more specific appearing in the short term, and those long term subtle effects which are difficult to be studied. The respiratory troubles are by far the most frequent effects of air pollution. Carbon monoxide produce very specific effects like suffocation due to its binding with oxygen carrying sites on the haemoglobin. Certain particulates present in the air also develop allergies in the people.

Air pollution affects the plant species in a variety of ways, reducing their growth and yield. Air pollution has resulted into great damage to our economic crops all over the world. Another aspect of the air pollution effect is the damage caused to the physical materials like the buildings, paper, textiles, leather, electricals, paints, and several such items of our daily use. It is now often talked of the cost of air pollution in context to the vast damage caused by it.

Meteorology is an important technical area in the study of air pollution which governs the accumulation of air pollutants in the atmosphere. The pollutants released into the atmosphere do not accumulate indefinitely, but tend to decrease with time due to their global sink. The halflife periods of different pollutants in the air can vary from few hours to several years. It is, however, the buildup of local concentrations of pollutants over a short period of time which is of most concern from the standpoint of human health and vegetation damage. Under certain conditions of meteorology like stable and windless atmosphere, the pollutant concentrations grow upto dangerous levels causing widespread effects. Most of the catastrophic air pollution episodes in the world like that of London and Los Angeles smogs have occurred only under adverse meteoroligical conditions.

Pollution problems cannot be tackled by technology alone, since social and economical aspects must also be considered. For any control strategy, the formulation of laws and regulations are must as the society cannot be governed without law. It should, however, be borne in mind that no environmental problem can be solved by scientists, technocrats, and law unless each individual understand his responsibility towards the society and personally involves in fight against pollution.

1.2 History of Air Pollution

The origin of air pollution on the earth can be traced from the time when Man started using wood fire as a means of cooking and space heating. With the discovery and increasing use of coal, the air pollution problems started to become more pronounced, especially in the urban areas, and it was recognised as long as 700 years ago in London the menace of smoke pollution which prompted King Edward I in 1273 to make the first antipollution law to restrict people using coal for domestic heating. In the year 1300 a further Act was passed banning the use of coal during the sessions of Parliament. The defying of the law led even to imposition of capital punishment in some cases.

The menace of smoke pollution remained, however, through the centuries but it started to emerge as a severe problem only from late eighteenth century with the start of industrial revolution in the west leading to the large scale burning of coal.

The first book on air pollution seems to be of John Evelyn, a writer-scientist, in 1661 who described the air pollution problems and attemted for their solutions. The measures used even today like shifting of industry from cities and use of green belts were first advocated in that book. The book was so informative that its second edition came even after almost a century later in 1772.

The air pollution problems started to further aggravate with the rise of chemical industry during the mid-eighteenth century which led to the dumping of acid fumes and other chemicals in the atmosphere. The first Alkali Act was passed in 1863 by Royal Commission to set the limits of acid discharges in waste gases.

When the air pollution problems in Europe, especially U.K., were surfacing fast, U.S.A. did not have much problems mainly because of the sparsely populated areas and lack of big cities and towns. The coal was also substituted by petroleum and gas little early and meteorological conditions were not adverse in several cities. It was only in the late nineteenth century that some realization was made of the presence of air pollution over certain cities, but it did not cause any concern because of the heavy demand of energy for domestic heating and industrial use. However, the air pollution levels, caused by the presence of smoke and sulphur dioxide rose in several cities for which the reports were filed first in 1907 for St. Louis, in 1910 for Chicago and in 1917 for Pittsburg. Smoke Control Laws in United States were passed in late 1800s with first Law in 1881 by Chicago. By 1912 almost all the big cities have passed such laws.

As the development and industrilization continued to take place all over the world, the rise in atmospheric pollution also continued finally culminating in the large scale deaths and morbidity due to air pollution disasters in 1930 in Meuse Valley, Belgium, 1948 in Donora, Penssylvania and 1952 in London. Alone in London more than 4000 deaths were reported due to accumulation of air pollutants over the city for about 5 days. As a consequence, the Beaver Committee on air pollution was established in 1953 and the Clean Air Act was passed in 1956 in Britain. Today, London, among the big cities, is considered as one of the cleanest cities in the world.

Another kind of air pollution problems emerged in the begining of twentieth century with the development of transportation system and large scale use of petrol and diesel. The severe air quality problems due to formation of photochemical smog from the combustion residuals of diesel and petrol were felt for the first time in Los Angeles. The problems of air pollution due to automobile exhaust are still quite serious in many cities of the developed as well as developing countries like India. The Air Pollution Control Act in India was passed only in 1981 and Motor Vehicle Act for controlling the air pollution, only very recently. The chronological sequence of some important events in the history of air pollution is given in Table 1.5.

Table 1.5 Important events in the history of air pollution.

Year (A.D.)	Event
1300	King Edward-I prohibited use of coal during sessions of Parliament
1578	Elizabeth-I, annoyed by coal smoke, complained to the Parliament
1661	John Evelyn book on air pollution
1772	Second edition of John Evelyn's books
1819	First English Select Committee to study air pollution
1843	Second English Select Committee to study air pollution
1845	Parliament passes law in U.K. requiring locomotives to consume own smoke
1866	First paper on effects on health due to air pollution
1875	Cattle deaths at London due to air pollution
1905	Dr. Des Voeux used term "smoke-fog" deaths. Presently it is called smog.
1919	First paper on automobile air pollution (carbon monoxide effects)
1930	Meuse Valley, Belgium air pollution disaster
1948	Donora, Pennsylvania air pollution disaster
1952	London smog disaster
1955	Frist U.S. Federal legislation
1956	British Clean Air Act
1963	U.S. Clean Air Act
1970	U.S. amended Clean Air Act
1975	U.S. Primary standards to be reached
1981	Air Pollution (Control & Prevention) Act in India

1.3 Air Pollution Disasters and Accidents

The continuous increase in the level of atmospheric pollutants in certain parts of the world resulted into some disastrous episodes leading to death and morbidity of a large number of people and animals. In all the cases, adverse meteorology played an important role promoting the accumulation of pollutants over the areas for several days.

Besides, accidental release of toxic or hazardous pollutants in the air can also result in mass death or morbidity. This, however, occurs as isolated incidents and cannot be compared, in effects, with the general air pollution. The usefulness of the detailed study of the air pollution disasters lies in the fact that they often throw light on the levels of pollution that can cause immediate health effecs and death.

1.3.1 *Air Pollution Disasters*

***Meuse Valley (Belgium)*, 1930**

Though the air pollution disasters had been taking place since early times due to volcanoes, or by smoke during the eighteenth and nineteenth centuries, the first major episode occurred in Meuse Valley in Belgium in 1930 killing more than 60 people. It is deep with hills 80-120 m high on either side, narrow and highly industrialized valley of the Meuse river. The city had several industrial plants including steel works, sulphuric acid plants, glass factories, zinc works, and a fertilizer plant.

Begining from Dec. 1,1930 in the winter, the adverse meteorology for 5 days with inversions and windless conditions resulted in the accumulation of smoke and abnormal pollutant levels in the valley over the population. By the third day many people became ill and started dying; most of the deaths occurred on the 4th and 5th day. Though, the people of all sex and age were affected but most of the deaths occurred in older people suffereing previously with heart or lung troubles. Cattle, birds and even rats were reported to be killed.

The symptoms of illness were acute pulmonary attacks with cough, throat irritation, shortlessness of breath, nausea and vomiting. The chief responsible factor for this episode was considered to be the abrnormal accumulation of SO_2 and SO_3 aerosols released from the industrial establishments. However, our current knowledge indicates that the levels of these pollutants present there were unlikely to cause that much damage. It seems possible that the hydrofluoric acid, originating from certain factories in combination with sulphur oxides might have caused this damage, though, the truth can never be proved.

Donora (Penssylvania, U.S.A.) 1948

Donora lies in a horseshoe shaped valley of the Monongahela river near Pittsburg. The major industrial plants in 1948 included a steel mill, a zinc plant and a sulphuric acid plant. It had a small population of about 1,41,000 people.

Due to adverse meteorological conditins of windlessness and temperature inversions, started from 26 Oct. 1948, the smoke and pollutants along with the fog started to buildup in the atmosphere over the city for about 5 days. Everything was black with gas and soot. This resulted in the death of 20 people; 43% of the population became sick, out of which 10% were severely affected. The symptoms of illness included irritation of eye, nose and throat; pulmonary trouble with coughing and respiratory irritation; vomiting and headache. No actual measurements of the pollutants were taken during the time of disaster but studies showed later that it might have been caused by the synergistic effects of two or more pollutants involving mainly sulphur dioxide, sulphuric acid aerosol, particulates and probably some oxidation products.

London, 1952

London, situated on the banks of river Thames, suffered perhaps from the most catastrophic air pollution in the history causing more than 4000 deaths. The city used large quantities of high sulphur coal for domestic heating, electricity generation (Thermal Power Plant) and other industrial establishments leading to the generation of high quantities of smoke and sulphur oxides.

The problem started with the development of adverse meteorological conditions with temperature inversions and windlessness for nearly 5 days from 4 Dec. to 8 Dec. 1952 during the winters. The air pollutants like smoke and sulphur oxides started to buildup in the atmosphere and the white fog accumulated over the city turned black forming a "Pea soup smog" with almost zero visibility. Within 2 days of the formation of this smog, peope started suffering from pulmonary disorders, cough, nasal discharges, sore throat, vomiting and irritation of bronchi and eyes which finally led to the excess death of people. The maximum sufferers were elderly people having history of heart and respiratory troubles.

The major cause of the episode is considered to be the unusually higher concentrations of sulphur dioxide and soot which reached upto the level of 4000 $\mu g/m^3$ each, several times higher than their normal concentrations of 50 $\mu g/m^3$.

Similar adverse meteorological conditions in London after 1952 resulted further in January 1955 (240 excess deaths), January 1956 (1000 excess deaths), December 1956 (400 excess deaths), December 1957 (800 excess deaths), January 1959 (200 excess deaths) and December 1962 (850 excess deaths). In December 1962, the SO_2 concentration was almost similar to that of Dec. 1952 but the number of excess deaths were quite lower. This was perhaps mainly because of the much reduced level of particulates after the enformcement of British Clean Air Act in 1956.

New York (U.S.A.)

The State of New York in U.S.A. has experienced several episodes of air pollution causing excess deaths, notable among them are those occurred during November 1953, November 1962 and November 1966.

All these episodes occurred as a result of the formation of a high pressure anticyclonic weather system over the area causing almost motionless wind conditions. The dispersion and dilution of pollutants diminished considerably resulting in their accumulation to high concentration over a period of days.

During November 1966, one such high pressure area developed over Thanksgiving in the New York State causing about 168 excess deaths of people. The 24 hour average concentration of SO_2 reached upto 0.51 ppm with maximum hourly values of 1.02 ppm associated with higher levels of particulates which were supposed to be the major cause of this disaster.

Los Angeles (U.S.A.)

Los Angeles basin in situated in the southern California in U.S.A. having mountains on north and east of the city. During 1940s it was realised that a grey haze develops frequently in the atmosphere which obstructs the mountain view, causes irritation and watering in the eyes, and mottling and wilting of the crops and flowers.

Initially, it was thought that the problems are mainly due to the presence of particulates and sulphur dioxide from the oil refineries in the area. In 1947, regulations were passed to limit the levels of SO_2 and particulates. The peculiar symptoms of the grey haze, however, still existed despite the diminishing of SO_2 and particulates levels, and it was soon realized that the nature of the air pollutants involved here is different from that of the pollutants caused disasters in St. Lewis, Meuse Valley, Donora and London. It was shown at the same time that the effects observed in Los Angeles can be reproduced by passing ultraviolet light through the mixture of nitrogen oxides and hydrocarbons produced by burning of petroleum. This resulted in the formation of several secondary pollutants like ozone, peroxy acetyl nitrate (PAN), free radicals and other such oxidants.

The problem in Los Angeles starts from production of higher quantities of autoexhaust pollutants due to plying of large number of motor vehicles. These pollutants, especially oxides of nitrogen and hydrocarbons, in the presence of sunlight (photochemically) are converted into various oxidants (see Chapter 3) which are responsible for the typical symptoms of eye watering and mottling of crops.

The problem in Los Angeles is aggravated during some parts of the year, mainly winters, due to development of subsidence inversions caused by the warm winds from the high pressure area over the Pacific. This results in trapping of the pollution in the inverted layer at quite low elevation from the ground.

The horizontal air movement is also quite low during this period and whatever winds prevail are obstructed by the mountains on the sides of the city, further preventing dispersal of the pollutants.

Tokyo (Japan)

Tokyo is one of the most populous cities of the world having a very large number of motor vehicles. The monitoring of air in the city indicated the rising levels of air pollutants, especially oxidants, during the day caused by photochemial reactions involving the pollutants from auto-exhaust. On 18 June, 1970 a thick fog was reported in the morning which disappeared by noon, but the visibility still remained quite low. During noon people complaned of eye irritation and several school children suffered from smarting of eyes and sore throat associated with difficulty in breathing. More than 6000 people were treated in the hospital for smog poisoning.

It was realised that the symptoms of this illness were chiefly because of the large scale formation of the photochemical oxidants in the atmosphere. The concentration of SO_2 was 0.39 ppm together with the formation of sulphuric acid mist that contributed maximm to the production of the health symptoms.

1.3.2 *Air Pollution Accidents*

Poza Rico (Mexico)

Poza Rico is a town in Mexico known for its oil refining and gas production business. On November 24, 1950 there was an accidental release of hydrogen sulphide gas from the oil refining establishment which left 22 people dead and more than 300 suffering from typical hydrogen sulphide poisoning with symptoms of loss of sense of smell, cough, irritation, nausea and headache. People of all ages and sexes were affected.

Though, the source of the spillage was closed within half an hour, the gas had already spread by that time and the adverse meteorological conditions facilitated its accumulation in the atmosphere for a longer period of time over the population.

Seveso (Italy)

On July 10, 1976, an accident occurred at Seveso near Milan in Italy when an explosion took place in a pesticide chemical factory manufacturing 2, 4, 5-T, resulting in release of a white cloud of poisonous gas containing a dioxin (TCDD). The dioxins are extremely poisonous to the organisms.

The gas cloud was settled over the city leading to a great damage to the population and ecology of the area. The whole episode resulted in severe illness and death of some people and small animals. About 187 people showed skin chloracne (boils & pimples), 46 showed other skin and liver complications, a few reported abortions, and many newly born children were found to have certain deformities.

Soil was contaminated in large area. The floods which followed the incident further spread the pollutants into the environment. The spread of the dioxin also helped by the sell of vegetables grown in the contaminated environment. Realizing gravity of the situation, the highly affected area near the factory was later completely evacuated.

Bhopal (India)

Bhopal gas leak disaster can be considered as the worst industrial disaster in the history of Mankind. On the night of 3/4 December 1984, an obscure town like Bhopal became internationally infamous when a poisonous gas, methyl isocyanate (MIC) was released from Union Carbide India Ltd., a subsidiary of Union Carbide, a multinational company based in U.S.A.

Although estimates vary, about 40 tons of lethal MIC escaped the tanks in the factory and was released into the atmosphere causing panic, death and havoc unparalleled in the world history. The gas quickly spread and caused severe eye, lung irritation and vomiting. People started running helter-skelter and thousands lay dead in the streets of Bhopal in the morning, and another 50,000 reported to various hospitals for minor to serious aliments. The worst effect was on poor slum dwellers living close to the factory. Th exact death toll is not known by anybody. The Indian Government's figure is 2,352 but people's guess vary from 3,000 to 20,000.

About 2,00,000 people have been seriously affected. Their woes ranging from temporary blindness to permanent disability. A large number of cases of abortions and stillbirth were reported. Even after many years people were suffering from various ailments. It caused serious socio-economic problems with thousands losing their livelihood due to various disabilities or losing the only earning member of the family.

Thousands of cattle also perished in the disaster and curious problems arose in their disposal. Having inhaled large quantity of MIC, they could release it during disposal. They were buried carefully 5 km away in a remote area using large quantity of salt, bleaching powder, lime and caustic soda to neutralize any release of gas after their decay.

Several studies were conducted on vegetation to observe the harmful effects on plants. In plants, MIC competes with CO_2 in photosynthesis resulting in suppression of growth. Several structural changes were reported in plant species like coriander, carrot, cabbage, cauliflower, spinach and some grasses. The reproduction and setting of fruits were also affected in almost all the plant species. The gas has also affected the soil microflora as well as waterbodies. The long term effects were studied under a CSIR, India sponsored programme of continuing studies on Bhopal gas leak effects.

The exact causes of Bhopal disaster are not yet known. Various theories including sabotage were contemplated, but it remains a fact that gas leaked even after 5 safety systems like water curtains, spare tank, vent gas scrubber, water spray and freezing chamber were available. MIC has been described as a dangerous chemical, lighter than water but twice as heavy as air. It has vigorous heat producing reactions with many substances, including water. In the presence of a catalyst, it can react with itself, producing a violent runaway reaction.

1.4 Air Quality in World and India

1.4.1 *The World Air Quality*

The World Health Organization (WHO) and United Nations Environment Programme (UNEP) are collaborating since 1974 on an urban ambient air monitoring project and their recent report shows that most of the megacities of the world are still quite polluted with certain air pollutants exceeding the specified limits.

Suspended particulate matter (SPM) is the single most threatening air pollutant with nearly 80% of the world's magacities exceeding its maximum permissible level of 60-90 μg/m^3. The three megacities of India, Bombay, Calcutta and Delhi figure in the list of polluted cities of the world mainly becuase of their higher level of SPM. For sulphur dioxide the WHO permissible limit of 40-60 μg/m^3 is exceeded by nearly 50% of these cities. According to a U.N. report appeared in its publication entitled "State the World's Environment 1972-92", 900 million people in urban areas are exposed to unhealthy levels of SO_2, which falls to the earth's surface as acid rain. More than one billion people in the world are exposed to excessive levels of soot.

The status of the six important pollutants, SO_2, NO_2, CO, O_3, lead and SPM in relation to the WHO limits in 20 megacities of the world are given in Table 1.6. Table 1.7 indicates the levels of SO_2 in 16 GEMS network cities between 1976 and 1980. While adequate data are available for others, limited data are available for NO_2, and O_3. The data indicate that the once highly polluted cities of the world like London, New York and Tokyo have now levels of SO_2 and SPM much bleow the WHO limits. With regard to these two pollutants the most polluted cities of the world are Beijing, Seol, Shanghai, Rio de Janeiro and Mexico city where the levels of SO_2 and SPM usually exceed the limits by a factor of two or above. Mexico city seems to be worst polluted in the world where all the six pollutants, SO_2, NO_2, CO, O_3, lead and SPM exceed the WHO limits.

Table 1.6 Status of air pollution in some metropolitan cities of the world, 1992 (based on a report of WHO & UNEP)

City	SO_2	NO_2	CO	O_3	Pb	SPM
Bangkok	C	C	C	C	B	A
Beijing	A	C	D	B	C	A
Bombay	C	C	C	D	C	A
Buênos Aires	D	D	A	D	C	B
Cairo	D	D	B	D	A	A
Calcutta	C	C	D	D	C	A
Delhi	C	C	C	D	C	A
Jakarta	C	C	B	B	B	A
Karachi	C	D	D	D	A	A
London	C	C	B	C	C	C
Los Angeles	C	B	B	A	C	B
Manila	C	D	D	D	B	A
Mexico City	A	B	A	A	B	A
Moscow	D	B	B	D	C	B
New York	C	C	B	B	C	C
Rio de Janeiro	B	D	C	D	C	B
Sao Paulo	C	B	B	A	C	B
Seol	A	C	C	C	C	A
Shanghai	B	D	D	D	D	A
Tokyo	C	C	C	A	D	C

A = Serious problem, WHO guidelines exceeded by more than a factor of two.
B = Moderate to heavy pollution, WHO guidelines exceeded by upto a factor of two.
C = Low pollution, WHO guidelines normally met with.
D = No data available or insufficient data for assessment.

Table 1.7 Mean annual concentration of SO_2 between 1976 and 1980 for cities in the GEMS network (Global environmental monitoring systems network).

City	Country	Annual mean SO_2 (pphm)
Milan	Italy	7.2
Sau Paulo	Brazil	3.7
Zaqreb	Ugoslavia	2.8
London	United Kingdom	2.8
Brussels	Belgium	2.7
Tehran	Iran	2.3
Madrid	Spain	2.3
Manila	Philippines	2.1
Tokyo	Japan	1.4
Montreal	Canada	1.4
Sydney	Australia	1.3
Calcutta	India	1.2
Amsterdam	Netherlands	1.1
Dublin	Ireland	1.1
Hong Kong	-	1.1
Aukland	New Zealand	0.6

Note : United States Environmental Protection Agency standard is 2.0 pphm
pphm = parts per hundred million

Source : Various GEMS Reports

Ozone is a secondary pollutant generated in the atmosphere by the photochemical reactions involving some of the constituents of auto-exhaust. The accumulation of this depends upon the local meteorological conditions. A number of cities especially Beijing, Jakarta, Los Angeles, Mexico city, New York, Sao Paulo and Tokyo have been found to buildup considerable quantities of ozone. Lead, also a product of auto-exhaust, seems to be problemetic only in the Asian cities of Bangkok, Cairo, Jakarta, Karachi and Manila.

Akland et al. (1992) indicated that the progress in controlling the air pollution sources has been reflected by the downward trends in the levels of SO_2 and particulates in many cities of the developed world, but the emissions are still increasing in the developing countries, which is likely to result in an increased risk to the public health of the city dwellers.

1.4.2 *Air Quality in India*

The data on Indian ambient air quality are available mostly on the sulphur dioxide, nitrogen oxides and suspended particulates (SPM) with some sporadic information on carbon monoxide, hydrocarbons and heavy metals. The air quality data in India are being regularly collected by Central Pollution Control Board (CPCB) and National Environmental Engineering Research Institute (NEERI) from several cities and industrial areas. The data obtained by CPCB during 1990 in various cities of India are given in Tables 1.8 and 1.9.

Table 1.8 Minimum and maximum values ($\mu g/m^3$) of various air pollutants for the mean annual ranges in India (data based on CPCB annual report, 1991-1992.

Area	SO_2		NO_X		SPM	
	Mean min	Mean max	Mean min	Mean max	Mean min	Mean max
Industrial	36.4 (Aupara)	81.8 (Howrah)	42.8 (Ahmedabad)	90.8 (Howrah)	378 (Gajraula)	837 (Dehradun)
Commercial	13.6 (Pune)	55.9 (Jamshedpur)	20.6 (Madras)	51.5 (Delhi)	273 (Pune)	594 (Bhopal)
Residential	19.5 (Calcutta)	78.2 (Jamshedpur)	36.6 (Ahmedabad)	101.2 (Kota)	329 (Bhilai)	566 (Kanpur)

CPCB = Central Pollution Control Board, India.

Table 1.9 Air quality in some important residential areas of India. (Based on annual report of CPCB, 1991-1992).

Area	SO_2	NO_2	SPM
Agra	5.8 - 43.8	4.2 - 20.8	120 - 942
Ahmedabad	2.0 - 204.5	6.7 - 195.8	1 - 1069
Bangalore	1.7 - 48.1	5.0 - 20.1	19 - 136
Baroda	2.5 - 165.1	3.0 - 87.7	45 - 911
Bhilai	1.0 - 57.3	9.7 - 41.8	94 - 702
Bhopal	0.0 - 34.1	4.5 - 49.5	52 - 454
Bombay	6.0 - 87.3	7.3 - 65.2	64 - 474
Calcutta	6.0 - 81.3	3.0 - 41.2	39 - 601
Chandigarh	0.9 - 15.0	2.7 - 55.2	50 - 663
Cochin	6.0 - 21.5	3.0 - 19.2	11 - 204
Delhi	2.0 - 62.3	3.0 - 81.8	26 - 1480
Dhanbad	7.9 - 122.7	10.9 - 73.4	29 - 699
Gajraula	18 - 128.8	7.5 - 137.6	162 - 422
Hyderabad	3.0 - 28.0	3.0 - 52.0	52 - 407
Indore	6.8 - 12.9	9.1 - 30.6	95 - 928
Jaipur	5.0 - 5.3	5.0 - 44.3	102 - 1329
Kanpur	2.8 - 19.8	3.0 - 42.2	44 - 1541
Kota	3.6 - 40.2	39.6 - 281.9	22 - 649
Ludhiana	0.0 - 53.2	2.8 - 78.5	78 - 859
Madras	0.5 - 94.9	3.0 - 118.9	27 - 306
Mysore	7.8 - 26.3	3.3 - 38.6	23 - 142
Nagda	2.2 - 51.7	3.4 - 73.4	78 - 713
Nagpur	2.2 - 37.0	3.0 - 71.8	29 - 499
Parwanoo (H.P.)	0.9 - 13.9	1.8 - 48.3	35 - 141
Pondichery	0.0 - 28.2	2.1 - 43.7	47 - 194
Pune	4.0 - 42.5	5.8 - 70.2	30 - 316
Satna (M.P.)	26.2 - 38.7	11.4 - 13.4	114 - 455
Silvassa (D & N)	1.0 - 22.5	1.2 - 11.8	1 - 273
Surat	5.8 - 71.8	7.5 - 119.2	8 - 776
Tuticorin	4.7 - 47.9	2.6 - 20.4	10 - 118

Units = $\mu g/m^3$

CPCB = Central Pollution Control Board, India.

Fig. 1.2 gives the data on SPM, SO_2 and NO_2 collected by NEERI. The data indicate that it is SMP that occurs outside the stipulated 24-hourly ambient air quality standards for the maximum period followed by sulphur dioxide and nitrogen oxides. It was found, however, that the maximum violations occurred in the industrial areas.

The air quality data of India further reveals the following facts.

1. For SO_2 and NO_2, the values are comparatively higher in the industrial and residential areas than the commercial areas.
2. For SPM, comparatively much higher values were recorded in industrial areas than the residential and commercial areas.
3. The mean maximum values for both SO_2 and NO_2 for the industrial areas were recorded at Howrah, while for SPM at Dehradan.
4. For commercial areas, highest mean maximum values were 55.9μ g/m^3 for SO_2 at Jamshedpur, 51.5 μg/m^3 for NO_x at Delhi and 594 μg/m^3 for SPM at Bhopal.
5. For residential areas, the Jamshedpur, Kota and Kanpur are the most polluted with regard to SO_2, NO_x and SPM respectively.

The data collected so far from the Indian cities show that at majority of the places SPM was above the specified standards for most of the period during the year. However, for SO_2 and NO_x the quality of air remains satisfactory at most of the places. Of the 146 total stations monitored by CPCB, 16 for SO_2, 11 for NO_x and as many as 104 for SPM showed some violations with respect to the standards.

The data collected on heavy metal air pollution in Delhi show that the lead occurs in air in the rage of 42 to 3619 ng/m^3 with greatest concentrations in industrial areas. Cadmium was found to range between 1 and 46 ng/m^3, and zinc between 364 amd 3313 ng/m^3. Some reports say that air pollution level in Chembur area of Bombay is so high that people call it often as "gas chamber" of Bombay. But the situation now seems to be improving because of the control measures taken by the industries situated there.

Cars in India produce nearly 4-times more carbon monoxide than the western cars. The incidence of chronic bronchitis is six to fourteen times higher than other places in the areas near thermal power plants in Delhi.

Air quality is greatly affected by the weather conditions during the year. Summer and winter are often considered critical periods for the accumulation of certain pollutants in the air. In summer the low humidity and high winds facilitate concentration of SPM in the atmosphere. Winter promote the conditions of inversion leading to the trapping of all atmosphere pollutants near the ground levels. Rainy periods are usually clean due to scrubbing action of the rain.

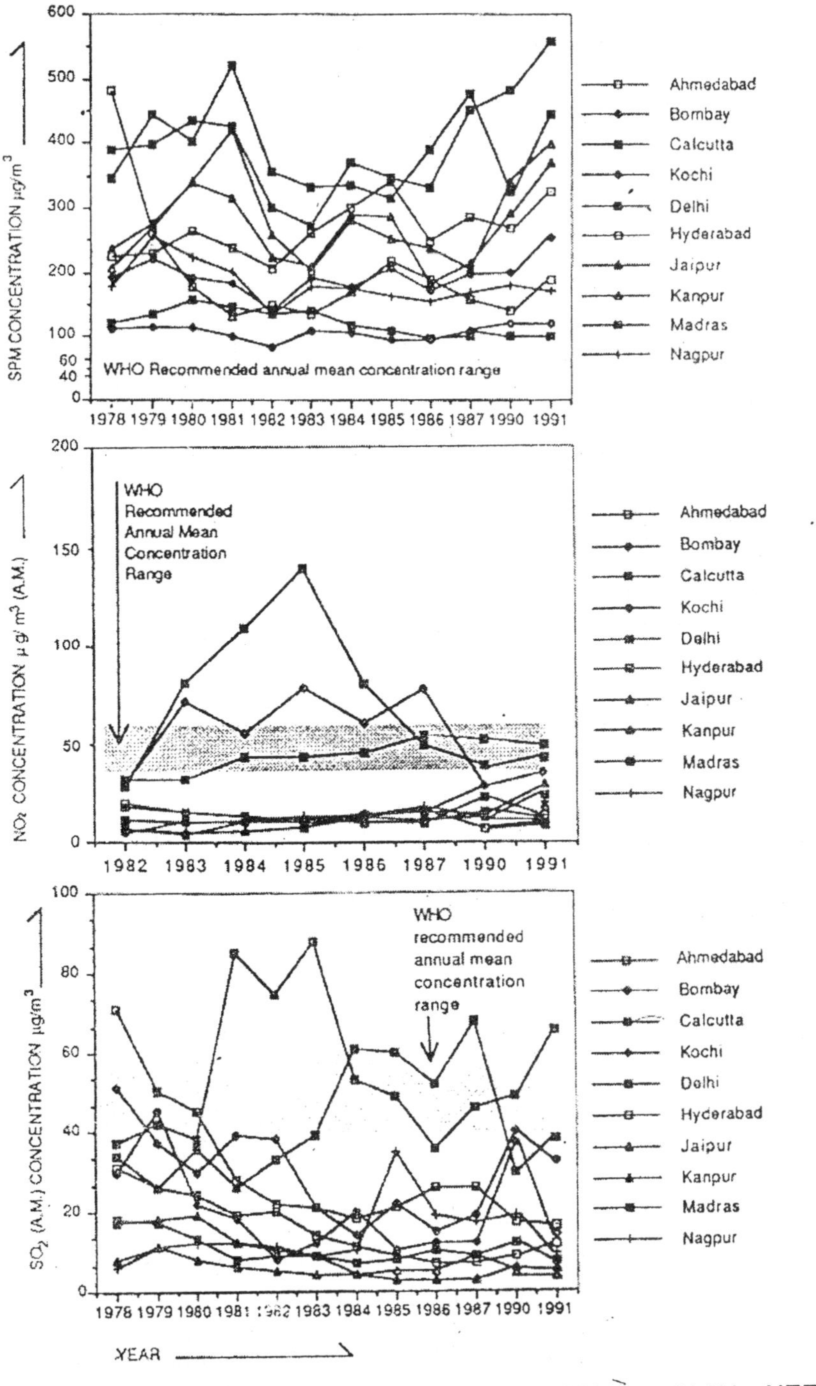

Figure 1.2 Annual average concentrations of SO_2, NO_2 and SPM recorded by NEEI some cities of India.

1.5 Classification of Air Pollutants

Air pollutants can be classified variously on the basis of their origin, state of the matter or chemical composition.

1.5.1 *Classification According to Origin*

On the basis of their origin, air pollutants can be grouped in two categories.

Primary pollutants

Primary pollutants are those emitted into the atmosphere as a result of some specific process, and remain for a long time in the chemical form in which they are emitted. Some important primary pollutants include particulates, SO_2, CO, hydrocarbons, H_2S, NH_3 (for details see chapter 2).

Secondary pollutants

These are the pollutants those formed in the atmosphere as a result of some reaction. This reaction may be photochemical or nonphotochemical and may take place between two pollutants, or between a single pollutant and natural constituents of the atmosphere. Well known examples of secondary pollutants are ozone, NO_x, peroxy acetyl nitrate (PAN), photochemical smog and acid rain. Properties and formation of these compounds are dealt with in Chapter 3.

1.5.2 *Classification According to the State of Matter*

According to this criteria, the air pollutants may be classified as follows (see Table 1.10).

Table 1.10 Classification of pollutants on the basis of the state of matter in their major classes and sub-classes.

Major classes	Sub-classes	Typical members of sub-classes
Organic gases	Hydrocarbons	Hexane, benzene, ethylene, methane, butane
	Aldehydes & Ketones	Formaldehyde, acetone
	Other organics	Chlorinated hydrocarbons, alchohols, nitrogen dioxide, nitric oxide
Inorganic gases	Oxides of nitrogen	
	Oxides of sulphur	Sulphur dioxide, sulphur trioxide
	Oxides of carbon	Carbon monoxide, carbon dioxide
	Other inorganics	Hydrogen sulphide, hydrogen fluoride, ammonia, chlorine
Particulates	Solid particles	Dust, smoke, fume
	Liquid particles	Mist, spray

Gaseous pollutants

Contaminants in the form of gases behave much as the air itself, without being settle out, e.g., SO_2, CO_2, NO_x, H_2S, NH_3, Cl_2, hydrocarbons etc. These may be organic or inorganic.

Particulate pollutants

These are finely divided solids or liquids. The larger particles tend to get settle out quickly and are called settleable or dustfall particulates (particles more than 1μ), while the smaller particles remain suspended for a longer period and are called suspended particulate matter (SPM; particle size less than 1μ). The smallest particles may behave almost like a gas and are readily transported by wind currents for longer distances without being deposited. Examples among solid particulates are dusts, smoke and fumes, while among liquid particulates, are mist and sprays.

1.5.3 *Classification According to Chemcial Composition*

According to chemical nature the pollutants can be divided into following categories.

Organic pollutants

They are organic in nature and contain mainly carbon and hydrogen, but may also contain some other elements. Carbon monoxide and carbon dioxide are excluded from this category as these contain only carbon and oxygen but no hydrogen. Examples are hydrocarbons, chlorinated hydrocarbons, aldehydes and alcohols etc.

Inorganic pollutants

Contaminants in the form of simple inorganics are compounds like CO, CO_2, NO_2, NO, SO_2, HF, H_2S metals, etc. Many of the most common pollutants of the atmosphere are of this category.

2 Primary Air Pollutants

Nature, importance, sources and abundance of some important primary air pollutants are given below. The details of their effects on life and physical matter are described in Chapters 7, 8 and 9.

2.1 Carbon Monoxide (CO)

It is a tasteless, colourless and odourless gas with slightly lesser density than air. The average background concentration, particularly in the northern hemisphere is 0.10 ppm. The mean residence time of this gas in the atmosphere has been worked out to be between 1 month and 5 years.

The main concern with its pollution effects is its ability to combine with haemoglobin, which reduce the normal capacity of blood to transport oxygen to the tissues. At higher concentration of 100 ppm it may cause people to experience dizziness, headache, lassitude and other symptoms. A concentration of 4000 ppm is lethal in less than one hour.

The major sources of CO include the incomplete burning of fuels and other carbonaceous matter. It is also generated in some industrial processes and solid waste combustion. Cigarette smoke also contain large quantities of CO. Natural sources of CO are mainly volcanoes, lightening and photochemical degradation of some reactive organic compounds. CO is also formed biologically by certain brown algae, various microorganisms, and some oceanic organisms.

According to some estimates 75.1% of CO is produced by total fuel combustion, 7.7% from industrial processes, 9.3% from agricultural burning, 4.9% from solid waste disposal and 3.0% from miscellaneous sources.

Carbon monoxide concentration in areas where traffic moves frequently range from 3 to 42 ppm, however, concentrations from 100 to 150 ppm have been found inside the vehicles.

Recent estimates of CO levels in urban areas average about 10-15 pphm but can increase under traffic stress. Williams et al. (1998) reported that CO in the central part of London averaged about 90 pphm in winter and 60-80 pphm in summer in the early 1980s. In USA, peak levels of 200 pphm have been found.

2.2 Sulphur Oxides (SO_2 and SO_3)

Sulphur oxides are most common air pollutants. These were recognized as major pollutants in several air pollution episodes in the world. Standards for sulphur dioxide are available from various localities all over the world. It is an integral part of most air quality monitoring programmes.

Smelting has been one of the greatest sources of SO_2 pollution. Ores of Cu, Zn, Pb and Ni etc., contain as much as 10% or more of sulphur. This waste product combines with oxygen in the air at high temperature of the smelter to produce principally SO_2, which is released into the atmosphere.

$$4\,FeS_2 + 11O_2 \rightarrow 2Fe_2O_3 + 6SO_2$$

$$2NiS + 3O_2 \rightarrow 2NiO + SO_2$$

$$Cu_2S + 2O_2 \rightarrow 2CuO + SO_2$$

Coal burning has been a traditional source of SO_2 pollution and on a global basis accounts for 75% of SO_2 production.

According to some estimates 103 trillion g SO_2 is produced in the world every year. The lifetime of SO_2 in the atmosphere is about 2-4 days. About 55% of SO_2 is lost due to photochemical conversion to sulphates and the rest is removed by wet and dry deposition.

It is, however, important to note that SO_2 levels in developed countries have been decreasing with changes in the characteristics of the fuels burnt and due to strict environmental laws. In new York in 1960, annual average concentration of SO_2 ranged between 14 and 21 pphm. By 1980 the average had dropped to 2.2 pphm.

SO_2 is a colourless gas possessing a pungent and irritating odour at higher concentrations above 300 ppm. The background concentration of SO_2 is 0.2 ppb. It can react photochemically or catalytically with other materials present in the atmosphere to form sulphur trioxide, sulphuric acid or the salts of sulphuric acid.

Sulphur trioxide, besides forming by oxidation of SO_2, can also be derived from combustion of sulphur containing materials. It may also exist in the form of vapour, and readily combine with water to form H_2SO_4.

The major concern with SO_2 and SO_3 in the atmosphere is their ability to form H_2SO_4, which declines the pH of rain water to result in the occurrence of acid rain. SO_2 has been reported to adversely affect the vegetation and productivity of several crops. The details of the effects of sulphur oxides on vegetation are given in Chapter 7.

Major sources of sulphur dioxide are smelting sulphide ores and the burning of sulphur containing fuels such as coal and petroleum. Out of the total sulphur discharged in the atmosphere, on an annual basis, one-third consists of gaseous SO_2 and remaining in other forms.

2.3 Oxides of Nitrogen (NO_x)

The most abundant and important oxides of nitrogen forming air pollutants are nitric oxide (NO), nitrogen dioxide (NO_2) and nitrous oxide (N_2O). Nitrous oxide, also called popularly as laughing gas, is not a very important air pollutant, though there is an evidence of its role in photochemical reactions.

Nitric oxide is a colourless and relatively harmless gas, but is gets readily converted into NO_2 by photochemical reactions. It is produced maily during high temperature combustion, particularly in automobiles and industries, due to reaction of atmospheric nitrogen with oxygen.

Nitrogen dioxide is a reddish-brown gas with pungent odour. The gas is corrosive, irritating and physiologically toxic. It reacts with water to form nitric acid, which may be a significant component of the acid rain. It is formed in the atmosphere primarily by photooxidation of NO.

Nitric oxide is also produced biologically in nature, and it is estimated that the natural production is 10 times greater than the anthropogenic sources. But, the importance of man-made sources lies in the fact that the urban areas have 10 to 100 times higher concentrations of NOx, which have been accumulated there from the human activities. In general, automobiles produce nearly 40% of the total NOx discharged in the atmosphere.

According to some estimates 48Tg/yr of NOx are produced in the atmosphere. Background concentration of these is 1000 pptv. Lifetime of NO_x is less than 2 days and its fate is oxidation to nitric acid, nitrates or photodissociation.

2.4 Ammonia (NH_3)

It is a colourless, pungent, suffocating, and highly soluble gas in water. With regard to the total production of ammonia, very high percentage of 99.9% (3.7×10^9 tons) is released from the natural sources during degradation of organic matter. However, in urban or industrial areas it may be important from air pollution standpoint because of its higher concentrations in certain localized situations.

Anthropogenic sources of ammonia include mainly the combustion of fuels in stationary and mobile sources, and incineration of wastes. It is also emitted from fertilizer plants, chemical plants, coke ovens and refineries. High concentration of ammonia is harmful to all kinds of life.

Typical background concentration of ammonia is 0.1 ppbv while concentration above 6 ppbv is found in the polluted areas. Lifetime of NH_3 in the atmosphere is 6 days. Its fate is conversion to ammonium salts.

2.5 Hydrogen Sulphide (H_2S)

It is a colourless gas with a foul odour. The natural processes account for nearly one-half of the total hydrogen sulphide released into the atmosphere (10×10^6 tones). Hydrogen sulphide in nature is produced mainly by bacterial decomposition of organic matter. It is also produced naturally from sulphur deposits, volcanic gases and sulphur springs. Man-made sources are mainly industrial such as kraft paper mills, petroleum refineries, coke oven plants, and sewage and industrial waste disposal ponds.

Hydrogen sulphide does not pose a widespread air pollution problem, but localized problems may be severe. The gas at higher concentration is toxic to humans and animals. It may also be corrosive to the metals.

Typical background concentrations of H_2S are 30-100 pptv and 330-810 pptv in polluted areas. Residence time in the atmosphere is 4.4 days. Hydrogen sulphide was responsible for death of 22 persons, while 320 others were hospitalized in Poza Rico, Mexico in 1950. They lived near the stack of a sulphur removal unit.

2.6 Hydrogen Chloride (HCl)

It is a colourless, strong, pungent, and irritating gas with a high solubility in water. It occurs naturally only in very minor quantities from volcanic fumes and in some rivers. It is emitted as an air pollutant from commercial production and use. It is also released during burning of paper products or from chlorine containing materials. Some chemical industries also produce HCl as a by-product during manufacturing processes.

The major concern with the HCl is mainly because of its great solubility in water producing fumes of hydrochloric acid in moist air. Hydrochloric acid is extremely injurious to the skin and mucous membranes. It is a potential air pollutant only in certain localized situations with relatively higher atmospheric concentrations.

2.7 Fluorides

Fluorine in nature is found quite abundantly in the mineral form as fluorspar and fluorapatite having a fluorine concentration of 49% and 3-4% respectively. All commercial fluorine is obtained from fluorspar. Fluorapatite, also popularly known as rock phosphate, is used for production of phosphoric acid and phosphatic fertilizers.

Fluorine as an air pollutant is found in the atmosphere in the form of solid particles as fluoride compounds, fluorine gas, and hydrogen fluoride. The predominant industrial sources of fluorides are processing of its minerals for production of fluorine compounds and phosphatic fertilizers. Significant quantities of fluorides are also emitted from coal combustion and manufacturing of steel, glass, bricks, tiles and aluminium.

Hydrogen fluoride is a highly corrosive gas affecting even glass. Fluorides cause fluorosis, and rubber legged conditions and corrosion of teeth and bones in cattle.

Threshold limit for hydrogen fluoride is 3 ppm. Fluoride concentrations in urban areas range from less than 0.05 μg to about 2 $\mu g/m^3$. Outside urban areas, concentrations usually do not exceed 0.1 $\mu g/m^3$.

2.8 Chlorine (Cl_2)

It is a dense greenish-yellow gas with an irritating odour. It is a strong oxidizing agent possessing bleaching properties due to which it may be extremely toxic to all forms of life. It is highly corrosive to metals and many other materials.

Many of the problems of chlorine pollution are localized due to leaks and accidental discharge or where it is formed in the industries. The major commercial source of chlorine is the electrolysis of chloride salts such as sodium and potassium chloride. Other sources include loading and cleaning tank, cars and barges and dechlorination of spent brine solutions.

Natural sources of chlorine are rare, but volcanic gases may contain some chlorine, and also it may be formed in small quantities by atmospheric reactions. Threshold limit value for Cl_2 is 1 ppm.

2.9 Carbon Dioxide (CO_2)

It is not a typical air pollutant of greater concern to human health. it is, perhaps, the only pollutant which is important on the global scale because of its ability to absorb long wave infrared radiation in the lower atmospheric layers that can increase the atmospheric temperatue. Much debate has been made in the recent years over the global warming as a result of excessive release of carbon dioxide of man-made origin in the atmosphere. The global increase in temperature, even to the extent of a faction of a degree, can lead to the melting of ice caps and polar ice resulting in submergence of low lying cities due to increase in sea level.

Naturally, CO_2 is present in the atmosphere comprising 0.03% of the constituent gases. Due to several-fold increase in the release of carbon dioxide in the atmosphere in recent years, its present concentration is estimated to be soared to nearly 0.033 per cent. Natural sources of CO_2 are chiefly the decay of organic matter and respiration of organisms. About half of the excessive quantities discharged into the atmosphere are absorbed by the oceans, while much are utilized in photosynthesis.

Man-made sources of carbon dioxide for the most part are the combustion of fossil fuels such as coal, oil and natural gas for the production of energy. This accounts almost up to 90% of the total anthropogenic discharges. The remianing 10% of CO_2 comes from the refuse disposal systems, burning of wood and forests etc. On a localized basis it may occur in greater quantites from coke ovens and smelting operations.

2.10 Boron

It is a non-metallic element occurring mostly in combination with other elements. It is a widely distributed element present in several minerals found commonly in nature. Important sources of boron in the atmosphere are boron dust and burning of borane fuels in rockets and jet engines. Boranes are highly toxic sususbtances. Some important boranes are diboranes, pentaboranes and decaboranes. Boranes are also used, sometimes, as additives in petroleum. Other important sources of atmospheric boron are coal burning, and manufacturing chemical industry using boron minerals and compounds.

Boron is a highly toxic element to humans causing damage to brain and even death in extreme cases. When inhaled as dust it leads to irritation and inflammation.

2.11 Phosphorus

It is a solid non-metallic element found commonly in two allotropic forms. The yellow form is highly inflammable, luminous in dark and poisonous. The other form, red in colour, is comparatively less inflammable and less poisonous. Many organophosphorus compounds are highly toxic and can be even lethal to man and animals at higher levels of atmospheric concentrations.

Phosphorus is emitted in the atmosphere in the form of phosphorus oxides, phosphoric acid and organophosphorus compounds. Many organophosphorus compounds are used commonly as pesticides. Its predominant atmospheric sources are oil-fired boilers producing significant quantities of phosphorus-bearing flyash, iron and steel industry emitting fumes of phosphorus pentaoxides, and transportation due to use of certain organophosphorus compounds as fuel additives. Chemical industry involved with phosphorus can also emit its appreciable quantities in air.

Elemetal phosphorus acts as a potent protoplasmic poison. It can cause skin irritation and nerveous symptoms at higher concentration.

2.12 Selenium

It is nonmetallic element, chemically resembling sulphur. Though, selenium is an essential nutrient for animals and possibly for human, but in excessive quantities it is a very powerful toxicant.

In nature, it is widely distributed in the earth's crust with an average concentration of 0.09 ppm. It is also found in coal and igneous rocks. Important atmospheric sources of selenium include the burning of trash, particularly paper. It is also emitted from copper refinery and use of fuels in industry.

2.13 Heavy Metals

Heavy metals are referred to those having a density more than five times to that of water. Many of them commonly occur as air pollutants and are quite toxic to life. A brief description of some of the important heavy metals is provided here.

Arsenic :

It is a highly poisonous element often found associated with the ores of copper, lead, cobalt, nickel, iron, gold and silver. The atmospheric sources of arsenic include the smelting of the arsenic-bearing ores, cotton ginning and burning of cotton trash, combustion of coal, and incineration. It is also released in various chemical forms during the glass and ceramic manufacturing. Some of its compounds are also used as pesticides.

Arsenic is a highly toxic element causing dermatitis and probably skin cancer. At higher concentration it may even lead to death.

Cadmium :

It is not found in free natural state. It often remians associated with the ores of zinc, copper and lead. It is a widely used element with several applications such as in electroplating; photography and dyeing; and manufacturing of glass, phosphorus, electrodes for storage batteries, semiconductors, silver alloys and photoconductors, etc.

The major atmospheric sources of cadmium are processing of the cadmium-bearing ores of zinc, copper and lead. Cadmium dust and vapours are often released from the mining and concentration of zinc ores. Metallurgical processing of ores such as roasting, sintering and smelting also volatilize cadmium in the vapour forms into the atmosphere. Some cadmium is also released during incineration of refuse containing steel, plastics, pigments and rubber. Gaseous emissions of cadmium as vapours are also produced when scrap steel is melted for recycling.

Cadmium is a highly toxic metal causing several disorders in humans and animals. It leads to the development of fibrosis of lungs; gastric troubles; and diseases of heart, liver and brain. It can also develop hypertension and cancers.

Chromium :

It is a lustrous brittle metallic element forming compounds with other elements. It does not occur in nature as a pure metal. Most soils and rocks contain small quantities of chromium as chromic oxide (Cr_2O_3). Its only commercial mineral is chromite ($FeOCr_2O_3$). It is used in production of stainless and austenite steels. High quantities of chromium are also used in electroplating.

It is introduced into the atmosphere from the metallurgical industry, chromate-producing industry, chrome plating, burning of coal, use of chromium chemicals as fuel additives and corrosion inhibitors, and chrome tanning. Chromium pollution occurs mostly as particulate emission, which can be controlled by employing common particulate control devices like electrostatic precipitators, bag houses and scrubbers.

Chromium is very toxic when inhaled from air. It causes irritation and perforation of nasal septum. It is also reported to be carcinogenic and causes ulcers on skin.

Lead :

It is a heavy, soft, malleable, bluish-gray metal. Its common ore is galena where it occurs in the form of sulphide. Most of the lead in the air comes as aerosols, fumes and sprays. it is very widely used in storage batteries and gasoline.

Auto-exhaust from gasoline powered motor vehicles is the major source of atmospheric lead in the urban areas. Other anthropogenic sources of lead include the combustion of coal, processing and manufacturing of lead products and manufacturing of lead additives such as tetraethyl lead for gasoline. Some lead is also introduced into the atmosphere during incineration of refuse and use of lead-containing pesticides.

Lead is a systemic poison causing anemia, kidney malfunction, tissue damage of brain and even death in extreme poisoning.

In America about 2 million tonnes of lead is consumed in a year. It is ubiquitous and its concentration is increasing in the world. The background concentration of lead is 0.5 to 1 $\mu g/m^3$, while the levels in the streets are often 6 - 11 $\mu g/m^3$, thus exceeding the WHO air quality standards (2 $\mu g/m^3$).

Manganese :

It is a hard, brittle, grayish-white metallic element. Though, it is required by body as an essential element in the trace quantities, its higher atmospheric concentrations lead to poisioning and diseases of various types.

Naturally, it is widely distributed in the earth's crust in the combined chemical form. In the atmosphere, it enters primarily in the form of oxides such as MnO, Mn_2O_3 or Mn_3O_4.

Its prime atmospheric entry occurs from the manganese and steel industries. The use of organic manganese compounds as additives in gasoline, fuel oil and diesel can also contribute significantly to the air pollution. Fumes containing manganese are also produced from the welding rods.

Mercury:

It is a dense, silver-white metal remaining in liquid state at the normal ambient temperatures. the chief ore of mercury is cinnabar (HgS) in which it is present in the form of sulphide. It also remains associated with many other minerals of common occurrence.

It is widely used metal with applications in several industries from where it is emitted in the form of an air pollutant. Paint industry seems to produce highest mercury emissions where it is used as an anti-fouling and preservative agent, especially in marine and latex paints. Other industrial applications of mercury include its use in rectifiers, batteries, mercury lamps, barometres, thermometers, flowmeters, switches, pressure-sensing devices and relays. The industrial use of mercury produces its droplets which vaporize in the air. Processing of ore, combustion of coal, and incineration of refuse also contribute significantly to mercury pollution. It is also used as pesticide in the form of certain compounds. Chlorine and caustic soda are usually manufactured employing mercury eletrodes.

Mercury is a highly potent nerve toxin. It is more toxic on inhalation than its entry through digestive tract. Chronic poisoning results in nervous symptoms which in advanced stage causes frequent tremors. It also leads to the development of gastrointestinal and pulmonary disorders.

Nickel :

It is grayish-white metallic element which is rough and resistant to oxidative corrosion. It is commonly used in making various metal alloys and stainless steel. It is released as an atmospheric pollutant mostly in the form of dust and vapours.

It is introduced in the atmosphere from a number of industrial activities. Burning of coal leaves significant quantities of nickel in the ash. However, its major source in the air is the processing of nickel for manufacture of various alloys. Nickel plating and its use in hydrogenation and dehydrogenation of organic compounds, and ageing of liquors also contribute to the air pollution.

It is relatively nontoxic but can affect proteins of alveolar tissues. Its occupational exposures have been linked to the development of cancers of lung and sinus, respiratory disorders and dermatitis.

Zinc :

It is a bluish-white metallic element resembling magnesium in chemicl properties. It exists in nature chiefly as sulphides, oxides, carbonates and silicates. Though, it is an essential nutrient for human and other organisms, it can be a toxic substance at relatively higher concentrations.

Zinc is widely distributed in the earth's crust, but its prime atmospheric sources are smelting of ores of zinc, lead and copper, recovery of scrap zinc, and incineration of zinc containing materials.

Fumes of zinc are highly corrosive, and irritate and damage skin and mucous membranes.

2.14 Hydrocarbons

Most of the hydrocarbons exist in the atmosphere as gases such as methane, ethane, propane, acetylene, butane and isopentane. Benzo-a-pyrene, a solid particulate hydrocarbon with carcinogenic properties, is also an important pollutant of the atmosphere. it is also an important constituent of the cigarete smoke. Methane constitutes about 90% of the hydrocarbons by volume, but is inert in photochemical reactions. The major concern with the atmospheric hydrocarbons lies in their ability to take part in photochemical reactions leading to the formation of several harmful secondary pollutants.

Naturally occurring hydrocarbons include terpene-type compounds emitted by vegetation. These hydrocarbons can get polymerized during photochemical reactions in atmosphere to form the aerosols responsible for the blue haze found in many forested areas.

The man-made sources of hydrocarbons are processing, distribution, storage, marketing and use of petroleum and some organic solvents. About one-half of the man-made hydrocarbons result from the incomplete burning of gasoline in internal combustion engines. Incineration of wastes is another important source of hydrocarbons in the atmosphere.

2.15 Aldehydes

These are organic compounds having a general formula of R-CHO. On oxidation, they yield acids; and on reduction, alcohols. Some common aldehydes of air pollution concern are formaldehyde, and acrolein-acetaldehyde.

Aldehydes are normally the product of incomplete combustion of hydrocarbons and other organic materials, and are produced from motor vehicles and during incineration of wastes. They are also formed by oxidation of hydrocarbons during photochemical reactions (see Chapter 3).

The aldehydes pose the problem of irritation of the mucous membranes of eyes, nose and other parts of upper respiratory tract. Threshold limit for formaldehyde is 2 ppm.

2.16 Organic Carcinogens

Several organic compounds, generated as air pollutants, have been reported to be potent carcinogenic in nature. These can be classified on the basis of their chemical nature into the following categories.

1. Polynuclear aromatic hydrocarbons (PAHs)

   Benzo (e) pyrene

   Benzo (a) anthracene

   Benzo (a) pyrene

   Benzo (e) acephenanthrylene

   Benzo (b) fluoranthene

   Chrysene

2. Polynuclear azo-hecterocyclic compounds

   Dibenz (a,h) acridine

   Dibenz (a,j) acridine

3. Polynuclear imino-heterocyclic compounds
4. Polynuclear carbonyl compounds
5. Alkylating agents

   Aliphatic and alifinic epoxides

   Peroxides

   Bactones

PAHs are produced at high temperature burning under incomplete combustion, pyrolysis and pyrosynthesis of organic matter. Azo-heterocyclic compounds are quite abundant in automobile exhaust. Nearly 85% of the carcinogenic compounds come from heat generation by burning of coal, gas or other carbonaceous matter. Benzo(a)pyrene is also found naturally to occur in bituminous coal. Alkylating agents are used as additives in liquid fueks like gasoline and diesel. All these compounds result in mostly the cancer of lung.

2.17 Odour Producing Compounds

Odour is defined as the sensation of smell perceived as a result of olfactory stimulus. Odours may or may not be toxic but most of the odourous compounds have unplesant and objectionable smells. Some of the common odour producing substances are hydrogen sulphide, chloride, hydrochloric acid, ammonia, aldehydes, organic acids (valeric, body odour, dirty feet, butyric), amines, acrolein (cooking fat), skatole (manure), putrescine (decaying putrescible matter), cadaverine (dead animals), and mercaptans (skunk musk, butyl, methyl, and ethyl).

The sources of odour producing compounds are many, including from a simple household activity like food preparation to large industrial sources such as coffee roasting, paints, solvents, plastics, fertilizer, rubber, foundry and petroleum industries.

A few odorous materials are highly toxic and their main danger lies not in their odour but in their toxicity. Some of the compounds whose maximum acceptable concentrations (MAC) are lower than their olfactory thresholds are ozone, acrolein, camphor, dioxane, methanol, methylformate, methyl glycol, sulphur dioxides and trichloroethylene.

2.18 Particulates

Particulate matter is any material, except uncombined water, that exists as a solid or liquid in the atmosphere or in a gas stream at ordinary conditions. The particulates present in air are generally of various sizes, and can be defined more specifically as any dispersed solid or liquid with the particles larger than a single small molecule (0.0002 μ) but smaller than 500 μ. Particles in this spectrum of size can remain suspended for a few seconds to several months. Size range of some common particles are provided in Table 2.1

Particulates in air are of various nature and on this basis can be defined as follows

Dusts :

These are consisted of solid particles larger than colloidal size and are capable of temporary suspension in air and other gases.

Aerosols :

These are solids or liquids of microscopic size dispersed in gaseous media. Examples are smoke, fog or mist.

Smoke :

It is the term normally applied to the visiblr products of imperfect combustion. Example is the smoke plume coming out of chimnies where fuel is burnt.

Fog :

It is consisted of visible aerosols in which the dispersed phase is liquid.

Table 2.1 Approximate size ranges of airborne particles. (Arranged in order of decreasing diameter).

Substance	Diameter (microns)	
	minimum	maximum
Rain drops	500	5000
Human hair	35	200
Stoker flyash	10	800
Pollen	10	100
Plant spores	10	35
Cement dust	3	100
Natural fog and clouds	2	60
Foundry dust	1	1000
Pulverized coal flyash	1	50
Metallurgical dust	0.5	100
Insecticide dusts	0.5	10
Bacteria	0.3	35
Sulphur trioxide mist	0.3	3
Alkali fume	0.1	5
Ammonium chloride fume	0.1	3
Oil smoke	0.1	1
Salt nuclei (from sea water)	0.03	0.5
Colloidal silica	0.02	0.05
Metallurgical Fume	0.01	2.2
Resin smoke	0.01	1
Tobacco smoke	0.01	1
Zinc oxide fume	0.01	0.5
Magnesium oxide fume	0.01	0.5
Carbon black	0.01	0.3
Combustion nuclei	0.01	0.1
Viruses and proteins	0.003	0.05
Gas molecules	0.0001	0.0006
Data based on ASTM (1962)		

Mist :

It is a low concentration dispersion of relatively small liquid droplets in air. Mists may result from the condensation of gases or vapours to liquid state. They can also be formed by breaking up a liquid through splashing, spraying or foaming.

Fume :

It is consisted of the particles formed by condensation, sublimation or chemical reaction, of which the predominant part consists of particles less than 1μ in size. Examples are tobacco smoke and condensed metal oxides.

Fly ash:

It is composed of finely divided particles of ash.

Soot :

It is made up of carbon particles impregnated with tar and formed during the incomplete combustion of carbonaceous material.

Major particulates in air are in the form of carbon and soot, acid droplets, metallic oxides, salts, silicates and others. The shape of the airborne particles may be variable, for example, spherical (smoke and flyash), irregular (minerals), or like flakes and fibres. particulates may also acquire an eletric charge in the air by several mechanisms. One such important mechanism is the collision of particulates with gaseous ions in air. The charge can also be acquired when they come in contact with a flame or other energy sources. Liquid particles may be charged when they are dispersed in air in the form of a shower spray.

The most significant property of particulates is, however, the size of the particles. Particles on the basis of their size and the time for which they remain airborne, can be grouped into following three main categories.

Condensation Nuclei (Aitken Nuclei)

All particles of the size below 0.1 μm are called condensation nuclei or Aitken nuclei. These particles are so small that they cannot be filtered or weighed. These can only be counted by special instruments in which the water vapours are condensed on their surfaces to facilitate the counting.

These finest particles are formed in nature by dust storms volcanic activity, fires and evaporation of sea spray leaving behind the salt particles. They have also been reported to be formed in the atmosphere by gas phase reactions between oxides of nitrogen and hydrocarbons. Industrial combustion may also release these small particles in the atmosphere. Because of their insignificant weight and difficulty in measurement, they are generally ignored in the study of air pollution.

Suspended Partcualte Matter (SPM)

These are the most abundant particles present in the atmosphere. They are of major concern for the health as they can enter deepest into the lungs, causing most severe effects on the body. The size of these particles range from 0.1 to 10 μ. The settling velocities of this particle size range are very low and, therefore, the particles remain suspended for long periods in air. The important examples of these particles are metallic fumes; droplets of oil, tar and acid; black soot; and local soil particles. Quantitative analysis of these particles can be made easily after their collection on specific filters.

SPM is most commonly measured parameter in all kinds of air quality monitoring and its standards are prescribed by pollution control authorities for a given area. Suspended particulates, being smaller in size, usually do not settle. They are important as they remain in the breathing zone of human beings. Besides, SPM are composed of several toxic compounds. Various activities like power generation, demolition, spraying, grinding, agriculture and stone quarrying generate suspended particulate matter. Cement, iron, steel and fertilizer industries significantly contribute to SPM. Automobile exhaust contains 40-50μg/L of particulates. Annual and 24-h peak total SPM concentrations in the GEMS network are given in Table 2.2.

Table 2.2 Annual average and 24-h peak total suspended particulate concentrations in various cities for the 1976 to 1980 period from the GEMS Network.

City	Country	Annual geometric mean TSP ($\mu g/m^3$)	Years	24-h Max. TSP ($\mu g/m^3$)
Lahore	Pakistan	678	1979	3415
Baghdad	Iraq	457	1979	1901
Delhi	India	447	1979	875
Calcutta	India	380	1976-80	917
Tehran	Iran	330	1976-80	885
Athens	Greece	247	1979	521
Jakarta	Indonesia	230	1979	654
Bangkok	Thailand	153	1979	433
Kuala Lumpur	Malaysia	151	1979	498
Zagreb	Yugoslavia	150	1976-80	587
Bogata	Colombia	140	1979	677
Bucharest	Romania	134	1979	721
Madrid	Spain	130	1979	1089
Hamilton	Canada	110	1976-80	801
Houston	U.S.A	100	1976-80	124
Manila	Philippines	90	1976-80	149
Sydney	Australia	90	1976-80	316
Toronto	Canada	76	1976-80	185
New York	U.S.A	64	1976-80	126
Tokyo	Japan	59	1976-80	337

Sources : Various GEMS Reports

Note: United States Environmental Protection Agency's standard is 260 $\mu g/m^3$.

Dust-fall Particles (Settleable Particulate Matter)

These are the particles larger than 10 μ which tend to settle out due to gravitational force. The major proportion of these particles in air is consisted of airborne soil particles, flyash and soot from industries. Industrial sources of these particles are incinerators, cement plants, steel mills, sulphuric acid, and kraft paper mills. Enormous amounts of dusts are also emitted in to the atmosphere from the mechanical processes such as grinding and abrasion, wind erosion, spraying and pulverizing of materials.

The dust-fall is less of a respiratory hazard than smaller particles, but it may affect vegetation, and contribute to degradation of strucures and buildings.

The major concern of the particulate matter lies in the fact that it is deposited on biological and non-biological objects. The particulates reduce the productive potential of plants and lead to the entry of several heavy metals, radioactive substances and toxic materials into food chains. Human beings are affected by particles due to induction of respiratory troubles and lung impairments. The detailed discussion on the effects of particulate matter on organisms and property is given in Chapters 7,8 and 9.

2.19 Asbestos

Asbestos is found in a variety of fibrous minerals occurring in rocks. Some of the important asbestos minerals are pyroxenes, chrysolite, crocidolite, amosite and anthrophyllite. Chrysolite is the most common asbestos mineral used in quantities of more than 90% of all. Asbestos is an important industrial material used in making a variety of products.

Its major atmospheric sources are asbestos mining, industries using asbestos, wearing of brake lining, roofing, fireproofing of buildings with sprayed asbestos, road surfacing, and asbestos cement. Large quantites of asbestos concentrations in the urban air are of the order of 10-100 ng/m^3. Asbestos is considered quite harmful because of producing "asbestosis", a kind of lung cancer.

2.20 Pesticides

The pesticides are the chemicals used for controlling the pests those destroy our crops or other biological objects of economic importance. These can be grouped as insecticides, herbicides, fungicides, namaticides, rodenticides, algicides, repellents and attractants on the basis of their specificity to destroy the pests.

Pesticides do not occur naturally in the environment. Their primary source is from their application during which they become airborne. Pesticides can also vaporize from the soil, water and treated surface. They may also become airborne with the blowing dust. The industries manufacturing pesticides may also produce the emissions containing these chemicals.

Pesticides tend to move from air to the other components of the environment like water and soil, and accumulate in the body of the organisms through food chains. They are damaging to the human and animal health after being accumulated in the body.

2.21 Radioactive Substances

These are commonly the isotopes of elements formed due to difference in the number of nuetrons, or the elements with higher molecular weight, especially those placed at the end of periodic table. Radioactive substances constantly emit energy in the form of alpha, beta and gamma radiations. These are also called radionuclides. They can remain present in the atmosphere in the form of both gases and particulates (dusts, fumes, smoke, mists). Their atmospheric sources can be natural as well as man-made. Naturally, they are present in soils and rocks and are also induced in the atmosphere by activation of normal gaseous consituents by cosmic rays, such as formation of tritium and carbon-14. Radon and thoron constantly emnate from the earth's crust and come to the atmosphere. Natural sources are considered most significant for atmospheric radioactivity. Important man-made sources include radioactive fall-out from nuclear explosions, nuclear fuel cycle (mining, milling and refinig of nuclear fuels), activation of atmospheric gases in nuclear reactors, and reprocessing of nuclear spent fuels etc. Certain fuels like coal, oil and natural gas also contain radionuclides in small quantities.

Radioactive substances are of grater concern because of their deleterious effects on health. Radiations lead to loss of hair, burns, ulcers, cancers, leukemia, genetic deformities and even death in extreme cases.

2.22 Aeroallergens

Aeroallergens are airborne substances those elicit an allergic response or hypersensitivity in susceptible individuals. The most common allergens occur commonly in the air are pollen (such as of ragweed and *Parthenium*), danders (small particulate organic materials such as feathers of fowl, hair of animals and house dust), fungi, bacteria, viruses and other particulates of various origin.

The pathologocal manifestations of allergic reactions developed by the airborne allergens are called "atopic allergies". Depending upon the specificity of the allergens, some important allergies are hay fever, asthma, skin disorders, and certain respiratory troubles.

3 Atmospheric Reactions and Formation of Secondary Pollutants

3.1 Introduction

Substances discharged into the atmosphere often get involved in a variety of physical and chemical reactions to form new products. The new chemicals formed by these atmospheric reactions are called *secondary pollutants*. The primary pollutants after transformations in the atmosphere can be converted into more toxic products or into relatively harmless ones. An evidence of occurrence of such atmospheric reactions comes from the fact that the oxides of nitrogen, sulphur dioxide, and hydrocarbons remain in quantities lesser than their total emissions, while the quantities of aldehydes and organic acids (oxidation products of hydrocarbons) increase above their calculated emissions in the atmosphere.

Most atmospheric reactions are induced by the absorption of light energy (photons) by the molecules. This results in their dissociation to form chemically active free radicals, which readily take part in many chemical reactions. These reactions where the light energy is absorbed by the molecules are called photochemical reactions, which often bring about the accumulation of several secondary pollutants into the atmosphere. Many secondary pollutants are also formed by non-photochemical reactions.

3.2 Primary Photochemical Reactions

The most important primary photochemical reaction in atmosphere is the dissociation of nitrogen dioxide (NO_2) into nitric oxide (NO) and oxygen atom (O).

$$NO_2 + h\nu \rightarrow NO + O$$

Other reactions of importance include the photodissociation of aldehydes into free radicals.

$$RCHO + h\nu \rightarrow R^{\bullet} + HCO^{\bullet}$$

Likewise, many other organic compounds, halogens and some inorganic compounds like metal oxides may also get photodissociated to form a variety of free radicals. These photodissociations later initiate several other chemical reactions in sequence owing to the production of highly reactive oxygen atoms and free radicals.

3.3 Formation of Free Radicals in Air

Free radicals are highly reactive chemical species and are formed by the photodissociation of several inorganic and organic compounds. The main compounds forming the free radicals of air pollution importance are aldehydes, ketones, peroxyacetyl nitrates, hydrogen peroxide, organic peroxides and nitrous and nitric acids.

$$RCHO + h\nu \rightarrow R^{\bullet} + HCO^{\bullet}$$
$$R_1R_2CO + h\nu \rightarrow R_1^{\bullet} + R_2CO^{\bullet}$$
$$RONO + h\nu \rightarrow RO^{\bullet} + NO$$
$$RONO + h\nu \rightarrow R^{\bullet} + NO_2$$
$$H_2O_2 + h\nu \rightarrow 2OH^{\bullet}$$
$$HNO_2 + h\nu \rightarrow OH^{\bullet} + NO$$
$$HNO_2 + h\nu \rightarrow H^{\bullet} + NO_2$$
$$HNO_3 + h\nu \rightarrow OH^{\bullet} + NO_2$$

Many free radicals such as hydrogen, alkyl or acyl groups, after combining readily with oxygen, form peroxy radicals.

$$R^{\bullet} + O_2 \rightarrow ROO^{\bullet}$$

These peroxy radicals are much more reactive and react further with nitrogen oxides, other primary pollutants and a number of derived secondary air pollutants to form again a variety of new products like more free radicals, alcohols, ethers, acids, peroxy acids, alkyl nitrates and peroxy acetyl nitrates. Some important chemical reactions involving peroxy radicals are given below.

$$ROO^{\bullet} + NO_2 \rightarrow ROONO_2$$
$$ROO^{\bullet} + C_2H_3R \rightarrow ROOCHR + CH_2$$
$$ROO^{\bullet} + SO_2 \rightarrow ROOSO_2$$
$$ROO^{\bullet} + O_3 \rightarrow RO + 2O_2$$
$$ROO^{\bullet} + NO \rightarrow RO + NO_2$$

The sequence of the reactions mentioned above is the chain reactions in which the products of one reaction are consumed in the next. Consequently, we may find that a large number of reactive free radicals are formed and accumulate in the air.

3.4 Formation of Ozone in the Atmosphere

We have seen earlier that the primary photochemical reaction dissociates NO_2 into NO and a free oxygen atom (O).

$$NO_2 + h\nu \rightarrow NO + O$$

The free oxygen atom, generated in this manner, reacts with O_2 present in the air to form ozone.

$$O + O_2 + M \rightarrow O_3 + M^*$$

Since, the ozone, formed in this way is unstable having too much energy to exist, it transfer this excess energy to some other molecule (represented as M in the reaction). This M molecule is more often N_2 or O_2 in the air. The ozone formed in this reaction, however, reacts again with NO, generated after dissociation of NO_2, to form again the original substrates, NO_2 and O_2.

$$NO + O_3 \rightarrow O_2 + NO_2$$

The cycle of these reactions is illustrated in Fig. 3.1, which shows that the ozone cannot be accumulated in the air through these reactions. In the presence of certain hydrocarbons, however, this equilibrium is destroyed and ozone begins to accumulate in the air. The mechanism of ozone buildup is shown in Fig. 3.2.

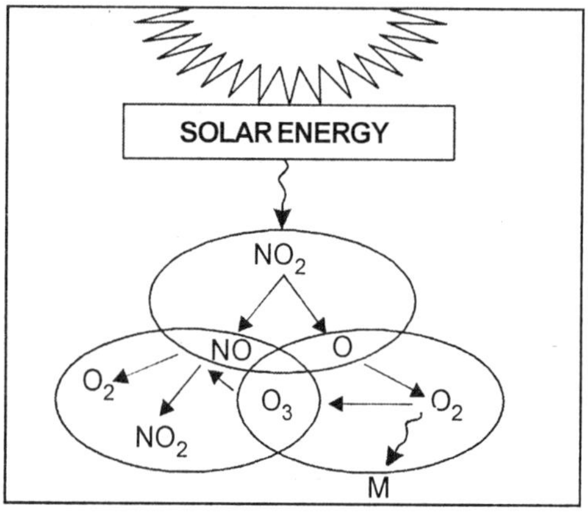

Figure 3.1 The cycle of chemical reactions initiated by photochemical dissociation of NO_2.

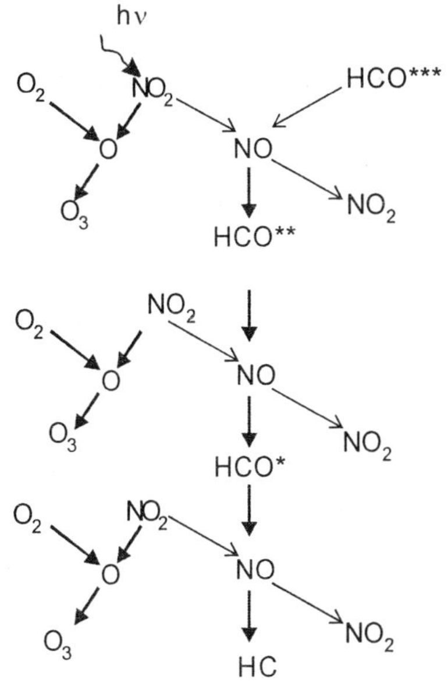

Figure 3.2 Buildup of ozone in presence of reactive hydrocarbons.

The ozone buildup is possible only when the ozone, formed by reaction of oxygen atom (O) with O_2, dose not get consumed again to restore NO_2 after reacting with NO as indicated in Fig 3.1. However, the reactive hydrocarbon molecules present in the air can perform this function of restoring NO_2 leaving O_3 to buildup in air. An example of the formation of these reactive hydrocarbons, which are must for ozone accumulation, is the reaction of oxygen atom with hydrocarbons like olefins having one or more C = C double bonds.

$$O + \text{Olefins} \rightarrow R^{\bullet} + R_1O^{\bullet}$$

Peroxy radicals are readily formed in the following way.

$$R^{\bullet} + O2 \rightarrow ROO^{\bullet}$$

The peroxy radicals are very efficient in converting NO into NO_2. Since, already one oxygen atom is consumed in breaking an olefin, which otherwise could have made the ozone, more than one NO should be converted into NO_2 by a peroxy radical. Peroxy radicals are capable of converting at least two NO molecules into NO_2, thus, facilitating the buildup of the ozone concentration in air.

The photodissociation of aldehydes in presence of oxygen atom and carbon monoxide is also capable of converting NO into NO_2.

$$CH_3CHO + O \rightarrow CH_3CO + OH^{\bullet}$$

$$OH^{\bullet} + CO \rightarrow CO_2 + H^{\bullet}$$

$$H^{\bullet} + O2^{+M} \rightarrow HO_2^{\bullet} + M$$

$$HO_2^{\bullet} + NO \rightarrow NO_2 + OH^{\bullet}$$

It can be seen from the above reactions that OH is generated in the end to start the reactions again. Likewise, there are many other organic hydrocarbons in the air, which have capability to convert NO into NO_2. A list of such chemicals is provided in Table 3.1.

Table 3.1 A list of common hydrocarbons capable of converting NO into NO_2 in the air.

2, 3-dimenthylbutane-2	n - heptane
2 - methyl-2-butane	Methylpentanes Isobutaines
Isobutanes	Pentanes
Propylene	2, 2, 4-trinethyl benzene
Ethylene	Butanes
1, 3, 5-trimenthybenzene	m - xylene
1, 2 3, 5-trimenthybenzene	1, 2, 4-trimethy benzene
0 - and p-xylene	Propylbenzenes
Toulene	Isobutanes

It is clear from the above mechanism that the only ingredient actually making the ozone in the air is oxygen (O_2). The hydrocarbons and nitrogen dioxide are not consumed in the reactions. NO_2 recycles in the reactions and hydrocarbons are just modified into other forms.

3.5 Formation of Peroxy Acetyl Nitrate (PAN) in Air

Peroxy acetyl nitrate (commonly called as PAN) is formed in the atmosphere by reaction of acetyl peroxy radicals with NO_2.

In effect, when the concentration of NO falls in the air, the peroxy radicals react with NO_2 instead of oxidizing NO.

$$ROCOO^{\bullet} + NO_2 \rightarrow ROCOONO_2$$

If R is a methyl group, then the resultant PAN will have a chemical formula as $CH_3OCOONO_2$.

3.6 Formation of Aldehydes in Air

Aldehydes are present in air as a result of both direct discharges and from photochemical reactions. Direct sources of aldehydes are mainly automobile exhaust and burning of organic fuel.

Photochemically, aldehydes are known to be produced by dissociation of olefins in presence of ozone or free oxygen atoms.

$$\underset{\text{(olefin)}}{CH_3CH = CH_2} + O_3 \rightarrow CH_3CHOO^\bullet + \underset{\text{(aldehyde)}}{HCHO}$$

3.7 Reactions Involving Oxides of Sulphur

When SO_2 is present in large concentrations in hot plumes coming out of the chimneys, it may get readily oxidized into sulphur trioxide (SO_3) in presence of metals [working as catalysts] already present in the smoke.

$$2SO_2 + O_2 \rightarrow 2SO_3$$

The sulphur trioxide formed in this way reacts with water vapours, present in the plume, to form sulphuric acid.

$$SO_3 + H_2O \rightarrow H_2SO_4$$

When SO_2 diffuses into the atmosphere from the plumes and its concentration is decreased, the dark oxidation (non-photochemical) in presence of metal catalysts is also declined to significant levels. In such conditions, however, the presence of photochemically produced reactive intermediate radical species or other oxidants may be important in oxidizing SO_2 into SO_3. The evidence of this comes from the fact that the rate of SO_2 oxidation increases in the presence of automobile exhaust where large quantities of hydrocarbons and nitrogen oxides are present.

$$SO_2 + ROO^\bullet \rightarrow SO_3 + RO^\bullet$$
$$SO_2 + O_3 \rightarrow SO_3 + O_2$$

The end result of these different reactions is the formation of sulphuric acid. Sulphuric acid in the atmosphere is later gets converted into sulphates such as ammonium sulphate and calcium sulphate.

3.8 Reactions Involving Oxides of Nitrogen

The main oxides of nitrogen present in the air are NO, NO_2 and N_2O. Nitrous oxide (N_2O), being a very stable compound, do not take part in the atmospheric reactions. Nitrogen oxide (NO) is by far the most important of the oxides of nitrogen, which is formed as a primary pollutant during high temperature combustion. Under normal conditions, it readily reacts with oxygen to form nitrogen dioxide.

$$2NO + O_2 \rightarrow 2NO_2$$

Substantial conversions of NO take place only when it is present in high concentrations. Ozone, however, if present in the atmosphere, can oxidize NO at a much faster rate.

$$NO + O_3 \rightarrow NO_2 + O_2$$

The NO_2 in presence of light is broken down into NO and free oxygen atom.

$$NO_2' \rightarrow NO + O$$

This starts a cycle involving NO_2, NO and O_3, as the free oxygen atom reacts with O_2 to from ozone as described earlier in this chapter.

$$O_2 + O \rightarrow O_3$$

No pollutant is accumulated by this cycle but, in presence of ozone, some NO_2 can get converted into NO_3.

$$NO_2 + O_3 \rightarrow NO_3 + O_2$$

The resultant NO_3 further reacts with NO_2 to form nitrogen pentaxide.

$$NO_3 + NO_2 \rightarrow N_2O_5$$

This N_2O_5 is converted into nitric acid by addition of water.

$$N_2O_5 + H_2O \rightarrow 2HNO_3$$

Nitric acid can also be formed by other mechanisms like direct hydration and catalytic oxidation of NO_2.

$$4NO_2 + O_2 + 2H_2O \rightarrow 4HNO_3$$

Nitrous acid has also been found to be formed in the air by the following reaction.

$$NO + NO_2 + H_2O \rightarrow 2HNO_2$$

Both , nitric and nitrous acids, can be photodissociated to again form the oxides of nitrogen.

$$HNO_3 + h\nu \rightarrow NO_2 + OH^{\bullet}$$

$$HNO_2 + h\nu \rightarrow NO + OH^{\bullet}$$

The atmospherically produced nitric acid is, however, gets often converted into both inorganic and organic nitrates.

3.9 Formation of Smog in Air

A natural fog is consisted of droplets of water suspended in air. The term "smog" was coined initially by Dr. Des Voeux in 1905 to denote trapping of smoke in fog. The particulate air pollutants provide the extra condensation nuclei to form the fine droplets of water which trap both particulates and gaseous pollutants in the stable air mass to form a smog. The smog usually allows high concentrations of pollutants to buildup in it under relatively stable atmosphere that may be responsible for vast ecological damage and adverse effects on the health. Most of the air pollution disasters (see Chapter 1) occurred in the world, were associated with the formation of smog. An incidence of formation of smog has also been reported in Bombay in November, 1986, where, though, no deaths were reported, but doctors had detected a phenomenal increase in complaints of chest pain, cough, burning in eyes and other ailments.

The fog is formed when the layer of air is cooled below the dew point, condensing water vapours to form droplets of fog. Fogs are produced mostly during the early morning, especially in the meteorological conditions of no clouds and no or light winds. Such conditions are also favourable for accumulation of pollutants in the atmosphere. Top surface of the fog reflects most of the light back to the space preventing heat to reach inside the fog that checks the evaporation of the droplets. The typical temperature profile in a fog is shown in Fig. 3.3. While there is normal temperature profile at the ground level, inversion persists at the top. Such type of temperature profile will mix the pollutants thoroughly at the ground level to form the smog. The pollutants in smog cannot escape due to the presence of inversion layer at the top.

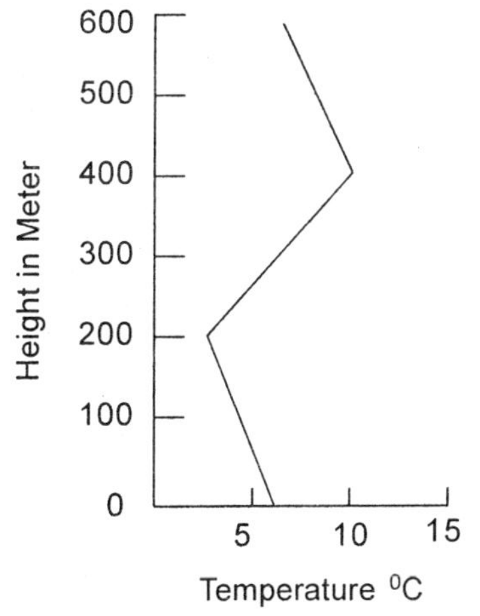

Figure 3.3 Temperature profile in a fog showing an inversion.

Smog basically contains two main types of components

1. Reducing components
2. Oxidizing components or photochemical components

Oxides of sulphur and particulates form the prime reducing components of the smog. Such type of reducing smog is more typical of eastern cities of United States and London.

The oxidizing components of the smog results from the photochemical reactions as described earlier in this chapter. The components of oxidizing smog are called "oxidants" and include mainly :

1. ozone
2. free radical oxygen forms
3. peroxy acetyl nitrate (PAN) and other monologues
4. oxides of nitrogen

As the main components of this type of smog are produced by photochemical reactions, it is commonly known as *photochemical smog*. The severity of this kind of smog is usually determined by its oxidizing properties such as capability of oxidizing iodine. Reducing components like SO_2 remain usually mixed with photochemical smog and may interfere in determining oxidizing properties of smog. The photochemical smog is most typical of Los Angeles where the conditions are ideal for its formation. The near dependence of automobiles results in high levels of nitrogen oxides and hydrocarbons, the prevalence of inversions keeps the pollutants together to allow them to react, and sufficient sunlight initiate the photochemical reactions.

4 Industrial Sources of Air Pollution

4.1 Introduction

Industry is considered to be a major culprit in polluting air. This is partly because of the utilization of enormous amounts of energy and partly due to handling of diverse kinds of materials which themselves, as their intermediates, or as by-products become air pollutants. Thus, the petroleum industry emits a number of hydrocarbons, hydrogen sulphide and sulphur oxides; while the chemical industry, a wide range of substances, usually specific to the processes, as air pollutants. The emission of pollutants in an industry is highly variable depending upon the nature of a specific piece of equipment, materials being processed, and operating procedures and conditions. Major air pollutants generated from different industries are given in Table 4.1.

Some sort of classification of industries is necessary if we wish to understand fully the processes by which the air pollutants are formed and released into the atmosphere. For this, the industries have been broadly classified into ten categories by their major characteristics. Industrial processes, production practices and operations remain more or less similar within each major category in terms of the source and emission characteristics of air pollutants.

4.2 Thermal Power Generation Plants

In India more than 60% of all the power generated comes from the thermal power plants. Huge quantities of coal are burnt in power plants for generating steam.

Concentration of air pollutants in the effluent gases depends largely on the constitution of coal. Analysis of typical Indian coal is given in Table 4.2. Sulphur content in coal is low varying from 0.2 to 2.2%. Practically all the sulphur comes out as sulphur oxides in air during the burning of coal. Ash content of Indian coal is comparatively higher and in some cases reaches up to 52.9%. Ash is the source of several kinds of particulates (Table 4.3). Burning of coal is estimated to mobilize more than 50 elements into the atmosphere, of which several are harmful trace elements. In general, the major air pollutants emitted from coal fired plants are particulates, sulphur oxides, nitrogen oxides, carbon oxides, hydrocarbons, mercury, chromium, zinc, cadmium, iron and carcinogens like benzo(a)pyrene. A 1000 megawatt (MW) coal fired power plant can emit carbon monoxide at the rate of bout 270 kg per second or 16 metric tons a minute. The total emissions of some important air pollutants from thermal power plants are given in Table 4.4, while the emission factors are provided in Table 4.5

Table 4.1 Major air pollutants emitted from various industries

Industry	Pollutants
Aluminium industries	Particulate matter, fluorides, gaseous chlorides
Ammonia manufacturing	CO, HC, NH_3 gas
Carbon black manufacturing	CO, HC, low NO_x
Cement manufacturing	Particulate matter
Charcoal making	CO, HC, particulates, methanol, acetic acid
Chlor-alkali	Chlorine gas, CO, CO_2 , mercury vapours
Coffee roasting	Dust, chaff, mists, smoke, organic acids, nitrogen oxides
Copper smelting	Dust, SO_x
Explosives making	Oxides of sulphur and nitrogen
Feero alloys	CO, dust
Fibre glass making	Particulates from glass melting operations
Glass industries	Particulates , fluorides
Gray iron foundry	CO, dust and fumes, smoke
HCI manufacturing	HCI fumes
Iron & Steel industry	Particulates, MgO, NO_x SO_2, chlorine gas
Lead smelting	Particulates, CO, lead oxides
Lime kilns	Particulates
Nitric fertilizers	NH_3, nitric oxides
Nitric acid	Nitric oxide, nitroge dioxide
Paint & varnish making	Particulates, lost solvents as hydrocarbons
Petroleum refining	SO_x NO_x HC, CO, odours, particulates, NH_3
Phosphatic fertilizers	Silicon tetrafluorides, CO, SO_x
Plastic making	Raw plastics, solvents, aldehydes, ketones, phenols, glycerines
Printing ink	Terpenes, carbon dioxides, aldehydes
Stone quarrying	Dust
Sugar factories	Particulates, CO, HC, NO_x
Sulphuric acid making	Acid mist
Synthetic fibre industry	Carbon disulphide, mists, HC
Wood pulping industry	Odours, SO_2 CO
Zinc smelters	Dust, fumes. SO_2

Table 4.2 Analysis of Indian coal on the basis of air dried weight (after Kumar, 1982).

Constituents	Range %
Moisture	0.6 – 13.7
Ash	6.0 – 52.9
Volatile combustible matter	6.7 – 49.2
Carbon	32.8 – 78.7
Nitrogen	0.7 – 2.1
Sulphur	0.2 – 2.2
Phosphorous	traces – 0.86

Table 4.3 Chemical composition of coal ash (after Kumar, 1982).

Constituents	Range %
Silica	41.62 – 70.0
Alumina	18.40 – 30.76
Ferric oxide	2.2 – 18.36
Titanium oxide	Traces – 2.6
Magnesium oxide	0.2 – 5.98
Sulphatas	Traces – 6.42
Lime	0.43 – 9.38
Phosphorous pentaoxide	0.02 – 5.1

Table 4.4 Total gaseous and particulates emissions from thermal power plants in India without control (after Kumar, 1984).

Components	1947	1970	1975	1980
Particulates (Mt)	0.54	4.21	5.86	8.06
Sulphur oxides (10^3 t)	32.40	250.97	349.28	480.70
Nitrogen oxides (10^3 t)	19.79	148.60	206.81	284.62
Carbon oxides (10^3 t)	1.01	8.26	11.49	15.87
Hydrocarbons (10^3 t)	0.32	2.48	3.45	4.74
Mercury (t)	23.27	180.18	250.71	345.11
Chromium (t)	36.90	285.74	397.68	547.30
Iron (t)	4906.8	38001.60	52889.04	72787.68
Zinc (t)	321.56	2452.45	4313.32	4697.39
Cobalt (t)	7.85	60.79	84.60	116.43

Table 4.5 Emission factors for gaseous air pollutants for coal combustion (kg/ton of coal burned).

	Type of unit		
Air Pollutant	**Power plant**	**Industrial**	**Domestic & Commercial**
Aldehydes	0.0022	0.0022	0.0022
Carbon monoxide	0.22	1.36	22.68
Hydrocarbons	0.09	0.45	4.54
Oxides of nitrogen	9.07	9.07	3.62
Oxides of sulphur	17.23 × S	17.23 × S	17.23 × S
Particulates	7.25 × A	7.25 × A	7.25 × A

S = per cent sulphur contained in coal. For example if sulphur content of the coal is 1.8% the emission factor shall be 17.23 × 1.8 = 31.01 kg/ton.
A = per cent ash content of coal
Data based on AP-44 and AP-66. U.S. Department of Health, Education and Welfare, Washington DC.

4.3 Food and Feed Industry

Odours and particulates are the main air pollutants emitted from the food and related industries. Pleasant odours may be released from coffee roasting plants, chocolates, bread making and others, but when they are in high concentration, persisting for longer periods, may be extremely nauseous. These odours are mainly complex chemical mixtures of aldehydes and related compounds with traces of amines.

Odours caused by biological decay of vegetable wastes, animal meats and fish are extremely offensive. Fish processing units produce obnoxious odours of hydrogen sulphide and trimethylamine. Dusts are produced from grinding, milling, storage and handling of grains. Cotton ginning also emits large amount of fibrous dust. The production of animal feed from alfalfa dehydration plant is also a source of huge quantities of dusts.

Emissions from the fermentation processes (preparation of fermented food, beer, whisky, wines, etc.) include gases like CO_2, and H_2 posing no specific air pollution problems, but the hydrocarbons emitted during the handling of the wastes may be of some concern. Emission factors of the pollutants from some industries of this group are provided in Table 4.6.

Table 4.6 Emission factors of parcitulates for some food and feed industry (Modified from Billings, 1974).

Industry/Process	Emission
Grain elevators	12.2 kg/ton grain handled
Cotton gins	5.4 kg/bale
Alfalfa dehydrators	22.7 kg/ton dry meal
Coffee roasting	
(a) Indirect fired roaster	0.8 – 4.0 kg particulates/ton of green beans
(b) Direct fired roster	3.0 – 5.0 kg/ton green beans

4.4 Pulp and Paper

In wood pupling, cellulose fibres of the wood are separated out by dissolving the lignin in heated caustic solution. There are three main chemical proceses for pulp production. The kraft proces is the most common where the wood chips are cooked in sodium sulphide and sodium hydroxide to dissolve the lignin. The chemicals present in the spent cooking liquor are recovered by a series of concentration steps. The inorganic compounds are recovered from the recovery furnace in a molten state and dissolved in a caustic tank supplied with slacked lime. The slacked lime is usually produced from a lime kiln situated nearby.

Particulate emissions primarily occur from the recovery furnace, dissolving tanks and lime kilns. The typical kraft mill odour is due to hydrogen sulphide, dimethyl sulphide and methyl mercaptan mixture arising mostly from the recovery furnaces. Carbon monoxide emissions may occur from the lime kilns as well as recovery furnaces. Emission factors for the various processes of pulp and paper industry are given in Table 4.7.

Table 4.7 Emission factors for kraft pulp industry (Kg/ton of dry pulp produced).

	Gaseous pollutants			Particulate pollutants
Source	**H_2S**	**methyl mercaptan**	**dimethyl sulphide**	
Digester blow sysem	0.05–0.32	0.4–2.4	0.4–1.72	negligible
Dissolving tank	–	–	–	9.1
Lime kiln	0.45	traces	traces	8.5
Recovery furnace	1.6–3.6	2.3	1.4	68.0
Multiple effect evaporator	0–0.2	0.001–0.013	negligible	negligible

→ Based on Kenline and Hales (1964)

4.5 Inorganic Chemicals

Chemical industry produces a wide variety of chemicals from a wide range of raw materials leading to the production of diverse kinds of air pollutants. Principal emissions are mostly consisted of raw materials, intermediates and reaction products.

The contact process of sulphuric acid production involves contact of SO_2 and SO_3 with water. The waste gas contains unreacted SO_2, SO_3 and sulphuric acid mists. Nitric acid manufacturing brings into the atmosphere nitric oxide (NO) and nitrogen dioxide (NO_2). HCl gas is emitted during the production of hydrochloric acid. The exit gas from hydrofluoric acid plants contains small quantities of HF, silicon tetrafluoride and CO_2. Phosphoric acid is consisting mostly of silicon tetrafluoride and hydrogen fluoride, arising when the phosphate rock is reacted with sulphuric acid. In the thermal process, the principal emissions are P_2O_5, acid mist and fairly large quantities of particulates.

Ammonia is produced by catalytic reaction of hydrogen and nitrogen at high pressure and temperature, resulting often in the emission of CO, NH_3 and hydrocarbons as air pollutants. Chloralkali manufacturing emissions include chlorine gas, CO_2, CO, H_2 and mercury vapours from diaphragm and mercury cells. The major emission from soda ash industry is ammonia. The emission factors for some industries of this group are provided in Table 4.8.

Table 4.8 Emission factors for some inorganic chemical manufacturing plants (modified from Billings, 1974).

Industry	Emission factors
Sulphuric acid (contact process)	Particulates (acid mists) - 0.5 – 2.3 kg/ton 100% H_2SO_4 SO_2 – 22.6 kg/ton acid
Phosphoric acid (Thermal process)	P_2O_5 – 2.3 kg/ton of P burned Particulates - 60.8 kg/ton of P_2O_5 Gaseous SiF_4 and HF - 9.1 – 27.1 kg/ton of P_2O_5
Nitric acid	NO_x – 13.6 – 45.3 kg/ton of acid

4.6 Organic Chemicals

Majority of the emissions from organic chemicals industry belong to the category of hydrocarbons that may be combustible, explosive and potentially toxic. Other air pollutants from this industry are various vapours, odours, SO_2, NO_2, CO, CO_2, and particualtes.

Organic vapour hydrocarbons constitute the major emissions from the industrial applications of organic solvents in manufacture of paints, varnishes, lacquers, adhesives, plastics, textiles, rubber, shoe polishes, floor polishes and waxes.

Carbon black is produced by burning of hydrocarbon fuel such as oil or gas at high temperature with a limited supply of air. The process results in a higher percentage of carbon monoxide and hydrocarbons in the emissions. Hydrogen sulphide and particulates are also present in appreciable amounts in the exit gases.

Plastics or resins are made by polymerization of basic monomers, usually a gas or a liquid. The emissions in this industry include the raw material monomers, solvent vapours and other volatile liquids, and sublimed solids such as phthalic anhydride. Printing ink production results in the formation of particulates and gases like terpenes, CO_2 and aldehydes. Significant emissions from adipic acid, used in manufacture of synthetic fibre, are of nitrogen oxides. Emission factors for this particular industrial group are not available.

4.7 Petroleum Refining

Petroleum refining consists mainly of four steps, separation (distillation), conversion, treating and bleding. The refinging and treatment of crude petroleum gives a variety of substances comprised of distillate fuels like gasoline, kerosene, diesel and jet fuels; lubricating oils; tars; asphalt; bitumen; and many raw materials for petrochemical industry. Essentially, the raw petroleum is distilled into different fractions which are either used directly or converted into more usable forms by breaking down and combining or rearranging the molecules to give the producs of desired quality. In catalytic cracking process, the large molecules are converted, in presence of catalysts, into lower boiling fractions such as gaseous hydrocarbons, gasoline and chemical feed stocks for other petrochemical industries. The final step is the blending of the basic refined stocks with each other and with other additives to meet the specifications of desired product.

Crude petroleum contains various hydrocarbons together with organic sulphur compounds, inorganic compounds containing iron and vanadium, and some alkali and alkaline earths. Depending on the place of origin, sulphur content of oils varies from 0.5% to 4%. Ash content of the oils is quite low at 0.1% or even less as compared to coal.

The sources of air pollution in refineries include the burning of low grade fuels in its own furnaces and boilers. There are particulate emissions from the catalytic cracking and catalyst recovery units. The hydrogen sulphides and mercaptans are originated at the time of their stripping from the lighter grades of fuels such as kerosene, light diesel oil and petrol. Potential of some specific emissions in a refinery are given in Table 4.9. Emission factors for important air pollutants are provided in Table 4.10.

Table 4.9 Potential sources of some specific air pollution from petroleum refineries.

Emissions	Sources
Sulphur oxides	Boilers, process heaters, catalytic cracking unit regenerators, treating units, H_2 flare burning, decoking operations.
Hydrocarbons	Loading facilities, sampling, storage tanks, waste water separatos, blow down systems, catalyst regenerators
Nitrogen oxides	Process heaters, boilers, compressor engines, catalyst regenerators, flares
Particulates	Catalyst regenerators, boilers, process heaters, decoking operations, incinerators
Aldehydes	Catalyst regenerators
Ammonia	Catalyst regenerators
Carbon monoxide	Catalyst regenerators, decoking, compressor engines, incinerators
Odours	Treating units, drains tank vents, waste water separators
Hydrogen sulphide, mercaptons	Stripping of these from light grade oils.

Table 4.10 Emission factors for various processes in petroleum refineries (Based on : Atmospheric emissions from petroleum refineries - A Guide for Measurement and Control. U.S.P.H.S. Publ. No. 763, NCAPC, Cincinati, Ohio).

Processes		Emission factors
Boilers and heaters	Hydrocarbons	63.5 kg/1000 bbl oil burned
	Particulates	363 kg/1000 bbl oil burned
	NO_2	1315 kg/1000 bbl oil burned
	CO	negligible
	HCHO	11 kg/1000 bbl oil burned
Fluid catalytic units	Hydrocarbons	100 kg/1000 bbl oil fresh feed
	NO_2	29 kg/1000 bbl of fresh feed
	CO	6214 kg/1000 bbl of fresh feed
	HCHO	9 kg/1000 bbl of fresh feed
	NH_3	24 kg/1000bbl of fresh feed
	Particulates	2 kg/ton of catalyst circulation (with electrostatic precipitators)
Moving bed catalytic cracking units	Hydrocarbons	39 kg/1000 bbl of fresh feed
	Particulates	2 kg/ton catalyst circulation (with high efficiency centrifugal separator)
	NO_2	2 kg/1000 bbl of fresh feed
	CO-	1723 kg/1000 bbl of fresh feed
	HCHO	5 kg/1000 bbl of fresh feed
	NH_3	2 kg/1000 bbl of fresh feed
Compressor internal combustion engines	Hydrocarbons	0.5 kg/1000 ft^3 of fuel gas burnt
	NO_2	0.4 kg/1000 ft^3 of fuel gas burnt
Miscellaneous process equipments		
1. Blowdown system	Hydrocarbons	136 kg/1000 bbl of refining capacity
2. Frocess drains	Hydrocarbons	95 kg/1000 bbl of refining capacity
3. Vacuum jets	Hydrocarbons	59 kg/1000 bbl vacuum
4. Cooling towers	Hydrocarbons	3 kg/10^6 gal. cooling water
5. Pump seals	Hydrocarbons	8 kg/1000 bbl refining capacity
6. Pipeline valves and flanges	Hydrocarbons	13 kg/1000 bbl of refining capacity
7. Vessel relief valves	Hydrocarbons	5 kg/1000 bbl refining capacity

4.8 Nonmetallic Mineral Industry

The nonmetallic mineral industry includes cement, glass, ceremics, asbestos, coal cleaning plants, concrete batching plants, asphalt plants, talc and lime processing, gypsum manufacturing, refractories, mineral wool production, and processing of crushed stone, gravel, sand and miscellaneous minerals such as phosphates and mica. The mineral processing industry is characterized by particulate emissions in the form of dusts. Most of the minerals are quarried in which material is usually blasted, crushed and later transported to the points of use. All these operations are associated with generation of large quantities of dusts, both coarse and relatively fine.

The production of particulates and gaseous air pollutants in cement industry have been disscussed in Chapter 14 in detail along with their control. Glass manufacturing involves melting of sand and other raw materials at higher temperature in furnaces with the emissions of large quantities of fumes and gases containing silica, carbonates, nitrates, chlorides and fluorides. Particulates in the form of coal dusts constitute the major air pollution problem from coal cleaning plants. Ceramic plants evolve considerable amounts of particulates with some fluorides and acid gases.

Fibre glass is made by drawing the molten glass into fibres, and then coating them with an organic material. The process results in the production of particulates during melting of glass and from the product coating line. Lime is manufactured by calcination of limestone ($CaCO_3$). The kilns are fired with coal, oil or natural gas. Atmospheric emissions are mainly particualtes and combustion products from kilns. The emission factors for some of the industries in this group are given in Table 4.11.

Table 4.11 Emission factors for nonmetallic mineral industry (based on Billings, 1974).

Industry	Emission factors for particulates
Crushed stone	8 kg/ton
Sand and gravel	0.5 kg/ton
Cement	
(a) Wet process	
1. Kilns	76 kg/ton of cement
2. Grinders, dryers etc.	11 kg/ton of cement
(b) Dry process	
1. Kilns	76 kg/ton of cement
2. Grinders, dryers etc.	30 kg/ton of cement
Lime production	
(a) Crushing, screening	11 kg/ton of rock
(b) Rotary kilns	82 kg/ton of lime
(c) Vertical kilns	3 kg/ton of lime
(d) Materials handling	2 kg/ton of lime
Ceramics	
(a) Grinding	36 kg/ton
(b) Drying	32 kg/ton

Table 4.11 *Contd...*

Industry	Emission factors for particulates
Refractories	
(a) Kiln fired	
1. Calcining	91 kg/ton
2. Drying	32 kg/ton
3. Grinding	32 kg/ton
(b) Castable	102 kg/ton
(c) Magnesita	113 kg/ton
Asphalt (Paving)	
(a) Dryers	15 kg/ton of materials
(b) Secondary sources	4 kg/ton of materials

4.9 Ferrous Metallurgical Industry

The ferrous metallurgical industry includes the manufacture of iron and steel from the basic iron ore (Fe_2O_3), and production of molds in the foundries.

Iron and Steel Mills

Iron is produced from the ferric oxide ore by its reduction with carbon. The reduction is carried out in a blast furnace where the iron ore with coke (almost pure carbon) and lime stone are burned to yield iron, a product which still contains some 6% carbon. This carbon containing iron is called pig iron and can be used in casting of products in combination with scrap iron. Pig iron can be further treated to produce steel by mainly three processes, the use of open hearth furnaces, basic oxygen furnaces or electric arc furnaces. In all these processes, the carbon percentage is reduced and some alloy elements are added to impart specific properties to steel such as hardness, tensile strength and corrosion resistance.

The basic air pollution problems in the iron and steel industry originate from the handling of huge quantities of iron ore and coal, and because of the involvement of high temperature furnace processes. Large amounts of dust are produced in mining and processing of ore before its introduction into the blast furnace. Blast furnace is a source of particulates and carbon monoxide. The gases from the open hearth furnace are mainly combustion gases. If the fuel contains sulphur, most of it comes out as sulphur dioxide. Fluorspar, it has been used as slag conditioner, is a source of fluorides. In basic oxygen furnace, a stream of oxygen is used to agitate the hot metal to promote combusion of impurities,. particularly carbon. The process results in generation of particualtes in the form of iron oxide. Likewise, electric arc furnace is also a source of iron oxide particulates.

Besides the above major processes, some other allied operations are also carried out in iron and steel mills. The coke, utilized in reduction of iron ore, is produced from the coal in coke ovens. The process is destructive distillation where all the volatile matter is burnt in the presence of restricted supply of oxygen, leaving behind practically pure carbon.

The coke ovens are source of several air pollutants such as a great variety of organic gases, smoke, dust, H_2S, phenols, cresols, pyridine, NH_3, CO, CH_4, C_2H_6, ethylene and several other ring structures. Due to presence of such valuable products, the coke oven gases, sometimes, are processed to recover useful materials.

Sintering is a process where the fine ore particles are converted into a cake to prevent their blow with the furnace gases. This is carried out by mixing the ore with crushed coal which burns and give a cake. The process usually results in emission of large quantities of particulates. The process called scarfing is the cleaning of hot surfaces of the billets and slabs before rolling. The scarfing machine uses oxygen to burn the surface impurities with the emission of particualtes. The emission factors for iron and steel plants are provided in Table 4.12.

Table 4.12 Emission factors for ferrous metallurgical industry (modified from Billings, 1974).

Process	Emission factors for particulates
A. Iron and Steel Mills	
1. Ore crushing	1 kg/ton of ore
2. Materials handling	5 kg/ton of steel
3. Sinter plants	19 kg/ton of sinter
4. Coke manufacture	
Beehive type	91 kg/ton of coal
By product type	1 kg/ton of coal
5. Blast furnace	59 kg/ton of iron
6. Steel furnace	
Open hearth	8 kg/ton of steel
Basic oxygen	18 kg/ton of steel
Electric arc	5 kg/ton of steel
7. Scarfing	1.4 kg/ton of steel
B. Iron Foundary	
1. Furnaces	7 kg/ton of metal
2. Materials handling	
Coke, lime stones etc.	2.3 kg/ton of metal
Sand	0.14 kg/ton of sand
All data are variable depending on the nature of a specific piece of equipment, materials being processed, and operating procedures and conditions.	

Foundries

The gray iron foundry uses a furnace called "cupola" where the pig iron and the scrap iron are melted together with limestone over an extremely hot bed of coke. The major emissions from cupola furnace are particulates and vapours from the charge materials, and CO, NO_x, SO_2, H_2, HF, CH_4 and some hydrocarbon compounds from the fuel. The molten metal from the furnace is casted in the sand molds. The preparation of sand molds also poses the problem of dust pollution. The emission factors for foundries are given in Table 4.12.

4.10 Nonferrrous Metallurgical Industry

Included in the nonferrous metallurgical industry are the operations of the production of copper, lead, zinc and aluminium besides some minor metals like Hg, Cd, Se, Be, K, Na, Ti and Mo, etc. from their primary ores. The industry also includes secondary recovery of metals from the scrap, and melting and casting operations in foundries. The major pollutants in this industry are particulates and sulphur dioxide, which arise from the handling of large quantities of sulphide and other ores of these metals.

In copper metallurgical operations, the copper sulphide ore is first roasted (oxidised) to remove a portion of sulphur as SO_2 which comes out in the proportion of around 8%, and can be catalytically converted into sulphuric acid. The resultant product, called calcine, is a mixture of sulphides and oxides of copper and iron. The calcine is then smelted in a reverberatory furnace in combination with limestone and /or silica. The slag, consisting of metal oxides with some impurities, float on the top of molten metal sulphides or the matte. The molten copper matte is transferered to a converter where air is blown to oxidize the remaining sulphur and iron leaving behind pure coper. The oxidized iron is removed in the form of slag. The copper, thus obtained is further purified by electrolytic refining. The principal emissions in copper metallurgy are dusts and fumes of Cu, As, Sb, Pb and Zn, SO_2, CO and oxides of nitrogen.

Lead and zinc are also obtained from their sulphide ores. These ores are also roasted forming large emissions of sulphur dioxide. The roaster gases also have impurities like arsenic trioxide (As_2O_3), HCl gas, HF and other such similar compounds which are volatilized from the ore. After roasting, the product is further processed to obtain the pure metals. The overall process of roasting and smelting generates dusts, fumes of primary metal oxide, and some quantities of many other metal impurities like As, Sb, Sn, Cd, Hg, Bi and Se present originally in the ores.

Aluminium is produced basically from bauxite ores (Al_2O_3 + Si, Ti, Fe). In the preliminary purification Al_2O_3 is separated in pure form by reacting the ores with NaOH. Pure aluminium is recovered by electrolysis in the Hall (Heroult) furnace process where Al_2O_3 is dissolved in fused mixture of fluoride salts to dissociate it into Al and O. The major emissions from this industry are particulates consisting of dusts, Al, C and solid fluorides, and gaseous hydrogen fluoride.

The secondary nonferrous metallurgical industry recovers Cu, Pb, Zn and Al from the scrap materials having coatings of various nature. Air pollution problems in this industry arise from the burning of coatings, and production of metal oxides. Nonferrous foundry industry is also associated with the emission of dusts, fumes, volatile metal oxides and combustion gases during melting operations. The emission factors for the whole industrial group are indicated in Table 4.13.

Table 4.13 Emission factors for non-ferrous metallurgical industry (modified from Billings, 1974).

Industry	Emission factors
1. Copper	
Ore crushing	Particulates - 1 kg/ton of ore
Roasting	Particulates - 76 kg/ton of copper SO_2 - 2-8% of waste gases
Reverberatory furnace	Particulates - 107 kg/ton of copper
Converters	Particulates - 19 kg/ton of copper SO_2 - up to 8% of waste gases
2. Zinc	
Ore crushing	Particulates - 1 kg/ton of ore
Roasting (Fluidized bed)	Particulates - 907 kg/ton of zinc
Sintering	Particulates - 82 kg/ton of zinc SO_2 - 4.5-7.0% of waste gases
Materials handling	Particulates - 3 kg/ton of zinc
3. Lead	
Ore crushing	Particulates - 1 kg/ton of ore
Sintering	Particulates - 236 kg/ton of lead SO_2 - 1.5-5.0% of waste gases
Blast furnace	Particulates - 113 kg/ton of lead
Dross Reverberatory furnace	Particulates - 9 kg/ton of lead
Materials handling	Particulates - 2.3 kg/ton of lead
4. Aluminium	
Grinding of ore	Particulates - 3 kg/ton of ore
Calcination of Al-hydroxide	Particulates - 91 kg/ton of Alumina
Reduction cells	
H.S. Soderberg	Particulates - 65 kg/ton of Al Fluorine - 0.04 g/m^3 of waste gases
Prebake	Particulates - 29 kg/ton of Al
Materials handling	Particulates - 5 kg/ton of Al

4.11 Miscellaneous Industrial Sources

In this group are the industries not classified in any one of the major categories described above. Charcoal production, woodworking, a wide variety of manufacturing and fabrication, finishing or coating operations, pharmaceuticals, biologicals and drugs, and textile etc. are some important industrial groups comprising this category of industries causing air pollution.

Charcoal is produced by destructive distillation (pyrolysis in absence of oxygen) of wood in which all the gases, tars, oils, acids and water are driven off leaving virtually pure carbon. Air pollutants released during the process are mainly CO, hydrocarbons, particulates, crude methanol and acetic acid. Most of the other industries of this category produce particulate dusts or mists emissions. The use of radioactive substances in various operations such as nuclear energy production, nuclear explosive service tests, submarine, chemical separation plants, and nuclear fuel reprocessing can also put substantial quantity of radionuclides in the environment.

5 Air Pollution From Automobiles

5.1 Introduction

Transportation is one of the most important sources of air pollution. The contribution of various pollutants from different sources of air pollution is given in Table 5.1. The pollution from automobiles may be highly significant particularly in congested and poorly ventilated roads. Congestion intensifies air pollution problems, increase communicating times, and raises vehicle operating costs, a major factor responsible for poor maintenance of vehicles. The major pollutants generated by the automobiles are hydrocarbons (HC), oxides of nitrogen (NOx) carbon monoxide (CO), smoke and lead.

Table 5.1 Sources of some man-made emissions in united states (percent of pollutants)

Source	CO	HC	NOx	Particulates	SOx
Transportation	92	65	42	14	4
Industry	4	26	21	44	32
Electricity generation	Tr	-	32	21	48
Space heating	3	3	5	14	12
Refuse burning	1	6	-	7	4

On an average basis, the transportation contributes more than 50% of the total pollutants emitted into the atmosphere. According to a report of EPA, the national emissions for 1969 in USA, show a contribution of 144.4 million tons of the total pollutants amounting 281.2 million tons. The quantities since then have been increased considerably.

A report, on the basis of the study carried out by Jawaharlal Nehru University, New Delhi, says that nearly 400 tons of pollutants are emitted every day from 5,00,000 different kinds of vehicles in New Delhi. Total number of vehicles in India have gone considerably higher from 3,06,313 in 1951 to 1,2347,000 in 1987, and growing presently at much more higher rate than this (Table 5.2). In 1990, USA has a record 190 million motor vehicles, almost 30 times higher to that registered in India. Motor cars are most preferred mode of transport in many developed countries (Fig. 5.1) over the rail and buses. An average Amercian drives about 12,000 miles per year in motor vehicles, almost double the distance travelled in most other industrial countries as indicated in Fig 5.1.

Table 5.2 Motor vehicles on road in India (in thousands).

Vehicles	1987	1986	1983	1971
Buses	247	228	178	94
Trucks	967	878	648	343
Jeeps	267	188	154	83
Cars	1442	1350	1061	539
Taxis	186	172	136	60
Two wheelers	7658	6264	3512	578
Three wheelers	437	374	230	37
Miscellaneous	1147	1027	800	134
All vehicles	12351	10481	6719	1868

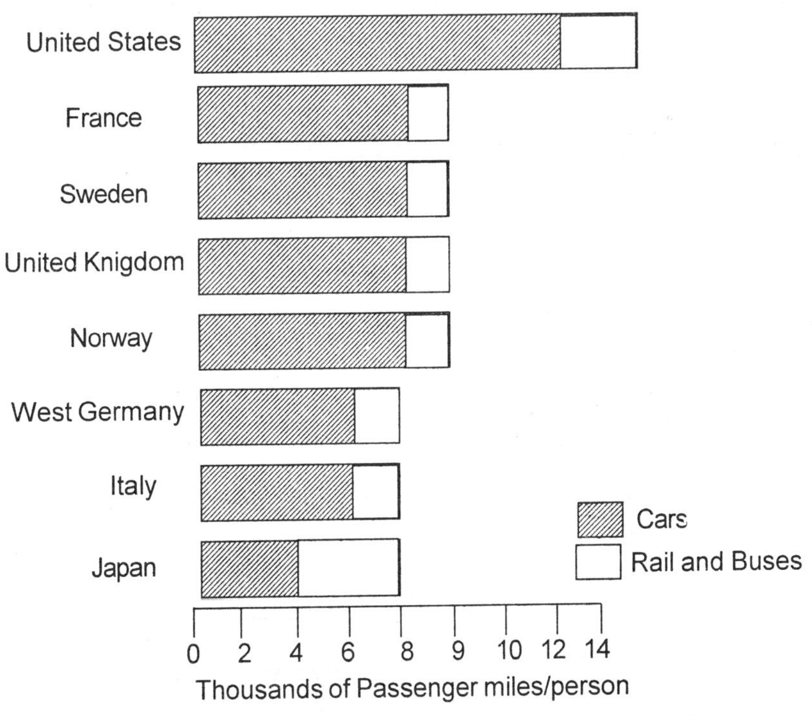

Figure 5.1 Per capita cars and other modes of travel in different coutries.

5.2 Major Auto Pollutants

Carbon monoxide is the major pollutant from the exhaust gases which comprises about 50% of the total weight of the pollutant. Hydrocarbons contribute nearly 8% of the total pollutants in the exhaust, while rest are NOx, particulates and other pollutants. Reports indicate that automobiles account for 70% of CO, 50% of hydrocarbons, and 30-40 per cent of particulates of the total air pollutant present in the big cities like Delhi and Mumbai. Emissions from vehicles in India are provided in Table 5.3

Table 5.3 Autoexhaust emissions in India in 1980 (Million Tonnes\Year).

Category	CO	HC	NOx	SPM	SO2	Total
Cars	0.380	0.036	0.031	0.003	negligible	0.450
Buses	0.209	0.034	0.034	0.012	0.025	0.314
Two wheelers	0.050	0.030	negligible	negligible	negligible	0.080
Three wheelers	0.90	0.050	negligible	negligible	negligible	0.95
Others	0.100	0.020	0.170	negligible	negligible	0.290
Total	1.639	0.170	0.235	0.015	0.025	2.084

Date based on NEERI (1980)

Hydrocarbons and carbon monoxide are the chemical products of combustion in the exhaust gases. Oxides of nitrogen are generated mainly by the chemical combination of nitrogen gas (N_2) and oxygen (O_2) at high combustion temperature. Particulates are produced because of improper combustion, and come out in the form of black smoke. Lead is the combustion product of inorganic additives. Considerable quantities of pollutants are also produced from the fuel tanks, carburettor and crankcase of the automobiles (Fig. 5.2). The contribution of hydrocarbons from various parts of the gasoline based motor vehicles is as follows.

1. Evaporation losses from tank and carburettor (20%)
2. Crank case blowby (25%)
3. Exhaust (55%)

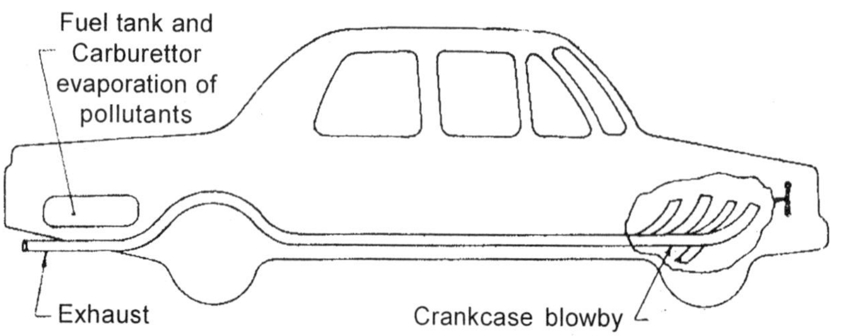

Figure 5.2 Origin of pollutants from various part of an automobile.

The important hydrocarbons present in the exhaust are paraffins, olefins (particularly the low molecular weight mono and diolefins), aromatics (mostly benzene and toluene) and acetylenes. Though, a total of more than 80 compounds have been identified from the auto-exhaust only olefins and polycyclics are of major concern. Olefins play an important role in the formation of photochemical smog, while polycyclics are the potential carcinogenic compounds.

Particulates from automobiles include salts of lead, alkaline earth compounds, iron oxides, soot, carbonaceous material and tars. This particulate material may vary in size from large flakes to submicron particles. Though the total eight of the particulates is comparatively low, considerable significance is given to auto-exhaust particles due to presence of lead and carcinogenic compounds.

Lead added in the form of tetramethyl or tetramethyl lead to the gasoline as an antiknocking agent up to 1 gram per litre of gasoline. The EPA has set a new guideline, on the basis of which, the lead concentration in USA has been reduced to 0.1 g per gallon of gasoline by 1986, and now its use is very restricted there. Lead appears in the atmosphere as a decomposition product in the form of lead chloride, lead bromide, lead sulphate, lead oxide and lead phosphate. Lead is an accumulative nerve toxin and may cause hypertension and heart attacks. It has been estimated that a reduction of lead in gasoline to 0.1 g per gallon in USA will prevent 1.8 million cases of hypertension, 5000 heat attacks and 1000 strokes. A short term survey carried out by the National Institute of Occupational Health, Ahmedabad, indicates that the lead concentration in the blood and urine of policemen and roadside shopkeepers remain particularly high as compared to the unexposed persons.

Switzerland was the first country in Europe to introduce lead-free petrol. Great Britain USA, and Japan, USSR have also completely banned lead in petrol. In India, these days only unlead petrol is sold.

Out of the several polycyclic particulate compounds, one of the most potent carcinogenics is benzo(a)pyrene. In fact, most polycyclic compounds including benzo(a)pyrene become active carcinogenics only after their metabolic activation or oxidation by ozone, NO_2 or PAN. Benzo(a)pyrene is usually present in high concentration in auto-exhausts, and is the product of high temperature combustion of carbonaceous matter.

5.3 Role of the Types of Fuels and Automobiles in Generating Pollutants

The percentage of various pollutants present in the exhaust differs from the types of the automobiles and kind of the fuels used. Automobile emissions also vary depending upon the altitude of the city, slope, and driving on freeway or congested city areas. Operating conditions of the driving have also been found to influence the quantity of emissions of different pollutants as indicated in Table 5.4. Table 5.5 gives the data on relative amounts of various pollutants released by different kinds of automobiles.

Table 5.4. Automobile emissions ($\mu g/m^3$) at various operating conditions during driving of vehicles (after Saranathan 1987).

Pollutant	Idle	Cruising	Acceleration	Deceleration
Spark Ignition Engine				
Hydrocarbons	750 (Less)	300 (Least)	400 (Less)	4000 (Max).
CO	52000 (Max.)	8000 (Least)	42000 (Less)	52000 (Less)
NO	30 (Less)	1500 (Less)	3000 (Max)	12-30 (Max)
Formaldehyde	(least)	(least)	(least)	(least)
Compression Ignition Engine (Diesel Engine)				
Hydrocarbons	250 (Max.)	65 (Least)	115 (Less)	250 (Max.)
NOx	60 (Less)	260 (Less)	850 (Less)	10-50 (Less)
Formaldehyde	Least	Less	Less	Max.
Smoke	Least	Less	Max.	Less

Table 5.5 Pollutant emissions from different kinds of automobiles (after Duprey, 1968). gasoline and diesel engines (in pounds/ 1000 gal. fuel) and air planes (in pounds/landing and take off).

Pollutants	Air Crafts		Motor vehicles	
	Jets	Piston	Gasoline	Diesel
CO	20.6	9.0	2300	60
HC	19.6	1.2	200	136
NOx	9.2	5.0	113	222
Particulates	7.4	2.5	12	110
Organic acids	-	-	4	31
SOx	-	-	9	40

– = data not available

Diesel engine produces much less CO, fewer hydrocarbons and no lead, but considerably higher amounts of NOx and organic acids are released mainly because of the high temperature combustion. Diesel exhaust is usually more odorous than others. High carbon load in diesel exhaust comes from unburnt carbon and higher SOx as a result of greater sulphur content of the diesel. Particulates in diesel exhaust are as high as 10 times to that of petrol exhaust. Composition of diesel exhaust is given in Table 5.6. On the other hand, petrol fueled automobiles produce considerably higher quantities of CO and hydrocarbons than the diesel fueled automobiles. Higher quantities of CO are attributable mainly to inefficient combustion of the fuel in spark ignition gasoline engines. Composition of petrol based auto exhaust is given in Table 5.7.

Table 5.6 Composition of diesel engine smoke (based on various reports).

Pollutant	Concentration
Carbon monoxide	less than 1000 ppm
Hydrocarbons	100-600 ppm
NOx	10-1000 ppm
Formaldehyde	5-20 ppm
Particulates	50 mg/m^3

Table 5.7 Composition of gasoline engine exhaust (uncontrolled engines).

Pollutants	Concentration
Carbon monoxide	3.5%
Hydrocarbons	900 ppm
NOx	1500 ppm

Air planes, both jet and piston types, are also significant producers of air pollutants. However, this source of air pollution is more important at airports and the vicinity. On a nationwide basis the aircrafts contribute only a very small percentage to the nation's air pollution problem. The pollutant loads generated by this kind of transport are provided in Table 5.5. The data clearly indicate that the jet planes are of more concern in producing the pollutants than the piston type planes. Developing countries do not suffer from severe automobile pollution problems because of relatively fewer number of vehicles. Yet according to a WHO report, the auto-pollution occurs at higher levels in certain big cities of India where the vehicles are old and there is poor maintenance due to expensive spare parts. Consequently pollution is out of all proportions to the number of vehicles present. Carbon monoxide levels of more than 100 ppm in ambient air have been recorded at street level in some cities.

The pollution problem by automobiles may be aggravated in hot climates. Consequently, there is an urgent need to study the effects of automobile pollution in relation to hot tropical climates, where till recently, a little work has been carried out.

5.4 Control of Automobile Pollution

We have seen above that the major automobile pollutants of concern are carbon monoxide (CO), hydrocarbons (HC) and oxides of nitrogen that are generated by the evaporation of fuel from carburettor and fuel storage tank; crankcase blowby (leakage between piston ring and cylinder wall); and combustion of fuel (exhaust gases).

Internal combustion engine is a very complicated machine, and much research work is going on for change in the design of the engine so as to minimize the generation of pollutants. The details of the engine design are beyond the scope of this book. Only some general considerations for controlling the automobile pollution are discussed here.

Role of Legislation

Enforcement of laws is an important tool in curbing automobile pollution. The auto emission standards can be promulgated at two stages i.e., at manufacturing and at road level. At the manufacturing stage, the emission of various pollutants like CO, HC, NOx and particulates is checked at the standard test conditions.

It is only very recently that a national level legislation on this subject has come into force after the amendment of the Motor Vehicle Act. Maharashtra Government has recently enacted the amended Motor Vehicle Rules, according to which a 3 per cent volume of CO limit for petrol engines, and a smoke density of 65 hartridge units for diesel engines have been fixed. In case of old vehicles of more than 5 years or which have already run oven 80,000 km, the limit for CO is 4.5 per cent of the total volume of exhaust gases. The details of the automobiles exhaust standards in India are given in chapter 18.

Devices for Automobile Air Pollution Control

Crankcase emission control

The pollution caused by crankcase is result of the leakage of hydrocarbons and other gases between piston ring and cylinder wall which are then released out into the atmosphere through a vent. A complete check on such emissions has been brought by a device called positive crankcase ventilation (PCV), which provides a return of crankcase blowby to the engine for burning again, instead of venting them out to the atmosphere.

Control of evaporative loses

Devices have also been developed for controlling the evaporative losses of fuel from the storage tank. One such device is an attachment of a vapour liquid separator to the tank, which return liquid back to the fuel tank and releases vapours in to a canister containing activated carbon. The stored vapours in this canister are then purged into the combustion chamber (cylinder) for burning.

Control of exhaust emissions

The exhaust emissions from an internal combustion engine can be minimized by following approaches.

Air-fuel ratio is one of the important factors that influences the emission from the exhaust. Normally, an increase in the air-fuel ratio, will facilitate the proper combustion of fuel as the oxygen supply is increased. This will decrease the concentration of CO and hydrocarbons in the exhaust, but unfortunately at the same time NOx concentration is elevated due to increase in combustion temperature. It is, therefore, felt that there is no possibility of controlling all CO, HC and NOx emissions at the same time by manipulating the air-fuel ratio. However, most auto manufacturers today prefer to make the design of engine for an air-fuel ratio which will reduce the emissions of CO and HC without much affecting the engine power.

NO_x emissions are controlled mainly by recirculating a part of the exhaust gases back into the engine and mixing them with fresh incoming air. The entry of exhaust gases back into the engine lowers the combustion temperature without affecting the combustion efficiency, thus reducing the formation of NO_x. Some efforts have also been made to control the NO_x emissions by their catalytic removal in the muffler. Most car manufacturers are now fitting the catalytic converters in their models.

The particulates have been controlled in exhaust by providing a small cyclone in the passage of the exhaust gases. Besides, the proper engine maintenance and proper ignition timings are also important in checking the excess emissions of air pollutants through the exhaust.

Recently, Moscow branch of the Institute of Tractor and Combine-harvester Engines has developed an exhaust purification device which is able to reduce carbon monoxide by 90%, hydrocarbons by 87.5% and NOx by 80-83%.

Alternatives to conventional Gasoline Engine

There are some effects to develop less polluting alternatives to the gasoline engines. There some devices where the conventional gasoline is replaced by LPG, natural gas or other such less pollution causing fuels. Some automobiles have also been developed which run on the solar or electrical energy. Some other types of engines such as stratified change engine or Wankel engine have also been used, but they suffer from some other limitations to make their use popular.

6 Natural and Other Sources of Air Pollution

6.1 Natural Sources

Many of the air pollutants in the form of gases, mists and particulates are naturally present in atmosphere as background concentration arising from various natural sources (Table 6.1). The residence times of these pollutants in the atmosphere remain usually much less in comparison to the principal gases varying from few days to several years. For example, while hydrogen sulphide and sulphur dioxide have only 2 and 4 days of residence time, methane can stay for about 4-7 years in the atmosphere. Natural concentrations of air contaminants are often harmless and do not pose any global problem. They can, however, originate in large quantities in certain localized areas, leading to severe air pollution problems. Some important natural sources of air pollution are given in Table 6.2.

The methane is generated naturally as swamp gas which amounts to nearly 1600 million tons annually. Besides, in salt marshes huge quantities of H_2S are produced from the anaerobic reduction of sulphate. The decomposition of organic matter in these marshes often result in the development of odorous conditions due to production of various decomposition gases.

Table 6.1 Background concentrations of some important air pollutants (after Strauss, 1977).

Pollutants	Concentration (ppm)
Carbon monoxide	0.1
Methane	1.4
Non-methane hydrocarbons	1×10^{-3}
Nitrous oxide	0.25
Nitric oxide	$0.2 - 2.0 \times 10^{-3}$
Nitrogen dioxide	$0.5 - 4 \times 10^{-3}$
Ammonia	$6 - 20 \times 10^{-3}$
Hydrogen sulphide	0.2×10^{-3}
Sulphur dioxide	0.2×10^{-3}
Chlorine	$3 - 15 \times 10^{-4}$
Iodine	$0.4 - 4 \times 10^{-5}$
Hydrogen fluoride	$0.08 - 18 \times 10^{-3}$
Ozone	0 - 0.05

Table 6.2 Some important natural sources of air pollution.

S.No.	Natural sources of air pollution
1.	Swamp gas (gases evolved due to degradation of organic matter and sulphate reduction)
2.	Salt sprays from sea
3.	Dusts pickup by winds
4.	Smoke from naturally set fires
5.	Terpenes and resins from forests, pollen from *Parthenium*, rag weed and other plants, yeasts, molds, animal hair, etc.
6.	Fog
7.	Photochemical ozone
8.	Gases, vapours and particulates from volcanoes, geysers etc.

Salt sprays originate mainly from the droplets of ocean water, injected into the atmosphere, by evaporation of water molecules leaving behind the salts. These particles travel across the coastal land masses and create severe problems of corrosion. They also promote rusting of ships.

For the production of dust, natural sources are considered quite significant, especially in the drier regions. An estimated 30 million tons of dust come from the natural sources each year in the atmosphere. Though, much of this dust is present in the remote areas, still significant quantities may be present in the populated areas after the dust storms. The dust level of air in many cities of Rajasthan in India, remains substantially higher due to the presence of loose sand which frequently becomes airborne.

Terpenes and resins are quite commonly secreted by many forest species. All of them usually have low vapour pressures and get easily vaporized into the atmosphere causing peculiar odours in certain areas. Nearly 170 million tons/year of terpenes have been estimated to be produced by the plant species.

Forest and prairie fires set out by lightening are quite common phenomena in the world. On one hand they destroy the large natural ecosystems, and on the other, generate huge quantities of smoke and other pollutants. The smoke is often produced in so large quantities that its drifting over populated areas produces severe health problems and even traffic hazards. Many of the wild animals, not killed by fire, are killed by inhalation of smoke. A recent forest fire in Indonesia, started in mid-July 1994, is feared to engulf nearly, 1,00,000 hactares of rain forest. Visibility has dropped to near zero in some parts, and people have been urged to wear protective masks. The pollution from this fire has even spread to other countries like Malaysia and Japan. In Malaysia, the air quality index has been recorded a high of 240 microgrammes of pollutants per cubic meter of air in some areas, making it hazardous to life.

Natural fogs are problem in itself on account of the visibility considerations, and further aggravate the air pollution problems by trapping already present pollutants in the air by forming smog.

The problems caused by pollen are quite severe in some parts as they frequently lead to the development of allergic reactions. Besides, certain molds, yeasts, hair, furs and other particulates present in air may also be capable of inducing allergies. It is estimated that each year some 1-2 million tons of pollen are released into the atmosphere in the world. The pollen of ragweed and congress grass have been reported to be culprit in many atopic allergies like asthma, hay fever and skin disorders.

6.2 Cigarette Smoking

Cigarette smoke can be considered a personal air pollution due to inhalation of tobacco smoke. The tobacco smoke contains high quantities of carbon monoxide, polycyclic aromatic compounds (PACs), aldehydes, hydrogen cyanide and lead. Benzo(a)pyrene is one of the important constituents of cigarettes smoke which has been recognized as an important carcinogenic substance.

Cigarette smoke usually provides an intermittant but high dose of pollutants, for instance, carbon monoxide in tobacco smoke may be present in the range of 400 ppm and an exposure to which for 5 minutes at a frequent interval can produce almost similar effects to that caused by community air pollution with exposure of 10-30 ppm for 4-8 hours. The presence of other air pollutants in the air usually have synergistic effects with cigarette smoke and make the problems more complicated.

Besides smokers, non-smokers are also exposed to significant air pollution. Carbon monoxide present in the rooms filled with cigarette smoke can reach, sometimes, beyond the permissible limits and may be quite harmful to the people already suffering from chronic broncho-pulmonary and coronary heart diseases.

6.3 Household Air Pollution

It refers usually to the production of smoke, soot, sulphur dioxide, carbon monoxide and nitrogen oxides from the burning of coal, wood and other fuels for domestic heating and cooking. Cooking fumes of various odours can also be included in this category of air pollution. The duration and level of exposure is highly varying from house to house.

Usually the levels of pollution in the houses remain lower than the community pollution, but in case of poor ventilation the pollutants can accumulate to dangerous levels. In India, there have been reports of people killed by accumulation of carbon monoxide from the burning of coal furnaces in the closed rooms for space heating during winters. The data on the magnitude of domestic air pollution in India is given in Table 6.3.

Table 6.3 Air pollution emissions from domestic sources in India.

I.	Total population in India in 1980				650 million
	Percentage of urban population 20%				130 million
	Rural population at 80%				520 million
	Assuming about 50% of urban population consume fuels except LPG				65 million
	Therefore, the population consume fuels like coal, firewood, kerosene, etc.				585 million
II.	Consumption of fuel				
	Type of fuel	per head/day	total/day		total/year
	Coal	0.3 kg	175×10^3 MT		63.9×10^6 MT
	Wood	0.2 kg	117×10^3 MT		42.4×10^6 MT
	Kerosene	0.25 L	150×10^3 KL		58.4×10^6 KL
III.	Total emissions from domestic sources (million tonnes/year)				
	Type of fuel	SO_2	SPM	NO_x	Total
	Coal	0.760	5.080	0.250	6.090
	Wood	0.080	0.640	0.170	0.890
	Kerosene	0.002	Negligible	Negligible	0.002
	Total	0.842	5.720	0.420	6.982

Data based on NEERI (1980)

6.4 Occupational Exposures to Air Pollution

Occupation exposure to air pollution is often encountered in industry, agriculture, mining and other working environments. This exposure, however, is limited to certain number of hours per day or week unlike community air pollution exposure, which may vary in magnitude but is more or less continuous. Occupational exposure affects mostly males of usually definite age group who are healthy and less susceptible.

The occupational hazards may be caused by physical, chemical and biological agents which may act singly or in combination. However, the chemical agents in the form of dusts, fumes, mists, vapours, gases and solvents are more frequently involved in health problems.

The entry of these agents into the human body from air can take place through respiratory inhalatin, skin absorption or ingestion (swallowing). Prolonged exposure to these airborne contaminats can lead to the development of chronic occupational diseases. Brief but high quantity exposure causes acute illness or even death as happens, sometimes, in case of gas leaks or other industrial accidents.

According to a joint ILO/WHO Committee on occupational health, the biological effects of occupational exposure to airborne toxic substance can be classified as under.

Category A : Exposures do not induce any detectable change in health and fitness of exposed persons during their life time.

Category B : Exposures that may induce reversible effects on health or fitness but that do not cause a definite state of disease.

Category C : Exposure that may induce a reversible disease.

Category D : Exposures that may induce irreversible disease or death.

Some important occupational chemical agents and their effects are described below.

Dusts :

Dusts are composed of solid particles originating usually from handling, crushing, grinding and disintegrating organic and inorganic materials like rocks, ores, metals, coal, wood and grains. The dusts have been reported to cause a variety of respiratory diseases like pulmonary fibrosis (formation of excessive fibrous tissue), obstructive lung disease and lung cancer. They may also cause certain allergies.

Silicosis and asbestosis are two important occupational diseases caused by dusts. Silica which may be in the form of quartz, tridymite or crystalobalite, causes fibrosis of the lung by formation of connective tissues around the particles in lung.

Asbestos is mixture of magnesium and iron silicates in fibrous form. Its dust remains in the form of fine fibres. Its exposure results mainly from asbestos mines, asbestos cement products, fireproof clothes and brake lining industry. Asbestosis develops after prolonged exposures of 5-10 years with symptoms of shortness of breath, chest pain and bronchitis. The particles in lung cause fibrosis, plural plaques (holes in outer covering of lungs), mesothelioma and lung cancer.

Asphyxiants :

These are the category of chemical agents which interfere with the use of oxygen by tissues in the body producing unconsciousness and death. Some important examples are carbon dioxide, methane, hydrogen, helium, carbon monoxide, cyanogen, hydrogen cyanide, arsine, aniline, toluidine, and nitrobenzene.

Irritants

These are the agents which produce irritation of respiratory tract, eyes and skin. Some of the important examples of this group are acrolein, sulphur dioxide, hydrogen chloride, chromic acid, formaldehyde, chlorine, bromine, ozone, phosgene, nitrogen dioxide and arsenic trichloride, inorganic and organic acids, inorganic alkalies, amines, organic solvents, detergents and salts.

Sulpur dioxide is a water soluble gas produced mainly from mines of sulphur or sulphur containing ores, smelters, paper and pulp industry, and sulphuric acid plants. It is powerful irritant of mucous membranes of the eyes and upper respiratory tract causing redness and tears from the eyes, cough, shortness of breath and spasm of larynx.

Skin irritation is mainly caused by several organic vapours like that of formaldehyde and various solvents as well as by chromium and nickel compounds. Fine arsenic powder from arsenic compounds can develop warts on skin which may become malignant. Other symptoms of skin irritation include itching, redness, soreness, blistering, thickening, cracking and dermatitis.

Anaesthetics and Narcotics

These depress the activity of the central nervous system and cause headache, dizziness, loss of consciousness, respiratory or cardiac depression and even death. Some of the important examples of these are acetylene, olefins, ethers, paraffins, ketones, alcohols and esters.

Systemic poisons

The agents of this category produce the injury at sites other than, or as well as, the site of contact. For example, halogenated hydrocarbons can affect a number of organs in human body. Other examples include benzene, phenols (brain and bone marrow), carbon disulphide (heart, nervous system), methanol (nerves and brain), organophosphorus compounds and tetra-alkyl lead compounds (brain), lead (bone marrow, brain), manganese (lungs), cadmium (testes, lungs), beryllium (lungs), mercury (kidneys), arsenic (blood and other tissues) and selenium (liver).

Carcinogens

These substances can produce cancers on frequent and prolonged exposure. Some important carcinogenic compounds are coal tar pitch dust, crude anthracene dust, crude mineral oil, polycyclic aromatic hydrocarbons, nickel, mustard gas, benzidine, vinyl chloride monomer, wood dust and benzene.

6.5 Chemical Weapons

Production and use of chemical weapons in war may be another source of highly toxic substances. Most of them are used in the form of gases or vapous and can be classified on the basis of their effects. Some important chemical weapons along with their effects on humans are given in Table 6.4.

Table 6.4 Chemicals used in chemical weapons and their effects.

Chemicals	Effects
Blood Agents (hydrogen cyanide, cyanogen chloride)	When inhales, they block the blood's oxygen carrying capacity, causing tearing, choking and sometimes, death.
Choking Agents (chlorine, phosgene, chloropicrin)	These gases, some of which smell like hay, tear the lining of the air passages. When plasma enters the lung from the blood stream, victims drown in their own fluids.
Blistering Agents (sulphur mustard, nitrogen mustard, lewisite)	These can linger for weeks causing vomiting, nausea, and eye and skin irritation. Temporary blindness and blisters typically result.
Nerve Agents (tabum sarin, soman, VX)	Substances that disrupt the function of the nervous system. The deadliest of the chemical poisons, they are inhaled or absorbed through the skin and kill within 15 minutes.

6.6 Coal Fires

Underground coal fires can pose severe environmental problems by producing huge quantities of air pollutants released through surface of the earth. One such incidence of coal fire has come to light in India at Jharia in Jarkhand where it is playing havoc with the lives of the people by releasing dangerous amounts of air pollutants in the nearby villages. The respiratory diseases among the people are continuously on rise, and it becomes difficult even to breath at times.

Such coal fires are often difficult to extinguish. They can remain alive for years together until all the coal is engulfed. Besides air pollution, they make a huge loss of natural resources in the form of coal.

7 Effects of Air Pollutants on Plants and Microoraganisms

7.1 General

Though, most gaseous pollutants are actively metabolized by plants, yet many species are susceptible to damage at even low concentrations of pollutants. For most pollutants, plants have been reported to be susceptible even to the concentrations that do not make any impact on animals.

Air pollution has caused a widespread damage to natural vegetation and economic crops. Historically, there have been reports of killing of entire plant life by ore smelters which were typically located in the rural areas and produced huge quantities of sulphur oxides from the sulphide containing ores. In Leeds (U.K.) the reports confirm substantial reduction in growth of lettuce and radish in heavily polluted areas. In California a widespread damage to the vegetation has been result of the air pollution by sulphur dioxide, oxides of nitrogen and ozone. Socramento valley in California has shown killing of the entire vegetation in 260 km^2 and reduced growth in further 320 km^2 area by the combination of sulphur dioxide and metallic pollutants. The pollution from smelters has resulted in complete destruction of vegetation at Ducktown, Tennessee. The air pollution from a copper smelter causing plant damage has led to an International dispute between Canada and the United States. Photochemical smog at Los Angles has also caused a widespread damage to certain crops like Citrus, and some of the surrounding forested area.

In India, though, we do not have any well documented data relating to the magnitude of economic loss as a result of plant damage by air pollution, but there have been several sporadic reports of the damage done to the plants by cement dust and sulphur dioxide.

Not all the plants are sensitive to air pollution. Some plants can resist fairly high levels of pollution and can be employed as indicators of air pollution (Table 7.1).

7.2 Structure of Leaf and Absorption of Pollutants

Before pursuing the effects of air pollutants on plants, we should consider briefly the structure of leaf (Fig. 7.1). The leaf has an outermost layer of epidermis on both the sides having relatively tough and inactive cells that provide protection to the leaf. Sandwitched between the two layers of the epidermis is present the chlorophyll bearing parenchymatous tissue, the seat of photosynthesis. The parenchymatous cells are of two structural types the elongated palisade cells and the irregular spongy cells. The palisade cells are arranged in regular layers and provide strength to the leaf, while the spongy cells are arranged in loose and irregular manner that creates open speaces through which air can circulate to various cells. For air to enter the leaf, there are openings in the epidermis called stomata. Majority of the stomata are usually present on the lower surface of the leaf. Each stomata is guarded by a pair of guard cells, whose turgidity variations regulate the opening and closing of these stomata. The leaf also has a network of veins (vascular bundles) consisted of xylem and phloem, for transportation of water and food. Most of the biological functions of a plant like photosynthesis, respirtation and transpiration takes place in leaves.

Table 7.1 List of plant indicators of air pollution.

SO_2 Indicators			
Non-Flowering Plants			
Alternaria tenuis			
Fusarium moniliforme			
Penicillum nigricans			
Rhizopus nigricans			
Flowering Plants			
Annual	**Herb**	**Shrub**	**Trees**
Amaranthus viridis	*Carthamus tinctorius*	*Nerium indicum*	*Adenia cordifolia*
Abelmoschus esculanuts	*Gosspyium sp.*		*Buchanania lanzan*
Arachis hypogea	*Helianthus annus*		*Butea monosperma*
Brassica nigra	*Hibiscus esculentus*		*Diospyros meleanoxylon*
Cyamopsis tetragonoloba	*Hordeum sp.*		*Mangifera indica*
Glycine max	*Lactuca sativa*		*Pyrus malus*
Hordeum vulgare	*Medicago sativa*		*Pinus sp.*
Ipomea crassicauli	*Spinacea oleracea*		
Medicago sativa			
Phaseolous aureus			
Phoenix sylvestris			

Table 7.1 Contd...

Annual	Herb	Shrub	Trees
Phaseolus radiatus			
Pisum sativum			
Raphanus sativus			
Solanum melongena			
Triticum aestivum			
Fluride Indicators			
Cyanodon dactylon			
Cement Dust Indicators			
Glycine max	*Calotropis procera*	-	*Cassia fistula*
Triticum aestivum	*Withnania somnifers*		*Dalbergia sissoo*
Fly Ash Indicators			
Triticum aestivum	-	-	
Petro-coke Indicators			
Phaseolus aureus	-	-	
Smoke indicatos			
	-	-	*Azadiracta indica*
Dust Indicators			
Triticum aestivum	*Helianthus annus*	-	
	-	-	*Mangifera indica*
	-	-	*Polyalthia longifolia*
	-	-	*Thespesia populnea*
Herbicide Indicator			
Cicer arietinum	-	-	
Combination of Pollutants			
Brasssica oleracea	*Croton sparasiflorum*	*Lantana camera*	*Aegle marmelos*
Chenoipodium album	*Withania sominifera*	*Nerium odoratum*	*Mangifera indica*
Cicer arietunum			*Melia indica*
Commelina benghalensis		*Tobernae montana*	*Tactona grandis*
Dolichos lablab		*Coronaria*	
Glycine max			
Helianthus annus			
Medicago sativa			
Sinchus asper			

Gases and vapours together with the air pollutants enter the leaves chiefly through stomata. The degree of opening of stomata shal! determine the quantity of air pollutants absorbed by the plant. The conditions that facilitate the opening of stomata are high light intensity, high relative humidity, moderate temperature and adequate soil moisture.

The cuticle present on the epidermis is also permeable to gaseous diffusion to some extent, but it is rather a slow process. Sulphur dioxide may diffuse through the cuticle in gaseous phase, or it may be absorbed into it to react either with the chemical compounds making up the cuticle or with a thin film of water present over there. Most of the pollutants can react with water in the substomatal cavity to get converted into other active species. For example, sulphur dioxide is rapidly oxidized to sulphite in the substomatal cavity from where it can move to the other tissues.

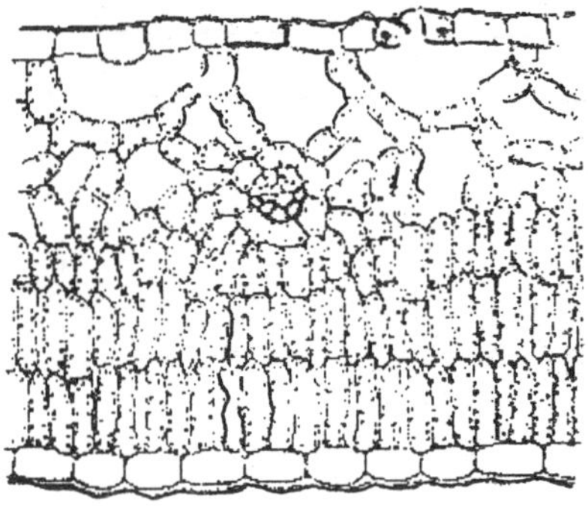

Figure 7.1 General anatomical features of a leaf

7.3 Factors Influencing the Plant Responses to Air Pollutants

The responses of plants to the air pollutants are not always same but vary with the change in environmental conditions like solar radiation, temperature, humidity, soil moisture, mineral nutrition, phenological stage of the plant, and the age of the individual leaf. Sunlight is an important factor in governing the opening and closing of stomata, thus influencing the direct uptake of gaseous pollutants. Temperature influences the rate of chemical activity and intake of gases by the plants. The increse in relative humidity is often associated with enhancing the severity of damage by air pollutants. According to Swain (1923) a critical point of injury by SO_2 is generally reached above 90% relative humidity.

A good mineral nutrition to the plants can suppress the effects of air pollutants as reported by some workers (Rao er al. 1985). The phenological stage of the plant and leaves can be a significant factor in determining the sensitivity of the plant. It has been observed that the younger leaves are quite resistant to SO_2 injury than the older ones (Halbwachs 1984). Guderian (1977) has reported that the age between flowering and fruit ripening is most critical for SO_2 injury in *Phaseolus* sp.

The degree of plant injury caused by pollutants depends not only on the quantity of pollutants emitted into the air, but also to a large extent on the meteorological factors. In Los Angeles district of the USA, greatly expanded industrial activity coupled with the persistant period of low wind velocity and atmospheric stability for sevaral days or weeks has led to the buildup of sufficient concentration of pollutants to make the large scale crop damage. The topographic features of an area can also aggravate the effects.

7.4 Kinds of Injury to the Plants

The injury to the plants can be attributable to the acute or chronic exposures of air pollutants. The acute effects relates to short term exposures to high concentrations of the pollutants as might occur under fumigation or sudden release of certain pollutants in atmosphere by industrial accidents. The chronic effects are the result of prolonged exposures to low concentrations as usually the case under normal ambient atmospheric conditions.

The responses of plants to air pollutants can be manifested in the form off :

visible injury

invisible or subtle injury

- effects on growth, reproduction and yield
- effects on physiology and biochemical reactions

Visible Injury

The visible injury usually occurs in the following forms.

1. *Necrosis* : Death and collapse of the cells due to plasmolysis that causes them to lose water leaving a discoloured dead area in the green tissue. There may be death of isolated cells, tissue or the entire plant.
2. *Chlorosis* : Loss or reduction of chlorophyll resulting in bleaching or fading of the leaf's green colour that makes the leaf to appear yellowish or pale green.
3. *Abscission* : Dropping of leaves
4. *Epinasty* : Downward curvature of the leaf due to higher rate of growth on the upper surface.

Invisible Injury

The invisible injury is result of the impairment of physiological and biochemical reactions. The most severe effects can occur on photosynthesis, respiration, photorespiration, nitrogen metabolism, pigment synthesis, enzyme structures and stomatal responses.

The reduction in growth, yield and reproduction is a measure of physiological and biochemical disturbances brought about by the pollutants in the plants.

7.5 Effects of Air Pollutants on Plants

Our knowledge of plant damage on visible injury, though,has been derived initially from the field observations in the affected areas, a great deal of information has come later from the laboratory or green house experiments carried out using different air pollutants with different concentrations and length of the exposure on various plant species. In many instances, however, the results were of purely theoretical importance as the concentrations used were too unnatural to be met within the ambient conditions. Never-theless, the results obtained from such experimental studies are of great significance as they may be able to define the mechanisms underlying the overall reduction in growth and yield of the plants.

Effect of sulphur dioxide

The concentrations of sulphur dioxide above 0.4 ppm causes an acute injury to the plants. The lower doses in the range of 0.1 and 0.4 ppm most often get oxidized inside the plant cell and may lead to chronic injury. Some plants are more sensitive to SO_2 than others. A list of some sensitive and resistant plant is provided in Table 7.2 Table 7.3 gives the sensitivity of various plant resonses to sulphur dioxide under laboratory conditions.

Table 7.2 Classification of some plant species on the basis of their relative sensitivity to sulphur dioxide

Sensitive	Intermediate	Resistant
ALfalfa	Cauliflower	Gladiolus
Barley	Tomato	Rose
Cotton	Brinjal	Potato
Lettuce	Begonia	Hibiscus
Beans		
Carrot		
Wheat		

Visible Injury

1. The chronic injury usually results in the form of chlorosis of leaves which may turn into necrosis. Sulphur dioxide enters the leaves through stomata attacking the spongy parenchymatous tissue and then spreading to the palisade layer. Since the cells near the veins are rarely affected, a damaged leaf often show a network of green veins on discoloured background (Fig 7.2).

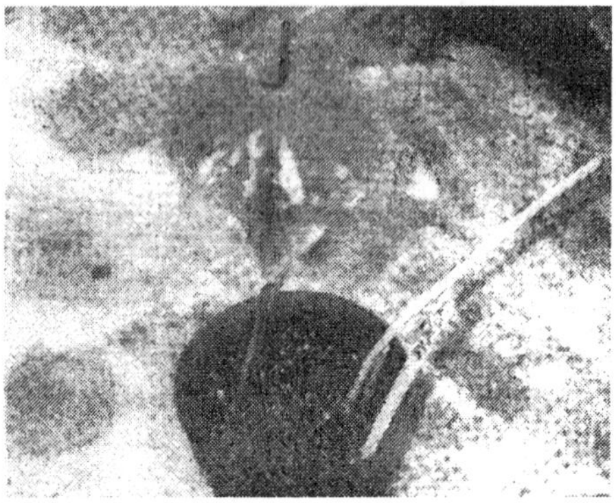

Figure 7.2 Sulphur dioxide (0.25 ppm) exposed cucmber plant showing symptoms as interveinal chlorosis and necrosis on either leaf surface (Photo courtesy Dr. Madhulika Agarwal)

2. The acute injury usually manifest itself in the necrosis of leaves. It starts from development of small irregular shaped greyish green areas with water soaked appearance due to collapse of mesophyll cells. These areas subsequently become dry to form brownish-red to black coloured necrotic spots. Fruits also develop necrotic patches when their surface is exposed to sulphur dioxide.
3. At higher concentration of SO_2, majority of flower buds become stiff and hard to fall subsequently from the plants because they are unable to flower.

Table 7.3 Sensitivity of various plant responses to SO_2 under laboratory conditions (after Varshney 1992).

System	Concentration	*Time (h) (cxt)	**Dosage	Time involved in evaluating the response in days	Reference
Chlorophyll content					
S. oleracea	9pphm	4	0.36	45	Boralkar & Chaphekar (1980)
A.esculentus					
P. Sawani, P. aureus					
Triticum aestivum	1 ppm	384	384	40-120	Prasad & Rao (1982)
Glycine max	1 ppm	144	144		
Pollen germination	1 ppm				
Cicer arietinum	1310μg/m3	1-5	0.5-2.5		Varshney & Varshney (1981)
N.indicum					
P. alba					
T. axillaris					
Proteins					
A. esculentus	9 pphm	4	0.36		Boralkar & Chaphekar (1980)
S. oleracea					
P.savani, A. viridius					
P. aureus					
Phaselus aureus	0.08-0.5 ppm			3	Nandi et al. (1980, 81)
Ascorbic acids					
Zea mays	1 ppm	2	20-62	30-80	Choudhary & Rao (1977)
Glycine max	0.7 ppm	2	70		
Zea mays	3 pphm	84	1.24	14-49	Varshey & Varshney (1984)
Breassica nigra					
P. radiatus					

Table 7.3 Contd...

System	Concentration	*Time (h) (Cxt)	**Dosage	Time involved in Evaluating the response in days	Reference
Enzymes					
Peroxidase					
P. radiatus	3 ppm	84	1.24	14-49	Varshney & Varshney (1984)
B. nigra					
Z. mays					
Phaseolus aureus	0.08-0.5			3	Nandi et al. (1980.83)
GDH					
B. nigra	3 pphm	84	1.24	14-49	Varshney & Varshney (1984)
P. radiatus					
Catalase					
Phaseoulus aureus	0.08-0.5 ppm			3	Nandi et al. (1980,83)

* Successive cycles of fumigation were converted into cummulative period expressed in hours.

** All values were converted into ppm h to calculate dosage.

Effects on phsyiological and biochemical reactions

1. At lower concentrations below 0.1 ppm, no injury occurs to the plants and many enzymes and reactions are, infact, activated. Pahlich (1975) suggested a general theory of the mode of action of SO_2 according to which it is converted into organic compounds at lower concentration, leaving the enzymes unaffected. But, if the dosage of SO_2 is such that its conversion into organic sulphur is not complete, then the residual inorganic sulphur leads to the inhibition of enzymes.

2. It is now fairly well known that the rate of photosynthesis in plants is greatly depressed by SO_2. The rate of photosynthesis, if decreased by that concentration of SO_2 which did not show acute effects, the plants can recover after discontinuation of the fumigation (Bennet & Hill 1973).

   The major cause of decrease in the rate of photosynthesis is the suppression of certain enzymes together with preferential incorporation of some metabolic intermediates of sulphur like sulphite, into the thylakoid membranes (Ziegler & Happm 1977). Sulphur dioxide also leads to the selective inhibition of photosystem-II and evolution of oxygen (Shimazaki & Sugahara 1979).

3. Sulphur dioxide alters the chemical composition and quantitatively reduces the chlorophyll pigments in almost all green plants, that may occur either by inhibiting the chlorophyll synthesis or by its destruction. There might be several mechanisms involved in destruction of chlorophyll. Chlorophyll *a* has been found to be converted into phaeophytin *a* (Rao & Le Blanc 1966); and chlorophyll *b*, into chlorophyllide *b* (Malhotra 1977). Chlorophyll can also be oxidized by formation of super oxide anion radicals (O_2-) and hydrogen peroxide. Formation of free radicals is an important factor in destruction of chlorophyll.

   Similarly carotenoids in some plants can also be damaged by SO_2, as they are comparatively more sensitive than chlorophyll (Shimazaki et al. 1980).

4. Sulphur dioxide causes inhibition of photorespiration by forming glyoxylate bisulphite, a potent inhibitor of glycollate oxidase (Zelitch 1957). Photorespiration can also be affected by formation of other toxic bisulphite compounds of glyceraldehyde, -ketoglutarate, pyruvate and oxaloacetate.

5. Though some workers have reported stimulation of respiration at certain concentrations of SO_2 in some plants, but most plants, however, show an inhibitory effect on respirtion. Sulphur dioxide affects the oxidative phosphorylation reducing the ATP formation (Miller et al. 1975).

6. Exposure of plants to SO_2 leads to an increase in levels of free amino acids and polyamines (Jager et al. 1972, Pierre & Queiroz 1981). The increase in free amino acids is often accompanied by a reduction in protein level.

7. Lipids and carbohydrates have also been found to be inhibited by SO_2 at slightly elevated concentrations. Lipids can be oxidised by peroxidase activity to form ethylene and ethane in the SO_2 affected plants (Bressan et al. 1979). An increase in phenol content, the indication of stress situation, and a decrease in ascorbic acid have also been reported in several species.

8. Sulphur dioxide causes inhibiton of the activities of certain enzymes like ribulose diphosphate carboxylase, phosphoenolpyruvate carboxylase, melate dehydrogenase, glocollate oxidase, glumate - oxaloacetate transaminase and catalase. Sulphur dioxide, on the other hand, can also enhance activities of the enzymes like peroxidase and glutamate dehydrogenase (Spedding 1978)
9. Stomatal activity of the leaves is greatly influenced by SO_2. Low concentration of SO_2 may induce opening of stomata while concentration to their closure. A high concentration of SO_2 can also damage guard cells. The effect on stomatal opening shall influence the normal gaseous exchange in photosynthesis and the rate of transpiration.

Effects on growth and reproduction

1. Both visible and invisible injury finally express themselves in the reduction of growth and yield of the plants. Visible injury hastens the senescence of leaves, flowers and fruits. Several workers have found reduced growth and yield of the plants by impairment of physiological and biochemical reactions even without any noticeable visible effects (Ashanden & Mansfield 1977, Ayazloo et al. 1980).
2. Sulphur dioxide affects reproduction in plants by supressing the pollen germination, pollen tube elogation and development of cones, fruits and seeds. Sulphur dioxide also interferes with nucleic acid metabolism by deactivation of DNA and RNA (Shapiro et al. 1970) and by inhibiting mitotic activity, that retards seed germination.

Effects of ozone

Around 1958, ozone injury was attributed to wide spread tobacco crop damage in America. Later it was found that it causes more damage to vegetation than any other pollutant in united States. O_3 has synergistic relation with SO_2 as it has been suggested that much lower O_3 (or SO_2) can produce symptoms if given in combination with the other gas. In case of these two gases it has been suggested that O_3 opens the stomata and allows SO_2 in.

Most of the work dealing with ozone injury on plants reveals that some plants are much more sensitive to O_3 than others. Heck (1968) has classified plants into three groups on the basis of their sensitivity to O_3 in producing minimal visible injury after one hour of exposure (Table .7.4) O_3. Damage to several plants species begins to occur at levels of 0.03 ppm or more for a few hours, a quite typical daily level in many urban areas.

Table 7.4 Classification of plants according to their sensitivity to O_3 based on the production of minimal visible injury after 1 hour of exposure (Heck 1968).

Sensitive (0.1 ppm)	Intermediate (0.2 ppm)	Resistant (0.35 ppm) Spinach
Radish	Onion	Beat
Musk melon	Chrysenthemum	Poinsetta
Oat	Dog weed	Black walnut
Pinto bean	Sweet corn	Strawberry
White pine	Wheat	Carrot
Potato	Lima bean	
Tomato		

Visible Injury

1. The ozone enters primarily into the plants through stomata. Size and opening of stomata play an important role in ozone diffusion into the leaf. Most workers agree that O_3 cannot diffuse into the plants when stomata are closed. High concentration of O_3 leads to the stomatal closure but cannot check its complete entry into the plant. Ozone penetrates through the stomata preferentially into the palisade layer, a major area of damage. Most symptoms of O_3 damage appear on the top surface of the leaves. Ozone reacts with some components of the cells in the leaf tissue to collapse them forming localized watery areas which get transformed later into necrotic areas. The injury causes a pattern of small spots or flecks, which appear first as black but slowly turn light as the tissue dies. On severe exposure, these spots often unite to form large areas of dead tissue. (Fig.7.3)

Figure 7.3 Ozone exposed (0.3 ppm) snapbean showing sysmptoms as interveinal yellowish flecks mostly on upper leaf surface. On left is the control plant (Photo courtesy Dr. madhulika Agarwal)

2. Ozone causes bleaching of chlorophylls within the injured cells with breakdown of leaf structure around them.
3. Ozone exposure injures leaves only at a certain stage of expansion with maximum palisade intercellular spaces. It is observed that neither very young nor very old leaves show visible injury.

Effects on Physiological and Biochemical Reactions.

1. There is a large amount of unknown material in the cell wall including amino acids, glacturonic acid residues, lignic acid and bound Ca^{++} which together form a gel-like substance inside the wall. The ozone can react with this gel to adversely affect the cell wall's ionic exchange properties and water permeability.

2. The enzymes responsible for cell wall synthesis are also inhibited by O_3.
3. Ozone has been shown to modify amino acids like cystiene, methionine, tryptophan, tyrosine. Histidine and phenyl-alanine; proteins; unsaturated fatty acids and sulphydryl residues (Mudd et al. 1969). Since all these substances are components of plasmalemma, its permeability is greatly modified by ozone.
4. Ozone leads to an increase in amino acids indicating that protein synthesis has either declined or its hydrolysis has triggered (Ting & Mukerji 1977).
5. The level of fatty acids is lowered in the tissue by O_3 exposure. Since the -SH groups are necessary for lipid metabolism, it is possible that all the lipid changes takes places as a result of -SH oxidations.
6. Ozone can lead to a fall in ATP levels in several plants.
7. Ozone depletes the levels of nitrate redyctade in soyabean (Tingey et al. 1973).
8. There is an increased anthocyanin formation (Koukal & Dugger 1967) and decrease in chlorophyll levels by ozone in several plant species.
9. Ozone causes a decline in leaf starch (Dugger et al. 1966).
10. Ozone promote disulphate formation due to oxidation of -SH groups. Most enzymatic effects are related to this due to impairment of protein structure.
11. Ozone inhibits synthesis of polysaccharides.

Effects on growth and reproduction

1. Cumulative injury by ozone results in premature senescence and ageing of the plants.
2. Ozone can reduce the growth of plant and fruit setting in many species. Studies by Manning & Feder (1976) have clearly revealed a reduction in growth and formation of fruits in certain tomato and beans species under green house conditions. Similarly, other crops like *Brassica oleracea, phaseouls vulgaris, Triticum aestivum, Gossuypium hirsutum, Spinacea oleracea, Glycine max* and several other plants have shown reduced growth under exposure of O_3.
3. Ozone can also lead to the reduction in nutritional quality of several vegetables and crop plants as a result of the decrease in total nitrogen content (Pippen et al. 1975).
4. Reproduction in plants is severely affected due to reduction in pollen tube elongation(Feder 1968).

Effects of Peroxy Acetyl Nitrate (PAN)

PAN is one of the important constituents of photochemical smog, and has ben found to cause widespread effects on crops and other vegetation due to its oxidative nature like ozone. Table 7.5 provides a list of sensitive and resistant plants to PAN type of injury based on the appearance of minimal visible symptoms. PAN damage can occur at levels as low as 0.01 ppm for a few hours or even within a few minutes with levels near 0.1 ppm. Several studies (Naegele 1974) have indicated that lettuce, potato and Petunia may get affected by four hours of exposure to 15 ppm PAN.

Table 7.5 Sensitivity of plant species to PAN type of injury.

Sensitive	Resistant Spinach
Oats	Cauliflower
Beet	Carrot
Corn	Cucumber
Pepper	Onion
Clove	Strawberry
Tobacco	Squash
Beans	Orchids
Alfalfa	Lily
Petunia	
Pig weed	
Wild oat	

The symptoms of PAN are not observed on very young or very old leaves. The most susceptible leaves are of intermediate ages. The uptake of PAN by the leaf is clearly related to its water solubility. The PAN which has more soluble alkyl groups, will be readily taken up by the leaves (Hill 1971). The requirement of light has also been noted for the plant injury to be caused by PAN. Dugger et al. (1963) have found that the maximum response for the injury occurs at the wavelength range of 420-480 nm.

Visible Injury

The major entry of PAN into the leaf takes place through stomata. It affects primarily the spongy parenchymatous cells particularly in the vicinity of stomata. The visible damage, attributable to PAN, is usually reflected in the form of glazing or bronzing of the lower surface of the leaves with involvement in some cases of the upper surface as well. This happens mainly with the collapse of protoplasts of the mesophyll cells resulting in the formation of air spaces which give rise to the glazed appearence. The maturity of the leaf cells has a significant bearing on the susceptibility to PAN, the frequent cause of the damage to occur in the form of strips or bands across the leaf. The lesions due to PAN are fairly characteristic but all plants do not show the same qualitative response.

Effects on physiology and biochemical reactions.

1. Many steps involved in the carbohydrate metabolism of plants (Fig .7.4) are disrupted by the exposure of PAN. Ordin and Hall (1967) reported the suppression of cellulose synthetase affecting the formation of cellulose. Enzymes, phosphoglucomutase and phosphorylase are also inhibited by PAN. According to Hansen and Stewart (1970), PAN can inhibit the mobilization of starch in darkness due to suppression of phosphorylase reaction.
2. PAN inhibits CO_2 fixation during photosynthesis (Dugger et al. 1963) and also damages the chloroplasts.
3. Several pigments present in the plants are susceptible ro PAN breakdown. Susceptibility of the pigments has been reported in the following order.

   Caretonoides $<$ chlorophyll $<$ chlorophyll *b*

4. Indole acetic acid can loose its hormonal properties due to reaction with PAN.
5. Like ozone, PAN also destroys the -SH groups leading to the breakdown of protein structures. Activities of several enzymes like glucose-6-phosphate dehyrdogenase and phosphoglucomutase are also inhibited by PAN.

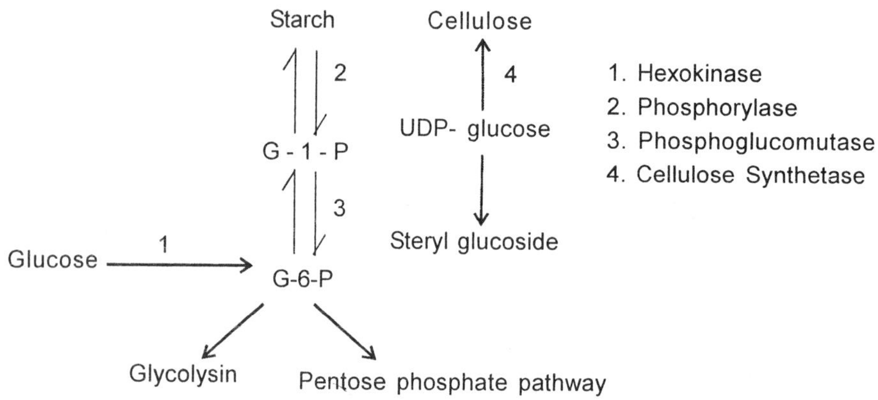

Figure 7.4 Steps of carbohydrate metabolism disrupted by PAN

6. PAN can also react with phytochrome fr.
7. Fatty acide synthesis is affected by PAN due to oxidation of NADPH (Mudd & Dugger 1963)
8. PAN interferes with activities of nicotinamide derivatives, sulphur containing compounds, purines, pyrimidines and amines

Effects on growth and reproduction

1. Most of the biochemical effects listed above manifest themselves into the reduction in growth and reproduction. Growth suppression without detectable leaf injury has been found in tomato with chronic exposures of PAN at lower concentrations.
2. The suppression of overall growth of the plant is greatly attributable to the impairment of cell wall sýnthesis. Ordin & Hall (1967) reported inhibition of cell wall polysaccharide synthesising system, while Ordin & Skoe (1964) found inhibition of metabolism of cell wall glucans and cellulose synthesis.

Effects of oxides of nitrogen

The oxides of nitrogen are commonly represented by nitrogen oxide (NO) and nitrogen (NO_2). The effects of these are usually independent and additive in nature. NO_2 can suppress the growth of plants at 0.5 ppm with several days of exposure. Acute doses for plant injury are usually higher. Except for the few studies made in the field, most of the information regarding NOx injury to plants comes from the experimental studies made mostly taking higher concentrations than those commonly encountered in the polluted environments (Mansfield & Feder-smith 1981).

Visible Injury

1. Chronic exposures of NO_2 at low concentrations usually do not show any visible injury to the plants. Acute injury with high concentrations in excess of 25 ppm can cause the characteristic leaf lesions appearing initially as water soaked areas on the upper surface of leaf, which later get converted into necrotic spots due to tissue collapse. These irregularity shaped necrotic lesions, appearing white to tan in colour, usually remain situated between large secondary veins near the leaf margins.
2. Bleaching or chlorosis of leaf also occurs by NO_2 injury associated with premature fall.

Effects on physiology and Biochemical Reaction

1. Protein content is found to be elevated by NO_2 fumigation in leaves (Zeevaart 1976) along with the total nitrogen content. However, nitrate -nitrogen may deplete due to promotion of nitrate reductase activity.
2. Chlorophyll and β–cartone can get'reduced by their conversion into phaeophytin (Kandler & Ullrich 1964). Synthesis of chlorophyll in developing leaves can also be inhibited owing to the photooxidative process. However, contrary to this, there have been some reports of greening of leaves by increase in chlorophyll content, especially in peas and tomatoes (Horsman & Wellburn 1975, Taylor & Eaton 1966).
3. Most of the enzymes remain unaffected or stimulated by NO_2.

Effects on growth and reproduction

Most plants show a suppressed growth due to chronic and acute exposures of nitrogen oxides.

Effects of carbon monoxide

Carbon monoxide affects the plants mostly at higher concentration than that can affect the animals and Man. Carbon monoxide strongly inhibits CO_2-fixation in certain plants at 5-8 ppm for 5-20 minutes (Bid-well & Fraser 1972). The same workers, however, also reported an enhanced CO_2-fixation at very high levels of CO at 200-300 ppm. Hill reaction and evolution of O_2 is also suppressed by CO (Vennesland & Jetschmann 1971).

Effects of hydrogen fluoride and other fluorides

Fluoride injury to plants is usually caused by hydrogen fluoride and silicon tetrafluoride, the common contaminants of industrially polluted air. Hydrogen fluoride behaves almost similar to sulphur dioxide. The plants are much more sensitive to fluoride than sulphur dioxide. However, the recovery of plants is slow in case of fluorides as compared to sulphur dioxide. The concentration of fluorides around I ppm can be quite damaging. The most sensitive species to fluoride injury are grapes and peaches.

Visible Injury

1. Fluorides enter the plants primarily through stomata, and tend to accumulate near the tip or margins of the leaf. The characteristic injury to plants appear in the form of necrosis at the tip and margins of the leaf where most of the fluoride has been accumulated.
2. Flowers are highly resistant to fluoride and blossom normally but 011 on the contrary fruits are much more sensitive.

Effects on physiology and biochemical reactions

1. Hydrogen fluorides and other fluorides reduce chlorophyll synthesis, Hill reaction, number of ribosomes, cellulose synthesis, and certain enzymes like phosphoglucomutase and polyphenol oxidase.
2. Fluorides can also stimulate some biochemical activities and metabolites under different conditions and concentrations. These include the rate of respiration, free sugars, pentose phosphate pathway, certain enzymes like enolase, catalase, pyruvate kinase, G-6-P dehydrogenase, cytochrome oxidase and peroxidase.

Effects of Ammonia Visible Injury

Foliar uptake of ammonia into amides, amino acids and proteins has been indicated by Porter et al. (1972) in plants. Ammonia, however, at higher concentrations may produce chlorotic and necrotic lesions on the margins of leaves.

Effects on physiology and biochemical reactions

1. Ammonia can depress respiration, NADH oxidation, free sugar levels, starch levels and glucan synthesis in several plants under experimental conditions with ammonium solutions.
2. Higher concentrations of ammonia reduces levels of chlorophyll, carotenoid and ascorbic acid in fumigated saplings of several fruit trees (Agarwal & Agarwal 1988).
3. Ammonia stimulates certain biochemical processes, metabolites and enzymes in the experimental conditions like glycolysis, glucose level, UDP glucose level, G-6-P dehydrogenase, enolase, peroxidase and cytochrome C oxidase as reported by Wakiuchi et al. (1971) and some other workers.

Effects of Chlorine (Cl_2)

Chlorine is relatively unimportant air pollutant with regard to its ambient concentrations. Concentration of chlorine in the atmosphere increase mostly at the time of leaks or accidents involving its storage. It is more toxic than SO_2 and can produce marginal or interveinal lesions on the leaves.

It produces symptoms very much like SO_2 (bleaching between veins, tip and margin burn). Mature leaves get affected. A concentration of 0.10 ppm can produce injury symptom in 2 hrs.

Effects of Hydrogen Cyanide (HCN)

It is less toxic than SO_2, and like Cl_2, is a rare pollutant causing widespread damage. It can, however, damage the plants by producing lesions on the margins of leaves at 10 ppm or above with the exposures lasting for few hours.

Effects of Ethylene

Among the hydrocarbons, ethylene can be an important air pollutant, but it is not of common occurrence like others. It can work as a plant hormone and at mild concentrations can cause epinasty and premature leaf abscission. In some sensitive plants, chlorosis, leaf curling and overall growth retardation have been reported. Can seriously affect vegetation even at a concentration of 1 ppm in some plants. Plants respond to ethylene toxcity by flower dropping and failure of flowers to open properly. According to Naegele (1974) cotton, marigold, tomato, cucumber and cream pea are sensitive to ethylene, while beet, cabbage, clover, Sorghum, oats, onion and radish are tolerant.

Particulates

Particulates in general are not considered very harmful to plants. However, a number of field and laboratory studies have shown that particulates can significantly reduce the yield of the plants.

A number of studies have been carried out on coal dust. Rao (1971) has shown that coal dust from a railway marshalling yard caused necrotic lesions in Mango and Lemon trees (*Mangifera indica* and *Citrus lemon*). Dust killed apical buds due to continual death of terminal buds. The lateral buds were activated leading to the development of an asymmetrical tree canopy. Deposition of coal particles inhibited pollen germination and ultimately fruit setting. Significant reduction in the yield was noted and out of two plants Mango was found to be more sensitive.

Cement dust contains varying quantities of Ca, K, Na, Si, AI, Fe, Mn, Mg and S. The size of cement particles ranges from 0.1 to 100 µm.1n presence of moisture; calcium aluminate (CaO Al_2O_3) and calcium silicate ($CaOSiO_2$) undergo slow hydration to form colloidal gel; which crystalize and solidify to form an impervious hard crust on the surface of soil and plant. A number of authors have reported injuries of cement dust on conifers in Germany. The crust developed by cement is difficult to be washed. In Germany a level of 1.0 $g/m^2/day$ dust deposition led to hard crust formation. Cement dust has been found to reduce stomata, starch formation and photosynthesis and rolling of the margins. Prominent chemical effects noted were reduction in CO_2 uptake. Many workers found no leaves and stunted growth in heavily dusted areas compared to those where no dust was observed. Dust also made plants susceptible to aphids attack as it removed the predators feeding on aphids. Many plants like *Acer rubrum*, *Quercus primus* and *Quercus rubra* reported 18% reduction in lateral growth. Particulates containing fluorides were found to be less injurious. Tip burn in *Gladiolus* has been reported due to fluoride containing dust.

Some of the major Indian studies on effects of dust on plants is summarized in Table 7.6.

Table 7.6 Indian studies on effect of dust on plants.

Authors	Plant species	Major conclusions
Das (1981)	Rice leaves	Concludes that evergreen trees with simple leaves, rough on hairy surfaces are most efficient dust collectors and hence recommends extensive cultivation of Ficus religiosa. Mangifera indica, Tectona grandis etc. for filtering dust
Rangaswamy and Jambulingam (1973)	Maize	Reduction in grain yield
Parthasarthy et al.(1975)	Maize	Noted that stem tip had more dust deposition on them than that on upper three leaves and cement covered plants showed reduction in leaf size, plant height as well as decrease in number and size of cobs.
Oblisami et al.(1978)	Cotton	Plant height, number of leaves and balls per plant were lower for polluted areas than for non polluted.
Yusuf & Vyas (1982)	*Calotropis procera. Cassia fistula, Delbergia sisso, Withonia somnifera*	Decrease in chlorophyll content
Singh & Rao (1978)	*Triticum aestivum* and *Glycine max*	Dusted plants showed a gradual decrease in chlorophyll and increase in potassium content. Wheat was more vulnerable than soybean
Chaphekar et al (1980) heavily	*Mangifera indica commelina bengalensis*	Leaves collected 10 g/m^2 dust in clean areas and upto 119 g/m^2 in polluted areas. Potted plants transplanted in polluted areas of Bombay city showed marked reduction in growth.

Naegele (1974) has provided list of sensitive and tolerant plants to fluorides. Asparagus, cotton, wheat, pear, Tomatos and Juniper were reported to be tolerant to fluorides, while Apricot, Gladiolus, Grape, peach and Tulip are sensitive. Soot deposition on plants clogs stomata and prevents gas exchange. Necrotic lesions develop on plants. Lead emitted from automobile exhaust is absorbed by the plants. Thakre and Rao (1985) have reported considerable absorption of lead by the leaves of various plants. (Table 7.7).

Table 7.7 Concentration of lead in leaf samples (μg/g of leaf sample) near Nagpur.

Plant species	Roadside vegetation		Control site	
	unwashed	washed	unwashed	washed
Annona squamosa	185.6	13.7	5.0	Traces
Lantana camera	70.6	35.0	Traces	Traces
Ziziplus jujuba	90.0	26.2	20.0	5.0
Cryptostegia grandiflora	65.8	39.1	12.5	0.5
Azadirachta indica	29.6	13.7	12.5	10.0
Tamarindus indica	55.8	16.6	5.0	Traces

Synergistic Effects of Pollutant Combinations

In most natural situations, the pollutants are not present alone, but usually remain associated with each other. The presence of pollutants in combination often results in the synergistic effects by enhancing their combined toxicities to the plants. Following are some important examples of this synergistic combination involving different pollutants.

1. Ozone and sulphur dioxide in combination at 0.028 and 0.28 ppm respectively after exposure of 2-4 hrs can damage the tobacco leaves, while no damage is caused by single pollutant at these concentrations. Similarly greater damage to radish, tomato and alfalfa is also caused by this combination at relatively higher levels.
2. A similar synergism with sulphur dioxide enhances the effects of NO_2 which alone at most realistic levels has almost no effects on plants.
3. The combination of NO_2 and O_3 can also work synergistically in suppressing the growth and yield of several plants like sunflower, alfalfa and maize.

A summary of important foliar symptons as visible injury caused by various air pollutants is given Table 7.8.

Table 7.8 Kind of visible injury caused to the plants by various air pollutants.

Pollutant	Foliar symptoms
Sulphur dioxide	Bleached spots, bleached areas between veins, chlorosis.
Nitrogen dioxide	Irregular, white or brown collapsed lesions on intercostal tissue and near leaf margin.
Ozone	Flecking, stippling, bleached spotting pigmentation, sometime tip brown & necrotic.
Hydrogen fluoride	Tip and major burns, dwarfing, leaf abscission, narrow brown red band separates necrotic from green tissue.
Peroxy acetyl nitrate (PAN)	Glazing, silvering or bronzing on lower surface (PAN) of leaf.

7.6 Effects of Air Pollutants on Microorganisms and Lichens

Air pollutants not only affect the higher plants, but also influence the microorganisms and lichens to a great extent. Microorganisms have important roles to play in the ecosystems and maintain the soil fertility. Some important observations on the effects of air pollutants on microorganisms and lichens, made by various workers, are given below.

1. Raviprakash & Naik (1988) have reported suppression of bacterial and actinomycetal populations. but an increase in fungal populations in the soils of Talcher industrial area of Orissa which has been affected by the substantial quantities of particulates, SO_2,. NOx and CO present in the air.

2. The low pH of acid rain causes severe effects on the soil microflora as well as phytoplankton in aquatic systems.
3. Sulphur dioxide has been found to suppress the activity of nitrogenase, an enzyme responsible for nitrogen fixation. A reduction in number of root nodules in leguminous plants has also been noted by Singh & Rao (1982) and Saxena (1983).
4. Bacterial nitrogen fixation is also inhibited at various carbon monoxide levels (Matsumoto et al.1971).
5. Vennesland & Jetschmann (1971) have reported an inhibition of oxygen evolution, nitrate reduction and Hill reaction by carbon monoxide in *Chlorella* in gassed suspensions.
6. Lichens are formed from the symbiosis of the fungal and algal associations, and have been reported to be much more sensitive to air pollution than higher plants. This may be perhaps due to their entire surface can involve in absorbing the pollutants from atmosphere in contrast to the higher plants where the major entry takes place through stomata. Not all the lichens are equally sensitive to air pollution. It has been noticed that the forms of fruticose and foliose lichens are much more sensitive to air pollutants than the crustose forms. The severity of the air pollution effects increase several-fold with the increase in the moisture. Out of the two partners, it is normally the alga which is more sensitive to the air pollution, though it makes up only about 5% of the thallus. Due to their high sensitivity, lichens have been variously employed as bioindicators of air quality (see Chapter 15).
7. Sulphur dioxide reduces the photosynthetic carbon dioxide fixation in several sensitive species of lichens (Nieboer et al. 1976).
8. Sulphur dioxide also releases substantial quantities of potassium from almost all kinds of lichens.
9. Sulphur dioxide in lichens has been found to cause bleaching of chlorophyll, and its conversion into phaeophytin is associated with a blue shift of the pigment spectrum. Protein structure and enzyme activity are also impaired by SO_2 in lichens.
10. Respiration rates are often reduced in lichens by SO_2 due to its reaction with fungal partner.
11. A study has been carried out by Pawar and Dubey (1985) on the changes in the microflera due to gaseous pollutants from a rayon industry. It has been found that areas which suffer from heavy air pollution for prolonged periods due to oxidation and gases dissolved in rain water result in increased acidity, sulphate and other components (Webster 1967, Babich & Stotzky 1978).

In the above study Pawar and Dubey have studied the microbial population in Nagda Industrial complex (M.P., India), a typical site for studying the impact of air pollution on soil microflora. The main industrial activity is sulphuric acid plant and other chemical factories. Samples were collected of the affected soils as well as 2.5 km. away from the source. The authors reported a 64.0% to 75% reduction in fungal population. Bacteria and actinomycetes also recorded similar changes. The decrease in actinomycetes was explained on the basis of reduction in pH (Dancer 1973). The higher salinity was also ascribed to the reduction in soil microflera.

8 Effects of Air Pollutants on Man and Animals

8.1 Introduction

According to the basic definition, the pollutants are the substances which have a deleterious effects on the human health, and his welfare, plants and property. In the preceding chapters, we have identified a large number of air pollutants and their sources. While the effects of these pollutants on the plants and microorganisms have been dealt with in the previous chapter, their effects on the human and animal health are discussed in this chapter.

The effects of air pollutants on human health are difficult to assess. This is not because of the effects are small, but because they are slow and get usually complicated by interaction of the other factors such as overcrowding, occupation, habits and the presence of more than one pollutant at a time in the air. The effects of these factors are not easily separable from the actual air pollution effects. Further, some groups within the population may be more sensitive to air pollution, particularly very young, very old, and those already suffer from respiratory or the other diseases, or exposed to other toxic materials or stress. Children are usually more prone because they breath relatively higher quantity of air per unit body weight than adults, and also have far fewer air sacs or alveoli in the lungs where oxygen exchange takes place. A whole spectrum of response to air pollution by Man and animals is shown in Fig. 8.1. Death and disease represent only the extreme end of this spectrum.

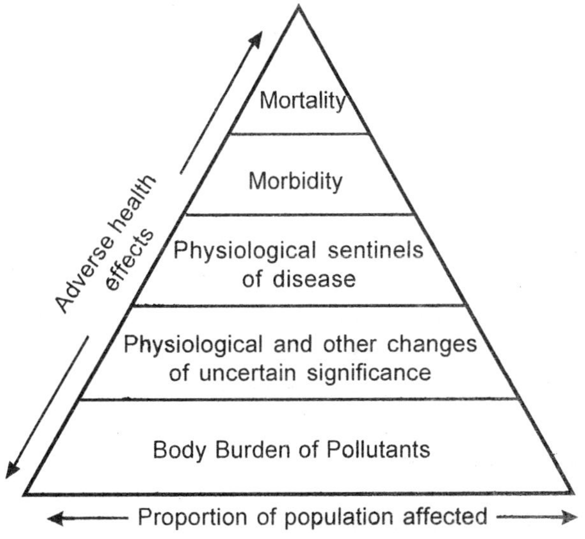

Figure 8.1 Biological responses of populations to air pollutants.

Much of our knowledge regarding the effects of air pollutants on Man and animals comes from three types of investigations.

1. Knowledge from air pollution disasters
2. Epidomiological studies
3. Laboratory studies

The study of the episodes of air pollution can give an evidence of the effects of pollution. These evidences may be both qualitative and quantitative. In the episodes of London smog, Meuse valley and Donora, there was a clear correlation between the death rates from cardiorespiratory diseases and the level of air pollution.

Epidemiological study is the scientific study of the distribution of diseases, where a correlation is established between a disease and the factors involved in its distribution and frequency in a population. There are two fairly distinct type of epidemiological studies depending basically on whether the data have been collected from the already existing records or from the extensive surveys designed specifically for the purpose. In the former, the data can be gathered from the hospital or other such records available usually in the form of the cases registered in hospitals, number of absentees in the industries, and deaths registered in Municipalities. In the other kind of epidemiological survey, studies are made on the basis of the medical examinations or questionnaire circulated in the populations. An epidemiological study made in Surat city of India reveals that Asthma is directly related to the dustfall and the levels of NO_2. Significant correlations were also reported between commond cold and sulphation rate; bronchitis and sulphation rate, NO_2 and dustfall.

In the laboratory studies, the effects of specific dosages are seen on the organisms in controlled conditions.

Though, we know that a large number of chemicals are damaging to health, but perhaps most worrisome of all are the immunotoxic chemicals that we inhale. Inhaled gases readily find their way into the blood stream and though the lungs swarm with scavenger cells, whose job is to engulf and devour particles from the air, some particles like absestos and silica, for example, cannot be digested and may seriously undermine this early line of defence. The substantial damage to the immune cells necessarily mean declining health due to appearance of serious infections in the same way as happens in case of AIDS when enough immune cells are killed by the AIDS virus.

8.2 Effects of Pollutants on Man

Target Organ Systems of Air Pollution

The human health is affectd by air pollution mainly due to inhalation of gases and particulates during respiration. A small quantity of air pollutants can also reach to Man by consumption of contaminated food. The effects of air pollution on human health have been concentrated mainly on the respiratory system and the eyes.

The Respiratory System

The overall basic function of respiratory system is to bring the air into close contact with a large number of blood capillaries, so as to facilitate the diffusion of atmospheric oxygen into blood, and carbon dioxide out from the impure blood. The parts of the respiratory system are show in Fig. 8.2.

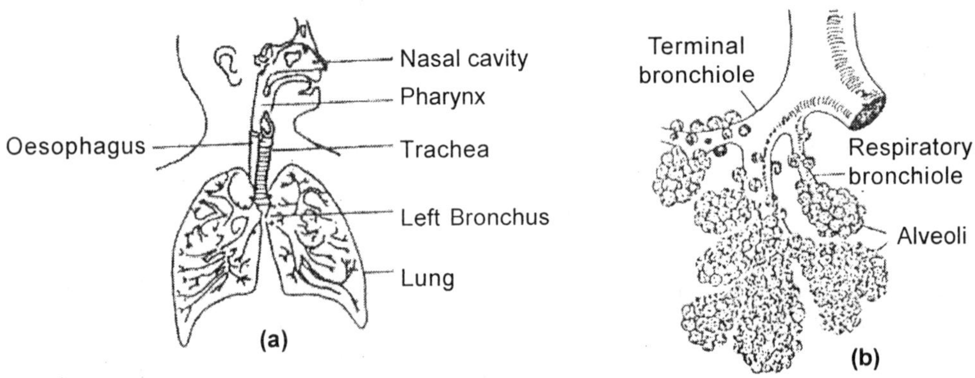

Figure 8.2 (a) Human respiratory tract (b) Bronchiole and alveolar structure

The upper respiratory tract consists of nasal cavity, pharynx and trachea. In the lower respiratory tract, the trachea branches out into two bronchi. These bronchi further subdivide into smaller bronchioles. At the end of the bronchioles are the alveoli which are arranged in clusters, with each cluster connected to bronchiole by an alveolar duct. The alveoli are very minute sac like structures surrounded by blood capillaries. The final division of the respiratory tract into alveoli increases the surface area for gaseous exchange. The two lungs with a volume less than 1 cu. feet have a surface area of well above 600 sq. feet for gas diffusion.

The inside of the whole respiratory passage is covered by the lining of mucous and cilia (minute hair like strucutres). The cilia beat back and forth in a precise rhythm. The mucous and cilia, besides performing other functions, also prevent the air pollutants entering into the alveoli. Though, only a small quantity of soluble gases, e.g., SO_2 can be absorbed and retained by the mucous, particualtes can be entrapped and retained to a greater extant by it. Very large particles are entrapped by the hair in the nasal cavity, and some of them are deposited on the sticky mucous due to inertial impact as the air is slowed down by several abrupt turns in the respiratory system. The smaller size particles are much more likely to be deposited in the lower respiratory tract. These accumulated particles are removed by the beating of cilia which move the mucous outward from respiratory tract to the throat (Fig. 8.3) from where they are swallowed or expelled by sneeze or cough.

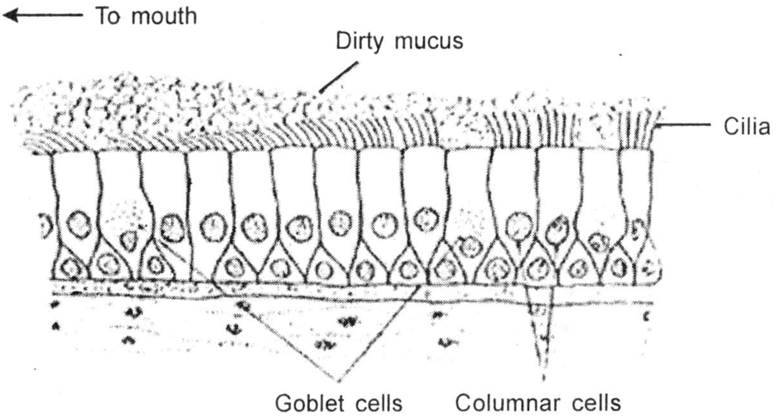

Figure 8.3 Traped particles by mucous are expelled by beating of cilia in the respiratory tract. (After National Tuberculosis and Respiratory Disease Association. 1968, Breathing - What you need to know, New York).

It has been reported that the lower respiratory tract is more efficient in removal of the particles in the range of a micron. The particles less than 10 microns may frequently enter into the alveolar sacs. However, there are certain mechansims by which these particles are removed from the alveolar sacs, but it is the continuous exposure to high concentrations that overloads these removal mechanisms leading to higher concentrations of deposited material in the lungs.

The Eye

The pollutants, both gaseous and particulates, contact the external coat of the eye and the internal mucous lining of the eyelid causing irritation. Physical damage to eyes may also result due to excessive rubbing of the irritated eyes.

Specific Diseases caused by Air Pollution

The epidemiological studies show that there are some common diseases which are often associated with the higher levels of air pollution. These are mainly chronic bronchitis, pulmonary emphysema, and lung cancer. Table 8.1 provides a list of important human diseases along with their etiological air pollutants.

Table 8.1 Human diseases caused by air pollutants with other contributing factors.

Diseases	Etiological pollutants
Accelerated ageing	Ozone and oxidant air pollutants
Allergic asthma	Airborne denatured grain protein etc.
Berylliosis	Airborne beryllium compounds
Bronchitis	Acid gases, particulates, respiratory infection, inclement weather
Cancer-respiratory tract	Airborne carcinogens and hereditary tendency
Dental caries	Selenium
Emphysema	Airborne respiratory irritants and family tendency
Mesotheliomas	Asbestos, associated trace metals, carcinogens in air, other fibres

Chronic Bronchitis

It is characterised by a persistent production of cough. The breathing is hampered by bronchial congestion and fluid often leading to the production of a bubbling sound as the air passes through this fluid. The condition usually worsens in cold and damp weather. In the damp and foggy climate of England in 1950s, a large number of deaths were recorded by this disease. 30,000 people alone died in 1950 in England and Wales. Researches show that the particulates and sulphur dioxide are the pollutants largely responsible for causing the chronic bronchitis.

Pulmonary Emphysema

It is the progressive breakdown of alveoli which leads to the joining of many small air sacs into one large volume. As a result, the surface area for gas diffusion into the capillaries is decreased causing a difficulty in breathing, which in extreme cases may even result in heart failure. This condision may be brought on by chronic infection of the bronchial tubes, chronic bronchitis, destruction of cilia, increased viscosity of mucous, and prolonged retention of inert air pollutants. Studies demonstrate that the patients of emphysema improve if they are protected from air pollution.

Lung Cancer

Cancer is complex multi-step process. The first step occurs when a single gene, an oncogene, is tansformed within a healthy cell. However, a single oncogene is not enough to produce cancer. According to the researches carried out at National Cancer Institute, USA, at least two or more mutations of oncogenes are necessary, and the chances of that are about one in a hundred trillion. Cancer experts now think that the real cancer danger may appear from the chemicals that favour the growth of mutated cells, thus promoting the likelihood that a second cancer-causing mutatin will occur. It is now increasingly felt that air pollution may be a factor in promoting certain skin and lung cancers. Some carcinogens like benzo(a)pyrene is believed both to register a cancerous gene change and promote the growth of these mutated cells.

Lung cancer is by far the common type of cancers induced by air pollution. When the carcinoma of lung breaks after enlargement, it spreads throughout the body, moving rapidly through lymphatic system and blood stream to spread cancer to other parts of the body. A number of carcinogenic compounds including benzo(a)pyrene present in the atmosphere may be responsible for development of lung cancer.

Other Respiratory Diseases

Some other diseases have also been found epidemiologically to relate with air pollution. Bronchial asthma is the narrowing of respiratory passage causing difficulty in breathing. Pulmonary edema is a condition where excess fluid is accumulated in lungs. Pulmonary fibrosis is toughening of the lung tissues. Pneumoconiosis is inflammation of lung tissues caused by retention of foreign particles. If the foreign particles are silica the disease carries the specific name silicosis, and if the particles are asbestos, it is called asbestosis. Both these diseases are, in fact, occupational diseases as there is no evidence that pneumoconiosis has ever resulted by breathing polluted urban air.

Effects of Some Specific Air Pollutants

Carbon Monoxide (CO)

Carbon monoxide is a systematic pollutant which reacts with blood and carries to the whole body. It is usually classified as an asphyxiant because of its strong combination with haemoglobin in blood. Normally, oxygen is picked up by haemoglobin in lungs and is carried as oxyhaemoglobin to all the tissues of the body through blood. In the tissues, the oxygen is freed and the blood returns to the lungs again through heart, to pick fresh oxygen. Haemoglobin, however, has a chemical affinity 210 times more for CO than that for oxygen. Consequently, it reacts with CO in the polluted atmosphere to form carboxyhaemoglobin, thus, reducing the oxygen carrying capacity of blood. The carboxyhaemoglobin in blood is fortunately reversible, and gets reduced with time as the CO concentration in the breathed air is reduced.

$$O_2Hb + CO \rightarrow COHb + O_2$$

Health effects of COHb blood levels are given in Table 8.2. The severity of effects of CO is related to the concentration and time of exposure. A continuous inhalation of CO from ambient atmosphere may result in several impairments and even death in extreme cases. At very high concentration of CO (in 100s of ppm), headache, drowsiness and death may occur as the brain is deprived of oxygen. At lower concentrations for longer periods, loss of visual acuity and mental alertness, loss of ability to accurately judge time intervals, and decreased muscular coordination are frequently experienced. Many deaths have occurred from CO in coal mines and unventilated garages where internal combustion engines have been left running. In rural areas, where people keep coal furnaces to keep the room warm in winter, may suffer if the room is not properly ventilated. The health standards for CO have been fixed at 35 ppm (40 mg/m^3) as 1-hour average and 9 ppm (10 mg/m^3) as 8-hour average.

Table 8.2 Health effects of COHb blood levels.

COHb blood levels %	Demonstrated effects
Less than 1.0	No apparent effect
1.0 to 2.0	Some evidence of effect on behavioural performance
2.0 to 5.0	Central nervous system is affected. Impairment of time interval discrimination and certain other psychomotor functions
Greater than 5.0, 10.0 to 80.0	Cardiac and pulmonary functional chanes. Headeches, fatigue, drowsiness, coma, respiratory failure, death

Sulphur Oxides (SO_x)

Much of the information on the effects of sulphur oxides on human health comes from the epidemiological studes carried out all over the world. Oxides of sulphur are not systemic pollutants, but are irritating substances of the respiratory system. The primary effect of sulphur oxides is to evoke constriction of bronchi, which leads to the suffocation due to increased airways resistance. Epidemiological studies reveal that there may be mortality at 1500 μg/m^3 (24-h average) of SO_2. Adverse health effects have been at concentrations of SO_2 exceeding 115 μg/m^3 (annual mean) or 300 μg/m^3 (24-h average levels). The main hazards of SO_2 on health are intense irritation, contribution to respiratory diseases and cardiac ailments.

A synergistic effect of sulphur oxides with particulates has been reported. Sulphur dioxide in presence of particulates may reach the lower respiratory tract in higher amounts adsorbed on the particulate matter. Studies show that a positive relation exists between air pollution and bronchitis, colds, influenza, and some other minor respiratory symptoms like production of increased sputum. The health standard for SO_2 has been kept at 0.14 ppm (365 μg/m^3) for 24-hour average and 0.03 ppm (80 μg/m^3) for 12-month average.

The dose related effects of SO_2 on Man are given in Table 8.3.

Table 8.3 Dose related effects of SO_2 on Man

Concentration, ppm	Effects
3-5	Least amount detectable by odour
8-12	Least amount causing immediate throat irritation
20	Least amount causing immediate eye irritation
20	Least amount causing immediate cough
20	Maximum allowable for prolonged exposure
50-100	Maximum allowable for short (30 min) exposure
400-500	Dangerous for even short exposures

Nitrogen Oxides (NO_x)

Of the nitrogen oxides, nitrogen monoxide (NO) is not an irritant and do not, as well, have adverse health effects at the ambient concentrations. Nitrogen dioxide is an immunotoxic chemical that damages the ciliated cells which line the airways and help expel bacteria and foreign debris. Nitrogen dioxide's injurious effects reach far beyond the lungs. When NO_2 hits the mucous membranes of the nose, mouth and airways, it reacts with water to form nitric acid and other chemical byproducts that spread immediately throughout the body. This impairs the function of macrophages, which alert other immune cells to the presence of potentially dangerous bacteria and viruses.

The primary toxic effects of NO_2 felt on the respiratory system, are dependent primarily on the concentration and the time of exposure. A dosage of 5 ppm (9.4 $\mu g/m^3$) for 10 minutes can produce a transient increase in the air flow impediment in the respiratory tract. Occupational exposures of more than 90 ppm led to pulmonary edema (a watery swelling). Acute bronchitis is common due to NO_2, particularly in the children. Oxides of nitrogen also cause toughening of the lung tissue. The lung tissue becomes leathery and brittle due to NO_x, and lung cancer and emphysema may also result. Since the inhaled NO_x remain in the body, they can also produce mutations in cells.

Like CO, NO_2 also has a high effinity towards haemoglobin, which is 30,00,000 times higher than that for oxygen. Death can occur after inhalation of high quantities of NO_2 due to lack of oxygen supply to the brain. The health standards for NO_2 have been fixed at 0.05 ppm (100 $\mu g/m^3$) for 12-hour average.

The odour of nitrogen dioxide can be detected at 0.12 ppm. A concentratin above 100 ppm or more for a few minutes can be lethal to Man. Serious illness and death has been known to result from high level of short term exposures of NO_2. NO_2 was responsible for 124 deaths in a fire at Cleaveland's Crile Hospital on March 15, 1929 when x-ray film containing nitrocellulose accidentally caught fire and produced NO_2.

Ozone

Ozone causes a variety of deleterious effects on health depending upon the concentration and the duratin of exposure. It is believed that the ozone leads to eye irritation above 0.1 ppm concentration. As believed earlier, the recent researches show that ozone is not a prime lachrymator (tear producing) in the photochemical smog. Ozone produces irritation of throat and nassal passage at higher levels, which may occur during occupational exposure such as at the time of welding. At concenrations around 1.5 ppm, choking, coughing and severe fatigue has been reported. In the experimental exposure of 1.5-2.0 ppm for 2 hours, chest pain, coughing, headache, loss of coordination, and difficulty in expression and articulation are the common symptoms. Such a high concentration of O_3 may reach in certain peak occupational exposures.

Some of the recent finding on the effects of O_3 are changes in blood biochemistry, soreness in chest, loss in the maximum volume of air one can exhail, slightly impaired distribution or ventillation within the lung, increased fragility of red blood cells, and slight loss in red blood cell activity. The symptoms of ozone are much more severe with pre-existing respiratory troubles in persons. The health standards for O_3 is 1.5 $\mu g/m^3$ for maximum daily 1 hour average.

Hydrocarbons

Of all the hydrocarbons present in the atmosphere as pollutants, only a few have any demonstrable direct effects on human health. Many hydrocarbons show the effects at higher concentrations which are never found in the open atmosphere. The primary importance of hydrocarbons lies in their role in formation of photochemical smog which produces a variety of hazardous effects.

The vapours of aromatic hydrocarbons cause odour irritation. Formaldehyde vapours are responsible for eye and bronchial irritation quite similar to that caused by SO_2. Acrolein is also an eye irritant. Some hydrocarbons can also cause systemic injury, such as benzene which is reported to produce certain blood disorders.

Peroxy Acetyl Nitrate (PAN)

It is one of the major components of the photochemical smog. It has been reported to be a major eye irritant and lachrymator. The eye irritation potency of PAN is about 200 times than that of formaldehyde.

Free Radicals

These are highly reactive molecules present in the urban smog, which have implicated in the ageing process. One effect of the free radicals is to hasen the loss of lung tissue elasticity that accompanies ageing, while the other may be to breakdown the immune system's lines of communication. Immune cells communicate with one another via protein receptors on their surfaces. If these receptors are damaged, the cell's ability to communicate may be knocked down.

Free radicals can also destroy connective tissue called elastin, which forms the scaffolding of the lungs and skin, supporting all other cells including immune cells. Once elastin is destroyed, it may be impossible for the body to restore the structure of lungs.

Hydrogen Sulphide (H_2S)

It produces an unpleasant odour like rotton eggs. Most of its effects are reported at higher concentration which may be associated only in certain occupational exposures or during industrial accidents. H_sS produces headache, sleeplessness, conjunctivitis and pain in eyes. At higher concentrations it can damage the nerves and block the oxygen transfer.

Hydrochloric Acid (HCl)

It has got a pungent and irritating odour. It produces coughing and choking, inflammation and ulceration of upper respiratory tract, and clouding of cornea.

Particulates

The effect of particulates on human beings is basically due to either intrinsic toxicity of the particle or the interference the particles cause with respiratory mechanisms in the body.

Size of the particle is supposed to be most important in determining its toxicity. Large particles are not all that harmful as they are blocked from entering into the respiratory system by hair like cilia. The smaller particles penetrate into the lungs and remain there for a long time. It is also well known that smaller particles are found in the lungs. A great many carcinogenic substances are found in these smaller particles and may cause 'scarring' or 'fibrosis' of the lung lining. This type of disease condition is well known in industrial settings, and is called as 'pneumoconiosis'.

Chronic bronchitis, bronchial asthma, emphysema and lung cancer are closely associated with particulates.

Many studies have found that higher level of particulate matter increase mortality and illness. Particulate matter as low as 80 μg per m^3 have been found to be causing serious diseases. However in such cases, the effect is usually synergistic. Higher SO_2 content has also been found in these areas. It is also otherwise difficult to separate the effect of particulates from that of gases.

The noxious gases and chemicals in the atmosphere may get absorbed into or adsorbed onto air borne particulates hence, significantly larger concentration of these chemicals result than would if they were inhaled alone. These noxious gases and chemicals get so deeply carried into the respiratory tract that they injure delicate tissues unprotected by the mucous linings. Chemicals found in atmospheric particles may include acids, bases, hydrocarbons and toxic metals like beryllium, cadmium, nickel, mercury, zinc and lead. A summary of the effects of toxic heavy metals and carcinogens together with some other important pollutants is provided in Table 8.4.

One mechanism by which particualtes can affect Man is by overloading the protective mechanism of our respiratory tract. As discussed earlier our respiratory tract can check entry of particulates due to presence of cilia and mucous, but when the mechanism is overloaded, entry cannot be checked further and they tend to reach deep into lungs. There is possibiity that some of the minor toxic materials, which would have been retained otherwise by cilia and mucous, will reach directly into the lungs.

The particulates are also able to enhance the effects of certain gases like oxides of sulphur by synergistic interaction. On the other hand they may also be antagonistic to certain gases like NO_2, which is adsorbed on the particles and retained with them by the protective mechanism of the body. The health standards for particulates (less than 10 micron in diameter) are 80 $\mu g/m^3$ for 12 month average, and 150 $\mu g/m^3$ for 24 hour average.

Asbestos

Asbestos is a naturally occurring fibrous mineral. Asbestos has a unique property of resisting heat transfer even at high temperatures. Asbestos dusts when generated are suspended in the air and may subsequently be inhaled into lungs. The size and shape determines the extent of damage. The fibres than get embeded into the lung tissue and cause mechanical irritation. It develops into a situation of 'mesothelioma' or 'lung cancer'. Asbestos is also associated with other types of cancers in the body and the safe limit for air for Crocidolite is 0.2 fibre/m^3.

Fluorides

Fluorides as particulats and HF as gaseous air pollutant are highly toxic and irritating. Only a fraction of the fluoride entering the body is excreted and larger amount of it is retained in the body. Fluorides are mainly deposited in bones and teeth. As one's skeleton is saturated with fluorides it starts accumulating in soft tissues. An overdose of fluorides may lead to mottling of enamels and bones. Mottled enamel is caused by fluoride at 2 ppm level in drinking waters in temperate regions but it occurs at much lower concentration of 0.4-0.7 ppm in tropics. Fluorides are repored to cause respiratory failure, lowering blood pressure and general paralysis. Continuous ingestion of non-fatal doses of fluorides causes permanent inhibition of growth (Parti & Naik 1994).

Other Pollutants

The effects of some other air pollutants like chlorine, ammonia, aldehydes, phosphorus, boron, radionuclides and pesticides are summarised in Table 8.4.

Table 8.4 Effects of some air pollutants on human health

Pollutants	Effects
Lead	Systemic poison; causes anemia due to reduction in the formation of heme; kidney malfunction; tissue damage of brain; death in extreme cases of poisoning
Beryllium	Systemic poison which can effect all organs (berylliosis); affect mucus membranes of eyes and lungs; pulmonary damae; skin damage
Asbestos	Fibrosis of lungs (the condition called asbestosis); calcification of pleura; pleural mesothelioma (a form of lung cancer); continuous contacts may lead to tumors; effects more pronounced in cigarrette smokers
Arsenic	Mild bronchitis; nasal irritation; dermatitis; probably skin cancer, a high levels may be fatal.
Nickel	Relatively nontoxic; affects proteins of alveolar tissues; occupational exposures have been linked to cancer of the lung and sinus; other respiratory disorders; dermatitis
Cadmium	Highly toxic; causes bronchitis and pulmonary emphysema; high levels may cause fibrosis of lungs; kidney damage resulting in proteinuria (protein in urine); gastric disorders; disease of heart, liver and brain; hypertension, carcinogenic.
Mercury	On inhalation mercury is more toxic than entry through digestive tract; highly toxic; enzyme poison, causes gastrointestinal and pulmonary disorders; chronic poisoning results in nervous sytem disorders, which in the initial stage are limited to nervousness and emotional feelings; at the advanced stage of poisoning tremors are reported.
Chromium	Carcinogenic; cause dermatitis and ulcers on skin; perforation of nasal septum; irritative and toxic to tissues.
Selenium	Causes irritation of nose, eye, upper respiratory tract and gastrointestinal tact; occupational exposures of high levels can cause long term effects on kidney, liver and lungs.
Zinc	Fumes are highly corrosive and damage skin; irritate and damage mucous membranes.
Vanadium	Effects on gastrointestinal tract and respiratory tract (mainly physiological effects); cholestrol synthesis inhibition; carcinogenic, causes heart diseases at higher levels.
Chlorine	Eye irritation; irritation of nose and throat, high levels cause damage to lungs resulting in edema and emphysema; bronchitis pneumonitis.
Ammonia	Damages eye at higher levels; damage to respiratory tract, corrosive to mocous membranes.
Aldehydes	Irritation of eyes, skin and respiratory tract; highly odorous
Phosphorus	Systemic poisoning; skin irritation; nervous symptoms at higher concentration.
Boron	Highly toxic; inhaled as dust causes irritation and inflammation; boron hydride cause damage to central nervous system and death in extreme cases.
Radioactive	Somatic effects include leukemia and other cancers and cataracts. Genetic effects are mainly mutations in gem cells; reduction in life expectancy.
Organic carcinogens	Are mainly of three types ; 1. Polynuclear aromatic hydrocarbons 2. Polynuclear heterocyclic compounds 3. Oxygeneted compounds and alkylating agents Most of these carcinogens are associated with lung cancers and increased tumor activity.
Pesticides	Include several inorganic and organic compounds, which can be grouped as insecticides, herbicides, fungicides, rodenticides, nematicides, algicides and repellants etc. depending upon the pests on which they are active; toxic to non-target organisms including Man; mild poisoning symptoms include headache, dizziness, stomach disturbances and irritation, in extreme cases muscular tremors with jerky movements; death is also reported in extreme poisoning.

Table 8.5 Effects of air pollutants on animals

Pollutants	Effects
Arsenic	Inflammation of respiratory and gastrointestinal tract; destruction of red blood cells; damage to kidney; salivation; thirst; uneasiness; ulcers in the nose of horses; horses may also have puffiness of the eyes, dilation of pupils, difficulty in breathing, and partial paralysis of the hind limbs; long term effects include the depression of central nervous system; loss of appetite; loss of weight and eventually death.
Cadmium	Decline in milk of cow, killing of pigs; depression of ciliary activity of respiratory tract.
Lead	Development of lameness in cattle and horses; in acute poisoning excileable jerking of muscles, frothing at the mouth, delirium, stupor and finally collapse of the animal; gastric troubles; paralysis of digestive tract and diarrhoea; long term effects are damage to blood forming system of the body.
Mercury	Protoplasmic poison which is lethal; damage to nervous system and brain; emotional response and muscular tremors.
Molybdenum	Highly toxic; death of cattle in extreme cases.
Selenium	Kills herbivorous animals, chronic poisoning called blind staggers; another poisoning is called alkali disease.
Zinc	Emaciation and swelling of limb joints in cattle and horses causing lameness.
Nitrogen dioxide	Morphological changes in living cells; tachypnea; terminal brochial hypertrophy; loss of cilia in rats; polychythemia; tissue changes in lungs, heart, liver and kidneys in monkeys; pneumonitis; alveolar distension and increased susceptibility to respiratory infection; structural changes in lung collagen in rabbits.
Ozone	Bronchioles severely damaged in monkeys; pulmonary lesions in rats; bronchitis; emphysema; pneumonia, loss of fertility.
SO_3 aerosols	Necrosis of alveolar tissues, edema of alveoli and bronchial ulceration in several animals.
Carbon monoxide	Reduced oxygen carrying capacity of blood.
Chlorine	Animals are killed at higher levels.
Asbestos	Lung cancer in experimental animals.
Hydrogen fluoride	Fluorosis; rubber legged condition of cattle; corrosion of teeth and bones.

8.3 Effects of Pollutants on Animals

Contrary to human beings, most of our knowledge of air pollution effects on animals comes from the experimental labortory studies rather than the epidemiological studies. The effects of the air pollutants on animals are usually dose related. Other factors, which may influence the effects are age, body weight, sex differences and strains of the animals. For eample, young animals are often more susceptible to air pollutants than the adults. A linear correlation between the indices of toxicity and the body weight has also been reported in several test animals.

Many air pollution episodes such as Meuse valley in 1930, Donora in 1948, Poza Rico (Mexico) in 1950 and London in 1952 have also witnessed animal illness and death along with human casualties. A large number of cattle had to be slaughtered in Meuse valley and London due to the development of incurable illness. Other animals got affected by the air pollutants in these disasters were dogs, horses, sheep, pigs and chickens.

Besides inhalation, a large quantity of air pollutants reach the animals by consumption of contaminated food. The effects of pollutants may also be different in different animals so as to make the generalization difficult. A broad summary of the air pollution effects on animals is given in Table 8.5. The result of several experimental studies have also been extrapolated to humans, where almost similar effects of pollutants are expected on both Man and animals.

9 Air Pollution Effects on Physical Structures and Materials

9.1 Introduction

Air pollution has been recognized long back as a source of damage to the buildings, monuments and other non-living materials leading to irreperable physical and economic loss. The process of the physical deterioration has been greatly accelerated after the setting of industrial revolution resulting into rise of the levels of air pollution.

The air pollution leads to widespread effects on physical structures mainly by way of corrosion of metallic surfaces, soiling and erosion of buildings and historical monuments, and damage to surface coatings, paints, fabrics, textiles, plastics and other materials of commerce. The common air pollutants responsible for this damage can include acid mists, sulphur dioxide, hydrogen sulphide, oxidants like ozone and particualtes of diverse nature (Table 9.1).

Table 9.1 Effects of various air pollutants on materials.

Pollutants	Effects
Ammonia	In association with $S0_2$ and moisture causes damage to varnish and paints, and discolours fabrics.
Carbon dioxide	Damage to building stones due to fomation of carbonic acid with moisture.
Chlorine	Corrosion and discolouration of metals, paints and textiles.

Table 9.1 Contd...

Pollutants	Effects
Chromium	Corrosion in form of chromic acid and discolouration of metals, paints, building materilas. paper, textiles.
Hydrochloric acid	Corrosion of metals and alloys.
Hydrogen fluoride	Etching of glass and metals
Hydrogen sulphide	Discolouration and tarnishing of lead based paints, copper, zinc and silver.
Iron	Stain in form of iron oxide and soiling of paint and other materials, textiles.
Manganese	Soiling of most materials, textiles.
Nitrogen oxides	Cause white textiles to turn yellow; fading of colours.
Odorous pollutants	Cling to skin, hair and clothing.
Ozone & oxidants	Fading of dyes, cracking of rubber.
Particulates	Abrasion and corrosion of most metals, paint, textiles.
Phosphorus	Corrosion of most materials in form of phosphoric acid.
Sulphur oxides	Corrosion of steel, zinc, electrical equipnent, limestone, roofing slate, mortal, statues, textiles, leather, book bindings; Electrochemical deterioration of iron, aluminium. copper, silver, building materials, leather, paper, textiles.

Though, comparatively little attention has been paid to this aspect of air pollution damage, nevertheless, some significant attempts have been made to understand the mechanisms and to correlate the material damage to the levels of air pollution in USA and some European countries. In India, though, we did realize the problem earlier, but attention was paid only few years ago after the controversy rose on Taj Mahal regarding the probable effects of air pollution originating from Mathura Oil Refinery. There are now increasing number of reports of the monuments being damaged by the deteriorating air quality at several places in India including Ajanta and Allora. It requires a detailed investigation of this problem together with a complete survey of the historical buildings, monuments and other such objects of archeological and national interest to assess the damage already made, and to take suitable steps to prevent their further deterioration.

9.2 Mechanisms and Factors Influencing the Damage

The damage to the physical structures by air pollution can be brought about by a number of mechanisms depending upon the nature of pollutant and environmental conditions.

Electrochemical Corrosion

Corrosion of various metals like iron, zinc, copper and aluminium can take place by the electrochemical mechanism which is brought about by SO_2 and corrosive particulates in presence of moisture.

Direct Chemical Reactions

In many cases the damage may take place due to direct chemical reaction between the pollutant and the surface material. The erosion of marble surface by sulphur dioxide and tarnishing of silver by hydrogen sulphide are two examples of this category.

Abrasion

Particulates travelling with high velocities, particularly during dust storms, can lead to the abrasion of surfaces.

Deposition or Settling of Particulates

The particulate matter present in air constantly gets deposited on the surfaces by gravity settling. Particles settled down can spoil the surfaces and reduce the aesthetic value of buildings. For example, the blackening of buildings near railway stations and factories have an adverse psychological effects related to aesthetics. Secondly, cleaning operations for removal of dirt from automobiles, clothes and other surfaces can also lead to the damage and loss of shining on the objects.

The important environmental factors influencing the damage are moisture, temperature, sunlight and wind. Moisture is essential for chemical reactions, corrosion of metals and erosion of other surfaces. The presence of higher humidity leads to an excessive damage to the structures and objects. Elevated temperatures can increase the rate of chemical decay of the objects. Tropical climate is quite favourable to air pollution damage owing to high temperature and humidity. Sunlight also enhance the damage of objects by fading colours of the dyestuffs and weakening the strength of fabrics and polymers. The presence of sunlight also causes photochemical production of ozone in the atmosphere. Wind action governs the direction and velocity of pollutants transport. A higher wind velocity will result in greater abrasive effects. The wind can also lead to the entry of air pollutants into the indoor spaces.

9.3 Damage to Physical Surfaces

Buildings and Monuments

The surface of buildings and monuments gets soiled, disfigured and damaged by air pollutants in a number of ways. Many of the particulates stick to the stone, brick, paint and glass structures forming a film of tarry soot and grit. Tarry substances of soot can be acidic in nature leading to the weathering by physico-chemical processes. The sticky materials pose further problems as they do not get removed by rains. The abrasion caused by high velocity moving particles causes gradual erosion of the outer surfaces.

The structures are also adversely affected by the presence of acidic gases like sulphur dioxide and carbon dioxide in atmosphere which cause physico-chemical degradation of the stone, concrete masonary, marble, limestone and bricks. The lime is commonly used in plastering and as a cementing agent. Almost all ancient buildings, Forts and other monuments have been constructed with lime.

The reactions of sulphur dioxide and sulphur trioxide with calcium carbonate and lime form calcium sulphate. In presence of carbon dioxide and moisture, appreciable quantities of calcuim bicarbonates can also be formed. All these are soluble materials and are washed away with the rain leaving behind the eroded surface exposed to further reaction.

Indian experiance

India has a rich historical tradition which is preserved in the form of our sculptures, monuments, manuscripts, paintings and wood carvings etc.

The cultural artifacts are mainly of three types.

1. *Inorganic chemicals :* Stone sculptures and buildings, stones of monuments, metallic objects, pottery and ceramic objects, glass and other inorganic objects of artistic and historical importance.
2. *Organic materials :* Books, manuscripts, wood carvings, furnitures, textiles, ivory, etc.
3. *Paintings :* Having both organic and inorganic materials.

Some prominent examples of damage to cultural property in India are given below.

1. Damage to the famous Victoria Memorial Hall by air pollution is well known. Damage to binding lime mortar of the blocks of marble has been caused by sulphation and chlorination. The marble blocks are becoming loose with the seepage of acidic rain water in the walls and domes. Various industries in the Garden Reach area of Kolkata are found to be responsible for the damage.
2. Terra cotta temples of Bishnupur and Hazardwari and Atpur temples near Kolkata are also found to be affected.
3. The 'Chenna Kerhara', world famous carvings of the 12th century near Belpur, and temples of Badami, Shrirangapatnam, Kotar and Nandi etc., in Karnataka are in danger due to air pollution.
4. The Taj Mahal is also suffering damage from the air pollution.

Threat to Taj Mahal in India

Taj Mahal is an old monument of nearly 350 years old and builtup almost fully of white marble. It is situated at Agra, the industrial town of foundries and leather. About 40 km from Agra an oil refinery was commissioned near Mathura. Since it is known that the oil refineries are the source of atmospheric pollutants like sulphur oxides, hydrogen sulphide, hydrocarbons and particulates, doubts were raised about the possible impact of these pollutants on the Taj Mahal. Sulphur oxides, in particular, can cause greater damage by forming acid in the atmosphere (acid rain) or in the thin water film on the surface of the monument. This sulphuric acid then can react with $CaCO_3$ to form $CaSO_4$ leading to the erosion and discolouration of the exterior surface. However, as the controversy arose, a greater attention was paid to the pollution control measures in the refinery, and an "environmental impact assessment" (EIA) was also made. The results of the EIA indicate that no or almost insignificant effects of air pollution shall be there after the proper pollution control measures have been taken.

A graver threat to Taj Mahal, however, seems to be from the pollution created by a large number of coal-fired foundries, a thermal power plant and railway yards rather than from the Mathura Refinery. The data on air pollution indicate that the air in the vicinity of Taj Mahal is already polluted with sulphur dioxide and SPM reaching to a maximum value of 43.8 $\mu g/m^3$ and 942 $\mu g/m^3$. Development of cracks, scaling, flaking, and dark spots have already been reported from the outer surface of the Taj. Sensing the danger, the Govt. has taken some precautionary steps. The Taj was sprayed with a chemical coating to check further damage, associated with other intensified cleaning operations. The shifting of foundries, discontinuation of the use of steam locos, development of a thick green belt, and monitoring of Mathura refinery are some prominent measures that have to be taken to save this monument from the threat of air pollution.

Corrosion of Metals

Air pollutants, both gaseous and particulates, accelerate the process of corrosion of metals. One of the important air pollutants responsible for corrosion of metals is sulphur dioxide which gets transformed into sulphuric acid in the presence of oxidants and moisture. Sulphuric acid acts as an agent to the corrosion of metals such as of iron and its alloys, zinc, copper, and aluminium.

Iron, in presence of oxygen and moisture, gets naturally rusted by formation of iron oxides, but the process becomes faster in presence of SO_2 due to formation of $FeSO_4$. Ferrous sulphate acts as an ionic conductor in the electrochemical mechanism of rusting. The rust on iron is flaky and falls off, exposing more metal to corrosion. A considerable damage is caused by such increased rusting to railway tracks, steel bridges, roofs, overhead wires and exposed steel structures of the buildings.

Copper corrosion is a problem in telephone-telegraph industry due to formation of corroded coatings causing problems in electrical contacts. Copper corrosion is also facilitated by SO_2 forming a blue-green layer called "patina" having composition like $CuSO_4.6Cu(OH)_2$ and $CuSO_4.3Cu(OH)_3$. Similarly aluminium also gets corroded due to formation of $Al_2(SO_4)_3.18H_2O$ in presence of moisture, probably by forming an acidic solution on the surface of metal.

Zinc is used as a galvanizing protective metal on iron and steel to prevent natural corrosion. In the atmosphere zinc forms a basic insoluble zinc carbonate ($ZnCO_3$) which acts as a means of protection to the surface. In presence of SO_2, a layer of soluble $ZnSO_4$ is formed on the outer layer of $ZnCO_3$ leading to the corrosion. The accelarated corrosion can also be a result of the action of the acidic solution formed from the reaction between SO_2 and moisture on the surface protective film of $ZnCO_3$.

Particulates and ozone can also bring about corrosion of metals. Ozone leads to the oxidation of metals. Particulates can accelerate the corrosion by adsorbing corrosion gases like SO_2 or they themselves can act as active corrosion agents. Particulates consisted of sulphates and chlorides can serve as corrosion nuclei to facilitate corrosion.

Textiles

Air pollution leads to soiling of cloths and curtains, and reduce their life and aesthetic appeal. It was found that during the London smog in 1952, the collar of a white shirt became almost black within a small time of about 20 minutes.

The presence of SO_2 and ozone causes the loss of mechanical strength of fibres of nylon, cotton, wool and rayon due to acid hydrolysis and oxidation. Nitrogen dioxide and ozone can lead to the bleaching of several dyestuffs resulting in fading of the colours of clothes.

Cotton, by virtue of its cellulolytic nature, is most susceptible to SO_2 attack. Gaseous air pollutants are directly sorbed by the fibres or by the particulates already trapped by clothes.

Leather

Leather is affected particularly by SO_2 due to formation of sulphuric acid in the surface water film, leading to its acid hydrolysis. Presence of iron can serve as a catalyst in acid formation. Leather bindings of books and documents are degraded by long exposures to the low levels of SO_2 usually encountered in the indoor spaces. Leather, gradually loses its resiliency, gets cracked, and finally disintegrates into a brown powder.

Rubber

Rubber is affected mainly by ozone losing its elasticity due to development of cracks. The mechanism of rubber damage involves the attack by ozone on the double bonds in the hydrocarbon polymers present in the rubber structure. Some synthetic rubbers having saturated carbon structures are quite resistant to ozone attack in the absence of double bonds.

The cracking is most pronounced where the rubber is under stretch as happens most commonly in tyres. In fact, the damage to the rubber was first noticed in tyres in Los Angeles, and presently the problem is so acute that most of the tyre manufactures have to use an anti-ozone coating on tyres.

The problem of rubber cracking has also been felt in rubber insulated wires used in telephone exchanges and power transmission.

Paper

Air pollutants, especially sulphur dioxide, also damage the paper by making it brittle and decreasing its folding resistance. The papers, made from both cellulose and artificial fibres, can be degraded by very low concentration of sulphur dioxide. The degradation takes place by acid hydrolysis and due to formation of lignosulphonic acids. Documents like books are particularly susceptible to attacks by sulphur dioxide because of their long life.

The modem paper, using various chemicals in manufacturing, appears to be more sensitive to air pollution because of the presence of metallic impurities which catalyse the conversion of SO_2 into sulphuric acid.

Paints

A large number of air pollutants like sulphur dioxide, ozone, hydrogen sulphide, fumes, mists and other aerosols including particulates can damage the paints and pigments used in art work and surface coatings. Fading of colours in the paints is a common problem caused by many pollutants. Hydrogen sulphide can react with the lead based pigments of the paints leading to their blackening by forming lead sulphate.

Fumes and mist of different chemical nature can also react with paints to damage art works and painted buildings. There are reports of even the damage of the ancient Ajanta paintings by increased air pollution caused by the tourist activity. Ancient frescoes have also been damaged by the air pollution in many European cities. Air pollution can also affect the paint of motor vehicles and hoardings by mechanical damage and chemical fading.

Glass and Ceramics

Glass and ceramics are comparatively more resistant to air pollution, but they can also be affected by long exposures of certain pollutants. Acidic air pollutants in presence of moisture lead to the damage of enamel polish in the long run. Hydrogen fluoride can react with silicon compounds affecting a wide variety of ceramics and glass. In the industrial areas with higher concentrations of fluorides, there have been reports of window glass turning opaque. The emissions of fluorides have considerably reduced in the recent years not because of their concern to the physical property, but mostly because of their injurious effects to vegetation and animals.

Electricals and Electronic Materials

Malfunctioning of electrical contacts is a major problem associated with air pollution. Low power electrical contacts, used in a variety of equipments, are quite sensitive as they can be affected by development of the insulating films by air pollutants. Particulates deposited in the switches, can result in improper electrical contact leading to the production of sparks. Direct chemical damage due to corrosion of metals used in electricals and power industry poses even greater threat due to frequent failure of equipments and electric transmission.

Sulphur dioxide and hydrogen sulphide can tarnish copper and silver contacts. Computers in the polluted indoor environments can also fail due to faulty electrical contacts. Nitrate present in dust can cause corrosion in nickel bases of palladium-capped contacts of crossbar switches causing electrically open circuits.

The particles deposited on the insulators of transmission lines, during conditions of high humidity, fog and rain, can cause electric conduction leading to the flashover of insulators and power failure.

Art Treasures

Air pollution has caused a great damage to the ancient monuments and invaluable art treasures all over the world. Ancient frescoes (kind of wall paintings) in several south European cities have shown severe damage due to air pollution. Cleopatra's needle, a large stone obelisk, which was brought to London from Egypt some 100 years ago, suffered more damage in the humid, smoky and polluted air of London in comparison to what even not caused in 3000 years before. The Parthenon in Athens has also been damaged during recent years by air pollution. Similraly, several other monuments of great acheological value like Colosseum in Rome and San Marco Basilica in Venice have been reported to be affected by air pollution. In France, the ancient statues outside the cathedrals have to be replaced by their replicas to save the original ones.

Much of this damage has been brought about by the crystallization of nitrate, sulphate and chloride, which has initiated formation of microcracks in stones leading to their crumbling due to greater pressures caused by the growth of crystals.

House-Hold Effects

Sulphur dioxide and ozone have been found to react with quite a large number of objects usually present in homes. At the concentrations usually found in indoor spaces, carbon monoxide, PAN and nitrogen dioxide have little or no effects on the nonliving materials. However, the commonly encountered concentrations of some other pollutants in the indoor spaces can damage the house-hold materials to a great extent.

Ozone can degrade objects made-up of different polymers, as well as fade a variety of dyestuffs. Sulphur dioxde is the most effective culprit in damaging numerous indoor materials and surfaces comprised of textiles, rayon, marble, concrete, metals and paints owing to its acidic nature. The objects like carpets, furnishing fabrics and wall papers are quite sensitive to air pollutants, with the effects more pronounced at higher relative humidity.

The air pollution level in the indoor spaces has a direct correlation with the maintenance costs in the form of cleaning, laundry, replacements, house painting and maintenance of hair and facial care.

10 Ozone Layer Depletion

Ozone depletion has also emerged as a major global environmental problem alongwith global warming in the last and present century. Our earth is surrounded by a layer of ozone about 15-40 km above the surface (Fig. 10.1) which keeps about 95% of the sun's harmful UV radiation from reaching the earth's surface. Short wavelength UV radiations in the range of 1800 A° to 2200 A° are absorbed by molecular oxygen which splits up into constituent atoms. These atoms combine with molecular oxygen to produce ozone

$$O_2 \rightarrow O + O$$

$$O_2 + O \rightarrow O_3$$

Another photochemical reaction which breaks down ozone molecules due to absorption of 2000 - 2900 A° radiations also occur.

$$O_3 \rightarrow O_2 + O$$

$$3O + O \rightarrow 2O_2$$

These two reactions balance each other and ultimately result in effective absorption of short wavelength UV radiation in the stratospheric region. This protects all life from the harmful effects of UV radiation. Most of the ozone (about 90%) is concentrated in the stratosphere at an altitude of 15-40 km.

However studies in the last thirty years have brought an alarming fact to the light that this ozone layer is depleting.

The concern over stratospheric ozone depletion was first aroused in the world when a US chemist Harol Johnson in 1971 declared that the supersonic aircrafts would introduce large quantities of nitrix oxide to break the ozone layer. Nitric oxide can catalytically attack ozone molecules and convert them to oxygen. Later Farmen and his co-workers in 1985 showed that the total overage quantity of ozone layer measured over the south pole in the month of October was gradually diminishing. A reduction of about 40% was recorded in ozone content over Antarctica. In 2000, seasonal ozone thinning above Antarctica was largest ever and covered an area three times the size of continental united states.

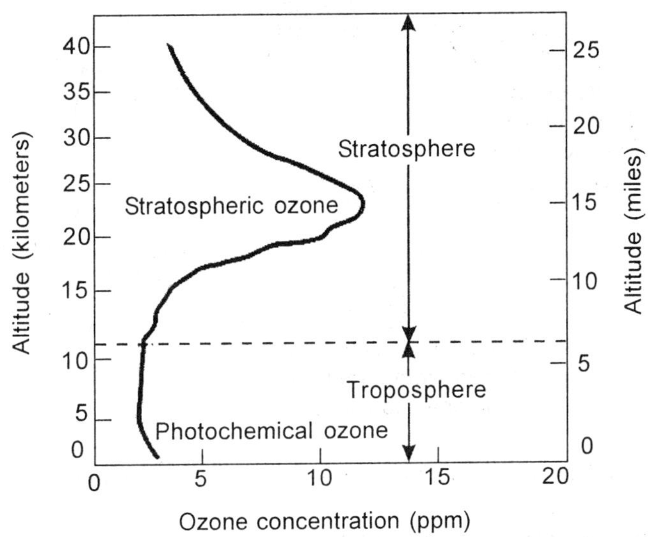

Fig. 10.1 Distribution and concentrations of ozone in the troposphere and stratosphere.

It was later realized that the main culprit for ozone layer depletion are chlorofluorocarbons (CFCS). CFCS were discovered in 1930 by Thomas Midgley Jr. and later a family of chlorofluorocarbons was created. The most widely used chlorofluorocarbons are CFC-11 and CFC-12 (Freons). CFCS are chemically non reactive, odourless, nonflammable, non toxic and non corosive compounds. They are extensively used as coolants in air conditioners and refrigerator, propellants in aerosol spray cans, as cleaners for various equipments, in insulation, packaging etc.

When disastrous consequences of CFCS came to light a worldwide ban was called on them.

Fig. 10.2 shows the mechanism of ozone layer depletion by CFCS. CFCS stay for a long period in stratosphere (65-38 years) depending on its type. During this period each chlorine atom is capable of converting up to 10×10^4 molecules of ozone to O_2.

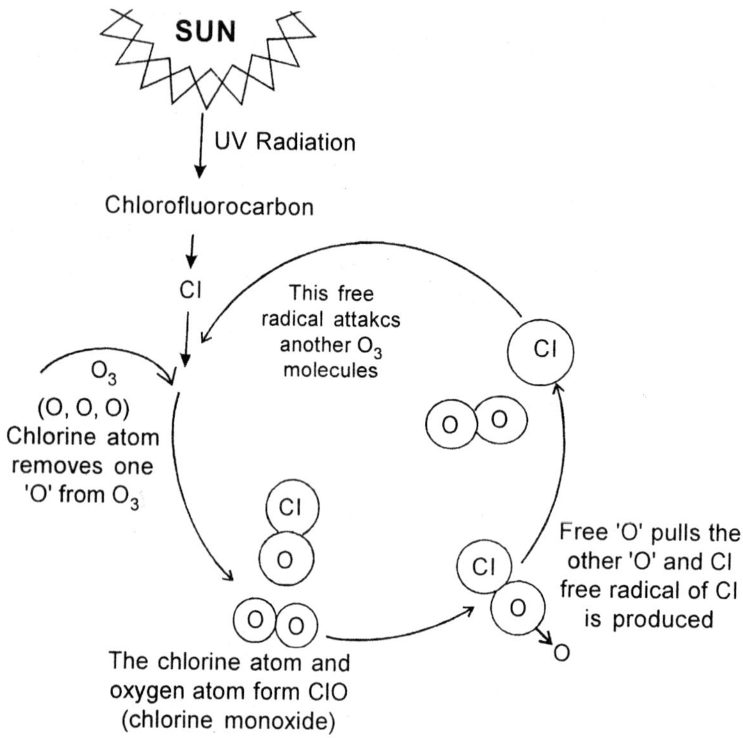

Fig. 10.2 Mechanism of repeated destruction of an O_3 one molecule by CFCS

Depletion of stratospheric ozone layer has been found to occur mainly due to following three constituents of the stratosphere.

1. ***Nitric oxide molecules :*** Nitric oxide reacts with ozone to form nitrogen dioxide which in turn reacts with atomic oxygen to produce nitric oxide again

$$NO + O_3 \rightarrow NO_2 + O$$
$$NO_2 + O \rightarrow NO + O_2$$

2. ***Chlorine atom :*** Chlorine atom react with ozone to yield chlorine monoxide which reacts with atomic oxygen to regenerate chlorine atom again

$$Cl + O_3 \rightarrow ClO + O_2$$
$$ClO + O \rightarrow Cl + O_2$$

3. ***Hydroxyl ion :*** Hydroxyl ions produced by photodissociation of water molecules in the stratosphere react with ozone molecules to produce HO_2 which reacts with another O_3 molecule to yield OH again

$$OH + O_3 \rightarrow HO_2 + O_2$$
$$HO_2 + O_3 \rightarrow OH + 2O_2$$

Causes of Ozone Depletion

1. ***Use of Chloroflurocarbons :*** As explained above CFCs are responsible for maximum damage to ozone layer.
2. ***Nitrogenous fertilizers :*** Microbial action on nitrogenous fertilizers produces nitrous oxide which escapes into atmosphere. As this gas is decomposed with difficulty it tends to accumulate in the atmosphere. The estimated trospheric load of nitrous oxide is 1.7×10^{18}g
3. ***Supersonic transport, rockets and space shuttles :*** Supersonic jetliners discharge various oxides of nitrogen, carbon, sulphur, hydrocarbons and particulate material. Ammonium perchlorate used in many of the rockets as oxidants releases plenty of chlorides.
4. ***Nuclear Tests :*** Nuclear explosions release high quantity of various gases and other materials which damage the ozone layer.

   Violent eruptions from the sun may also be responsible for producing ozone depleting substanes.

Consequences of Ozone Layer Depletion

With depleting ozone layer in the stratosphere the consequences will be drastic. More biologically damaging UV-A, UV-B and even UV-C radiation will reach the earth's surface.

Some major consequences are outlined below :

1. Skin cancers of various types including the dangerous malignant melanoma which occurs in the pigmented area of the body. Every year about one lakh people die of this cancer studies suggest that about 90% of the sunlight's melanoma causing effect may come from exposure to UV-A and 10% from UV-B.

   Some estimates suggest a 100% rise in incidence of skin cancers for a 25% reduction in stratospheric ozone content.
2. A direct correlation has been observed between cataract formation in eyes and ultraviolet radiations. Immune system suppression can also occur.
3. There will be considerable damage to lower animals which do not have and can not use protective device. The entire ecosystem may collapse due to such effects.
4. Even in wild life increased eye contract may occur, the population of sensitive species may reduce.
5. It will also lead to increased acid rain, increased photochemical smog and degradation of outdoor paints and plastic.
6. It will also lead to accelerated global warming because of decreased ocean uptake of CO_2 from atmosphere by phytoplankton and CFCS acting as greenhouse gases.

International Action to Protect Ozone Layer Depletion

Considerable activity is going on in the world for the past many decades for protecting the ozone layer however, the recent models suggest that it will take about 50 years for the ozone layer to return to 1980 levels and about 100 years for recovery to pre - 1950 levels.

Montreal Protocol

A large International convention was organized in Montreal city of Canada in 1987 where an International agreement was signed known as "Montreal Protocol". The Montreal Protocol was made effective from 1 Jan 1989. Only 48 countries signed this protocol. Developing countries mostly stayed away from this protocol. Its goal was to cut emissions of CFCS (but not other ozone depleters) into atmospheres by about 35% between 1989 and 2000. After hearing more bad news about seasonal ozone thinning above Antarctica in 1989, representative of 93 countries met in London in 1990 and in copen hagen. Denmark in 1992 and adopted the copenhagen protocol which accelerated the phasing out of key ozone depleting chemicals.

These landmark International agreements now signed by 177 countries are important examples of global cooperation in response to a serious global environmental problem. Without these agreements, ozone depletion would be much more serious threat.

Action in India

Being a signatory to Montreal protocol India has taken a number of steps in phasing out ozone depleting substances. Ministry of Environment and Forests, Govt. of India has an ozone cell which has been receiving the grants from International agencies and is coordinating the programmes at National level. A timebound programme has also been made in this regard as follows.

Ozone Depleting Substances (ODS)	Percent cut
1. CFC - 11	50% by 1994
2. CFC - 12	85% by 2007
3. CFC - 113	100% by 2010
4. Helon - 1211	50% by 2005
5. Helon - 1301	100% by 2010
6. Tetrachloromethane	85% by 2005
7. Trichlorethane	30% by 2005
8. HCFC	100% by 2040

A number of alternatives for CFCS are now available. Prominent among them are HCFC 22, ammonia, HFC 134 A and Hydrocarbons.

11 Air Pollution Meteorology

Meteorology is the science of the atmosphere and the study of characteristics of weather elements. Meteorological parameters are of great significance in transport, diffusion, and natural cleansing of pollutants in the atmosphere. Meteorological information is, thus, very essential in locating the industry and planning control measures for air pollution.

11.1 The Earth's Atmosphere

The atmosphere stores and distributes the contaminants which have been released into it, and it is this function which is of interest in air pollution. The behaviour of atmosphere determines whether the pollution released into it will remain around us or shall be blown away. Before going into the details of the atmospheric behaviour, we shall study its structure that will enable us to understand the meteorological processes.

The atmosphere is a fluid mixture of gases surrounding the earth in several layers of varying thickness and density (Fig. 11.1). The layer nearest to the earth is called troposphere, which extent from the earth's surface to about 10-12 km. In general, the atmosphere is not heated by the sun's rays, rather is heated from below by the warm earth. Temperature, therefore, decreases with altitude in this layer along with the decrease in density and pressure of gases. The lower troposphere up to 2 km is of most interest in air pollution meteorology. About 80% of the mass of atmosphere is contained in the troposphere.

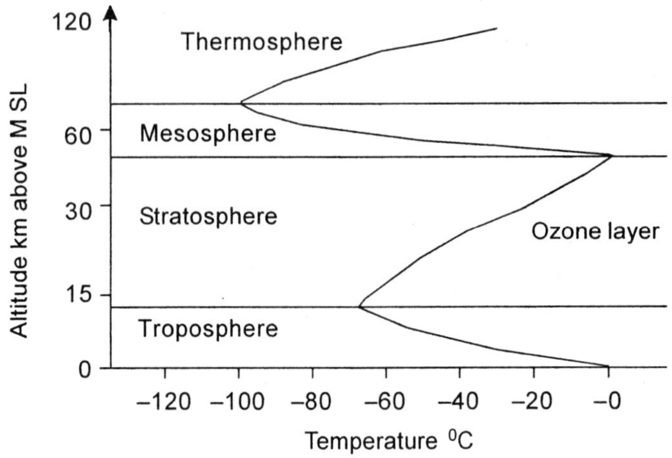

Figure 11.1 Temperature profile of earth's atmosphere.

The next layer, the stratosphere, is characterized by the increasing temperature, since near top of this layer is a layer dominated by ozone, which absorbs ultra violet solar radiation and gets heated. U. V. radiation, in fact, dissociate the ozone into an oxygen atom (O) and a molecule of oxygen (O_2), and their reunion again in ozone, releases energy in the form of heat. This makes the stratosphere a warm area and a shield to prevent the entry of harmful U. V. radiation and cosmic rays into the lower atmosphere near the ground level.

The layer above the stratosphere is called mesosphere, in which the temperature decreases with altitude falling up to 110 °C at the top. Above this, is a layer where ionization of the gases is a major phenomenon, thus, increasing the temperature again. This Layer is called as thermosphere.

Only lower troposphere is routinely involved in the determination of weather, and hence in air pollution. The other layers are of least significance in determining the fate of air pollution.

11.2 Effects of Meteorological Parameters on Transport and Diffusion of Air Pollution

The air pollution cycle can be considered to be consisted of three phases, i.e., release of air pollutants at the source, their transport and diffusion in the atmosphere and reception of air pollutants by people, plants, animals and other objects. Meteorological factors have the greatest influence on the diffusion and transport phase. The factors of most concern in transport and diffusion of pollutants are the wind and atmospheric stability.

Wind Effects

The horizontal motion of air, that we sense as wind, is the most familiar aspect of air, and plays a significant role in air pollution. While the speed of the wind determines that how the pollution is diluted and blown away, the direction of the wind decides the line along which this dilution takes place. The effect of wind is actually two-fold. Wind speed determines the travel time of a pollutant from source to the receptor. For example, if a receptor is situated 1000 meters downwind from a source and wind speed is 10 m/sec, then it will take 100 sec. for the pollutants to travel from source to the receptor. The other effect will determine the magnitude of the dilution of pollutants in the windward direction. If a continuous source, for example, is emitting a pollutant at a rate of 10 g/sec and the wind speed is 1 m/sec, then a downwind plume of 1 meter in length will contain 10 g of the pollutant. The concentration of pollutants in the air decreases with the increase in the speed of wind, since a wind of high velocity quickly disperse the pollutants within the air mass.

The motion of the air at any point is the composite result of many motions of different sizes ranging from global circulations to small dust devils. For convenience in discussing such a wide range of motions, meteorologists have arbitrarily classified them into groups by size or scale as follows.

Planetary motions	1,000-10,000 km
Synoptic motions	100-1,000 km
Mesoscale motions	1-100 km
Microscale motions	1 cm-1 km

Wind data at a given point are usually represented by a wind rose. A wind rose is a graphic display of direction and velocity of the winds at a given location over a period of time (Fig. 11.2). The spikes plotted in a wind rose in the given direction indicate the direction from where the wind is blowing. The width and colour of the spike indicate the wind velocity, and the length is proportional to the per cent of times a given velocity and directions are observed.

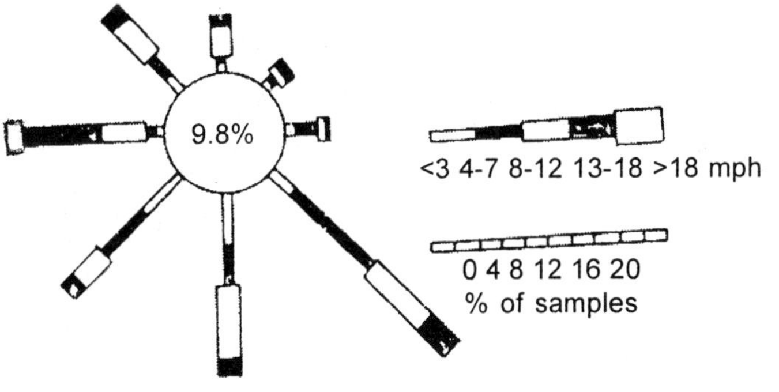

Figure 11.2 An 8-arm wind rose

Planetary Wind Motions

They are the largest motions of air over global-scale distances. They are the direct result of the temperature imbalance between equator and the poles. These motions transfer the excess heat from the equator to the poles. If we assume the earth as stationary, these motions will appear as vertically circulating air masses or thermal cells. At the equator, the warm air would rise and move towards the poles. The air at equator then would be replaced by cooler air coming along the surface from the poles.

The rotation of earth, however, break these thermal cells into three smaller circulations as shown in Fig. 11.3. The middle cell is the weakest of the three smaller cells, and the temperature differences between oceans and the land masses further break-up it into two large, semipermanent, circulating high pressure systems. One high pressure system is located in the North Atlantic and the other over the North Pacific as shown in Fig.11.4.

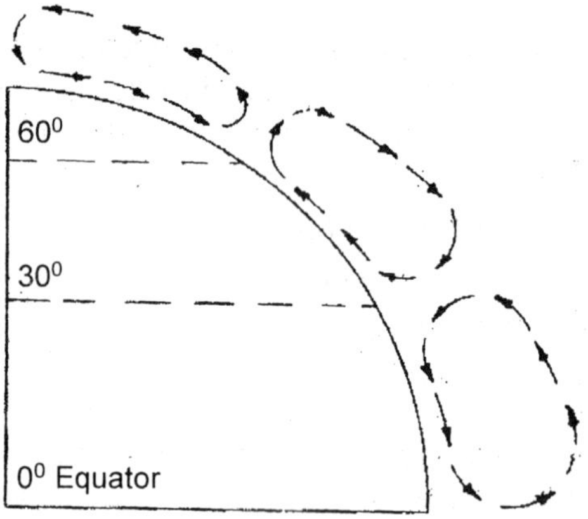

Figure 11.3 Global air circulations in the form of thermal cells

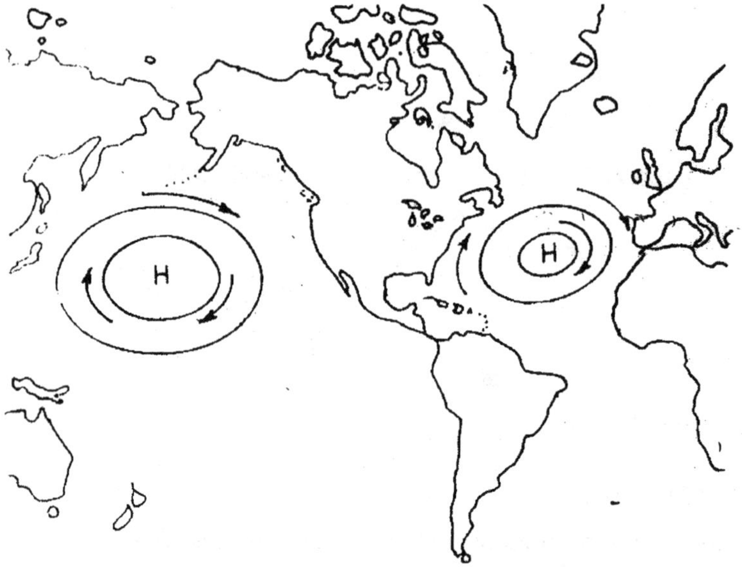

Figure 11.4 The two global high pressure systems in North Atlantic and North Pacific Ocean

These two semipermanent air masses of high pressure areas have their effects on air pollution. When the North Pacific high travels slightly southward near the western America in winter and fall, it brings peculiarly adverse meteorology to the Los Angeles basin that helps make its smog problem. Similarly the Atlantic or Bermuda high has an effect on air pollution in the western coasts of England and Europe. This high pressure system is also partly responsible for London smog problems. The effects of high pressure systems on meteorology are described later in this chapter.

Synoptic Wind Motions

These are the rotational motions of air ranging in size from 100 to 1000 km. These rotational motions are, in fact, travelling weather systems often distinguished as either high or low pressure systems, or simply just 'highs' or 'lows'. A low pressure system is also called as cyclone; whereas a high pressure system, an anticyclone. Low pressure systems or cyclones in the Northern hemisphere have anticlockwise rotations, with the air flowing generally in towards the centre and then upward (Fig. 11.5(a)). This rising trend of the air in lows leads to the precipitation, which is often associated with stormy weather.

In contrast to the lows, high pressure systems or anticyclones rotate clockwise in the Northern hemisphere in which the air tends to diverge in a spiral manner out-ward towards the lower pressure (Fig. 11.5(b)). The air subsides from higher altitudes into the centre of the highs, therefore, they are often associated with pleasant weather having no precipitation and no winds. The high pressure systems are supposed to bring adverse meteorology as far as dissemination of air pollutants is concerned. On the other hand, low pressure systems are considered favorable to air pollution dissemination as the wind and rain help removal of pollutants from the air.

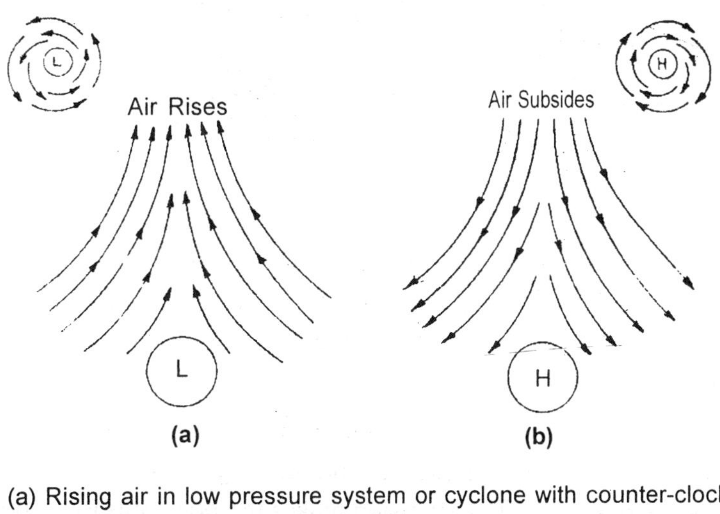

Figure 11.5 (a) Rising air in low pressure system or cyclone with counter-clockwise wind movement in northern hemisphere.
(b) Subsiding air in high pressure system or anticyclone with clockwise air movement in northern hemisphere.

Mesoscale Wind Motions

These are the motions of rather smaller scale, approximately of the size of our urban areas, driven primarily by the temperature imbalances. With regard to air pollution significance, only two motions in this category, the land-sea breeze and mountain-valley wind, are important. Both these motions have considerable impact on the local air pollution.

Land-Sea Breeze

These wind motions are often encountered in the coastal areas, where the air is driven primarily by the temperature differences between land and the ocean (Fig. 11.6). In morning, the sun warms the land much more rapidly than it does the water resulting in a higher temperature of air over the land than air above the ocean surface. This makes the warmer air above the land to rise to be replaced by cooler air from the ocean resulting in a sea-breeze. When the sun sets in the evening, the land is cooled faster than the ocean to cause its temperature to fall below the ocean temperature. This results in rise of the warmer air over the ocean to be replaced by cooler air from the land causing a land-breeze.

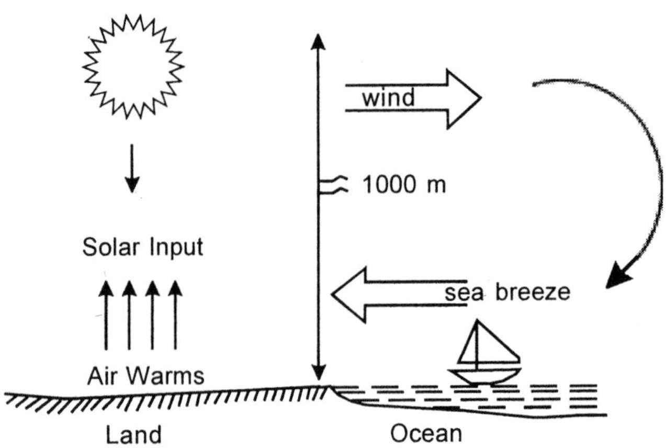

Figure 11.6 Formation of land-sea breeze

The sea-breeze can have its impact on air pollution in two ways. The morning sea-breeze can bring the pollution to upland areas from the sources located in downtown areas. Secondly, it can bring back the pollution from the sea which has been carried away by the land-breeze during the previous evening.

Another effect of sea-breeze is to cause a temperature inversion as shown in Fig. 11.7. This occurs when the warm air rises from the land drawing in cool air from the sea which remains below the warmer layer. The inversion makes the pollutants to accumulate in air. Details of inversions are provided later in this chapter.

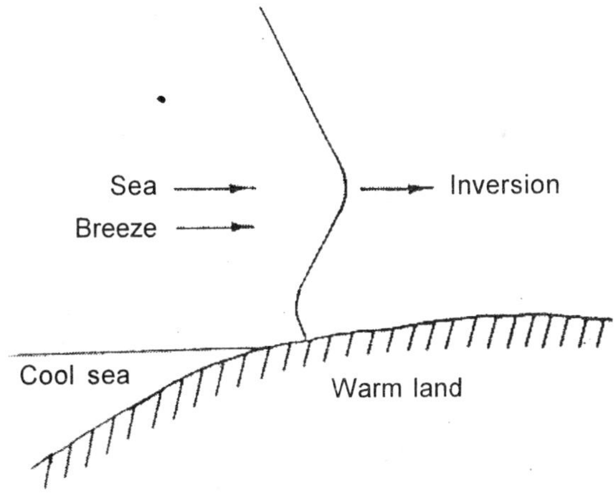

Figure 11.7 Formation of inversion due to land sea breeze

Mountain-Valley Winds

The mountain-valley winds are driven primarily by the temperature differences between different heights. In Fig. 11.8, the point A is nearer to the ground than the point B, and hence the air at point A would be warmer and move up creating a morning breeze up the side of the valley, but the reverse, however, occurs in the evening. Since the pollution sources are often located in the valley floors, the mountain-valley winds are likely to move the pollution up in the valley along the slope, exposing the people to these pollutants. Secondly, the pollutants carried up during the day may return at night with the wind as it shifts its direction towards the floor of the valley. In such circumstances the valley is filled with cool air during the night, and light warm breeze pass over the valley without disturbing the valley air (Fig. 11.9). Under these conditions, the concentrations of pollutants can buildup to dangerous levels in the valleys.

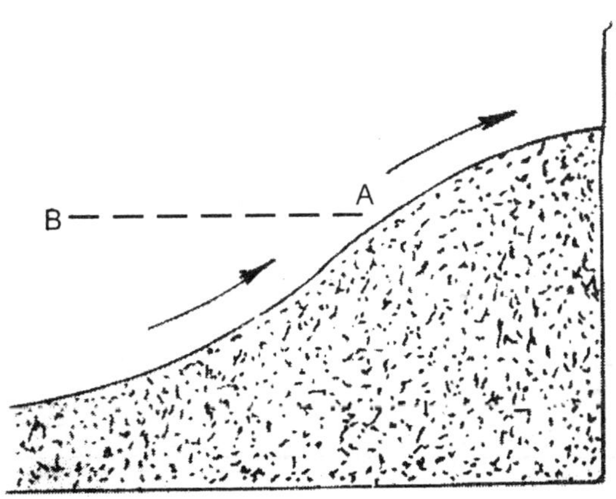

Figure 11.8 Formation of mountain-valley wind.

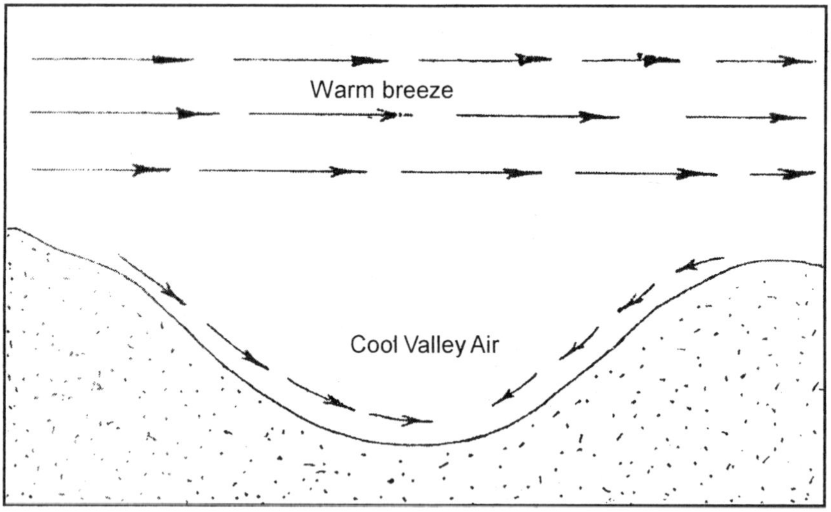

Figure 11.9 Durig night, the valley is filled with a stagnant cool air with warm breeze flowing above it.

During morning with the start of solar heating of the valley slopes, the air rises and after striking the warm inversion layer at the top, flows back towards the centre of the valley resulting in its circulation within the valley as shown in Fig. 11.10. These factors were major determinants in air pollution disasters of the Meuse valley in Belgium and Donora in Pennsylvania (U.S.A.).

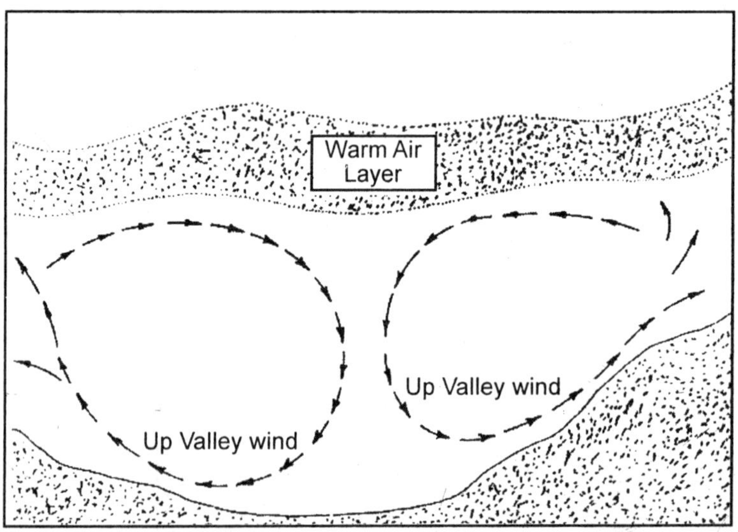

Figure 11.10 In the morning, due to heating of slopes, the air circulates within the valley with the warm air still above the valley.

Urban Heat Island

Cities are always warmer than their surrounding areas. The temperature differences between urban areas and their surroundings are particularly large at night than during the day. This temperature difference forces the air to circulate, as the warmer city air tends to rise to make the surrounding cool air to flow towards the city (Fig. 11.11). Such type of air circulation do have some effects on the local air pollution.

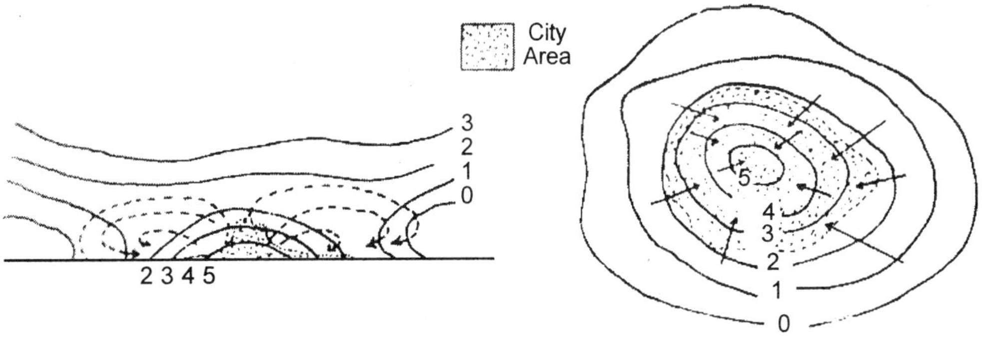

Figure 11.11 Formation of urban heat island.

Microscale Wind Motions

Microscale motions of air are of much smaller size, and include dust devils and small scale mechanical turbulence caused by the roughness of the surface. The surface roughness is provided by the non-uniform height of the buildings, presence of trees and other such roughness providing elements. In general, the turbulence of air rises with the increase in the surface roughness and the prevailing wind velocity. The mechanical turbulence consists of turbulent eddies which are the major factor in mixing the pollutants. An eddy refers to a piece of air which moves randomly in a fluctuating manner.

Another aspect of the surface roughness is separation of flow. The separation of flow can cause high concentrations of pollutants around the buildings. To understand the process of separation consider Fig. 11.12 showing the air to pass around a cylinder. Around the cylinder the flow is not uniform, and close to the cylinder on its back the velocity of air falls considerably to shed eddies from the cylinder. This is called as separation which is caused by the presence of an object, leading to obstruction of the uniform flow of air that results in its velocity to be decreased just on the back side of that object.

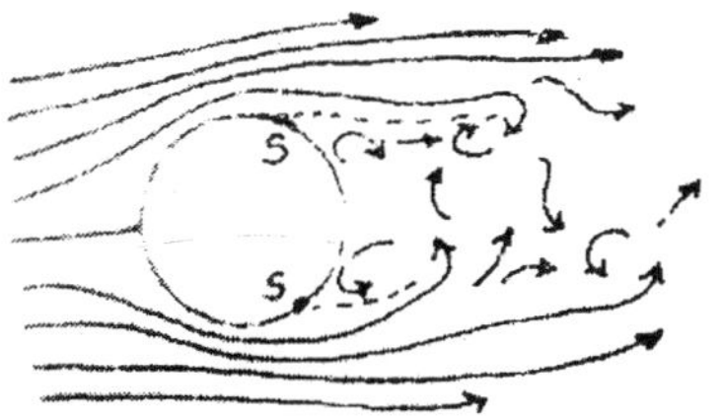

Figure 11.12 Air flow separation around a cylinder.

The phenomenon of separation is one of the important aspects of the air pollution problems in some particular situations. For example, downwash of effluent gases arising out of a chimney is one such phenomenon caused by separation (Fig. 11.13). This happens when the emitted effluents are trapped in the separated region backside of the chimney. Fig. 11.14 shows that how the plume is carried to the ground when the wind blows over a cliff. If the plume is emitted into the eddy very little mixing occurs, and pollutants tend to concentrate in that region. Figs. 11.15 (a-c) show, that how the separation of air flow caused by buildings can affect the plume dispersion. In this situation, a high concentration of pollutants is buildup backside of buildings. To avoid such a situation, the height of stacks near buildings should be 2.5 times or more than that of the height of the tallest building.

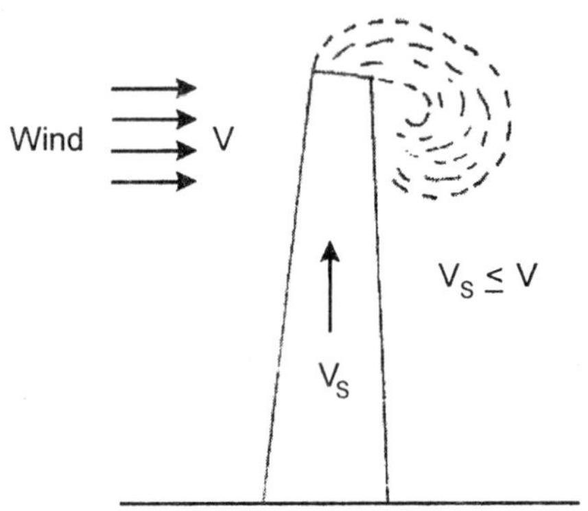

Figure 11.13 Downwash of pollutants behind a stack in the separatd region.

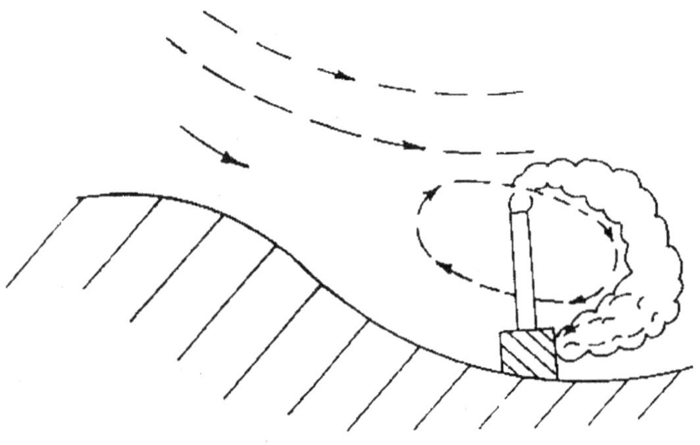

Figure 11.14 Plume is carried to the ground if it is released into the eddy formed by separation when air flow over a cliff.

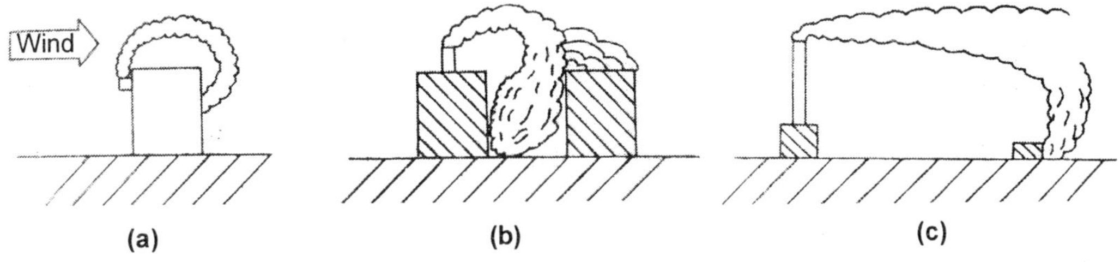

Figure 11.15 (a-c) Plume is carried to the backside of the buildings by separation of air flow caused by them.

Atmospheric Stability

Atmospheric stability is governed by vertical motions of the air. Atmosphere is called to be unstable when there is appreciable vertical turbulence in the air. The unstable atmosphere facilitates dispersion of pollutants vertically in the air. Reduction in the vertical turbulence will result in a stable atmosphere. The vertical turbulence of air is caused mainly by the solar heating of the ground which produces convection currents of the air.

Vertical turbulence also determines that how much depth of the atmosphere shall be available to disperse the pollutants. The vertical motion of the air is dependent primarily on the temperature gradient or the lapse rate prevailing in the atmosphere.

Temperature Lapse Rates

The rate of change of temperature with the height of the atmosphere is called the temperature lapse rate. On the basis of the temperature gradients, the lapse rates can be classified into different categories. The fundamental lapse rate is dry adiabatic lapse rate, which is characterized by a temperature decrease at the rate of 1°C per 100 meter. Any rising parcel of dry air is always cooled with the adiabatic lapse rate with no transfer of heat either form parcel to the surrounding air or *vice-versa.*

The rate of temperature decrease of more than 1°C per 100 m is called superadiabatic lapse rate; and the temperature decrease with less than 1°C per 100 m, subadiabatic lapse rate. Inversion is caused when temperature actually increases with height. No change in temperature with the height is called isothermal lapse rate. Fig. 11.16 represents various types of lapse rates, encountered manually in the atmosphere.

Significance of Lapse Rates to Air Pollution

To understand the significance of lapse rates in atmospheric stability and dispersion of pollutants, consider Fig. 11.17. If there persists a superadiabatic lapse rate, the rising air parcel, cooling at the adiabatic rate, remains always warmer and lighter than that of its surrounding air causing it to move continuously upward as a result of buoyancy. In such a case the parcel of rising air will be unstable, and mix and stir about violently dispersing the pollutants fairly evenly through a large volume of air.

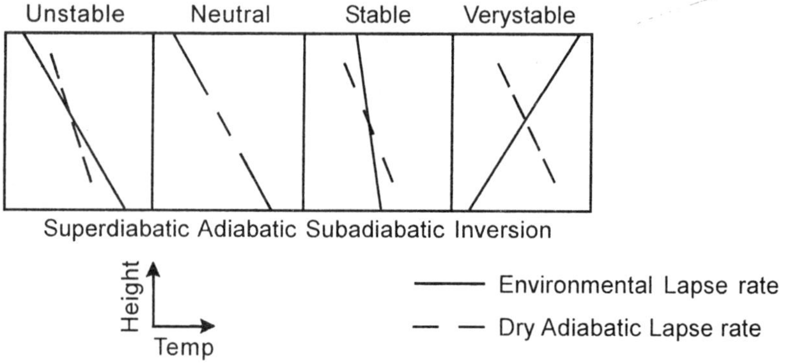

Figure 11.16 Various lape rates in different atmospheric temperature gradients.

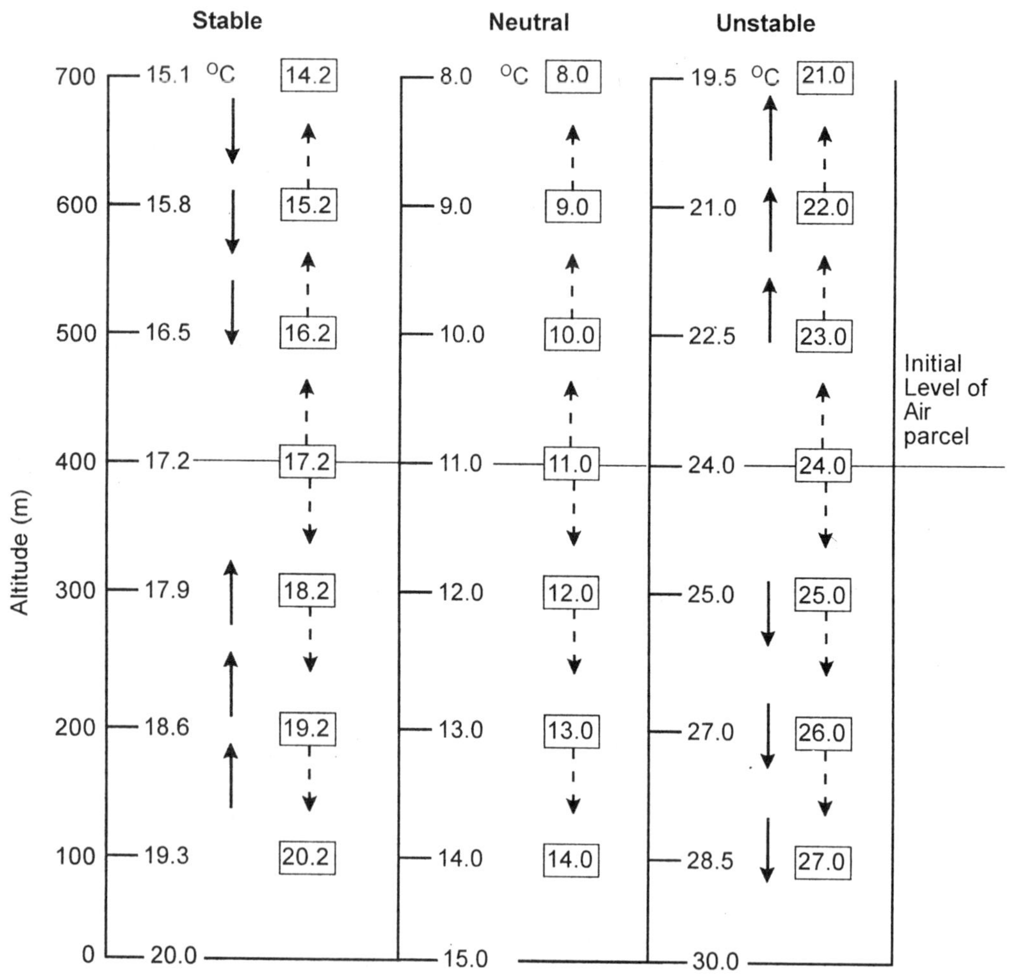

Figure 11.17 The behaviour of a rising air parcel in super-adiabatic atmospheric conditions.

In case of subadiabatic lapse rate, a rising air parcel becomes cooler and denser than its surrounding air, and tends to return to its starting point The air parcel in this case is stable and, in fact, will not be able to rise. The atmospheric conditions in this case are called stable, and pollutants will not be dispersed vertically. In adiabatic condition of lapse rate the atmosphere is neutral to vertical mixing. When the isothermal or inversion conditions prevail, the atmosphere becomes highly stable with complete stoppage of vertical mixing of pollutants.

Inversions

Inversion conditions are responsible for creating strongly stable atmosphere that is considered to be highly unfavourable for the dispersion of pollutants. Inversion can be of various types based on the prevalence of different causative factors. They can occur at different heights with various depths and for variable durations.

Nocturnal Radiative Inversions

These are one of the most common types of inversions occur during the night owing to radiative cooling of the ground. They are ground-based and are of short duration which burn off in the morning. The development of these inversions is illustrated in Fig. 11.18(a).

At night, the earth radiates heat escaping it to space that causes the surface temperature to fall. With the cooling of the earth's surface, the air in immediate contact with it also cools, in turn cooling the next layer and so on. This results in the decrease of temperature just near the surface of the earth resulting in an inversion. When solar heating starts the next morning, inversion is burnt off as the surface is gradually warmed to make the profile normal again.

The radiative inversions have several effects on air pollution. Due to these inversions, there is considerable accumulation of pollutants at the night time. They also cause an interesting morning phenomenon called fumigation, where the pollutants emitted from a chimney suddenly come to the ground level. Such type of inversions may be more dangerous, particularly in the winters as they persist for a longer period of time in the morning because of lower solar heating. At the same time the early morning activity, such as rush-hour traffic, can bring a tremendous increase in the pollutants level.

Frontal Inversions

They usually develop at the boundary between two air masses, called a front. When the two travelling air masses of different temperature meet, the warmer air mass, being slightly lesser dense, tries to ride over the edge of the heavier cooler air mass as shown in Fig. 11.18(b). This causes to develop an inversion at the mixing boundary. Such type of inversions are often associated with the subsequent rains which may cleanse the atmosphere.

Subsidence Inversions

The subsidence inversion occurs in the centre of a high pressure system or anticyclone. In such systems, the air at the edges spirals out and is replaced by air sinking down into the certre. The subsiding air is warmed as it descends forming an inversion at a height as shown in Fig. 11.18(c). The high pressure systems are, thus, considered to bring an extremely adverse meteorology for air pollution, as in these systems the winds are minimum, rains are absent, and conditions for both radiative and subsidence inversions are favourable. Such type of inversions develop quite frequently in Los Angeles because of the north Pacific high pressure system as discussed earlier in this chapter.

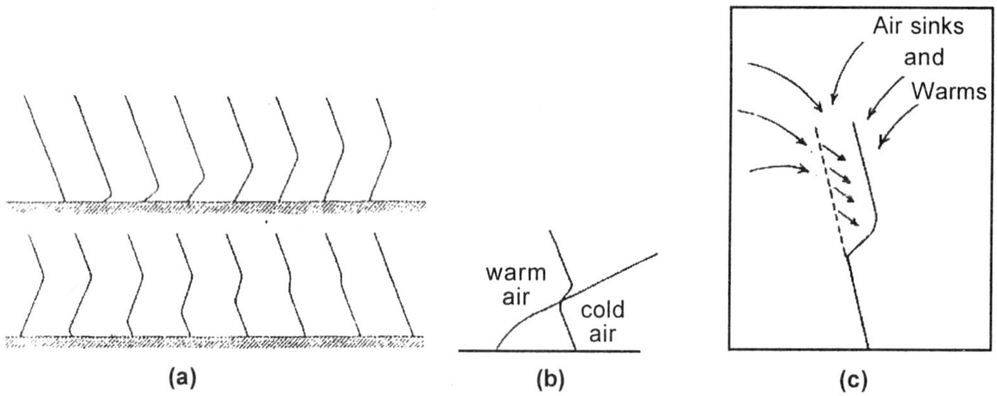

Figure 11.18 Inversions : (a) Noctumal radiative inversion (b) Frontal inversion (c) Subsidence inversion.

Plume Types

Atmospheric stability is an important factor in dilution and dispersion of pollutants in the atmosphere. Depending upon the temperature profiles (lapse rates) and other meteorological conditions, different types of plumes are formed as shown in Fig. 11.19. Details of the conditions of the atmosphere and weather responsible for various plume types are given in Table 11.1.

Table 11.1 Types of plumes formed in relation to different weather conditions

Plume type	Temperature profile	Wind conditions & turbulence
1. Looping	Adiabatic or superadiabatic	Light winds with intense thermal turbulence
2. Coning	Lapse rate between dry adiabatic and isothermal	Moderate to strong winds, turbulence mainly mechnical due to surface roughness
3. Fanning	Inversion or isothermal	Light winds, very little turbulence
4. Lofting	Adiabatic lapse rate at stack top and above, inversion below stack	Moderate wind, high turbulence aloft and no or less turbulence below
5. Fumigating	Adiabatic or super adiabatic lapse rate at stack top and below, inversion or isothermal lapse rate above	Winds light to moderate, thermal turbulence in lower layer, little turbulence in upper layer
6. Trapping	Inversion aloft	Wind light to moderate

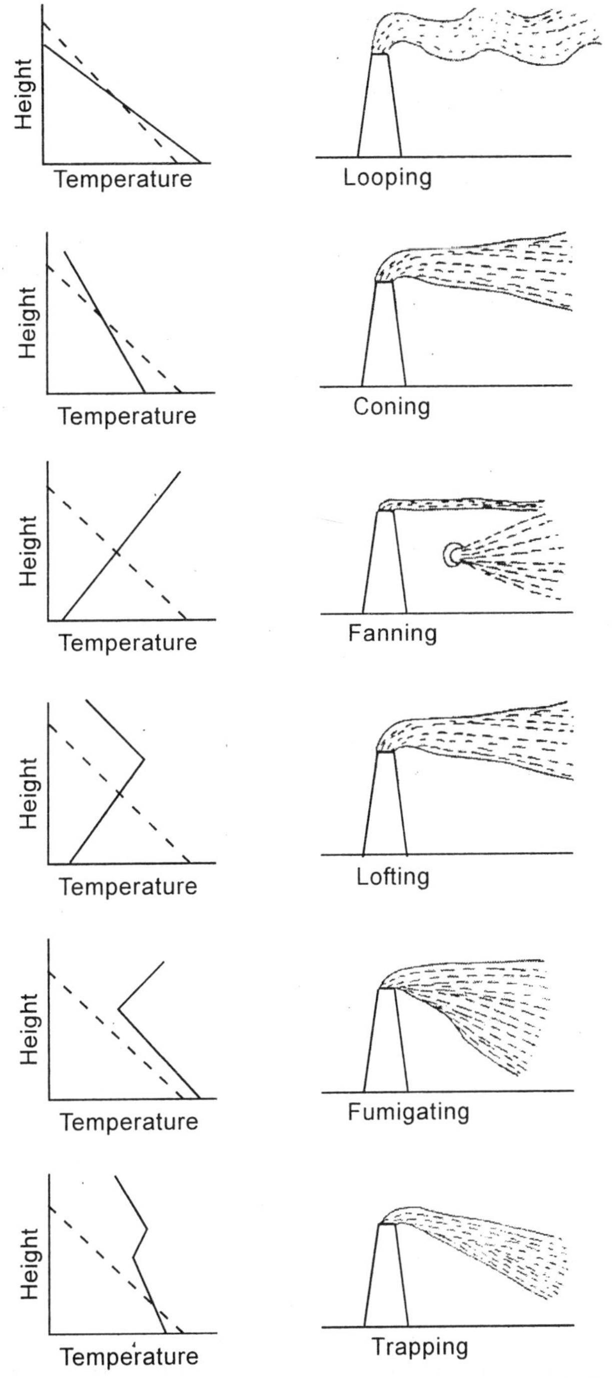

Figure 11.19 Formation of various plume types.

Very stable atmosphere forms a fanning plume. In the morning with the warming of ground surface, the radiative inversions are burnt off and atmosphere becomes unstable. When this unstable layer reaches the level of stack height, the fanning plume is forced to the ground by the turbulence creating a fumigating plume.

When inversions are present aloft with light winds and a moderate turbulence below, the plume is trapped and unable to rise, resulting in a trapping plume. At the time of highly unstable atmosphere, particularly during clear hot days, a looping plume is formed. A lapse rate between isothermal and dry adiabatic, associated with the turbulence due to surface roughness, forms a coning plume. In the evening, when the near ground temperature begins to lower, highly unstable conditions of atmosphere may still persist above the stack height, causing a plume to become lofting.

11.3 Effects of Air Pollution on Climate

This is not only the climate and weather which affect the air pollution, but air pollution itself too can modify the local and global climate. The climate of the earth has been changing over past millions of years due to operation of several factors such as volcanic erruptions, mountain building, modification in the composition of air and many more, of which some are still unknown. The joint effects of these natural forces are only incompletely understood, making it difficult to distinguish the effects caused by anthropogenic activities from other effects. However, some regional or local effects may be extremely prominent which can be ascribed purely to the Man-made air pollution.

Global Effects

Impact of Carbon dioxide and other heat absorbing gases (Green House Effect)

The basic effect of CO_2 on climate is due to its property that allows to pass through it the short-wave radiation from the sun, but absorbs the outgoing long wave radiation as heat from the earth. This results in the rise of atmospheric temperature with the increase in CO_2 concentration. The phenomenon is known as green house effect (Fig. 11.20). Some other gases like Nitrous oxide (N_2O), methane(CH_4), ozone(O_3) and chlorofluoro carbons(CFCs) also produce green house effect. However, the role of carbon dioxide is much more significant than these gases on account of its uniform and higher atmospheric concentrations. Since, CO_2 decreases the quantum of the radiation going back to the space, the upper atmosphere may get cooled as a result of an increase in CO_2 concentration in the lower atmosphere. The details of the green house effect are given separately in Chapter 12.

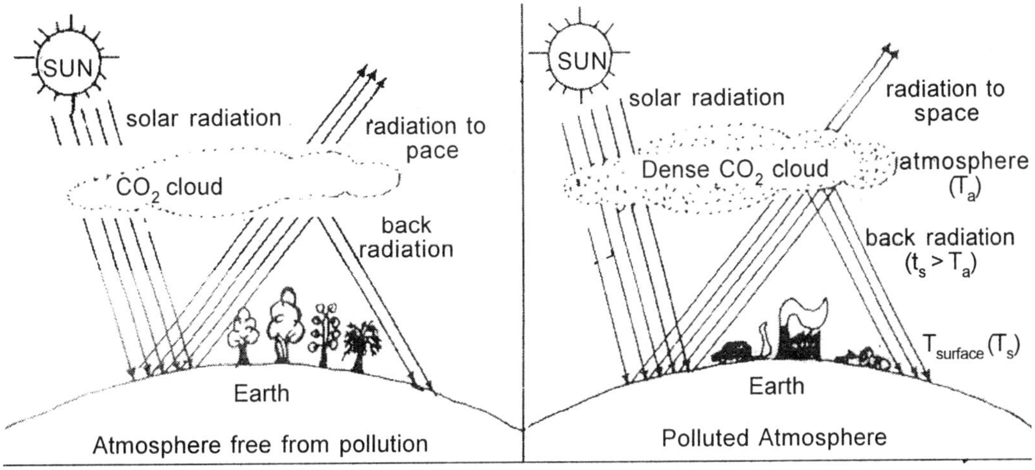

Figure 11.20 Absorption of radiation by green house gases to produce atmospheric warming.

Local Effects

Thermal Influence

As discussed earlier, the urban areas generally have a higher temperature than their surrounding country areas. The reduction in vegetation, a higher heat absorption because of the lowered albedo, and a ready storage of heat in concrete structures are the major factors those lead to an increase in the temperature of urban areas. A large amount of heat is also poured by industrial combustion and air conditioning processes, which account for nearly 80% of the temperature increase in urban areas. The formation of 'urban heat island' and the resultant wind effects and cloudiness have been discussed earlier in this chapter. The temperature increase in urban areas may be significant at local levels, but unlikely to cause any global change.

Visibility

One of the most obvious effects of the air pollution is the reduction in visibility. The decreased visibility occurs mostly as a result of the discharge of particulates from industry and automobiles. A substantial reduction in the visibility may also occur, sometimes, by the water droplets produced by industry. Large quantities of water are also vapourized in the cooling towers. Warm water discharges into the bodies of water lead to an increased evaporation. In some industrial areas this extra evaporation reaches upto 30% of the natural surface evaporation. The problem of visibility is more serious during winters, when the air is nearly saturated and little addition of water vapours make them to condense forming fog.

The excessive particulate matter in atmosphere also facilitates the condensation of atmospheric water vapours. Sulphur dioxide after its conversion into sulphuric acid causes the formation of droplets even before the saturation of water vapours is reached. At the higher relative humidity SO_2 influences the visibility considerably.

Sunshine Intensity

The presence of haze, smoke and other particulates cut the light intensity reaching to the earth's surface. It is estimated that there may be, on average, a 15 to 20% reduction in sunshine over the cities due to pollution.

Precipitation

It has been noted that the downwind regions of industrial areas experience comparatively more rainfall. It is still not clear whether the effects are due to increased convection of air as a result of excess heat, or increased condensation nuclei in the form of water vapour.

Summarily, there is no evidence that human activities and increase in air pollution have caused any global climatic changes, but large effects may occur in future. Nevertheless, measurable local climatic changes in the industrial and urbanized areas have been reported as a result of air pollution. Unfortunately we do not have the means to estimate the magnitude of these climatic changes very precisely, and some of these disappear in the natural climatic fluctuations. However, the pollution of air may put earth to the serious risk climatically, unless proper measures to contain the levels of air pollution are taken at this stage.

12 Climate Change and Green House Effect

Green house effect or global warming has emerged as one of the most important ecological problems in the modern world which has threatened to make this planet unsurvivable in future. Although various theories are proposed, many of them contradictory, and some scientists have even gone to the extent of giving the earth only 50 more years.

What is green house effect ?

Our earth is surrounded by a gaseous cover of mainly nitrogen and oxygen and many other gases in small concentration including water vapour and carbon dioxide. This atmosphere provides the vital oxygen to the living beings, maintain heat balance of the earth and protects us from the harmful radiations. Low wavelength radiation coming from sun is reflected back in the form of infrared long wavelength radiation, however, all of it is not reflected but part is intercepted by the gases in the earths atmosphere and in turn provides heat on this planet to keep it perpetually warm.

This phenomenon has been termed as green house effect, while some scientists are of the opinion that it should have been termed as troposphere heating effect. Table 12.1 gives details of various green house gases in the atmosphere. This phenomenon maintains the average temperature of the world and governs all life processes. The sea level is maintained and polar ice caps remain intact. Although vast changes and variations are noted in temperature all over the world and even in a day time at any given place, but the average temperature should remain constant. However, it has been noted for the past hundred years that the earth is gradually getting warmer.

Table 12.1 Important greenhouse gases (Miller 2004)

Gas	Human Source	Average Time in Troposphere	Relative Warming Potential Compared to CO_2
Carbon dioxide (CO_2)	Fossil fuel burning, especially coal (70-75%), deforestation and Plant burning	50-120 yrs	1
Methane (CH_4)	Rice paddies, guts of cattle and termites land fills, coal production, coal seams and natural gas leaks from oil and gas production and pipelines.	12-10 yrs	23
Nitrous oxide	Fossil fuel burning, fertilizers, live stock wastes and nylon production	114-120 yrs	296
Chlorofluoro carbons	Air conditioers, refrigerators, plastic foams.	11-20 yrs	900-8300
Hydrofluorocarbons	Air conditioners, refrigerators, plastic foams	9-390	470-2000
Halons	Fire extinguishers	65	5500
Carbon tetra fluoride	Cleaning solvent	42	1400

Although it is not a new phenomenon to our earth, the speed at which it is increasing is likely to have far reaching effects like sea level rise, change in climate, effects on crops, plants, forests, animals and microbes threatening the whole survival of earth. For example, it is predicted in June 2004 that 1 meter sea level rise will displace 8 million Indian people. The main reason of the global warming is increase in the concentration of green house gases due to human activities mainly burning of fossil fuel, rise in cattle population and industrialization. The other reasons are deforestation, burning of vegetation, and cultivation of paddy and use of inorganic fertilizers, which release N_2O into the atmosphere. There is conclusive evidence of this global rise in temperature. Scientists have noted slow but not noticeable changes in the average temperature of earth in the last 20,000 years. A rise of 0.3 to 0.7 °C is noted in the last century only, which is a major change. Results from recent climatic models suggest that mean global temperature shall rise by 2-6 °C during the next century if we assume that CO_2 concentration in the troposphere increases by 600 ppm.

Major Green House Gases

Carbon dioxide (CO_2) : Eighteen billion tonnes of CO_2 is added to the atmosphere annually. A rise of 26% has already occurred in a period of 200 years. It is rising at a rate of 0.5% per year.

Methane (CH_4) : Produced by organic matter decay under anaerobic conditions. Its concentration was 1.1 ppm in 1950. 1.7 ppm in 1985 and is registering a rise of 0.1 % per year.

Nitrous oxide (N_2O) : Preindustrialization, its concentration in the atmosphere was 285 ppb (parts per billion), which has increased to 315 ppb. It is rising at a rate of 0.3% per year.

Water vapours : It is an important green house gas. 14000 m^3 of water is present in the atmosphere as vapours. As there is more heating, there is more evaporation and more trapping of heat.

Chlorofluorocarbons (CFCs) : Chlorofluorocarbons were discovered about 70 years back but their concentration in atmosphere up to 1960 was negligible. Now their concentration has increased to a very high level. Their concentration in 1985 was around 0.045 ppm which has increased to nearly 0.8 ppm and at the present rate may go to 1.0 ppm. They are, however, being phased out.

Ozone (O_3) : Increasing use of CFCs is causing a depleting in the ozone layer but its concentration increasing in the lower layer of the atmosphere causing atmospheric warming.

Evidence for Global Warming

Are we really experiencing global warming ? Evidence comes from analysis of ice core samples, temperature measurements at different levels in several hundred boreholes in the earth's surface and atmospheric temperature measurements (Miller 2004). The findings show that the concentration of CO_2 in the troposphere is higher than it has been in the past 4,20,000 years. The 20th century was hottest in the past 10,000 years. Since 1861, the average global temperature of the troposphere near the earth's surface has risen 0.6 ± 0.2 °C with most of the increase taking place since 1946. Nine of the ten warmest years since 1861 have occurred since 1990. The hottest year was 1998 followed by 2002 and 2001. There is an apparent correlation between increase is fossil fuel, atmospheric concentration of CO_2 and global temperature 1970 and 2002 in fossil, fuels. The earth's poles and in greenlands as well as glaciers on the top of mountains in the Alps, Andes and Himalayas have begun shrinking and melting.

Impact or Climate Change on India

A study sponsored by the Asian Development Bank (ADB) reveals that although India is not a major contributor to global greenhouse gas emissions, its geographical location renders it particularly vulnerable to the impacts of global warming.

Crop yields in India could be disturbed by changes in temperature and altered concentration of CO_2. Wheat yields will be hit hard. Rice yields in coastal areas, where the productivity is low, will not be affected, but yields in the more productive regions of Haryana and Punjab are likely to drop.

Experts expect that with a rise in global temperature, sea levels will rise with adverse impacts. Vast tracts of crop land and valuable mangrovers which are unique to this region, could be innundated. Besides, damage to coastal infrastructure, this could result in the loss of freshwater supplies due to percolation of seawater. According to this report over 7 million people are at risk and the impact of sea level rise could be as much as Rs. 184,767 Crores. However the impact on forests will be minimal (Mallik 1994).

Currently, the issue of global warming has assumed diplomatic significance with the debate over the fixing of responsibility on developed countries which produce bulk of the green house gases (USA, 32.44% and Europe, 49.54% in 1990). However, all countries should jointly work to fight the menace.

The ultimate consequences of global warming could be second only to a nuclear war. Some of these important consequences are discussed below.

1. One of the disastrous consequences of global warming is the melting of polar ice resulting in the rise of sea level. Small islands would be affected badly by even a small rise in sea level.

   The IPCC's projections indicate that if emissions of green house gases continue in the same way they have increased in the last 10 or 20 years it would mean by 2030, the sea level will be rising 2-5 cm or 0.8-2 cm per decade. So far in the current century the rise has been one centimetre.

   Polar ice melting as a result of temperature rise can be considered a positive feedback which causes the incoming heat from the sun to be less efficiently reflected back (lower albedo) into space with more heat retained. Oceans also warm-up releasing more CO_2 and so on.

2. An average temperature rise of only 3 °C could mean increase of more than 10 °C at high latitudes in some seasons. In temperate zones winter would tend to be shorter and warmer, summers longer and hotter.

   Increase in global temperature may lead to a reduction in vertical temperature gradient in the urban areas affecting the surface-atmosphere exchange of energy. Consequently, the nature of inversion layer in the urban areas may also change.

3. It is expected that humidity will increase with global warming due to increase in the rate of evaporation and evapotranspiration, and temperature-led air expansion creating more room for water vapour in the air.

4. Rainfall would be affected on account of higher evaporation rates which may increase by 7-11 per cent a year in certain areas.

5. Temperate winters might be wetter, and summer drier. The tropics would also become wetter but the sub-tropics, already dry, could become drier still.

6. Wind is influenced by atmospheric temperature and pressure. Numerous changes are expected to take place in atmospheric wind system because of the climate change. Global warming may alter the pressure gradient in some areas affecting wind speed and causing wind direction to change.
7. Studies indicate an increase in the rate of desertification as a result of global warming, foiling the efforts taken for its reversal.
8. Decrease in grain production is likely in certain areas, though it is difficult to anticipate the way in which global warming will affect agriculture.
9. Climatic changes can also influence the human settlements in diverse ways. There is a strong relationship between climate and socio-economic activities such as construction, transportation, communication and climate related accidents. Climate also affects energy consumption, outdoor recreation, psychological discomfort, urban agriculture and agro-based industrial activity. Human health and the prevalence of certain disease vectors are also controlled by climatic factors.

Large quantities of CO_2 are produced in decomposition and volcanic erruptions, but the Man-made air pollution caused by combustion of fossil fuels is no less and adds a huge quantity of CO_2 into the atmosphere. It is estimated that about 1×10^{10} tons per year of CO_2 is discharged into the atmosphere by anthropogenic activities, but nearly 50% of this added CO_2 is absorbed by the oceans, and the rest stay in the atmosphere. Generally accepted figures indicate that CO_2 has increased from 270 ppm in the nineteenth century to 350 ppm at present with an increased rate of approximately 0.6 ppm per year currently. It is believed that the concentration of CO_2 in the atmosphere in the year 2000 would be about 380 ppm.

The UN sponsored "International Panel of Climate Change" (IPPC) has concluded that the global mean surface air temperature has already increased over past hundred years with five global average warmest years in 1980s. It predicts the rate of increase of global mean temperature during the next century to about 0.3°C per decade. This would result in an increase in global mean temperature by about 1°C by the year 2025 and 3°C before the end of the next century. It is interesting to note here that the average earth's temperature was only SOC colder than now during the last ice-age.

In order to stabilize the rising atmospheric concentrations of CO_2 at 1990 levels, immediate minimum 60% cuts in the emissions of CO_2 are required, according to IPCC. However, scientists assume that the concentrations of CO_2 would keep rising for 200 years even if global emissions were stabilized currently.

However, these estimates are only theoretical, as we ignore the effect of most atmospheric motions and other factors such as changes in ice cover, that affect the distribution of solar radiation. Nevertheless, the monitoring of CO_2 is of great importance as its rising concentrations can pose serious climatic problems at a future date.

In tropics, the demand for energy consumption and the level of heat-related discomfort may increase. The reverse is likely to be the case in the temperate and polar regions. In the tropics, heat-related diseases may increase while cold-related one may reduce. The rate and intensity of heat waves may rise in the temperate areas. The pattern of clothings will also change in relation to the change in

An intergovernmental panel on climatic change (IPCC) was established in 1988 by United Nations and World Meteorological Organization. A large number of studies have been undertaken since then and major conclusion with regard to future are : There will be significant increase in the emissions of CO_2, CH_4 and N_2O during the 21st century and such increase is very likely to enhance the earth's natural greenhouse effect. There is 90-95% chance that the earth's mean surface temperature will increase by 1.4 - 5.8 °C between 2000 and 2100.

Possible Effects of Global Warming

Fig. 12.1 gives a broad effects of global warming.

The projected change in the mean surface temperature may appear insignificant because variations of this magnitude are experienced in the course of seasonal or even daily weather. In fact, it is not so, during the last ice age about 12,000 years ago when much of the North America and Europe was covered with a sheet of ice, the mean surface temperature were only about 5 °C lower than today. It has taken 12,000 years to give a rise of 5 °C but such changes now may occur only in the next 100 years.

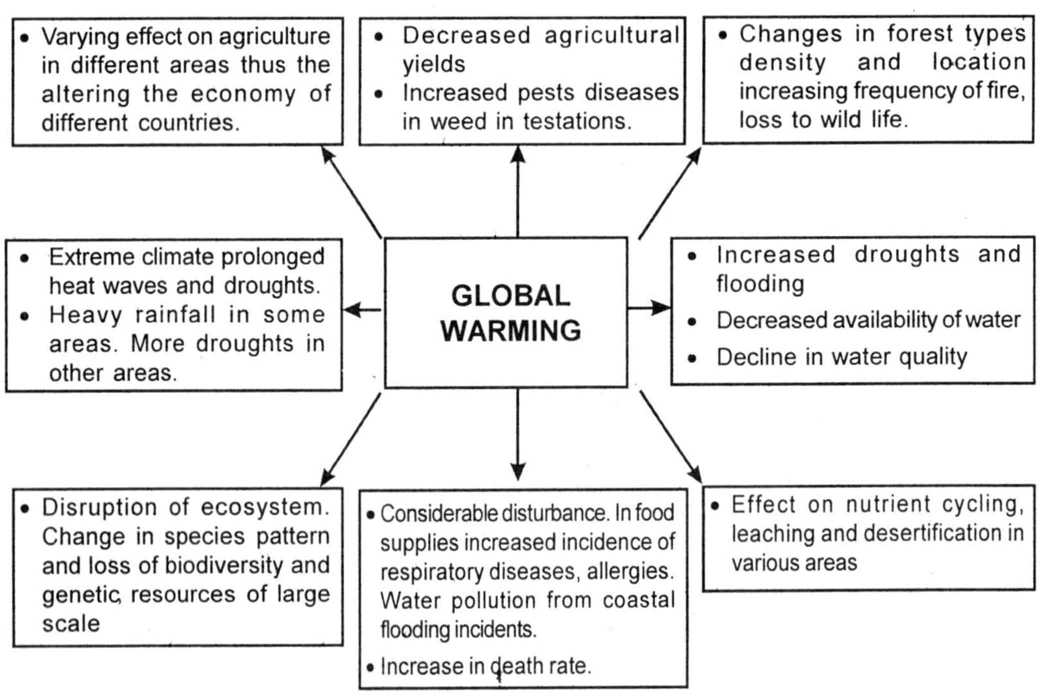

Fig. 12.1 Effects of Global Warming

Although there are considerable uncertainties regarding the precise consequence of global warming, one obvious results of general heating up shall be rather rapid rise in the mean sea level. The mean sea level has been rising for the past fifteen years. Evidence suggests that about 12000 years back it was 100 m lower than the present day level. It is expected that the global rise in temperature shall further enhance the rate of already rising sea level in two ways. Firstly, large deposits of ice present on the earth's surface shall melt which will add more water to the oceans. Secondly, rise in temperature shall also thermal expansion of the upper layer of water. An increase of 4-5 °C could cause enough expansion of this enormous surface of water so as to raise the mean sea level by 5-6 m. If all ice on the earth was to melt, sea level could rise by about 60 m. Low-lying areas shall go underwater. Large percentage of the world's population lives near the shores. This population will come under threat. About 60 island countries shall face deep encroachment by seawater and some, like Maldives may completely disappear.

Impact of Climate Change on India

Fig. 12.2 provides a clue to controlling global warming.

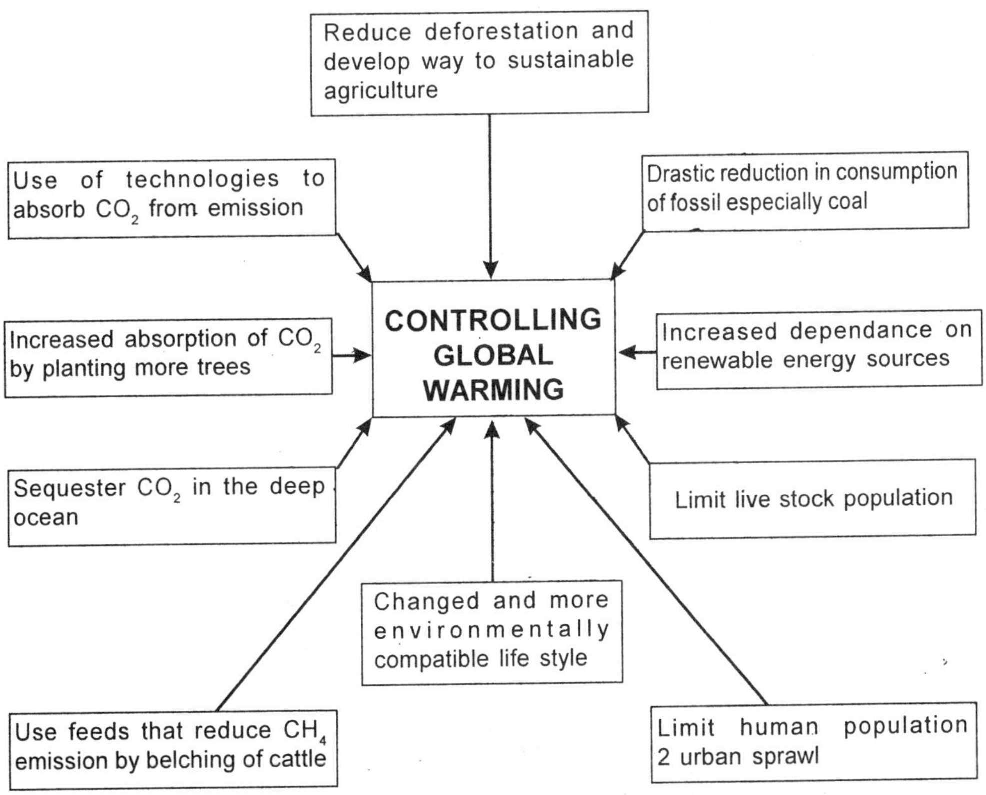

Fig. 12.2 Controlling Global Warming

International Action to Reduce Green House Effect

As per Kyoto treaty 1997, 38 developing countries are to cut green house emissions to an average of 5.2% below 1990 levels by 2012 because they are responsible for 36% of the world CO_2 emissions.

According to Muller (2004), China, the third largest emitter of CO_2 after US and European Union, is voluntarily improving energy efficiency and increasing use of renewable energy resources even though she is exempt from cuts under the first round of the Kyoto treaty.

According to a 2001 study by Natural Resources Defence Council, China reduced its CO_2 emissions by 17% between 1997 and 2000. The period during which CO_2 emissions in the United States rose by 14%, China accomplished the reduction.

Major global companies such as Alcoa, Dupont, IBM, Toyota, BP and Shell have established targets to reduce their greenhouse gas emissions by 10-65% from 1990 levels by 2010.

More than 500 cities around the world have taken up programmes to reduce their greenhouse gas emissions.

13 Acid Rain

13.1 The Problem

Acid rain refers to the presence of strong mineral acids like sulphuric acid, nitric acid, and in some locations even hydrochloric and hydrofluoric acids, which bring down the pH in the atmospheric precipitation. The water in the cleanest rain or even distilled water can have a low pH of around 5.6 when it is in equilibrium with atmospheric carbon dioixe. It is logical, therefore, to call the precipitation as acidic only when the pH is below this threshold level of 5.6. It will be appropriate to call it as acid deposition as the acid rain not only occur through rainfall and snow but quite often the acidic substances also get dry deposited when present in the form of mists in the atmosphere.

The acids in the atmosphere react with ammonia and other cations forming sulphates and nitrates which fall on the surface of the earth in the form of particulates. It is estimated that about 40% of the particles present in the atmosphere over the north polar regions are in the form of sulphates. A general outline of the atmospheric processes in acid rain deposition is given in Fig. 13.1.

The problem of acid deposition is primarily related to the use of high-sulphur coal and oil, the combustion of which produces considerable quantities of sulphurdioxide (SO_2) and nitrogen oxides (NO_x). These gases react with atmospheric moisture to form sulphuric and nitric acids, which eventually precipitate to the earth. Much of the SO_2 comes from the electric generation using coal energy. In the United States electric power plants are responsible for nearly 70% of SO_2 and 33% of NO_x emissions. The generation of 25 million tons of SO_2 along with substantially larger quantities of NO_x are major factors responsible for the acid rain over some parts of the U.S. (Ellison 1993).

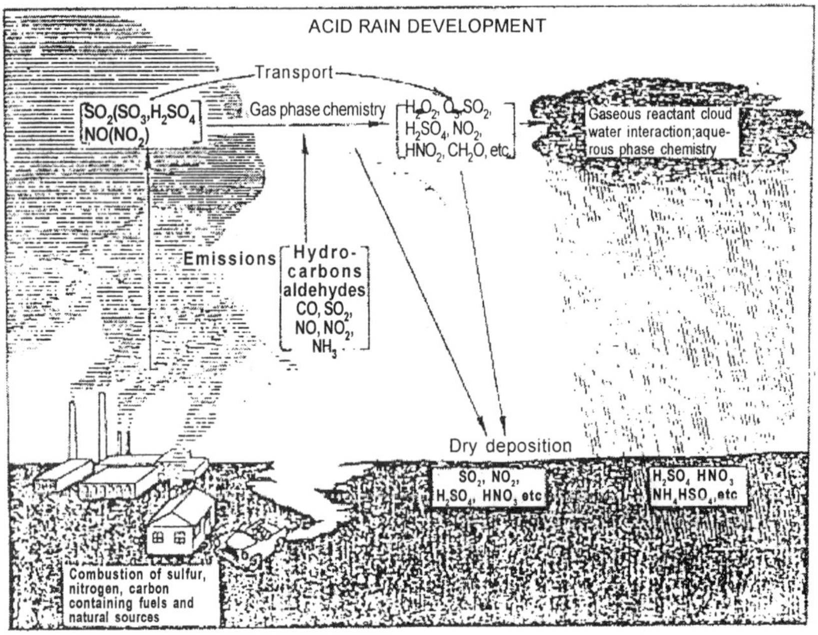

Fig. 13.1 Atmospheric processes in acid deposition (After Sridharan and Saksena, 1990).

13.2 Extent of the Problem

Acid precipitation is not a recent phenomenon, but has been reported as long ago as 1852 in Manchester, England. However, the greater scientific attention to the problem was paid only during the recent past in 1950s.

With rapidly growing consumption of coal energy, serious problem of acid rain have surfaced in various parts of the northern hemisphere, especially northeastern U.S., eastern Canada, northern Europe and China. Surveys have shown that the acidity of rain has dramatically increased in northern Europe. Until 1956 the low pH area was quite confined and the pH value remained mostly above 4.5, but by 1966 the low pH area increased considerably, and there were several regions in southern Netherlands and Rhine Valley in Germany with a pH lower than 4.0 (Oden, 1971). The rain in south China has been reported with a pH in the range of 4.3 to 5.5. In North America and Canada a pH of 4.2 is frequently met with in rain water.

The acid forming gases not only affect the areas of their origin but also cause problems in the regions of neighbouring countries. The incidence of increased acid precipitation in certain Scandinavian countries cannot be explained alone by the level of emissions of SO_2 and NO_2 in these countries. The increase in acidity in lakes and rivers in Sweden, Finland, Norway, Austria and Switzerland has been transported from the highly industrialized areas of U.K. and central Europe. Similarly, the pollution generated in the U.S. is frequently transported over the regions of Canada with the winds.

According to Sridharan and Saksena (1990), pH values of precipitation in India vary between 5.18 and 9.00 indicating that the problem of acid rain has also begun to surface here in some parts. Annual SO_2 emissions have almost doubled in the last decade due to increased fuel consumption, and considerably low pH values in rain have been reported from many metropolitan cities and industrial areas of India. Average pH value in the acid rain was reported to be 5.80 in Calcutta, 5.73 in Hyderabad, 5.85 in Madras, 6.21 in Delhi and 4.80 in Bombay. The acid rain status in ten cities of India during 1991 (monsoon), based on the data collected by NEERI, is given in Table 13.1.

Table 13.1 Rain water status in ten cities of India during 1991 (monsoon).

City	pH	Conductivity μS/cm	Chlorides	Sulphates	Nitrates
Ahmedabad	6.3 (6.5-6.1)	100 (154-27)	14 (21-3)	21 (34-4)	1 (1.7-0.7)
Bombay	6.5 (6.8-6.4)	54 (85-32)	16 (19-8)	7 (12-3)	3 (5-2)
Calcutta	6.4 (6.8-6.1)	45 (83-23)	7 (11-2)	6 (14-2)	4 (8-2)
Delhi	6.4 (6.8-6.1)	19 (40-5)	4 (6.8-2)	5.5 (12-2.6)	3 (6-2)
Hyderabad	7.2 (8.1-7.1)	36 (107-7)	5 (13-1.2)	14 (24-2)	1.2 (5.0-0.1)
Jaipur	6.7 (7.4-6.4)	20 (55-3)	3 (9.4-0.5)	2 (5.6-0.3)	1.3 (4.3-0.1)
Kochi	6.2 (6.9-4.8)	54 (415-10)	15 (20-8)	15 (125-2)	1 (2.6-0.07)
Kanpur	7.6 (8.1-7.1)	104 (183-62)	13 (21-8)	20 (47-6)	2.4 (5.2-0.8)
Madras	6.2 (6.7-6.1)	33 (101-7)	12 (15-5)	8 (30-0.08)	0.8 (3.4-0.2)
Nagpur	6.4 (6.6-6.1)	25 96-9	2 (6.2-0.7)	5 (26-1)	0.4 (1.2-0.06)

Effects of Acid Deposition

Problems caused by acid rain in the form of long-term and regional impacts on ecosystems, health and materials along with the associated political ramifications of transboundary air pollution have become very serious. The long term effects of SO_2 and NO_2 cannot be visualized in their gaseous forms, but in the acidity of rain-fall which they cause. The harmful effects caused by the acid deposition can be categorised under the effects on water bodies, soil, vegetation, health and materials.

(a) *Effects on Water Bodies*

One of the most severe problems of acid rain is the acidification of lakes and rivers. In southern Scandinavia thousands of lakes and streams show acidification and even more are threatened in Canada and northeastern U.S.A. In northern England several lakes with lime poor sediments have gone acidic by 1950s.

Soft water lakes lack the chemical species that can buffer the acidic change and, therefore, are highly vulnerable to acidification. Acid deposition brings about drastic changes in aquatic communities and reduction in diversity. An increase in transparency is usually seen in acidified lakes due to suppression of algal growth, which often results in the decline of fisheries potential by eliminating the sensitive fish. There have been reports of the existence of 15000 fishless lakes in Sweden and some 100 in Adirondak in USA as a result of acidification. Not only surface waters, but ground waters can, also be affected by acid deposition as has been found at some places in Sweden.

(b) *Effects on Soil and Terrestrial Vegetation*

Soils with low buffer capacity are the most sensitive soils to the acid deposition. Such soils include mainly the sandy soils having low lime, which frequently loose their fertility by acidification due to accelerated leaching of nutrients like potassium, phosphorus, magnesium and calcium. The acid rain also brings about the mobilization of heavy metals like aluminium, zinc and manganese from the soils.

Development of acidity can influence the chemistry and biology of the soils to a greater extent. It adversely affects the microorganisms whose activity is responsible for maintaining the soil fertility. Agricultural production is greatly affected by the acidification of farm lands. Increased acidity of soils can lead to greater absorption of cadmium by plants, which may be dangerous to humans after consuming such produce. An incidence of cadmium poisoning in Japan has resulted in the death of several people from a painful bone disease after consumption of cadmium rich rice.

In Japan damage to ceder trees in more than 5000 km^2 area has resulted due to acid rain. In the long run it is feared that the acid rain may further deteriorate the forest soils, especially those developed on sandy substrate poor in lime. However, the soils with low sulphur and high carbonate may get benefited by deposition of acid sulphates.

(c) *Effects on Materials*

One of the important consequences of acid deposition is the physical damage to the buildings, monuments, bridges and other structures by corrosion. Calcium and magnesium carbonates in the limestone are converted into their respective sulphates forming a hard surface skin which blisters and scales off.

In sandstone, calcite cement is attacked by the acid to make the silica sand grains loose, which later get washed away by wind and rain. Stone is also corroded by the presence of excessive quantities of carbon dioxide that form carbonic acid in rain. Carbonic acid form the soluble calcium and magnesium hydrogen carbonates.

There have been doubts raised by several environmentalists about probable damage to Taj Mahal by the increase in the acidity of rain due to SO_2 generation from Mathura oil refinery and local foundries. Similarly, several ancient monuments all over the world have been destroyed by acid rain.

Sulphur dioxide, dissolved in droplets of water, forms sulphurous acid which can bleach the chemical dystuffs. The reaction is accelerated in the presence of ozone. Several other items like paper, fabrics, leather and wood are greatly affected by the production of acid from sulphur dioxide. More details of the damage to physical property and materials by air pollution are given in Chapter 9.

(d) Healh Effects

Human health can also be affected by acidification of air, water and food. While the consumption of low pH water in itself is dangerous, it can also release heavy metals from the pipes of the distribution systems into the potable water supply.

The sulphate particles formed from sulphuric acid in the atmosphere can enter deep into the lungs causing severe lung diseases including lung cancer. Another aspect of the generation of acid mists in the atmosphere is reduction in visibility, especially in fogs, which might lead to the accidents. Acid rain mobilizes a number of heavy metals in the soil, which may get accumulated in the plants to cause health effects in the consumer as seen earlier by the example of cadmium.

13.4 Mechanisms of Acid Formation in Atmosphere

A brief outline of the reactions involving various precursors for acid formation is given in Table 13.2. Some important acid forming reactions from sulphur dioxide and nitrogen oxides are given in detail in chapter 3.

Table 13.2 Acid forming reactions in atmosphere

Pollutants	Reactions	Products
1. Sulphur dioxide	(a) SO_2 with water	(a) Sulphurous acid
	(b) Oxidation of sulphurous acid	(b) Sulphuric acid
	(c) Oxidation of SO_2	(c) Sulphur trioxide
	(d) SO_3 with water	(d) Sulphuric acid
2. Nitrogen dioxide	(a) NO_2 with waler	(a) Nitrous and nitric acids
	(b) HNO_2 wilh waler	(b) Nitric acid and nilrogen monoxide
3. Carbon dioxide	CO_2 with waler	Carbonic acid
4. Hydrogen sulphide	Oxidalion	Sulphur dioxide
5. Hydrogen flouride	HF with water	Hydrofluoric acid
6. Silicon tetrafluoride	with water	Hydrofluoric acid and SO_2

Sulphuric acid in the air can be formed from SO_2 in a number of ways depending upon the level of air pollution and environmental conditions of light and humidity. Sulphur dioxide is oxidized to SO_3 in the presence of certain metals like Mn, Fe, Cu, Cr, Al, Pb and Ca which act as catalysts. These reactions are, however, more pronounced in the plumes coming out of stacks since the concentration of these metals is great enough there to perform the oxidation of SO_2. The resultant SO_3 reacts readily with water to form sulphuric acid. The presence of oxidants and peroxy free radicals in air also facilitate the oxidation of SO_2 to SO_3. Sulphur dioxide can also react directly with water to form the sulphurous acid which later gets oxidized into sulphuric acid.

It is seen that the rate of oxidation and solubility of SO_2 in water is the function of pH where both are suppressed at lower pH values with more and more production of acid. However, the acid generated in the atmosphere gets reduced by its conversion into the aerosols of ammonium and calcium sulphates facilitating further generation of the acid.

$$2SO_2 + \dot{O}_2 \xrightarrow{\text{metals}} 2SO_3$$

$$SO_2 + O_3 \rightarrow SO_3 + O_2$$

$$SO_2 + ROO \rightarrow SO_3 + RO$$

$$SO_3 + H_2O \rightarrow H_2SO_4$$

$$SO_2 + H_2O \rightarrow H_2SO_3$$

Nitrogen oxides in the atmosphere are present mainly in the forms of nitrogen dioxide (NO_2) and nitrogen monoxide (NO). Nitric acid can be formed by direct hydration and catalytic oxidation of NO_2. NO_2 can be readily converted into NO_3 by oxidation with ozone which can react further with NO_2 to form nitrogen pentoxide. This N_2O_5 is converted into nitric acid after reacting with water. Sometimes, NO and NO_2 can also react together with water to form nitrous acid.

$$4NO_2 + O_2 + 2H_2O \rightarrow 4HNO_3$$

$$NO_2 + O_3 \rightarrow NO_3 + O_2$$

$$NO_3 + NO_2 \rightarrow N_2O_5$$

$$N_2O_5 + H_2O \rightarrow 2HNO_3$$

$$NO + NO_2 + H_2O \rightarrow 2HNO_2$$

The nitric acid produced in the atmosphere often gets converted into both inorganic and organic nitrates.

13.5 Control Strategies For Acid Rain

Acid rain abatement programmes are most often directed towards the control of sulphur dioxide emissions together with some quantities of nitrogen oxides. Following are some commonly employed strategies for controlling the emissions of these gases.

1. The use of low sulphur coal
2. Coal cleaning and gasification
3. Substitution of coal by other fuels
4. Alternative methods for power generation
5. Fuel gas desulphurization

Coal in the nature is found always associated with some quantities of sulphur. The use of low-sulphur coal will greatly help reducing the emissions of sulphur dioxide.

The sulphur in coal remains present in the form of pyritic materials, sulphate and organic-S. The quantities in the form of sulphates are, however, quite meagre and often difficult to be removed. Pyrites can be removed by pulverization and later washing the coal with water. Organic sulphur is bound with the molecules and can be removed only by changing the chemical nature of the coal by gasification, liquefaction or carbonization. It is possible to recover almost 99% of the sulphur in a pure usable form by coal gasification.

Substitution of coal by other fuels, producing lower emissions of acid gases, can also be a good strategy for control of acid rain. Natural gas is one of the fuels which produces insignificant quantities of sulphur dioxide and can be a best substitute for coal. It is found in abundance in this nation and now gas-based thermal power plants and energy requiring industries are coming up fast.

The power can also be generated by using other methods instead of thermal power plants. Streets (1990) opined that in South Asia, development of large hydropower facilities can be a better strategy, as one of the policy options to replace thermal generation, to control acid rain. The production of nuclear power shall eliminate the generation of SO_2 but some inherent problems of environmental safety and availability of fuels limit its use.

Installation of flue-gas desulphurization systems in large power plants can reduce emissions of SO_2 by 90% or more. Wet scrubbing by lime generates sulphite and sulphates of calcium. The huge quantities of these chemicals can be disposed off as land fill or can be converted into usable gypsum and its high value sister compounds like anhydrite (anhydrous calcium sulphate) or alpha hemihydrate. The high quality gypsum cake, so recovered, can also be used in manufacture of plaster cement and other construction materials. In countries like USA, where sufficient land is available, most of these scrubbing wastes, amounting to nearly 86%, are disposed off as land-fill. In Japan and Germany more than 70% of these wastes are used for production of pure usable gypsum and its compounds.

The flue-gas desulphurization programmes can also be directed towards the production of elemental sulphur, sulphuric acid, liquid sulphur dioxide and ammonium sulphate. The sulphur recovery can be made by use of alumina beads of 1.6 mm diameter impregnated with sodium carbonate in fluidized bed which can absorb up to 90% SO_2 and 70% NO_x. The spent sorbent is regenerated at 650 °C with a reducing gas converting the captured SO_2 into a mixture of SO_2, H_2S, S and COS, which can be later converted chemically into elemental sulphur. Sulphur dioxide can be converted into sulphuric acid by oxidation using a catalyst like vanadium pentoxide.

Ammonium phosphate is usually manufactured by reacting ammonia and phosphate rock after its digestion with sulphuric acid. Technology has been developed to make ammonium phosphate by wet scrubbing of SO_2-containing flue gases with ammonia and phosphate rock.

One of the latest technology to control the acid gases is 'Electron Beam Technology' which converts SO_2 and NO_x into ammonium sulphate [$(NH_4)_2 SO_4$] and ammonium nitrate [BH_4NO_3] respectively on a dry mode basis generating no liquid wastes. The process involves the reaction of ammonia, which is injected from outside into the flue gas, with SO_x and NO_x in a process vessel under the influence of electrons produced by an electron beam gun. It is possible to remove 95% of SO_x and 80% of NO_x simultaneously from the flue gas under normal operating conditions by this process.

Several countries have developed their own plans to control the acid rain. The Environmental Ministers of European Economic Community (EEC) nations have in 1988 agreed upon to take appropriate steps in their countries to reduce overall quantities of SO_2 by more than 3 million tons by the year 1993 and 7.5 million tons by 2003 from the level of 1980. They also agreed for the ultimate reduction of NO_x by 30% from the emission inventory of 1988.

14 Air Pollution Control

This chapter is divided into two major sections. The first section deals with the general principles and working of common devices and techniques employed for control of diverse gaseous and particulate pollutants particularly for stationary sources as the abatement of pollution from mobile sources has already been discussed along with automobile pollution in Chapter 5. The other section gives the control of air pollution in some specific industries.

14.1 Air Pollution Control from Stationary Sources

Painter (1974) has given an excellent classification of the conventional approaches and principles used for air pollution control from stationary sources. Under each category a number of devices and equipment with different engineering designs are available. The description of all these is beyond the scope of this book. However, description of only most commonly used devices and equipments is given here following the Painter's classification.

Air pollution from stationary sources such as industries can be controlled by following two fundamental approaches.

(i) Preventive techniques

(ii) Proper effluent cleaning

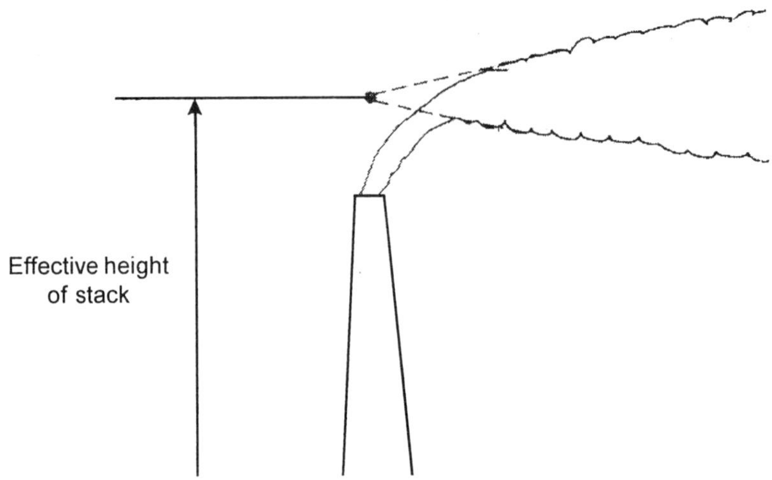

Fig. 14.1 Effective height of stack.

14.2 Proper Effluent Disposal

The most effective method of air pollution control in atmosphere is to properly dilute and disperse the air pollutants as they are released from the source. This can be achieved by providing a greater height to the stacks. The long stack will reduce the ground level concentration of pollutants by facilitating their discharge away from the ground, and making available more ground, and making available more depth of the atmosphere for their dilution. The effective height of the stack (Fig. 14.1) should be more than two and a half times of the height of the tallest building near the source. In 1984 the U.S.A. has 179 smoke-stacks 500 feet or higher including 20 that reach upto 1000 feet.

The dilution and dispersion of the pollutants in air is also dependent upon several micrometeorological factors such as the velocity and direction of wind, and the prevailing temperature profile. Siting of industry should also be decided after taking into consideration the local meteorological features so as to avoid the exposure of pollutants to a greater proportion of the population.

14.3 Control at the Source

Control at the source is achieved by minimizing the formation of air pollutants or by destroying, modifying or trapping before they are released into the atmosphere. Following are some of the common methods employed to control the pollutants at source.

Preventive Techniques (Source Corrective Methods)

Shift of the Source

It is possible to control air pollution by relocating the industries in such a manner as to minimize the effects of pollutants on the population. For example, if an industry is situated in a heavily populated area, it can be shifted to some other area outside the city, or where population is sparce. This may be the situation in many big industrial cities like Mumbai and Ahmedabad where several polluting Textile and other industries are located in most densely populated areas. Steps can be taken to shift such industries away from the human population at a safe distance. The financial cost of such shifting, however, may be a constraint.

An industry can also be shifted elsewhere on the considerations of meteorological conditions. As we have seen earlier that meteorology plays an important role in local air pollution problems, hence, it is necessary to locate industries in those areas where meteorological factors do not allow concentration of pollutants near the ground level in the populated areas. In India, for example, the winds are normally northerly to north-east during winter, the season which supports several adverse meteorological factors for air pollution. Industries, therefore, can be shifted to, south of the cities, so as to avoid the drift of the pollutants along with the winds over the populated areas. Mention may be made here of some large industrial cities like Mumbai, Baroda and Bhopal whose industrial areas are located at north of the city that helps bringing the pollutants over the residential areas with the winds. Bhopal tragedy could have been minimized had the Union Carbide Plant was situated in south of the city.

Temporary Shutdown of the Source

The source can be shutdown for a period of time when there is a danger of heavy accumulation of pollutants on account of the adverse meteorological conditions.

Substitution of Raw Materials and Fuels

Some raw materials cause more pollution than others and, therefore, can be substituted by materials causing less pollution. For example, reactive organic solvents can be replaced by nonreactive aqueous solvent systems, which can help preventing the release of organics into the atmosphere.

Use of low sulphur coal shall reduce the emissions of sulphur oxides during combustion. Washing of coal can remove pyrites (sulphur containing inorganic compounds) to some extent help reducing the sulphur. However, much of the chemically combined sulphur in the organic form still remains after washing which cannot be removed by physical treatment. Partial desulphurization of coal and fuel oils can reduce sulphur oxides emissions. Grading of coal to remove coal dust from other sizes shall reduce particulate air pollution. Worst potential sources of flyash and grit are pulverized fuels which burn while still in suspension in the combustion chamber.

Coal can also be gasified into synthetic fuel gas containing mainly methane with a simultaneous recovery of sulphur. Substitution of greater pollution-producing fuels by others is also an important method to reduce the emissions. Soft coal, for instance, can be replaced by hard coal, oil or natural gas. Even fossil fuels can be substituted by electric, hydroelectric, solar, nuclear, or geothermal energy. Replacement by low sulphur containing coal in a thermal power plant in central London for several years had resulted into lowering down of the levels of air pollution. Similarly, restrictions are in force on sulphur content of oil in central districts of Paris for abatement of pollution.

Process Modifications

Formation of some of the pollutants can be controlled by new or modifying processing methods. For example, nitrogen oxides are formed by combination of nitrogen (N_2) and oxygen (O_2) of the air at high combustion temperatures, but by suitably modifying the operations, their formation can be minimized. Some of the important process modifications for controlling nitrogen oxide pollution are fuel gas recirculation, water injection, two stage combustion and low excess air firing. The two stage combustion has been found to be very effective in bringing down the nitrogen oxides by 90%. In the process of two stage combustion, all the fuel is fired in the first stage with insufficient air, and then more air is introduced in the second stage to completely burn the fuel. Due to heat loss between the two stages, higher temperatures are prevented reducing the formation of nitrogen oxides.

Nitrogen oxide emissions can also be lowered by use of fluidized bed for boiler heating instead of ordinary furnaces. The lower flame temperature in fluidized bed will reduce the formation of oxides of nitrogen.

In petroleum refinery, instead of burning hydrogen sulphide in flares, it can be reclaimed chemically in the form of elemental sulphur.

By use of exhaust hoods and special ducts over the various industrial ovens, several solvents can be recovered which otherwise would have been released in the air as pollutants.

Alteration of Equipment

Alteration of certain equipments can also bring down the pollution levels of air. For example, open hearth furnaces in steel industry can be replaced by less polluting electric or oxygen furnaces. Hydrocarbon pollution caused by evaporation from the storage tanks can be cut down by using floating roof tanks rather than vented tanks.

Good Operating Practices

Good operational practices of the equipment may play an important role in reducing the formation of air pollutants. For example, if too much thick layer of coal is introduced into the furnace it will lead to the entry of greater quantities of unburnt coal particles into the flue gases. Similarly, the scarcity of oxygen in furnace can be responsible for the formation of excessive flyash and smoke. But, if excess air is introduced into the furnace, it will result in entrainment of small coal particles, thus increasing the dust load of flue gas. Introduction of excess amounts of liquid sulphur in the burner of sulphuric acid plant can emit higher quantities of sulphur dioxide.

Proper Effluent Cleaning

In addition to the techniques described above, devices for removal of pollutants from the flue gases have to be used prior to their disposal into the atmosphere. Though, these techniques or devices are usually different for gaseous and particulate pollutants, some of them can also remove both these pollutants simultaneously. Some devices have been designed specifically for removal of a particular gas or particulate matter of a definite size.

Control of Gaseous Pollutants

The selection of devices to control gaseous air pollutants depends mainly on the characteristics of the gas. The commonly available devices are based broadly on the following five principles.

(a) Absorption

(b) Adsorption

(c) Combustion

(d) Closed collection and recovery systems

(e) Masking and counteraction

Gas Absorption

The technique of gas absorption is based on the principle of contact between the pollutant gas and a liquid in which the gas is soluble or makes some reaction with it. The technique involves the gases to be passed through scrubbers (absorbers) containing the absorbing medium that retains the pollutants, while allowing the passage of clean gases.

The absorbents used in scrubbers can be classified into two categories of reactive and nonreactive based on whether the gas makes some chemical reaction with the absorbent or simply gets dissolved in it. For example, SO_2 can be removed by reactive absorbents like calcium hydroxide, which form calcium sulphate as a result of the chemical reaction between the two.

An absorbent may be nonregenerative if it cannot be regenerated after removal of pollutant for recycling. for example, water. An absorbent is called regenerative, when it can be separated from the pollutant for recycling. For example, carbon tetrachloride after absorption of chlorine can be separated from it, and is available again for recycling, while freed chlorine is recovered to be used again.

Absorption is carried out in variously designed scrubbers. The various designs of scrubbers are based on the consideration to provide maximum contact between absorbent and the gas so as to achieve a high efficiency of gas removal. An account of some common type of scurbbers is given below.

1. *Packed tower scrubbers :* The design of a packed tower scrubber is given in Fig. 14.2. It consists of a long tower packed with a suitable inert packing material such as polyethylene. The absorbent trickles down from the top to downward, while the gases pass in the opposite direction from downward to the top, thus allowing the maximum reaction time. The presence of packing material makes the absorbent to trickle down in thin films to provide maximum surface area for contact. The packed tower is usually more economic for corrosive gases and vapours in view of the lesser quantities of corrosion resistant materials required for its construction.

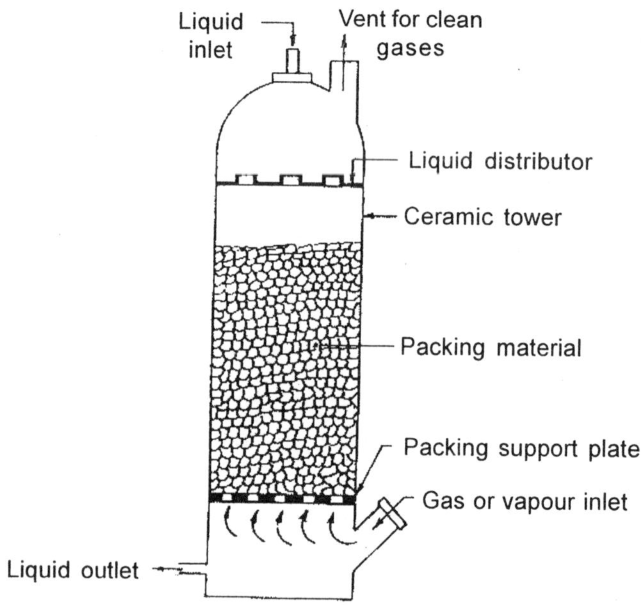

Fig. 14.2 A packed tower gas scrubber.

2. *Plate tower scrubber :* The construction of a plate tower scrubber is shown in Fig. 14.3. It consists of a long vertical chamber fitted with perforated circular plates at equal spacing. The gases or vapours pass from downward to the top of the tower making a contact with the liquid present on the each perforated plate. The liquid does not fall through the pores on the plates as it is held by the pressure created by the velocity of the gases. Each plate is provided with a pipe to carry the excess absorbent downward from plate to plate.

   The plate towers are most suitable when a frequent cleaning is required particularly in case of the liquid which after absorption contains high quantities of particulates and relatively insoluble and offensive gases.

3. *Spray tower scrubber :* The design and construction of these scrubbers is given in Fig. 14.4 (a-c). In these type of scrubbers, the liquid is sprayed on the pollutant gases that provides the turbulence to the gases for better absorption. The method

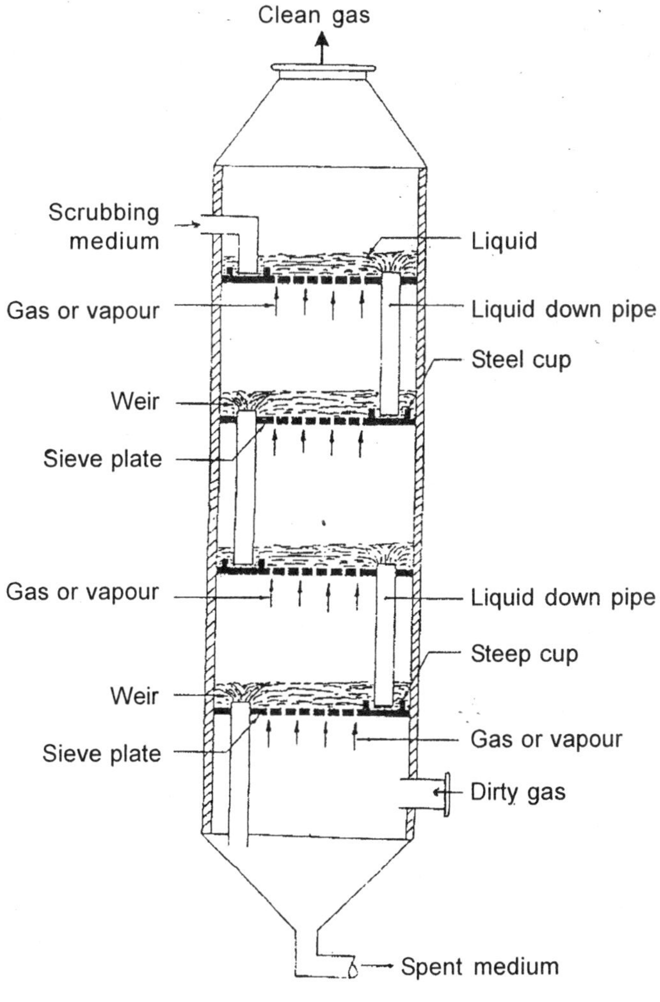

Fig. 14.3 Impingment plate tower gas scrubber.

is best suited for soluble and offensive gases. The design of the scrubber can be so made to give a centrifugal force to both liquid spray and the gas to achieve maximum contact between the two for higher efficiency of removal. The spray tower scrubber can also be used for removal of both solid and liquid particulates.

4. *Liquid jet scrubber :* The device is most suitable for the condensable gaseous pollutants. The scrubber is shown in Fig. 14.5 and consists of two vertical chambers. In one of the chambers, a liquid jet is sprayed which atomizes and produces small droplets of the absorbent. Gases are also introduced into the same chamber from the upper end. Non-condensable clean gases are removed from the other chamber.

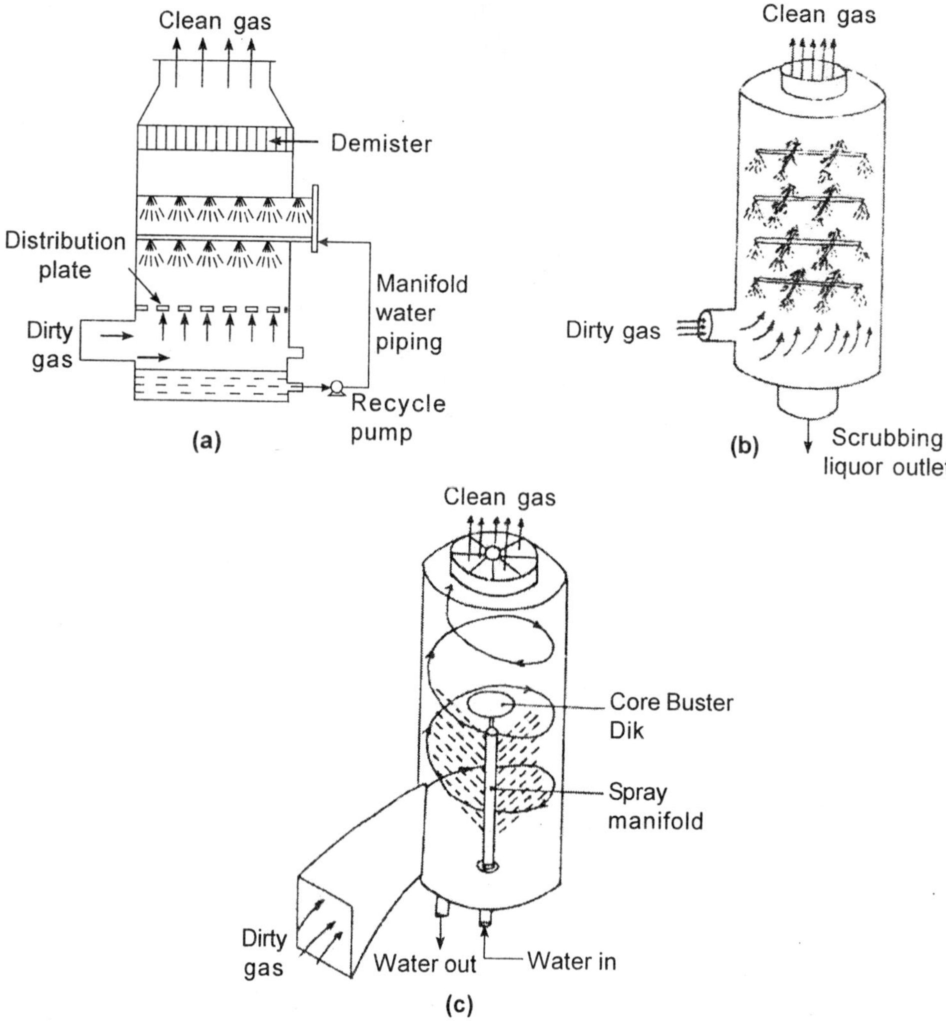

Fig. 14.4 (a-b) Spray tower gas scrubbers (c) Cyclonic spray tower gas scrubber.

5. *Agitated tank scrubber :* The effluent gases, in this type of scrubber, are agitated together with the absorbent in a tank against baffle plates fitted on the sides of the tank as shown in Fig. 14.6. The turbulence caused by stirring provides greater absorption efficiency when particulates are also present.

All these scrubbers described above, operate efficiently at a temperature below 100 ^{o}C that avoids the undue loss of the absorbent by evaporation, and keeps it in the liquid state. For this, the scrubbers are always preceded by some cooling devices to bring down the temperature of effluent gases to the desired level. The treated gases have always a lower temperature, and contain large quantities of water vapours and absorbent droplets. Demisters or some other suitable devices are installed in sequence after the scrubber to

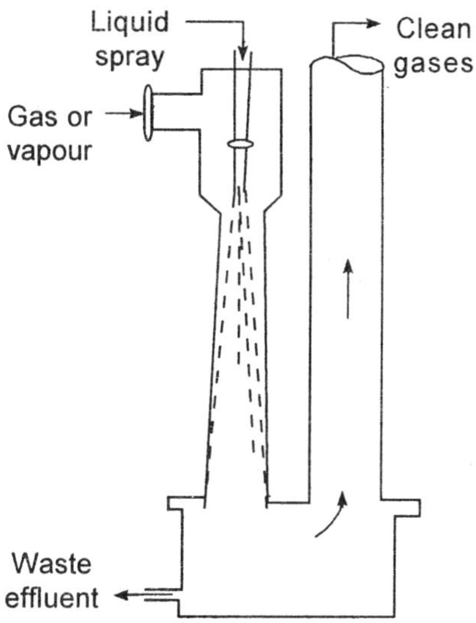

Fig. 14.5 Liquid jet scrubber.

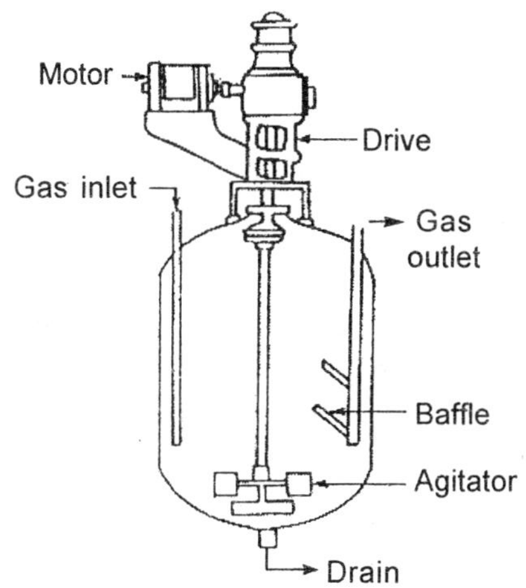

Fig. 14.6 Agitated tank gas scrubber

remove water vapours and the traces of the absorbent from the effluent gases. Reheating of the gases is also necessary in most cases to provide a required buoyancy to the gases for their escape from the long stacks.

The method of scrubbing the gases is most suitable for removal of the oxides of sulphur from coal based units (e.g., thermal power plants) and smelters, fumes of sulphuric acid from paint, pigment and sulphuric acid plants, chlorine, oilier halogens, CO_2 and NO_2 from nitric and sulphuric acid plants, HCl gas from plating industries and H_2S from petroleum refineries.

Gas adsorption

The technique of gas adsorption is based on the reaction of gases on the solid adsorbents. The adsorption may be physical or chemical. In this method the gases are passed through adsorbents packed in the specially designed towers to allow the maximum contact between the two.

The physical adsorption is dependent upon the temperature and pressure conditions in the system. Adsorption is promoted by the increase in pressure and decrease in temperature. The chemical adsorption depends on the reactivity of the gases and their bond forming capacity with the surface of the adsorbent. The adsorption depends also on the available surface area of the adsorbent, which provides surface for the reaction.

The adsorbents can be recycled by desorption (removal of adsorbed gas) of the gases. However, the desorption is suitable only when the freed gaseous pollutants are of some economic use, otherwise a problem may occur to handle them again. In the cases where the pollutant is not economically utilizable, it is better to dispose the pollutant together with the adsorbent.

The adsorbents are mostly pollutant specific. For example, activated alumina, silica gel and diatomaceous earth are suitable for adsorption of water vapours from a gas-phase mixture of water vapours and organic contaminants, thus, may be useful in drying of gases. These polar adsorbents can also adsorb other polar molecules like SO_2 and NH_3.

Activated carbon with a surface area usually in the range of 200-1200 m^2/g is capable of adsorbing a large number of nonpolar and less-polar organic compounds. It is often used for removal of organic solvent vapours. A brief description of the activated carbon adsorber is given below.

A common design of the absorber is shown in Fig. 14.7, where the gases are passed from below the activated carbon bed contained in a vertical chamber. The gases are sucked from the top to allow their rapid flow through the bed.

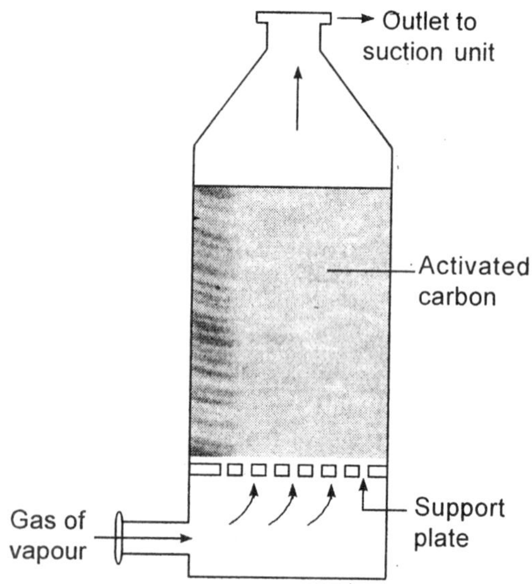

Fig. 14.7 An activated carbon adsorber.

The use of activated carbon adsorber is most suitable to remove odorous organic compounds, such as methyl chloroform from the film processing plant vapours of ethyl alcohol from whiskey warehouse, cleaning of kitchen exhausts, mercaptans, cresols and butyric acid etc.

Combustion

The process of combustion is most suitable for organic contaminant, whereupon by burning, they are converted into carbon dioxide and water vapours. The combustion, however, depends on four factors.

Combustion of pollutants can be accomplished in three different ways depending upon the combustion characteristics and the concentration of the pollutant gases.

(a) Furnace combustion

(b) Flare combustion

(c) Catalytic combustion

1. *Furnace combustion :* It can be divided into two types on the basis of combustibility of the pollutant gases.

    (i) thermal oxidation

    (ii) direct flame combustion

In thermal oxidation, the pollutant gases are burnt by the rise in temperature with the help of burning some other fuel in presence of oxygen in a combustion chamber (Fig. 14.8). The organic compounds are completely converted into CO_2 and water vapours at the high temperature of 540-820 °C. The direct flame combustion technique is employed when the pollutant gases are themselves combustible, and are present in high quantities to produce a flame (Fig. 14.9).

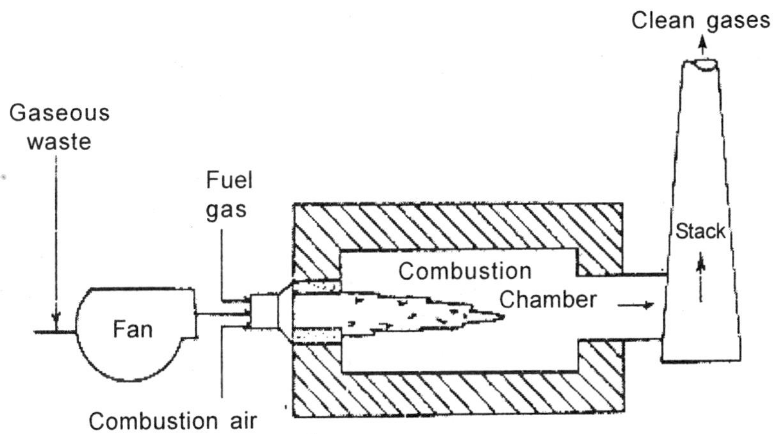

Fig. 14.8 Furnace combustion : Thermal oxidation of gases with the help of some fuel.

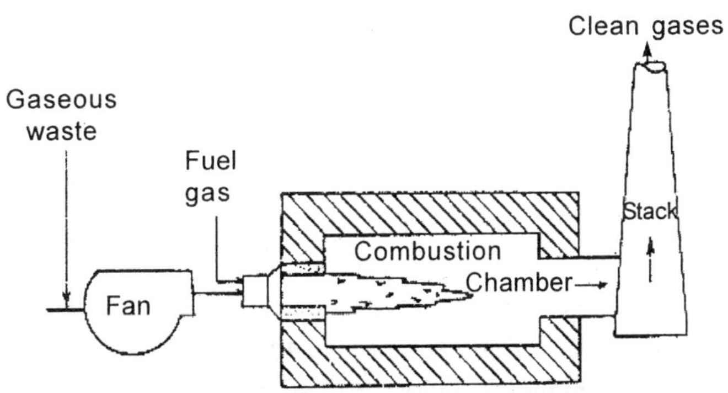

Fig. 14.9 Furnace combustion : Direct flame combustion of gases without fuel.

The furnace combustion is suitable to remove methyl mercaptans, hydrogen sulphide, and methyl sulphide (all producing odours) from kraft pulping process, and organic vapour odours from paint and other industries.

2. *Flare combustion :* Here combustion is a technique which involves the production of an open flame by burning the combustible gases in presence of open air. The method is usually employed to remove hydrocarbons and organic vapour odorous compounds in refineries and chemical works. Here combustion can also be used in burning hydrogen, ammonia, HCN or other toxic or dangerous gases. The pollutant gases are burnt on the top of a stack by providing a suitable burner. If aromatic hydrocarbons are present in the effluent gases, they burn with a smoky flame. This difficulty can be overcome by injecting steam into the flame which results in a water-aromatic hydrocarbons reaction producing hydrogen and carbon monoxide, both of which burn smokelessly. However, such steam injected flares are little noisy. A steam-injected flare burner is shown in Fig. 14.10.

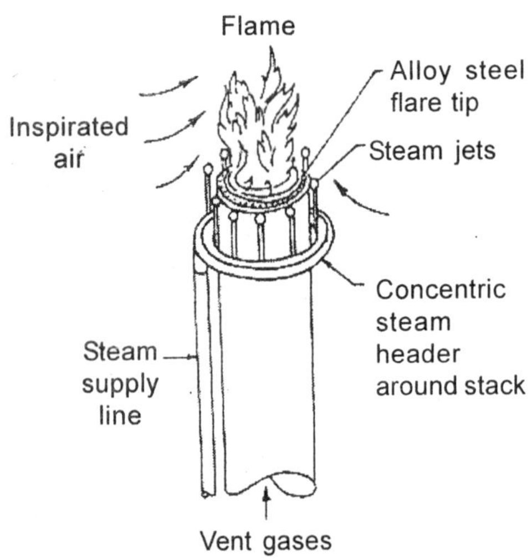

Fig. 14.10 Steam injection flare for smokeless hydrocarbons combustion.

3. *Catalytic combustion :* Catalytic combustion is carried out in presence of some catalyst; the combustion is flameless and required relatively low temperature of 300-400 °C. The process is suitable when the effluent gas contains vapourized or gaseous combustible materials with comparatively low quantities of particulate matter. The effluent gases are passed through a catalyst and temperature is raised to accelerate the oxidation process. Some of the common catalysts, widely used, are oxides of metals, platinum alloys and vanadium pentoxide.

Control of Particulates

Particulate matter is controlled in the effluent gases adopting the following common methods.

(a) Dry type mechanical collectors

(b) Wet collectors

(c) Filters

(d) Electrostatic precipitators

The selection of a specific device to control particulate pollution shall depend on factors like physical and chemical characteristics of the particulates and the carriers gas, flow rates, size of the particles and their concentration, besides the characteristics of the source itself.

Dry Type Mechanical Collectors

Some important gas cleaning devices in this category are described below.

1. *Settling chambers :* A settling chamber is merely an enlargement in the form of a chamber in a duct carrying the effluent gases (Fig. 14.11) in which the gas is slowed down to allow settling of dust and mist particles by the force of gravity. This device is normally suitable for the particles of larger size and mass (>40 μ). These are often used as precleaners to remove coarse particles prior to employing some other efficient device. The efficiency of this device depends on the residence time of the gas in the settling chamber which is related to the velocity of gas flow and the chamber volume. The increase in size of the chamber and reduction of gas velocity below 10 ft/sec shall considerably increase the efficiency of settling chambers. The main application of this device is in removing coarse particles in kilns and furnaces.

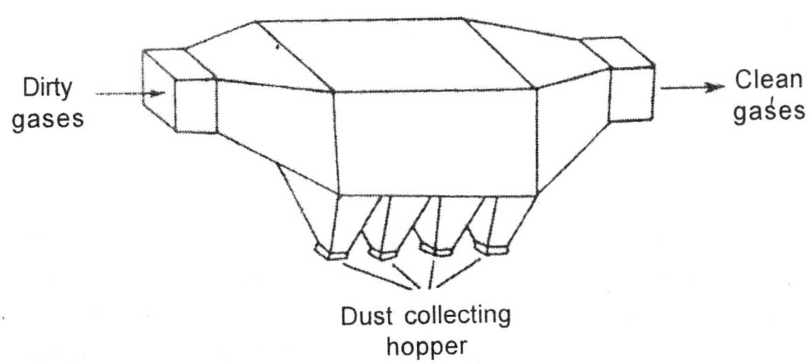

Fig. 14.11 A simple gravity settling chamber.

2. *Cyclones :* The main principle applied in cyclone is the spinning of particles by a centrifugal force to separate them from the carrier gas. The dust particles, by virtue of their inertia, move outward to the periferal wall, from where they fall to a receiver. The devices used for this type of centrifugal separation are called cyclones. Cyclones are widely used in different type of industries to remove particles above 10 μ. Cyclones can be of two types based on the direction of the flow of gases.
   (a) Reverse-flow type
   (b) Straight-through type

Fig. 14.12 shows a reverse-flow type of cyclone. It is consisted of a cylindrical shell with a conical base and a hopper at the bottom and a tangential inlet at the top for the effluent gases. The gases enter the cyclone through this tangential inlet moving downward spinning around the periphery, and then reversing and forming another spiral within the previous downward spiral. Finally, the gases are removed from the centrally placed exit pipe. The particles which are thrown to the walls, settle down in the hopper.

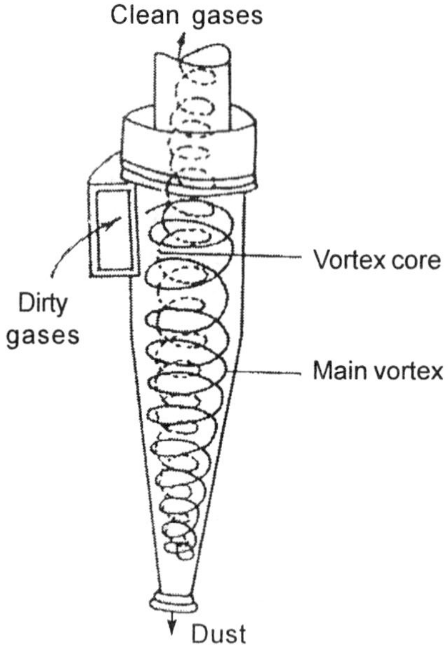

Fig. 14.12 A reverse-flow cyclone dust collector.

In the straight-through flow type of cyclones, the gases do not reverse back but go straight downward. As the gases spun, the dust is collected in the outer layers around the periphery of the base of the cyclone. These outer layers of the gases with concentrated particles, are removed off to a secondary collector such as a settling chamber or a reverse-flow type cyclone. This type of cyclone is mostly used as a flyash collector or as a precleaner device before the application of other efficient devices.

A multicyclone is a collection of a number of cyclones in parallel.

The major application of cyclones is when the particles are of larger size (10 μ) such as in cement industries, metal industries, foundries, steel mills, food and grain mills, asphalt plants and petroleum refineries.

Wet Collection

Wet collectors are commonly called as scrubbers, where the gases are passed through the water to remove the particles. Wet collectors are capable of cleaning hot and moist gases, which are difficult to be treated by other devices. Scrubbers are available in a variety of designs, shapes and sizes.

Wet collectors can be classified according to the method of collection. In one method, the particles are first conditioned so as to increase their effective size for enabling them to be collected more easily. The conditioning of particles may be accomplished by condencing the water upon the particles or by intercepting of fine dust particles by liquid droplets, resulting in the formation of a heavier dust-liquid agglomerate. In another method of collection, the liquid traps the particles, and the body of liquid with the trapped particles is taken outside the collector for disposal.

Has recognised some 14 types of wet srcubbers with variously designed units in each type. Description of all these wet scrubbers is beyond the scope of this book, and only some important and common type of scrubbers are described here.

1. *Gravity spray tower :* This is one of the most simple devices consisted of a tower in which the dirty gases rise from the bottom, while water is sprayed from a number of nozzles as shown in Fig. 14.13(a-b) given earlier in connection with the removal of gaseous pollutants. The spray produces large number of water droplets falling due to gravity in the path of rising particles. Particulates, as they come in contact with the droplets, become heavier and fall at the bottom of the tower from where they can be removed along with the water.
2. *Venturi scrubber :* A venturi tube is a narrowed section of a duct as shown in Fig. 14.13(a). The narrowing causes the acceleration of the velocity of the gases to a high level in the Venturi section with a simultaneous drop in pressure. Water sprayed into the Venturi section is quickly atomized by the high velocity gas under low pressure, to form millions of small droplets. These droplets collide with the dust particles to form dust-water agglomerates. These entrained water droplets in the form of agglomerates are removed from the gas stream by a cyclonic separator attached with the Venturi as shown in Fig. 14.13(b).
3. *Disintegrator scrubber :* The design of a disintegrator scrubber is shown in Fig. 14.14. Water is disintegrated into small droplets by alternate rows of stator and rotor bars present in the scrubber. Water is introduced axially and due to rotation of rotor bars, it is effectively atomized into fine droplets. These droplets collect the particles allowing the clean gases to be released out.

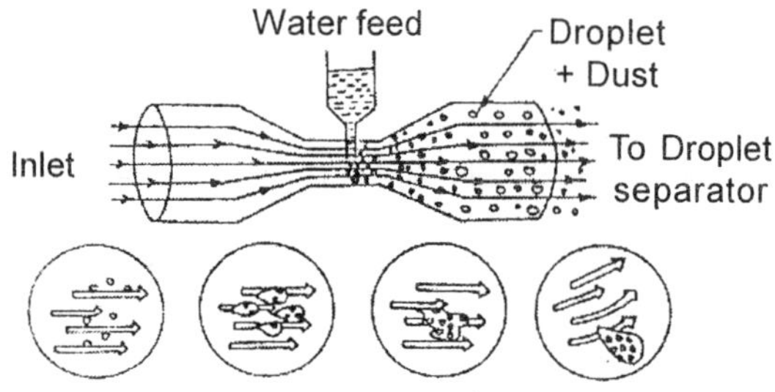

(a)

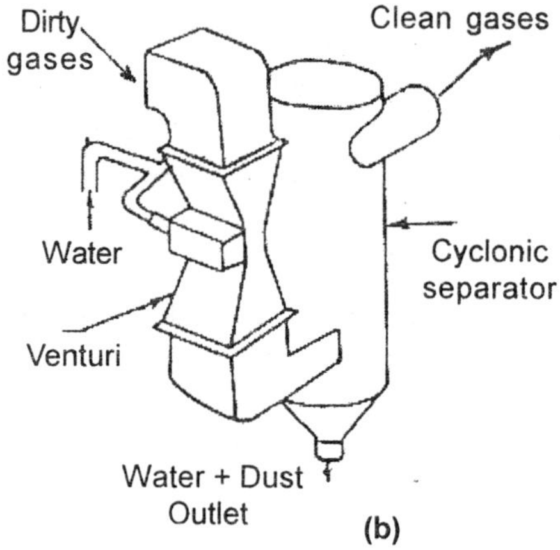

(b)

Fig. 14.13 (a) Venturi section showing the formation of liquid droplets and trapping of dust particles by them (After S.J. Williamson.1973. Fundamentals of Air Pollution. Addision-Wesley) (b) A Venturi scrubber with cyclone separator

4. *Wet impingment scrubber :* Wet impingement scrubber is the same as a plate tower scrubber (Fig. 14.3) described earlier in connection with the removal of gases. It is consisted of a Vertical tower containing several circular perforated plates mounted at equal spacings. The water falls from one plate to another by means of a downspout pipe provided at one side of the each plate. As the gases pass from below the plate, water is atomized at the edge of orifices (perforations) to form small droplets which impinge the particles of dust, and clean gases are passed.

5. *Wet centrifugal scrubbers :* One of the scrubber of this type is called cyclonic gas scrubber and is shown earlier in Fig. 14.4(c). In this type of scrubber the particles upon impaction on the droplets are moved to the perifery by the centrifugal force due to spinning movement of the gas. The clean gases are passed out, and the slurry is removed from the bottom of the scrubber to be disposed off.

   Wet scrubbers have been successfully applied to the industries such as steel industry, sulphuric acid plants, foundries, coal dryers, kraft paper mills, asphalt plants, mining, pickle liquor concentrators, fertilizer plants, hydrogen plants, sintering plants, chemical industries, Cevient kilns, aluminium furnaces, and ore roasting.

Fabric Filter Systems

In the fabric filter systems for collecting particles, the dirty gases are passed through woven or felted fabrics so as to retain the particles, and allowing clean gases to pass out.

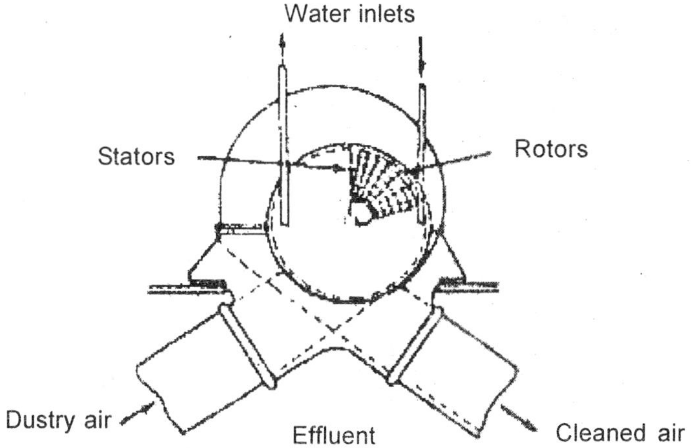

Fig. 14.14 A disintrigator scrubber.

The filter systems are consisted of several thin, long bags hanging in an enclosure, called a bag house. The air in a bag house flows through the open ends of the bags and passes out from their sides to be finally released out of the filter system as a clean effluent. With time, a cake is formed on the filter surface that further improves the efficiency of filtration. But, as this cake grows and become thick, it can lower the filter efficiency by a pressure drop across the filter, and hence to be removed periodically. The cleaning of filters to remove the deposited dusts is carried out by shaking the bags, reversing the flow, rapping, pressure jets or by gentle collapsing. The fallen particles are collected in a hopper from where they can be removed for final disposal. A common fabric system with inbuilt devices for periodic cleaning, without stopping the filtration, is shown in Fig. 14.15.

The baghouses are quite efficient in collecting smaller particles and are often placed in series after mechanical collectors. The use of fabric filters is limited, however, by the availability of fabrics that can be used in hot temperature and corrosive gases. Other factors important in selecting the fabrics are their acid or alkali resistance, air permeability and resistance to abrasion and shrinkage. Some common materials used in preparation of filter bags are cotton, wool, nylon, nomex (a kind of fibre), asbestos, teflon, orion (a kind of acrylic fibre), dacron (a kind of polyester fibre), microtain (acrylic fibre), polytain (olefin fibre), and silicon-treated woven glass.

Baghouses have found major applications in the industries including cement plants, flour mills, building materials dust removal, soap powders, dry chemical recovery, talc dust recovery, dry food processing, pneumatic conveying, metal dust recovery, and fertilizer dust removal.

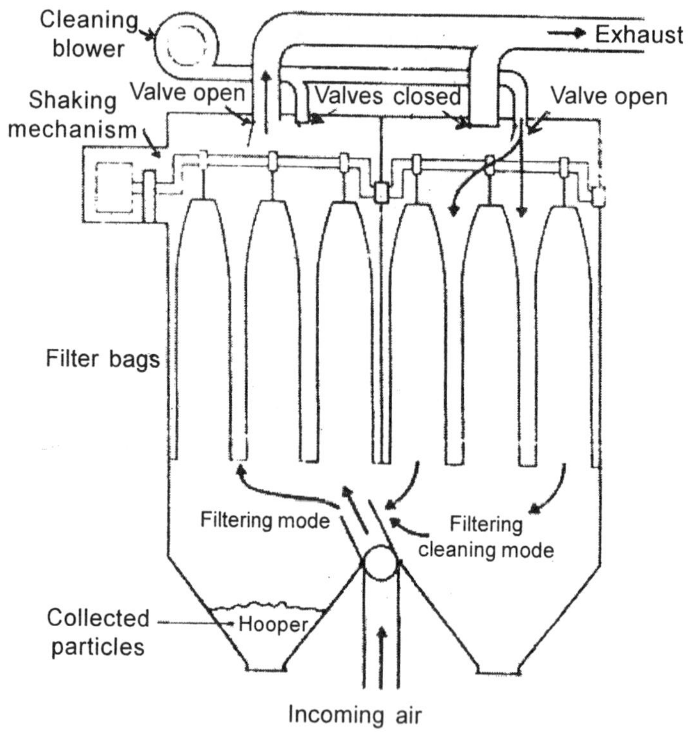

Fig. 14.15 High efficiency fabric filter baghouse provided with the mechanism of reverse flow of air for cleaning the filter (After S.J. Williamson. 1973. Fundamentals of Air Pollution, Addision-Wesley).

Electrostatic Precipitator

In electrostatic precipitators, the dust particles are electrically charged by producing a high voltage discharge, and then collecting them on the collecting plates by electrostatic forces. The electrostatic precipitators are consisted of sets of parallel collecting plates with discharge wires hanging between them by weights (Fig. 14.16(a-c)). These collecting plates are kept in a chamber provided with hoppers at the base to collect the dust. Proper inlets and outlets (parallel to the plates) are also provided for the gases.

A corona discharge (an arch discharge) is produced on discharge wires by a negative D.C. high voltage, which breaks down the air gases electrically to form the ions. These gaseous ions with negative charges collide with dust and other particles charging them negatively. These negatively charged particles then migrate to the positively charged collecting plates. The particles after getting deposited on the collecting plates get neutralized and fall by gravity into the hopper. A cake of dust on the plates is formed periodically which is to be removed for efficient working of the electrostatic precipitator. This cake is removed by hammering the plates, a technique called rapping.

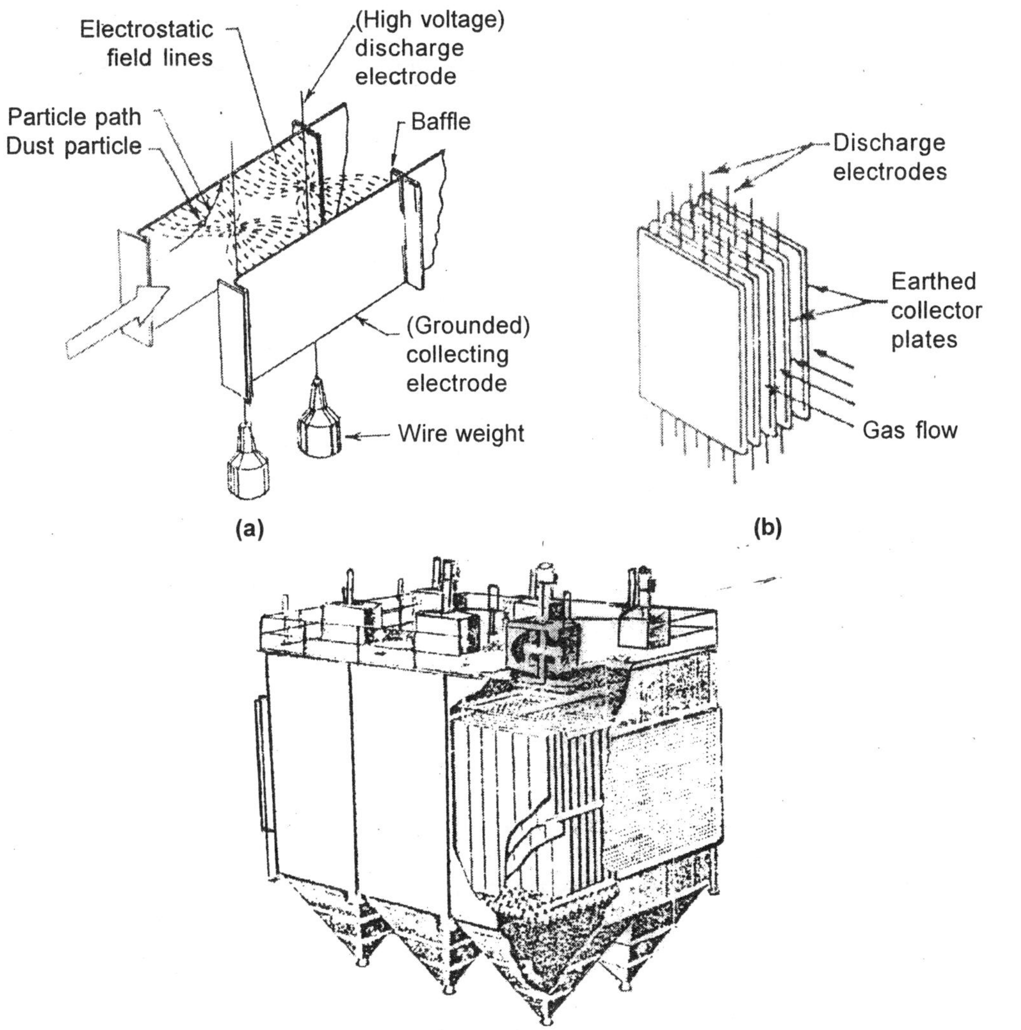

Fig. 14.16 Electrostatic Precipitator (a) Electrostatic charging of dust particles by corona discharge and travel of the particles to the collecting electrodes; (b) A cluster of collecting electrodes (c) A full electrostatic precipitator with dust collecting hopper.

These devices are very efficient in collecting small particles. In case of high dust load, a mechanical device can re placed before it. The electrostatic precipitator is very much suitable for high temperature and corrósive materials which are difficult to be removed by other techniques such as a baghouse.

The electrostatic precipitators are widely used in coal fired thermal power plants, steel plants, cement industries and pulp and paper industries.

14.4 Control of Air Pollution in Some Specific Industries

In the previous section, we have dealt with the general air pollution abatenent techniques for the control of air pollutants. The present section discusses the air pollution control of some specific industrial air pollution sources.

To control air pollution from any source, three basic approaches can be followed :

(a) preventive techniques

(b) proper effluent disposal in air

(c) proper effluent cleaning

For efficient control of air pollution, it is necessary to consider all the three approaches together. Though the techniques for the first two approaches remain basically same for almost all sources, there may be variation in application of gas cleaning devices depending upon the types of pollutants, their quantities and characteristics, and the processes by which they are generated. The important considerations for control of air pollution in three industries are discussed below.

Coal based Thermal Power Plants

In a thermal power plant, the main process is the production of steam by coal fired furnaces and then its feeding into a turbine to produce electricity. All objectionable air emissions in a thermal power plant come from the combustion of coal in the furnace. The major pollutants from a thermal power plant are particulates (fly ash), SO_2, CO, hydrocarbons and NO_x.

Fly ash is formed due to presence of non-combustible matter in the coal, and consists chiefly of silica and other metal oxides. Fly ash emissions increase with the higher ash content of the coal with finer ash particle size, and increased in stack gas velocity as a result of more boiler firing rate. Most coals contain 10-15% of ash. There is no commercial method to remove the ash from the raw coal. The measurable quantities of particles of fly ash cover a size of 1 to 300 μ.

The control of air pollution in thermal power plants is mainly carried out for the particulates and sulphur dioxide only. The other pollutants such as CO, NO_x and hydrocarbons are not controlled because of their very low emissions rates, and lack of suitable technology to control them in low quantities. Following options can be considered to control air pollution in thermal power plants depending upon the finances, size of the units and the quality of fuel used.

I. Proper preventive techniques and effluent disposal (All the techniques discussed earlier under sections 13(A). I and 13(A).2.1 are applicable here).

II. Proper effluent cleaning

(a) Control of particulates and SO_2 with some NO_x; together by lime injection process.

(b) Removal of particulates separately by cyclones or electrostatic precipitators (or both) and then removal of SO_2 by lime scrubbing or by other methods.

(c) Control of only particulates by cyclones or/and electrostatic precipitators.

Lime injection process

The lime injection process is carried out in two ways by dry and wet processes. In the dry process, limestone ($CaCO_3$) is injected into the high temperature combustion zone where it reacts with SO_2 to form calcium sulphate ($CaSO_4$). The dry process is followed by the wet process, where a scrubber containing lime slurry completes the removal of SO_2. During scrubbing, both particulates and SO_x together with some NO_x are removed, and 110 separate removal of particulates is required. However, in case of large quantities of particulates present in effluent gases, a separate particulate removal device such as cyclone or electrostatic precipitator can be employed before lime scrubbing. The process of lime injection is given in Fig. 14.17.

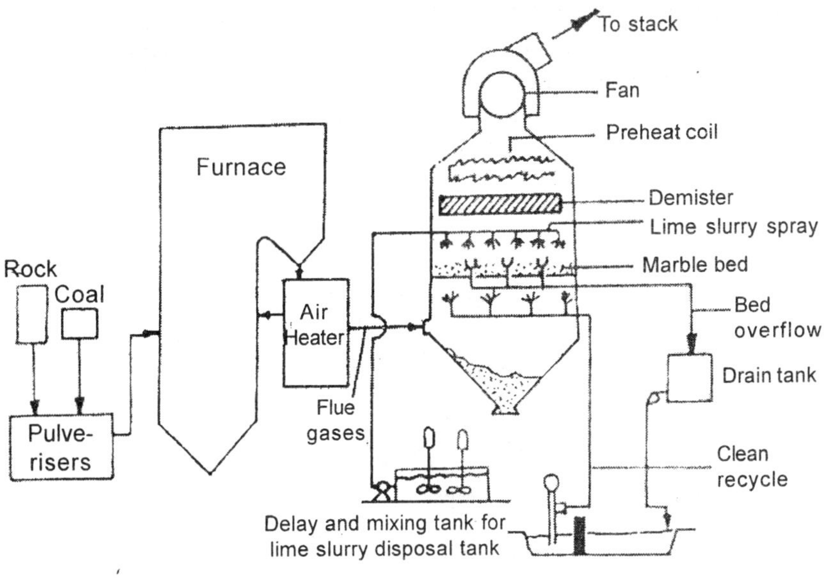

Fig. 14.17 Lime injection process for removal of SO_2 (After Miller, D.M.Experience with wet scrubber for SO_2 removal at the Lawrence station of the Kansas and Light Company, Kansas State Univ. Bull. Special Report 85, September.

Limestone is injected into furnace as a mixture with coal, where $CaCO_3$ is calcined into calcium oxide (CaO) at high temperature.

$$CaCO_3 = CaO + CO_2$$

The CaO reacts with SO_2 in furnace to form calcium sulphate

$$2CaO + 2SO_2 + O_2 = 2CaSO_4$$

The stack gases containing particulates, unreacted limestone and reacted limestone ($CaSO_4$) are then enter the scrubber having a bed of marble pieces. A lime slurry flows down through the bed and the reaction between the slurry of lime and SO_2 is completed to form $CaSO_4$. The lime slurry falling through the bed is recycled above marble bed to use the unreacted limestone.

After scrubbing, the gases are passed through a de mister to remove the mists and moisture, and then reheated to provide sufficient buoyancy for escaping them out through the stack.

Removal of particulates and SO_2 separately

The gases coming out of the furnace are first cooled to about 275-300 °C by use of an economizer and air preheater. The economizer is used to preheat the boiler feed water and the air preheater is used to heat the incoming combustion air (Fig. 14.18). Generally, mechanical collectors and electrostatic precipitators are used for control of particulate matter. Electrostatic precipitators are normally used in combination with mechanical collectors. The mechanical collectors such as cyclones will remove the coarse particles and reduce the dust load in the air entering the electrostatic precipitators. Electrostatic precipitators are highly efficient in removal of smaller particles.

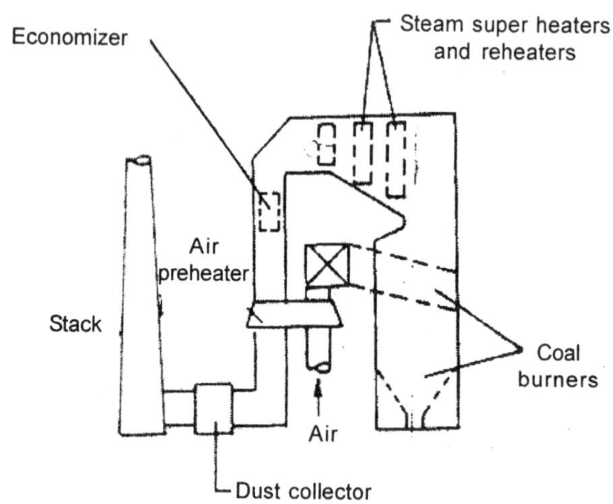

Fig. 14.18 The use of economizer and preheater to cool the effluent gases in a thermal power plant. (After Perkins, H.C. 1974. Air Pollution, Mcgraw-Hill Kogakusha, Tokyo).

After the removal of particulates, the effluent gases are passed through a device to remove SO_2, such as a lime slurry based wet scrubber (described previously), or any other SO_2 removal device. One such SO_2 removal technique described here takes into consideration the conversion of SO_2 into sulphuric acid by catalytic oxidation process.

Catalytic oxidation process

The catalytic oxidation process converts SO_2 to sulphuric acid by passing the effluent gases through a catalyst bed of vanadium pentoxide (V_2O_5) which promotes the oxidation of SO_2 to sulphur trioxide (SO_3). The SO_3 then reacts with water vapour to form a dilute concentration of sulphuric acid. The process is outlined in Fig. 14.19.

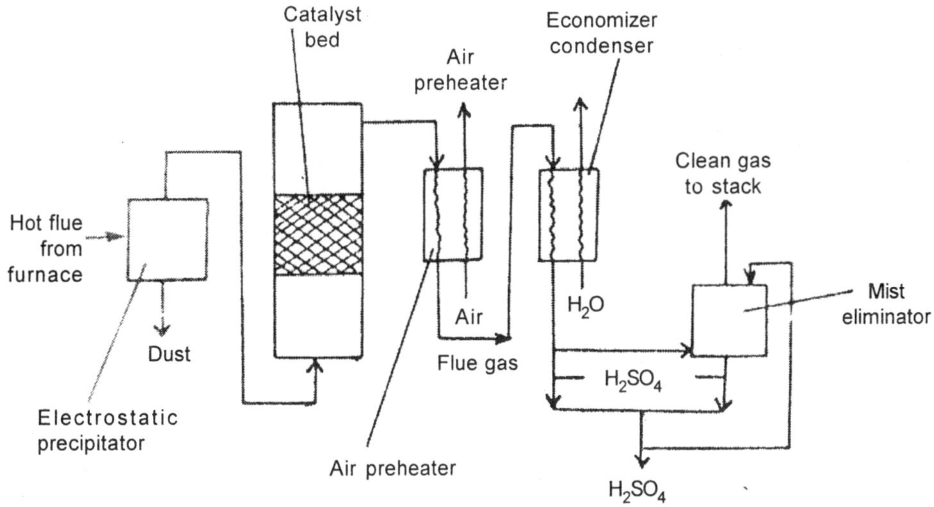

Fig. 14.19 The use of economizer and preheater to cool the effluent gases in a thermal power plant. (After Perkins, H.C. 1974. Air Pollution, Mcgraw-Hill Kogakusha, Tokyo).

During the process, the gases after removal of the particulates, are passed through the catalyst bed, and then through the air preheaters for cooling. The cooled gases then enter the economizers (condensors) for condensation of the acid. A demister is used for removal of acid droplets carried over with the gases before the clean gases go up the stack.

Removal of only particulates

Most of the thermal power plants go only for the control of particulate matter by employing mechanical collectors and electrostatic precipitators. The control of SO_2 in these cases is most often carried out by following preventive measures and proper disposal of effluent gases by higher stacks rather than empolying gas cleaning devices.

Cement Plants (Portland Cement)

Cement plants emit particulate matter as the main air pollutant together with relatively smaller quantities of SO_2, CO and NO_x. Control for only particulates is necessary in cement plants, as the quantities of gaseous pollutants are relatively insignificant. We shall first discuss the process of cement manufacturing in brief, to understand the steps responsible for generating pollutants.

The manufacturing process and generation of pollutants

The process of portland cement manufacturing is outlined in Fig. 14.20. The process consists mainly of four steps. In step I, the main operations are quarrying, rock crushing and raw material storage. Step 2 has two alternatives, one is dry and the other is wet process, for preparation of the material for kiln feed. In the dry process, materials are dried and grinded, while in wet process, the grinding is carried out in presence of water to form a slurry. Step 3 involves the burning process of the materials in kiln to form a fused product called clinker. The kilns can run on coal, oil or gas as a fuel. The clinkers so produced in the kilns are transferred into an air cooler to cool them as well as preheat the boiler fed air. In step 4, clinker and gypsum are mixed and ground to form the final product, the cement. The operations where the particulates are formed and need to be controlled are indicated in Fig. 14.20. The particulates are formed chiefly in the kiln, clinker cooler, dry grinding circuits, material dryers, and the materials handling.

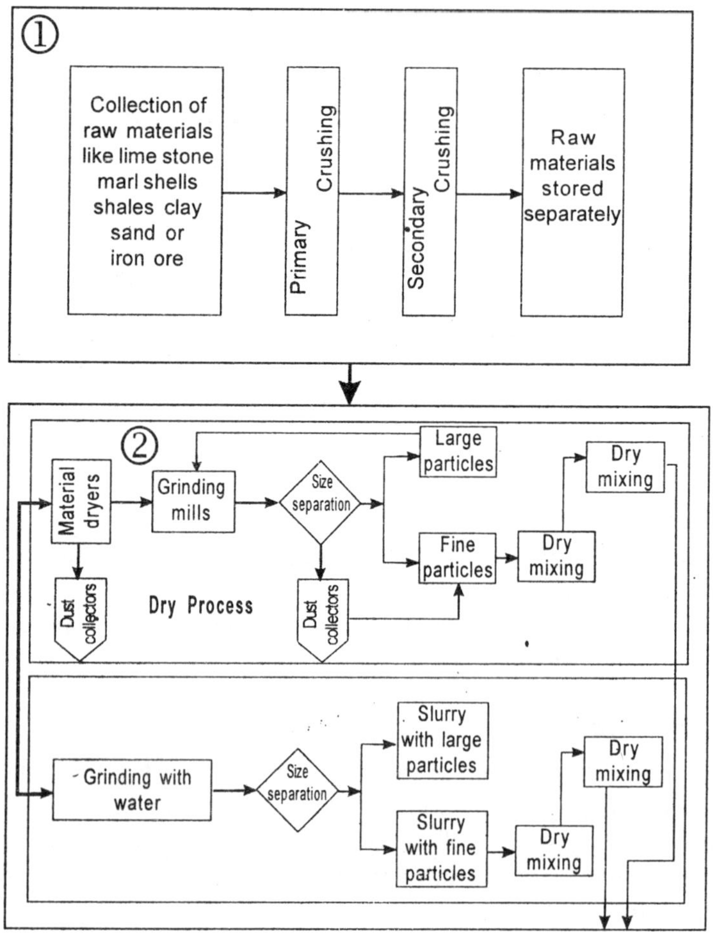

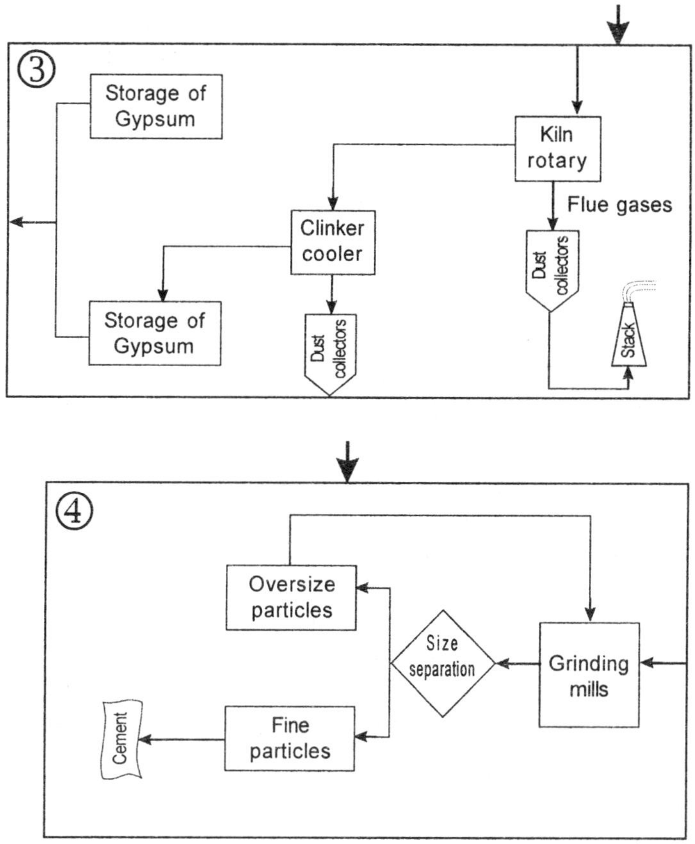

Fig. 14.20 Diagrammatic representation of the cement plant process showing the formation of pollutants.

The gaseous pollutants such as SO_2 and NO_x are produced during the combustion in the kilns, but they react with the alkaline particulates, and are trapped with them. Therefore, only a very little quantity of these gaseous pollutants is emitted from the cement plants.

Application of control devices

Three main devices of particulate pollution control-cyclones, electrostatic precipitators and bag houses are commonly used in cement plants. Cyclones have been used in older plants alone for particulate collection from kiln and clinker coolers. However, these days, the cyclones are employed mainly as precleaners for bag houses or electrostatic precipitators.

Bag houses are widely used in cement plants. Choice of fabric material depends mainly upon the operating temperature, for instance, glass fabrics are suitable for kilns and clinker coolers, while high temperature synthetic fabrics for dryers. Baghouses, however, are rarely used in wet process kilns due to problem of pressure drop because of fabric blinding.

Electrostatic precipitators are applied chiefly to control emissions from the kilns, but they are also useful for dry grinding circuits, material dryers and clinker coolers. Gases from the dry process are first moisture conditioned before they enter into the electrostatic precipitator, to maintain their electrical conductivity.

Petroleum Refineries

There are various units in a refinery, from where different kind of pollutants are produced. From the main refinery unit (distillation unit), the major pollutants are hydrocarbons and hydrogen sulphide (H_2S). The catalytic cracking and reforming units produce mostly particulates, hydrocarbons, CO, H_2S and NO_x.

In a refinery the control is carried out mainly for particulaters, hydrocarbons, CO and H_2S. Other pollutants, particularly NO_x are normally not controlled. For control of particulates the most common devices are mechanical collectors such as cyclones, and electrostatic precipitators which are often used together in series.

The control of hydrocarbons, CO, and H_2S in refineries is made by the technique of combustion where they are burned and converted into CO_2 and H_2O. The common combustion technique employed in refineries is the flare burning. It is accomplished by directly burning a gas in air to produce an open flame. A pilot light at the top of the stack is used to initially ignite the flame. Steam is also injected in the flame to check the smoky flame. The open flame results as the oxygen in the surrounding air diffuses into the flame to facilitate burning of hydrocarbons. Instead of flare burning, hydrogen sulphide can also be converted into elemental sulphur as a refinery by-product by Claus process as illustrated in Fig. 14.21.

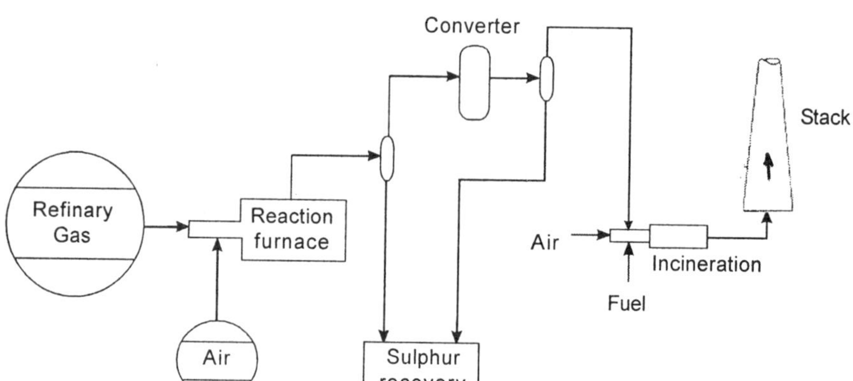

Fig. 14.21 Clauss process for removal of H_2S.

15 Sampling and Analysis of Air Pollutants

15.1 Introduction

Sampling of air is the first step in analysis of air pollutants. The air pollutants in the form of gases, vapours and particulates may be present either alone or in combinations. Due to the differences in physical states and the variability in ambient concentrations, common sampling devices cannot be applied for all kinds of pollutants. For example, the devices suitable for particulate sampling cannot be employed for collecting gases and vapours.

Since, the air pollutants often occur in low concentrations, a large sample is required to be drawn for their quantitative analysis. In such cases the pollutants are concentrated by means of some devices before analysis. If a pollutant can be analysed in low quantities such as by chromatography, infrared gas analyser or by any other means, a small air sample without any concentration may also be collected.

15.2 Sampling of Particulate Matter

Filtration

The particulate matter from air can be sampled by passing the air through a filter whose pore size is small enough to retain the particles. The selection of filter depends on the objective of sampling and size of the particles. If the particles are to be collected for the study of their sizes and morphology alone, membrane filters tend to embede the particles which are difficult to be removed. A nonhygroscopic filter such as a glass-fibre filter is most suitable for the particles to be collected for measuring their weight. When chemical analysis of the particulate matter is the objective, a filter is selected which do not have appreciable quantities of the substances being collected.

Of the various filters commercially available, the glass-fibre filters are most common for quantitative analysis of particulate matter. These glass-fibre filters are also commonly employed in a sampler called "high volume sampler" described later in this chapter.

Sedimentation

The technique of sedimentation is suitable for comparatively larger particles having a size more than 10 μ. The jar method for dustfall (described later in this chapter) is based on this principle. Greasy slides can also be used for trapping the sedimented particles.

Impaction on Solid Surfaces

When an air stream is deflected after stricking a surface, the particles are impacted due to the inertial forces. The collection efficiency is usually greater for larger particles of more than 1 μ. One of the widely used sampler is Anderson impactor which has a series of plates with perforations having progressively decreasing pore sizes. Petri plates provided with some sticky substances are kept below these perforated plates. The air passes through the larger pore size plate to smaller pore size plate. At each stage, as the air passes through the plates it strikes the sticky surface of the petri plates impacting the particles thereon. The variation of the perforation sizes of the plates makes the velocity to vary, which facilitate the separation of particles of different sizes on different plates.

Impingement in Liquids

In the samplers based on the priniciple of liquid impingement, the particles are separated from the air by the force of inertia as the air is deflected after stricking the liquid surface. The bubblers or impingers used for collection of particles are the same those used for collection of gaseous pollutants as described later in this chapter. The most suitable devices are, however, Greenburg-Smith standard and Midget impingers. The impingement in liquids is not a widely employed technique for collection of particulates because of the limitation of low sampling rates.

Electrostatic Precipitator

The electrostatic precipitator, used for collection of particulates, works essentially on the same principle as described for the control of particulate pollution in industries.

The electrostatic precipitator for collection of particles is, however, of much smaller size and has usually a circular plate on which the particles are collected (Fig. 15.1). The high voltage corona discharge, produced on a central wire, charges the particles, which later drift towards the circular collecting electrode plate. The particles, thus, collected can be used for weighing, chemical analysis or morphological studies.

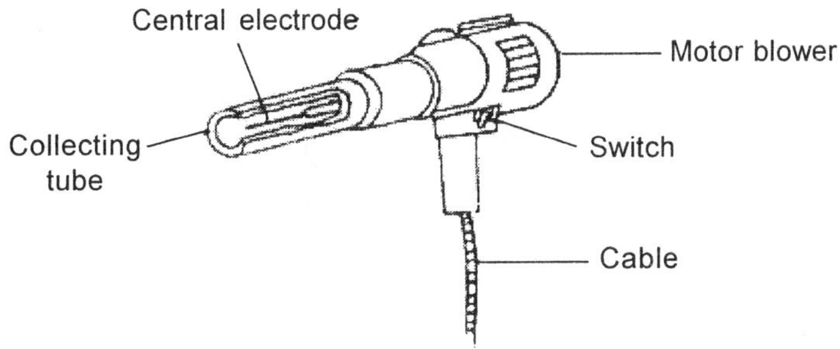

Fig. 15.1 Electrostatic precipitator for collection of particulates.

Thermal Precipitation

The collection of particles is based on the principle of thermal force, which deflect the particles from the zone of higher temperature to the zone of lower temperature to be deposited there. The method is suitable for collection of the particles of all sizes ranging from 0.01 to 10 μ. Because of the weak thermal forces, a large thermal gradient of more than 750 °C/m and a slow sampling rate is required for efficient collection of the particles. Only a small quantity of particles is collected which may be subjected only to microscopic studies.

15.3 Sampling Gases and Vapours

Bags and Containers

The use of bags and containers allows the collection of air in its natural state without any concentration of pollutants. The technique is not suitable for collection of samples of large quantities of air, but may be convenient for the collection of pollutants those are present in relatively larger quantities or those permit the determination by chromatographic or infrared gas analysis or other such instrumental techniques where only a small quantity of pollutants is required. For example, carbon monoxide can be collected in small bags from different locations and analysed in the laboratory by infrared gas analyser. Some of the collection devices are shown in Fig. 15.2.

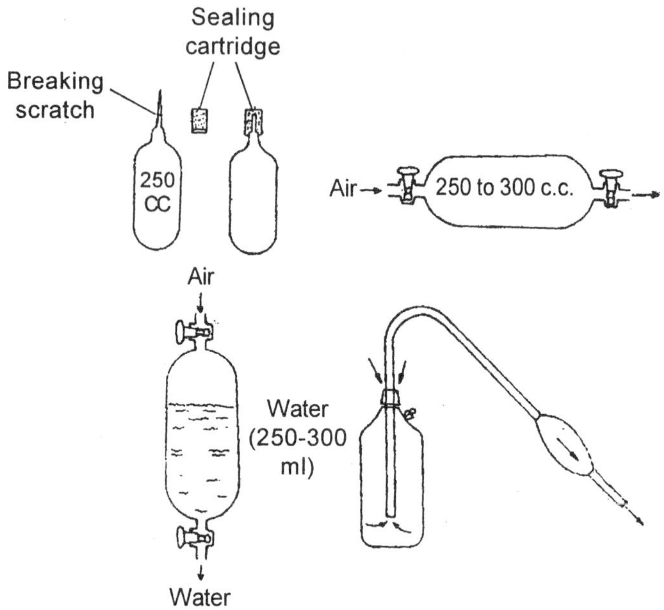

Fig. 15.2 Various devices for collection of gaseous air samples.

The rigid container or a bottle can be filled with polluted air by evacuation of the original air by pumping the polluted air by filling the water and then emptying it to permit the entry of outside polluted air. These bottles are sealed before transferring to the laboratory. Flexible plastic bags can be filled by means of a squeeze rubber bulb fitted with special valves to prevent escape of the filled gases. Special syringes may also be employed for collection of small volumes of air samples, especially in case of the odorous pollutants.

The rigid container or a bottle can be filled with polluted air by evacuation of the original air by pumping the polluted air by filling the water and then emptying it to permit the entry of outside polluted air. These bottles are sealed before transferring to the laboratory. Flexible plastic bags can be filled by means of a squeeze rubber bulb fitted with special valves to prevent escape of the filled gases. Special syringes may also be employed for collection of small volumes of air samples, especially in case of the odorous pollutants.

Absorption

Sampling of air by absorbing the gases in a suitable liquid absorbent is by far the most popular method of collection of gaseous air pollutants. The resulting liquid solution is later subjected to the chemical analysis for the pollutant of interest.

Sampling is carried out in suitable devices ranging from simple bubblers to complex gas washing devices allowing the air to pass through the absorbing liquid to absorb the pollutant. Some common gas absorbing devices are shown in Fig. 15.3. Impingers are most widely used devices, which configuratively have an entrance tube terminating in a jet orifice dipped in the absorbing media. As the air passes through the jet, its velocity is increased and it strikes to the bottom of the vessel forming an intense bubbling. The bubbling helps increasing the efficiency of absorption. In some cases solid absorbents can also be used, but their application is limited. For example, carbon dioxide can be absorbed by a solid bed of some alkali.

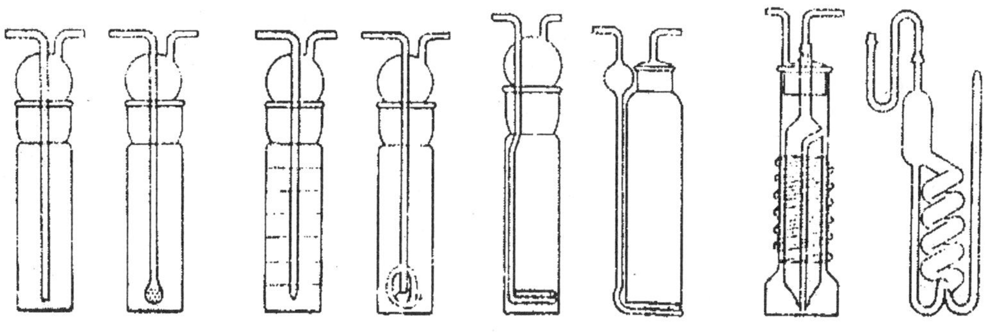

Fig. 15.3 Various gas absorbing devices. (A-B) simple bubblers (C) Midget impinger (D) Greenburg-Smith standard impinger (E-F) Fritted absorbers (G-H) Spiral type absorbers.

The degree of absorption depends upon several factors such as the duration of contact between liquid and the gas, the degree of solubility of the gas in liquid and the rate of chemical reaction. Table 15.1 indicates the absorbing capacity, sampling rates and other information of the various absorbers.

Table 15.1 Utility and specifications of various absorbers for air sampling (After Katz 1969)

Type of absorber	Absorbent capacity (ml)	Sampling Rate (L/min)	Remarks
Sample bubbler	10-100	1-30	General propose; short contact between gas and liquid
Standard impinger	50-100	28 or less	Useful for readily soluble gases and vapours
Midget impinger	10-25	2.8	Useful for readily soluble gases and vapours
Scrubber with fritted glass or other diffuser	25-100	5.20	Good gas-liquid contact. bur diffuser has a tendency to glass or other diffuser plug
Spiral scrubber	10-100	0.004-0.5	Effective only at low flow rates
Packed tower	5-50	0.5-2.0	Variable resistance; effective only at low flow rates
Spray absorber	50-100	1-30	Capacity of absorbenl depends on design and size of absorber; useful for large-volume sampling

Adsorption

Adsorption permits the retention of gases or vapours on the solid surface by the forces of physical adsorption. The adsorption is a temperature dependent process, and for a particular pollutant, based on the adsorbent selected, a specific temperature is required for optimum efficiency. Most widely used adsorbents are activated carbon, silica gel, activated alumina and activated earth.

For the collection of air pollutants the adsorbents are kept in a tube through which the air is passed. For subsequent analysis, the pollutant is desorbed either by heating or eluting with a suitable organic liquid. The desorbed pollutants are later quantitatively analysed by gas chromatography or infrared and ultraviolet spectroscopic methods depending upon the nature of the collected pollutant.

Freeze-out or Condensation

This method is usually employed when the given pollutant is extremely low in concentration, but can easily be condensed at low temperatures. In low temperature sampling, a prior removal of particulate matter is essential, which can be achieved by applying some suitable method such as filtration. The method involves use of a sampling train so designed as to permit the progressive cooling of air in two or three stages by use of different coolants. The low temperatures that can be achieved by different coolants are given in Table 15.2.

Table 15.2 Temperature of various cooling materials

Cooleant	Temperature °
Ice	0
Ice +salt (NaCl)	-21
Dry ice	-79
Liquid air	-149
Liquid oxygen	-169

In the first stage at the temperatures of ice or ice-salt mixture, the water vapours, hydrocarbons and other such gaseous contaminants are readily condensed. As these condensed materials may get converted into solids, creating problems in the sampling train by chocking, they have to be removed by using some filter such as a glass wool plug. If analysis of these fractions is also to be made, they can be added to the other condensed fractions collected progressively.

Due to the general inconvenience and other limitations, the freeze-out method is not applied routinely. The collected pollutants are mostly analysed by gas chromatography, infrared or ultraviolet spectrophotometry or by mass spectrograph methods.

15.4 Measurement of Pollutants

Dust-fall Determination

Dust-fall is that fraction of particulates in air which settles down quickly by virtue of their larger size. The measurement of dust-fall is relatively simple and does not require any specialized sampler. The assembly used for dust-fall determination is shown in Fig. 15.4. It consists of a simple open top cylindrical container having a flat bottom. The diameter of the cylinder is normally more than 15 cm with a height of about 2 to 3 times of it. The container is made-up of any suitable material such as of glass or plastic, and is kept little above the ground on a stand with a protection provided by a guard frame.

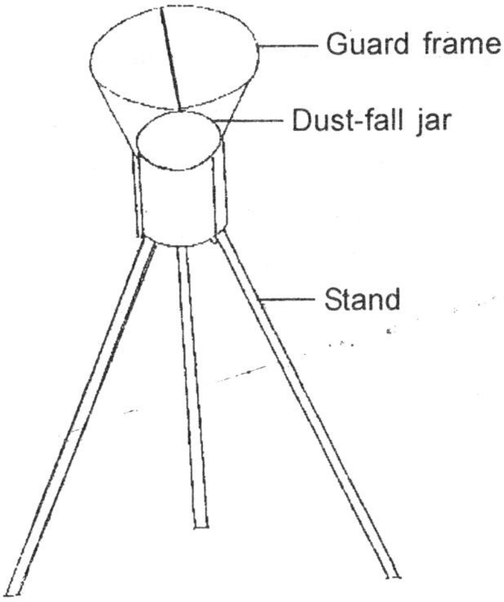

Fig. 15.4 Dust-fall jar with guard frame and stand.

The container is filled about half the volume with distilled water, and preferably, a small quantity of fungicides and algicides (such as $CuSO_4$) is added to prevent the biological growth. The container is then kept on the stand in open to allow the dust to settle in it, at least for a period of one month. In the areas of higher dusl-fall, the exposure may be reduced to a less number of days. After the exposure, the container is removed from the frame and is taken to the laboratory for further analysis.

The water in the container is sieved through a sieve No. 20 to discard any larger objects. The volume of the contents is made to some suitable quantity with distilled water. From this, the following fractions of the dust-fall are measured.

(a) Total insoluble matter
(b) Inorganic insoluble matter
(c) Volatile insoluble matter
(d) Total water solubles
(e) Total dust

The insoluble matter is determined by the difference between the initial and final weights of the filter paper after filtering the contents through it. The inorganic insoluble matter is obtained as the residue left after igniting the filter paper at 600°C for 15 minutes. The volatile matter will be equal to the difference between total insoluble matter and inorganic insoluble matter. Total water soluble fraction is determined from the filtrate after evaporation of a suitable aliquot on a borosilicate or silica evaporating dish. After obtaining these fractions of particulate matter, total dust can be calculated as the total of insoluble matter and water soluble fraction.

The dust-fall rate, reported as metric tons/km^2/month, is calculated by taking into consideration the surface area of the collecting jar and number of days for which the exposure was made.

Measurement of SPM by High Volume Sampler

High-volume sampler is the most popular device for measuring the suspended particles in the range of 1 to 10 μ which do not settle by gravity. A large volume of air is passed through a filter at a very high rate by applying suction.

The apparatus is consisted of two basic units (Fig. 15.5). The upper unit is the filter adapter unit to keep a glass fibre filler paper of 20 × 25 cm. The filter adapter unit is protected by a hood to prevent it from rain or any other direct fallings in the form of dust fall. The another unit, called blower unit, is situated below the filter assembly to apply suction for making the air to pass through the filter. For measuring the flow rate of air, a manometer or a rotameter is also fitted to the blower unit. The sampling rate for the calculation is taken as the average of the initial and final readings of the flow rates.

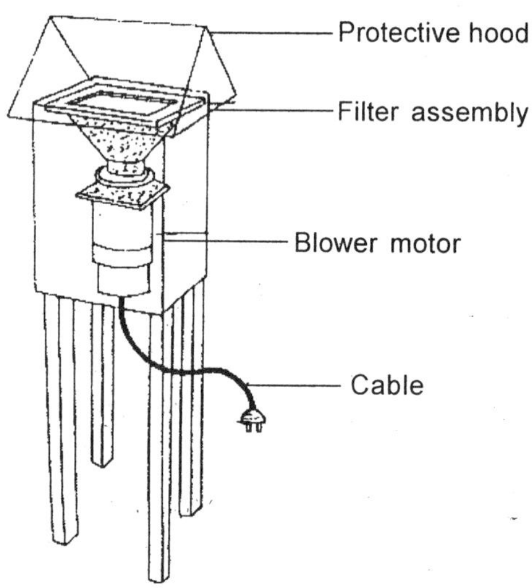

Fig. 15.5 High volume sampler.

A preweighed glass fibre filter paper is kept in the adapter assembly and the air is drawn for 24 hours at the rate of 1-3 m^3/min. Power failure or otherwise stoppage of the sampling is also taken into consideration to get the exact time for which the sampling has actually taken place. The filter is removed after the sampling is over and its final weight is determined. The difference in the initial and final weights is taken as the amount of SPM. The results are expressed as $\mu g/m^3$. The filter paper can later be used for further analysis of the chemical nature of particulate matter by following the standard analytical techniques.

Measurement of Sulphation Rate

Sulphation rate gives an indication of SO_2 present in the air and is measured with the help of a lead peroxide candle. Sulphur dioxide in air reacts with lead peroxide to form lead sulphate which can be chemically analysed in the laboratory.

For determining sulphation rate, a cloth is impregnated with a paste of Gum Tragacanth and lead peroxide and then rapped around a cylindrical tube or the candle which has a surface area of 100 cm^2. The prepared candle is dried in a pollution free desiccator.

The candles are taken to the field in the carrying cases, and installed there in louvered boxes for exposing them to at least 30 days. After the exposure, the candles are removed and taken to the laboratory for chemical analysis. The chemical analysis for sulphation rate is made by dissolving the impregnated material in hot distilled water containing sodium carbonate. After dissolution, the sulphate is converted to sodium sulphate. The resultant solution is filtered through a Whatman No. 42 filter paper, and the filtrate is chemically analysed for sulphate by using any standard procedure such as turbidimetric method. The sulphation rate is finally calculated as mg SO_4-S/100 cm^2/day.

Measurement of Sulphur Dioxide

West & Geake Method

The method is based on the principle that sulphur dioxide reacts with sodium tetrachloromercurate to form dichrolosulfitomercurate ion which gives a red-purple colour with acid-bleached pararosaniline and formaldehyde. The intensity of the red-purple colour is proportional to the concentration of SO_2, and can be detected spectrophotometrically.

The sampling train for collection of the gas is shown in Fig. 15.6. Samples are collected in the impinger containing the absorbing reagent, sodium tetrachloromercurate. The sampling is carried out at a flow rate of 200 mL - 2.0 L/min for 30 minutes to 24 hours. Duration and rate of sampling depend upon the concentration of SO_2 expected in the ambient air. After collecting the gas in the absorbent, proper volumes of sulphamic acid, formaldehyde and pararosaniline hydrochloride are added to develop the red-purple colour. The intensity of the colour is measured after half an hour by taking optical density at the wavelength of 560 nm.

Standard curve, for obtaining the unknown concentration, is made with sodium metabisulphite in the range of 2 to 25 μg of SO_2. The concentration of SO_2 is represented in μg of SO_2/m^3 which is calculated as follows.

$$SO_2 \ \mu g/m^3 = \frac{\mu g \ SO_2 \times 10^3}{\text{Total volume of air sampled (L)}}$$

Automated Sensors for SO_2

Several automated sensors for SO_2 measurement are available. These sensors are based mainly on colourimetric, conductimetric, correlation spectrometry, coulometric, electrochemical, flame photometric, infrared or ultraviolet spectrometric techniques.

The sensors employing colourimetric principle use the reaction between SO_2 and tetrachloromercurate, which upon addition of formaldehyde and pararosaniline yields a strong purple colour.

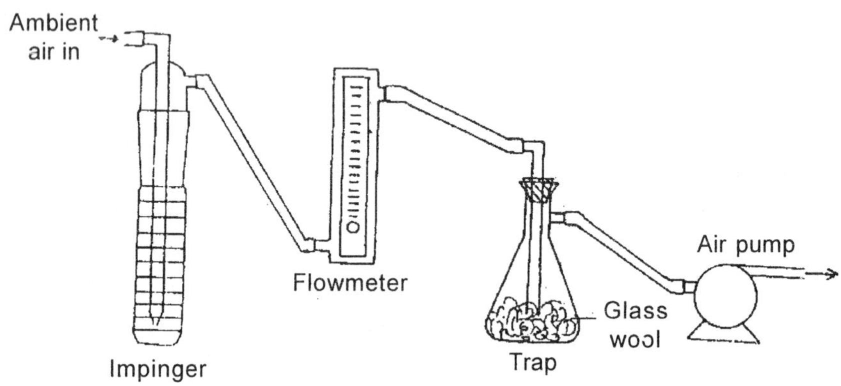

Fig. 15.6 Sampling train for SO_2 measurement by West & Geake method.

In the conductimetric analysis, SO_2 is dissolved in a weak solution of sulphuric acid and hydrogen peroxide or distilled water. The dissolution of SO_2 makes the conductivity of the solution to change, which can be calibrated directly on the SO_2 concentration scale. In this technique other acidic gases like HCI create a positive error, while the basic gases like ammonia, a negative error.

In the coulometric analysers the SO_2 electrogenerate free bromine or iodine from their solutions. This free bromine or iodine is later detected to give a measure of SO_2.

The flame pholometric sensors are based on the principle that when SO_2 is burned in a hydrogen rich flame, a radiation in the wavelength of 394 nm is generated, the intensity of which can be calibrated on a scale as the measure of SO_2 concentration.

Measurement of Nitrogen Dioxide (NO_2)

Analytical Method

Nitrogen dioxide is dissolved in sodium hydroxide-sodium arsenite solution to form sodium nitrite, which can be analysed in solution by any conventional method.

The NO_2 is collected in an impinger containing the absorbing reagent (sodium hydroxide-sodium arsenite). The sampling train is similar to that used for SO_2 measurement as given earlier in Fig. 15.6. In the absorbed air sample, hydrogen peroxide (H_2O_2) is first added to eliminate the interference of SO_2 by converting it into sulphates. Colour is developed by adding sulphanilamide solution with phosphoric acid and N(1-naphthyl) ethylenediamine dihydrochloride. Intensity of the colour is measured after 10 minutes by obtaining optical density at 540 nm. Standard curve is made with sodium nitrite, ranging from 0.04 to 2.0 μg NO_2 per mL. The concentration of NO_2 in the air can be calculated by the following formula.

$$\mu g\ NO_2/m^3 \text{ of air} = \frac{\mu g\ NO_2 \text{ in absorbent} \times 10^3}{\text{Volume of air sampled (L)} \times 0.82}$$

Where, the value 0.82 is a factor for collecting effeciency.

The sampling rate is usually kept at 200 mL/min, and the sample is collected for 24 hours for the air containing NO_2 in the range of 20 to 750 $\mu g/m^3$.

Automated Sensors for Nitrogen Oxides (NO_x)

Automated sensors for determining nitrogen oxides may be based on colourimetric, coulometric, chemiluminescence, gas chromatography or electrochemical techniques.

In the colourimetric method, NO_2 reacts with sulphanilic acid to form a diazonium salt which couples with N(1-Naphthyl) ethylenediamine dihydrochloride to form a deeply coloured azo dye.

In chemiluminescence determination, NO reacts with ozone (O_3) to form nitrogen dioxide (NO_2) with chemiluminescence. The emitted light can be measured photometrically.

Measurement of Total Oxidants and Ozone

The term oxidant refers to those substances in air, other than oxygen, which exhibit oxidizing properties. The oxidants have oxidizing potential greater than oxygen and include some important urban pollutants like ozone (O_3), nitrogen dioxide (NO_2) and peroxy acetyl nitrate (PAN). Oxidants can be divided into two categories for the purpose of measurement, total oxidants and ozone.

Total Oxidants

(Neutral buffered KI method)

The method is based on the principle that the oxidants react with potassium iodide (KI) to liberate iodine in equivalent quantities. The absorbing reagent is made by dissolving potassium iodide in buffer solution of potassium dihydrogen phosphate and disodium hydrogen phosphate having a pH of 6.8.

Air is passed through the absorbing reagent using impinger as a collector. The sampling period is usually 30 minutes. The absorbence of the liberated iodine solution is measured at 352 mμ. The concentration of iodine is determined from the optical density values by employing a standard curve. The standard curve is prepared between optical density and equivalent ozone values. The ozone equivalents can be calculated from iodine values. The method can measure the oxidants in the concentration range of 20 - 20000 $\mu g/m^3$.

Interference to the method results from SO_2, H_2S or any other reducing agents present in the air. Sulphur dioxide can be removed by passing the air sample through a glass-fiber filter impregnated with chromium trioxide (CrO_3).

Ozone (O_3)

Ozone alone is seldom measured by wet chemical analysis because of the presence of other oxidants which give the same reaction as ozone. In practice ozone is determined in combination with other oxidants by chemical methods such as neutral buffered potassium iodide method as described above.

But, if ozone alone is to be determined, some instrumental methods involving ozone sensors have to be followed.

Ozone sensors may be based on chemiluminescence, ultraviolet spectroscopy, coulometric or thermal conductivity principles. One of the common principles employed for ozone measurement is chemiluminescence that has been used for developing automated sensors. In this method ethylene is made to react with the gas phase ozone to produce a shortlived ozonide that emits light upon decomposition. The intensity of the emitted light is related to the concentration of ozone, and can be measured photometrically. The method works for a wider range of concentration from 10 to 2000 $\mu g/m^3$ of ozone.

Measurement of Carbon Monoxide

Determination of CO is rarely performed by wet chemical analysis techniques. It is estimated mostly by instrumental methods. The most reliable instrumental technique is based on the principle of specific absorption of infrared radiation by CO molecules. Carbon dioxide and water vapours interfere with this technique, but their interference can be minimized by adopting certain measures.

Several automated sensors have been developed based on this principle. These sensors are usually insensitive to flow rate, require no chemicals, independent of air temperature, measure wide range of CO concentration and have short response times. One such analyser is shown in Fig. 15.7. Infrared radiation is produced from a hot filament, and is passed alternately through a sample and a reference cell with the help of a chopper. The radiation, after passing through the two cells, reaches a detector cell divided by a pressure sensitive diagphram. Carbon monoxide, if present in the sample, will absorb some infrared radiation causing a lower pressure exerted on the diagphram as a result of the greater heating of the detection cell portion than the reference cell portion. The resulted distortion of the diagphram is converted to an electric signal for rectification and amplification to be read on a scale calibrated for CO concentration directly.

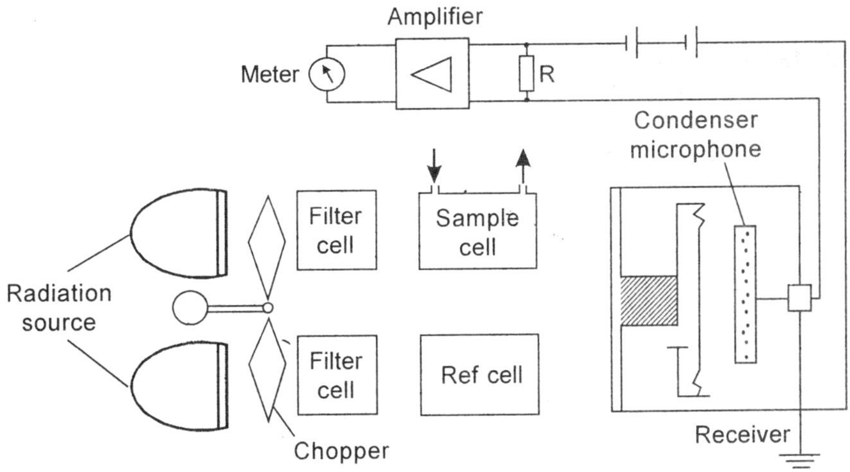

Fig. 15.7 Infra-red gas analyser for carbon monoxide measurement.

Measurement of Smoke Density

(Ringelmann chart scale method)

The density of black smoke can be measured by using the Ringelmann smoke chart that gives the shades of gray with which the density of smoke is compared. The chart is made up of graduated gray shades varying by five equal steps between white and black. The chart is, in fact, consisted of black cross lines of various thickness to provide the different gray shades as shown in Fig. 15.8. The smoke density is related to the Ringlemann chart number as given in Table 15.3.

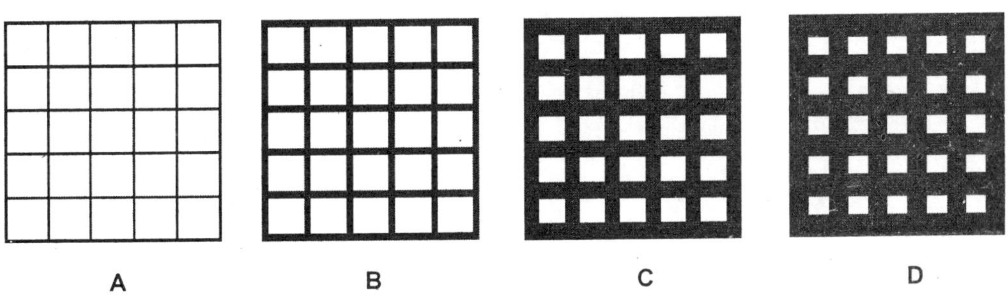

Fig. 15.8 Ringlemann's scale chart. (A) Card 1, equivalent to 20% black, (B) Card 2, equivalent to 40% black, (C) Card 3, equivalent to 80% black. Card 0 and Card 5 are not shown in the figure which are preferably white and black respectively.

Table 15.3 Calculation of % smoke sensity from Ringlemann chart number.

Ringlemann % Chart Number	Black density
1	20
2	40
3	60
4	80
5	100

For finding the smoke density, the chart is kept at eye level at a distance so that the cross lines on the chart merge into gray shades. The observer views the black smoke and compare its shade corresponding most nearly to the gray shade number of the Ringlemann chart. A large number of observations are taken at short intervals of 1/4 to 1/2 minutes.

The accurate results can be obtained if the observer is positioned more than 100 feet away from the source, but not more than 1/4 mile away. The smoke should be viewed at right angles to the direction of the plume. Sun should be at the back of the observer to prevent any direct glare in the eyes. The results can be calculated as follows.

$$\% \text{ Black smoke density} = \frac{\text{Total of Riglemann chart numbers observed } \times 0.2 \times 100}{\text{Total number of observations}}$$

16 Air Quality and Stack Monitoring

16.1 Ambient Air Monitoring

Air monitoring is usually referred to as long term, systematic and routine measurements of air pollution that may be carried out for diverse purposes. The sampling sites together with the equipment involed in acquiring and analysing the data constitute the monitoring network. The monitoring of air forms an important part of any air management programme. In the past, air monitoring used to be carried out at one or a few stations using chiefly static or manual analytical methods, but now with the rapidly growing demand for comparable data, automatic monitoring is fast replacing the older one.

The monitoring of air may be carried out broadly for the purpose of research, surveillance or any other specific reason. The major aim of the air monitorning in most cases is to aquire data on existing air pollution levels for compliance with the air quality standards. The air pollution trends as influenced by the planning, growth of industry, density of traffic and population from year to year can also be worked out with the help of air monitoring. The monitoring is also helpful in making epidemiological studies and determining the effects of pollution on surrounding areas. Assessment of any control measure can also be made by air monitoring. The monitoring is also useful for research purposes such as to study a new atmospheric phenomenon, a new atmospheric pollutant or a new air pollution sensor. Sometimes. The air monitoring becomes a necessary tool to locate an unidentified source of pollution, such as of odours in an urban area. A variety of air pollution warning systems have been developed in many countries on the basis of the data acquired by air pollution monitoring.

Air Quality Monitoring Around Isolated Sources

Meteorological data are very important in monitoring air pollution around an isolated source such as an industrial plant. Wind rose (see Chapter 11) can be prepared after obtaining the wind data over a period of at least 1 year. The wind rose helps determining direction of the principal drift of air pollutants from the source. Determination of the point of maximum ground level concentration is also important. This point lies approximately at a distance ten times of the stack height downwind for the stacks with height between 50 and 350 feet. At least one sampling station should be located at this point. A few (at least 2 or 3) sampling sites are also taken between 100 and 200 times of the height of stack downwind. For finding out the background concentration for comparison, additional sampling is made upwind beyond a distance of 100 times of the stack height.

Data of the air quality for an isolated source should be obtained for a period of at least 1 year to determine the impact of the source on the surrounding area. If the study is being made to see the effect of the process changes in the industry, it may be necessary to carry out sampling for 2 to 5 years before any worthwhile statistically significant information is obtained.

Air Quality Monitoring In Urban Areas

Air quality monitoring in urban areas is of major interest since most of the population is concentrated in the cities, and a diverse kind of sources of air pollution are situated there. Depending upon the resources available and the objective of the monitoring, three basic air quality networks can be set up.

Uniform Area Based Network

This is also called rectilinear grid system of air pollution monitoring. In this system, the sensors are located uniformly over the urban areas in a rectilinear grid.

The number of locations shall depend upon the size of the urban areas. A large number of Sampling sites may be required for a big metropolitan area to get the correct picture of air pollution. Normally static or manual methods of air quality monitoring are used in this system.

Pollutant Concentration Based Network

This set-up is based on the concept that the air quality is normally below the standards where the pollution sources are located. On the other hand cleaner areas do not have any air pollution problems. Most of the sensors in this network are located in the areas of higher pollutant concentrations. One or two sites are also selected in the cleaner areas for obtaining background concentrations for the purpose of comparison.

Population Distribution Based Network

In this network, the sensors are placed in the most populated areas without taking into consideration the most polluted areas, which, in fact, can be left out as they may have the least population. This system of monitoring will give the levels of air pollutants to which bulk of the population is exposed. The data obtained here are important from the view point of public health.

The necessary number of sampling sites and their locations depend upon several factors including the objective of the monitoring, the size of the study area, the proximity of sources of pollution, topographical features and weather. Sampling sites must be carefully selected so as to be representative of the areas under study. The presence of tall buildings, canyon effect of streets, and concentration of pollutants near ground level are some of the important factors which pose a difficulty in locating sites for placement of sensors.

The objective of the study may be important in obtaining a representative air sample. If the data are being collected for obtaining average pollutant concentration levels on area-wise basis, the sampling should be carried out in the open areas such as parks or on the roofs of one or two story buildings to avoid the effect of streets. For the study of health effects, the samples should be collected at the breathing level which in most circumstances can be taken 3-6 meters above the ground as an optimum height. Sampling site should be easily accessible for the operation and maintenance, and should be safe from any kind of disturbance.

Methods of Air Analysis

Methods of air analysis can broadly be divided into three categories namely static, manual and instrumental methods.

Static Methods

The air pollutants are made to collect or react with the reagents at the sites without actually drawing the quantitative air samples. The sampling times are usually longer in terms of weeks with sensitivity, in general, low. The most common static methods are dust-fall jars, lead peroxide candles, sodium carbonate cemented filter papers and biomonitoring using certain plants. The details of some of these methods are given in Chapter15, while that of biomonitoring later in Chapter 17. Though, these methods cannot be applied for quantitative measurement of the ambient air concentrations, they do provide a low cost indicator of relative levels of air pollutants in an area.

Manual Methods

The samples of air are first collected from a given area and then transferred to the laboratory for analysis. Suspended particulate matter (SPM) is usually measured by a most widely used device called High Volume Sampler. For the gaseous pollutants, a wet sampling train is employed where the pollutants are dissolved in some collecting medium after drawing the air for some period of time. The exposed collecting medium is then analysed in the laboratory for finding out the concentration of the pollutants. The details of the analysis of some important air pollutants are provided in Chapter 15.

Instrumental Methods

A variety of sensors have been developed for individual air pollutants which directly measure the concentration with a fair degree of accuracy. These sensors work on different principles depending upon the kind of air pollutants they measure. The use of sensors avoid the cumbersome exercise of sample collection, laboratory transfer and chemical analysis. The use of instrumental sensors gives a quick reading and is also helpful in obtaining a continuous data. The detailed description of different sensors is beyond the scope of this book, however, a brief description of some important sensors is provided in Chapter 15.

Modern Automated and Continuous Monitoring Systems

The use of automated monitoring systems is increasing rapidly due to a rising demand of continuous air quality data with quick analysis and processing. Table 16.1 provides a summary of the various techniques used for automated air quality monitoring.

Table 16.1 Principles and techniques for determination of various air pollutants in automated moniotoring.

Pollutant	Principle and Technique
Sulphur dioxide	Colourimetry using p-rosaniline; conductimetry; coulornetry using I_2 generation
Hydrogen sulphide	Conductimetry; potentiometry; colourimetry using paper tape
Carbon monoxide and carbon dioxide	Spectranetry by infrared absorption
nitrogen oxides and nitrates	Spectrophotometery by sulphanilamide diazotization (NO_2); Griess-Ilosvay method of spectrophotometery (NO); colourimetry ($NO+NO_2$ combind)
Ozone and Oxidents	Spectrophotometry employing phenolphthalein; coulometry by I_2 generation
Ammonia & its salts	Potentiometry
Hydrogen cyanide	Potentiometry

The principle of the selection of sampling sites remains the same as for the other techniques described earlier. In the automated and continuous monitoring network, the sensors kept at the sampling sites provide the data in continuous form which can be recorded on the strip charts or magnetic tape. Comprehensive laboratory trailers which are fitted with the sensors of the pollutants like NOx, SO_2, CO, hydrocarbons, oxidants, aldehydes, CO_2 and particulates are placed at important sites. These laboratory trailers may also be fitted with some meteorological instruments to measure temperature, relative humidity, wind speed, wind direction, precipitation and atmospheric pressure. Remaining of the sampling stations may have sensors only for some important pollutants like SO_2, CO and particulates. The data recorded by the sensors are collected and taken to the headquarters for further analysis and processing.

In the fully computerised systems, the continuous data from the sensors are directly telemetered to the central headquarters by an on-line data transmission system. Normally, two computers are employed at the headquarters for handling the data. The first computer converts the signals into the digital values and provides the 15 minutes average of the continuous data. These 15 minutes averages are then fed into the second computer which process the data further and gives hourly, daily and monthly averages. The data are also analysed statistically on the second computer. The fully processed data come in the form of a printout, and at the same time are stored in the form of a magnetic tape or other device to facilitate its retrieval later at the required time.

Expression of Results

To avoid the confusion and complexity, the data in air pollution should always be expressed in C.G.S. units. This also improves the comparability of the data. Using C.G.S. system, the concentration of pollutants is reported in terms of mass per unit volume at a standard or reference temperature and pressure. The units suggested by a WHO scientific group (Katz) 1969) are given in Table 16.2

Table 16.2 Units recommended for expression of results in air pollution monitoring and research.

Item	Recommended units	Alternative or derived units
Particulates (liquid or solids) of known concentration.	mg/m^3	$\mu g/m^3$
Suspended or air borne particles	mg/m^3	$\mu g/m^3$
Gases of vapoors	mg/m^3	$\mu g/m^3$, ppm
Gas volumes	m^3 at standard conditioos (temp. = 0°C. pressure 760 mm Hg)	-
Volume emission rates	m^3/sec	-
Mass emission rates	kg/sec	g/sec
Velocity	m/sec	-
Air sampling rates	m^3/min or cm^3/min	L/min
Temperature	°c	-
Pressure	millibars (mb) or mm Hg	-
Visibility	km	-
Light transmission	% T (per cent transmittance)	-
Light reflection	% R (per cent reflectance)	-
Particle size	microns (μ) (10^{-6} m)	-
Wavelength of light	millimicrons (m μ) (10^{-9} m)	angstrom (A)
Time of day	in terms of 24-hours clock	

The purpose of data processing is to condense a large number of observations into the information that can be understood and utilized effectively by the user. Various techniques can be used for data analysis and presentation depending upon general or specialized objectives. Some of the important ways of data analyses are discussed below.

The most simple type of data analysis is the data summarization. The data summarization consists of calculating simple 1-hour, 3-hour, 24-hour, weekly, monthly or annual arithmetic averages and rearranging them in a form which is convenient to be understood. Table 16.3 shows one such method of summarization of air pollution data in a tabular form presenting the data collected over a period of one month. The form is also suitable for storage of data and their retrieval later when required.

Table 16.3 Summarization of air concentrations of sulphur dioxide (ppm obtained by automated instrumentation over a period of one month. The summary columns and rows give daily mean at the right, diurnal variation at the bottom and the monthly mean (0.9 pphm in this case) at the corner.

Day of		A.m												P.m.												D	N	M
Month	Week	12	1	2	3	4	5	6	7	8	9	10	11	12	1	2	3	4	5	6	7	8	9	10	11			
1	Thu	0	0	0	0	1	1	1	1	1	0	0	0	0	0	0	3	0	0	0	0	0	0	0	0	0.2	24	2
2	Fri	0	0	0	0	0	0	0	0	1	3	4	1	0	0	1	1	3	5	0	0	0	0	0	0	8	24	22
3	Sat	0	0	0	2	4	3	3	3	3	1	0	0	0	0	0	0	0	0	0	0	0	0	0	0	0.8	24	6
4	Sun	0	0	0	0	0	0	0	0	0	0	0	0	0	0	0	0	0	0	0	0	0	0	0	0	0.0	24	1
5	Mon	0	0	1	0	0	0	1	2	2	-	-	0	0	0	0	0	0	0	0	0	0	1	0	1	0.3	22	2
6	Tue	0	0	0	0	0	0	0	1	5	1	2	3	3	1	0	1	0	0	0	0	0	0	0	0	0.7	24	14
7	Wed	0	0	2	0	0	0	0	0	0	0	-	0	0	0	0	0	0	0	0	0	0	0	0	0	0.1	23	13
8	Thu	0	0	0	0	0	0	0	1	0	0	0	0	0	0	-	-	-	-	-	-	-	0	0	-	0.0	16	1
9.	Fri	-	-	-	-	-	-	-	-	-	-	-	-	-	-	-	-	-	-	-	-	-	-	-	-	-	-	-
10.	Sat	-	-	-	-	-	-	-	-	-	-	-	-	-	-	-	-	-	-	-	-	-	-	-	-	-	-	-
11.	Sun	0	0	0	0	0	0	0	1	5	5	3	1	0	1	3	2	0	0	0	0	0	1	1	1	1.0	2.4	16
12	Mon	0	0	0	0	0	0	0	1	3	7	-	3	3	3	2	0	0	3	4	1	0	1	2	2	2	1.5	23
13	Tue	1	0	0	0	1	2	1	0	0	0	0	0	0	0	0	0	0	0	0	0	0	0	0	0	0.2	24	5
14	Wed	0	0	0	0	0	0	1	0	0	0	0	0	0	0	0	0	0	0	0	0	0	0	0	0	0.0	24	1
15	Thu	0	0	0	0	1	0	1	2	1	1	0	1	0	0	0	0	0	0	0	0	0	0	0	0	0.3	24	2
16	Fri	0	0	0	0	0	0	0	3	9	5	0	0	1	2	1	0	5	5	3	0	0	1	0	0	1.6	24	39
17	Sat	1	2	4	4	3	1	4	1	1	1	1	1	1	1	-	-	0	-	-	-	-	-	-	-	1.7	15	12
18	Sun	-	-	-	-	-	-	-	-	-	-	-	-	-	-	-	-	-	-	-	-	-	-	-	-	-	-	-
19	Mon	-	6	10	2	2	1	0	0	-	-	1	0	0	0	4	3	2	1	1	1	1	0	1	0	1.7	21	15
20	Tue	0	0	0	0	0	0	0	0	0	0	0	0	0	0	0	0	0	0	0	0	0	0	0	0	1.2	24	22
21	Wed	0	0	0	0	0	0	1	1	4	5	5	2	4	3	1	0	0	1	0	0	0	0	1	0	1.2	24	24
22	Thu	0	0	0	0	0	0	1	1	5	5	42	10	11	2	5	1	1	1	1	0	0	0	0	0	3.1	24	29
23	Fri	0	0	0	0	0	0	0	1	2	10	5	0	0	-	0	0	0	1	0	0	0	0	0	0	0.8	24	16
24	Sat	0	0	0	0	0	0	0	0	0	0	1	3	2	3	2	3	2	1	0	0	0	0	0	0	0.7	24	6
25	Sun	0	0	0	0	0	0	0	0	0	0	0	0	0	0	0	0	0	0	0	0	0	0	1	1	0.1	24	1
26	Mon	1	0	0	0	1	2	1	2	2	-	2	1	0	0	0	0	0	4	0	0	0	1	1	1	0.8	23	21
27	Tue	1	1	2	1	2	2	2	3	3	-	-	-	-	-	-	1	1	1	1	1	1	1	1	1	16	19	5
28	Wed	1	1	1	1	1	1	1	2	3	4	11	15	2	2	1	0	4	17	9	6	1	0	12	9	3.9	24	35
29	Thu	10	2	1	0	0	1	3	2	1	1	1	1	0	0	0	0	0	0	0	0	0	0	0	0	1.0	24	35
30	Fri	0	0	0	0	0	1	3	3	2	1	1	0	0	0	0	0	0	0	0	0	0	0	0	0	0.4	24	3
31	Sat	1	1	1	1	1	1	1	2	2	1	1	0	0	0	0	3	0	0	0	0	0	0	0	0	0.6	-	-
Monthly mean		1	0	1	1	1	1	1	1	2	2	3	1	1	1	1	1	1	2	1	0	0	0	1	1	0.9	-	-
No. of days		27	28	28	28	28	28	28	28	28	24	24	27	27	27	26	26	27	26	26	26	26	27	27	26	-	642	-
Max. hrly mean		10	2	6	10	4	3	4	3	9	10	42	10	4	3	5	4	5	17	9	6	1	2	12	9	-	-	-

– = data could not be recorded

D = Daily mean, N = No. of hours, M = 5 -min max.

Data can also be summarized in the form of diurnal variation patterns. frequency distribution and pollution roses. The diurnal data variation pattern is useful when a continuous data over a period of 24 hours or less have lo be analysed. This analysis is the most simple in the way that the averages are first obtained for each time period during the daily cycle and then are plotted against the line as indicated in Fig. 16.1. The presentation is very helpful in understanding the variation of pollutants through the day with regard to the variation in human activity and micrometeorological conditions.

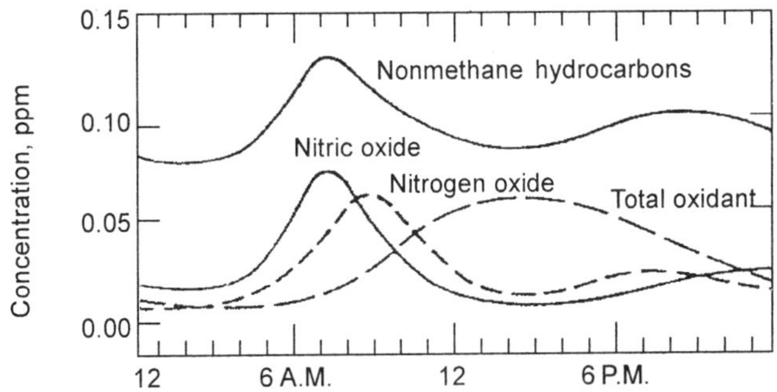

Fig. 16.1 Presentation of diumal variation data in the form of curves.

The frequency distribution method is applied when a huge number of observations are to be condensed. The frequency distribution of data, in fact, indicates that how often the concentrations of a specified magnitude occur. Frequency distribution, which can be presented in the form of a one-line summary, is given in Fig. 16.2.

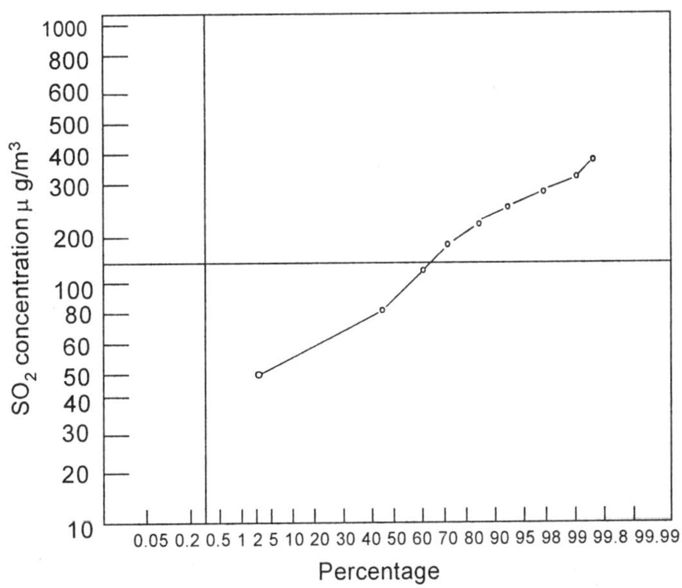

Fig. 16.2 Frequency distribution of air pollution data of SO_2 concentration in the form of a one line summary.

For drawing such a summary line. The total number of measured concentrations during a certain period are arranged in the form of cumulative frequency distribution as shown in Table 16.4. The cumulative class intervals are then plotted against their probabilities of occurrence (per cent occurrence as in Table 16.4) to get the one-line summary.

Table 16.4 Cumulative frequency distribution of 24-hour average of SO_2 concentrations measured at a site in Enschede, Netherlands for a period over six months.

Class interval (g/m^3)	Percent occurrence
< 30	3.79
<60	40.15
< 90	61.36
< 120	73.48
< 150	83.33
< 180	93.94
< 210	97.73
< 240	98.48
< 280	99.24.

The concentration of many air pollutants has been found lo follow a log normal rather than a normal distribution. Suspended particulate matter (SPM) concentrations are an important example of such log normal distribution. The log distribution, in fact, can be shown by any set of data which is dominated by a few occurrences of higher values. Such type of situations are rather common in air pollution studies. In such cases the frequency distribution should be plotted on a log-normal graph paper instead of a simple one. The data given in Table 16.4 have been drawn in the form of a graph as shown earlier in Fig. 16.2. The scale for the pollutant is logarithmic, while the per cent scale is spaced according to the probabilities of a standard normal distribution.

The air pollution data can also be presented in the form of a pollutant rose (in the pattern of a wind rose), provided a simultaneous wind data are also available. The analysis is made by grouping the data according to the prevailing wind direction. After grouping, the data are averaged and plotted in the form of a rose as explained in Fig. 16.3

Other ways also exist for presentation of air pollution data such as 3-dimentional pictorial form and iso-pollution lines on a map in the form of contours. Statistical tools are also available which help eliminating the erroneous observations and finding the means, variability, correlations and comparisons. The description of the statistical parameters is beyond the scope of this book, and the reader can refer any standard text of statistics for details.

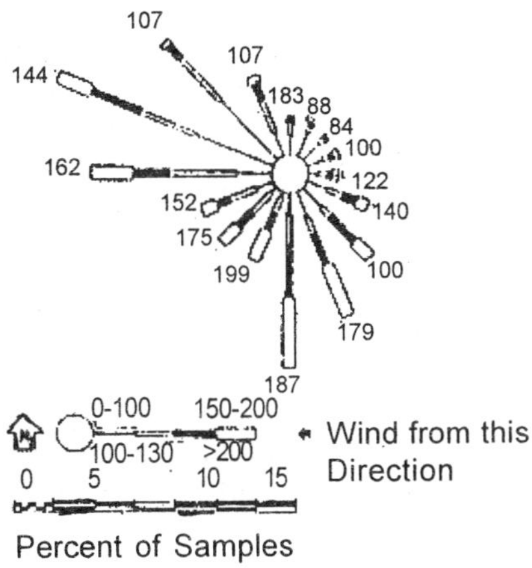

Fig. 16.3 Presentation of air pollution data in pollution roses (After Farmer, J.R and Williams, J.D. 1966. Interstate air pollution study:Phase II Project report -III. Air Quality Measurements. US P.H.S., Cincinnati, Ohio, Dec. 1966.

16.2 Stack Monitoring

The immediate aim of the monitoring of stack gases is to find out the total amount of the pollutants released into the atmosphere in a given time that is called as emission rate of pollutants. The sampling of the stack may also be useful for the following purposes.

1. For determining the kinds of pollutants emitted from the source.
2. For measuring the efficiency of control measures.
3. For measuring the efficiencies of different control devices.
4. For determining the effect of changes in raw materials and processes on the emissions.
5. For checking compliance of the emissions with the emission standards.
6. For preparing the emission inventories.

Stack sampling differs from the ambient air sampling in many respects. It samples the gases that are confined to a stack and, therefore, needs an opening in it to be made for the sampling. The flow rates vary considerably across the stack that necessitates the sampling at a number of traverse points in the stack. For sampling the particulates, isokinetic conditions (i.e., sampling rate equal to stack gas velocity) must be maintained for collection of representative samples from the stack. A brief discussion of these considerations is given below.

Sampling Location

The sampling point should be located, as far as possible, away from any source of flow disturbance such as a bend, expansion, contraction, valve, elbow, baffles or visible flame. It should be kept apart from a disturbing element by a distance of 5 to 10 times downstream; and 3 to 5 times, upstream of the diameter of the stack. For rectangular stacks, the equivalent diameter can be calculated by the following equation.

$$\text{Equivalent diameter of a rectangular stack} = \frac{2\,(\text{length} \times \text{width})}{(\text{length} + \text{width})}$$

For sampling, an opening is made in the stack at the appropriate location. The size of the opening should be sufficient to accommodate the probes, and normally kept in the range of 7 to 10 cm in diameter. This opening is covered with a lid, and opened only at the time of sampling.

Traverse Points

There is a considerable variation in the temperature and velocity along with the concentration of pollutants across the stack. For a representative sample, it is necessary that the sampling is carried out at several points across the stack, which are called traverse points. The number of traverse points depends upon the area of the stack and can be selected according to the following scheme:

Cross-sectional area (m^2)	No. of traverse points
0.2	4
0.2-2.5	12
2.5 and more	20

The layout of the traverse points in the cross-sectional area of the stack is as follows:

Circular stacks

The traverse points should be located on two perpendicular diameters as shown in Fig. 16.4 (A).

(A) (B)

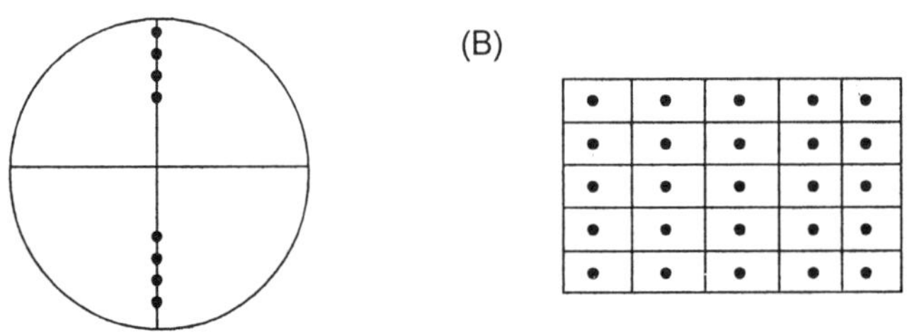

Fig. 16.4 Selection of transverse points in circular stacks (A) and rectangular stacks (B).

Rectangular stacks

The cross sectional area is divided into several equal rectangular areas preferably as many in number as traverse points as indicated in Fig. 16.4 (B). The traverse should be carried out in the centre of at least nine hypothetical rectangular areas on minimum three lines.

Isokinetic Conditions

Isokinetic conditions can be achieved by maintaining the velocity at the nozzle of the probe (V_n) equal to the velocity of gas stream (Vs) in the stack. The isokinetic conditions are important, particularly, while taking the representative sample of the gas for measuring particulates. As shown in Fig 16.5, if the sampling velocity is too high, an excess of lighter particles enter the nozzle deflecting the heavier particles outside as a result of the development of a convergent stream. This will result in the collection of particles with a weight on lower side. Conversely, if the velocity of sampling is lower than the stack gas velocity, the lighter particles will be deflected outside, while the heavier particles will continue to move into the nozzle by virtue of their inertia, resulting in the collection of particles with a weight on higher side.

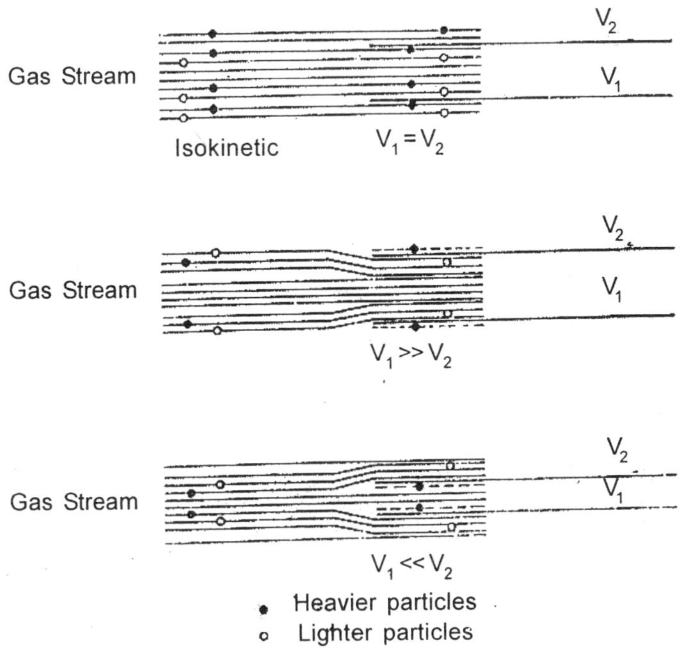

Fig. 16.5 Movement of particles in isokinetic and non-isokinetic conditions of sampling (V_1 = Velocity of sampling and V_2 = Velocity of stack gas).

Determination of Mass Emission Rate

The determination of mass-emission rate of pollutants is the overall objective of stack sample which can be determined according to the following equation.

$$X_s = C_{st} \times Q_{st}$$

Where,

X_s = average pollutant mass emission rate

C_{st} = average pollutant concentration

Q_{st} = average volumetric gas flow rate

The stack monitoring measures the quantities of C_{st} and Q_{st} which are used for calculation of mass emission rate of the pollutants.

Measurement of Average Volumetric Gas Flow Rate (Q_{st})

The average volumetric gas flow rate (Q_{st}) is calculated by multiplying the velocity of stack gases (V_s) and the cross sectional area of the stack at sampling location.

Qst = average velocity of gases × cross-sectional area of stack

The velocity of the gases is calculated from the following equation.

$$V_s = K_p \cdot C_p \sqrt{\frac{T_s \cdot \Delta P}{P_s \cdot M_s}}$$

Where,

V_s = Velocity of gas stream (m/sec)

ΔP = Velocity head in mm of water

T_s = Temperature of stack gases (K)

P_s = Absolute stack gas pressure in mm of Hg

M_s = Molecular weight of dry gas

K_p = Dimension constant (34.96 for metric units)

C_p = Pitot coefficient (Pitot correction factor)

The quantities K_p, C_p, P_s and M_s are usually constant for a particular stack and pitot tube, whereas the factors T_s and, ΔP are variable. Once the former four factors are known, then only T_s and, ΔP are to be measured in routine. The measurement of only ΔP, M_s and T_s is discussed here. P_s is obtained from the barometric and stack pressures. Average velocity can be obtained by taking mean of the velocity values measured at various traverse points.

Velocity Head (ΔP) Determination

The velocity head is the difference between the impact pressure (measured against the gas flow) and the static pressure (measured perpendicular to the gas flow). It is obtained with the help of a pitot tube attached with an inclined manometer assembly. The pitot tube used for this purpose is called 'Type-S' or 'reverse type' which consists of two opposite openings as illustrated in Fig. 16.6. The pitot tube is inserted into the stack up to the desired level and velocity head is obtained from the manometer reading.

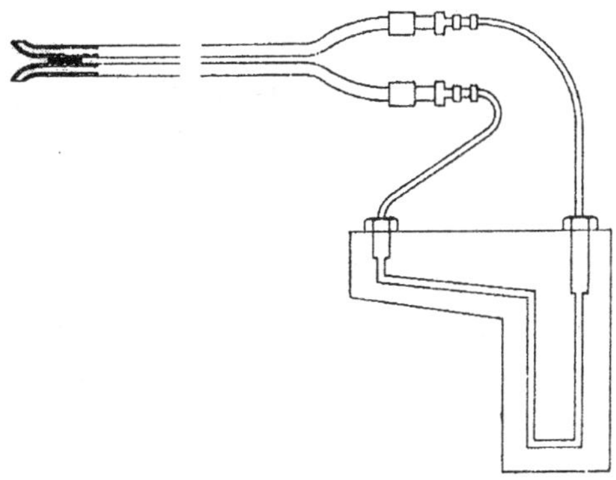

Fig. 16.6 A Pitot tube.

Molecular Weight Determination (Ms)

The major atmospheric gases present in the stack (CO_2, CO, O_2 and N_2) are measured with the help of an Orsat apparatus. The Orsat apparatus contains different reagents for the absorption of these gases, such as 20 to 40% KOH solution for CO_2, alkaline pyrogallol for O_2 and acidic cuperous chloride for CO. As the rest is only N_2 gas, it can be measured by calculation. The sampling train for collecting gas for determination of composition is given in Fig. 16.7 which consists of a filter for removal of particulates, an air cooled condensor for removal of excess moisture, a vacuum pump for drawing the gas, a flow rate meter, and a flexible bag for collecting the gas sample. The average molecular weight of the gases can be calculated by the following equation.

$$M_w = \Sigma M_x \times B_x$$

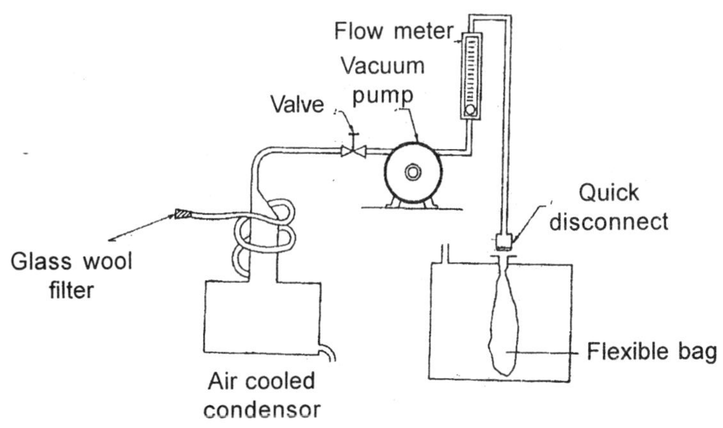

Fig. 16.7 Sampling train for collection of gas for finding its composition.

Where,

M_w = average molecular weight of the gases present in the stack.

M_x = individual molecular weight of the gases (CO_2 = 44; O_2 = 32; CO = 28; N_2 = 28)

B_x = volume fraction of the individual gas

The molecular weight, thus, obtained is corrected for moisture content to get the dry gas molecular weight, by measuring moisture content of the gas with the help of wet and dry bulb temperature technique.

Temperature Determination (T_S)

Temperature is determined by use of a thermocouple, which is inserted in the stack at desired points. Though, several types of thermocouples are available, the most common in use is alumel/chromel type. The average temperature is taken as the mean of the readings obtained at various traverse points.

Measurement of Average Pollutant Concentration (C_{st})

Particulate Matter

The sampling train: The sampling train for the collection of particulate matter is shown in Fig.16.8. The probe, which is made up of either Pyrex or stainless steel is inserted into the stack. The probe is connected to the filter assembly which allows to pass the gases but retains the particulate matter. The filter assembly is followed by a series of four impingers. The first and second impingers are filled with 100 mL deionized distilled water. The third impinger is kept empty, and the fourth one contains 200g of precisely weighed predried

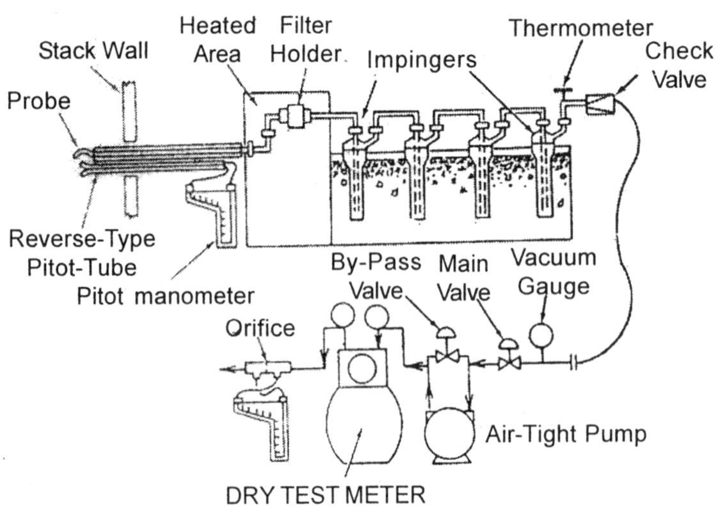

Fig. 16.8 Sampling train for particulate matter collection.

silica gel. All the four impingers are kept in an ice bath. Their main function is to completely remove the moisture from the gases. Tne last impinger is then connected with a vacuum line to a vacuum pump dry test meter and a flow measuring device. The dry test meter gives the integrated gas volume which has been sampled. Flow measuring device may be a simple rotameter or a calibrated orifice with a manometer as shown in the above sampling train. A temperature measuring device is also fitted to the inlet and outlet of dry test meter to find out the temperature at which the gas has been collected.

Procedure: The particulate measurement is always carried out in isokinetic conditions as discussed earlier. The velocity of gases is first determined and the flow rate of the gases through the sampling train is adjusted equal to it. The particulates are measured as the difference between the initial weight of the thimble of the filter assembly and its final weight after the sampling is over. Some of the particulates are also deposited in the nozzle of the probe; they are also removed carefully and added to the weight of the particulates. Temperature, manometer pressure, and total dry gas volume are also recorded at each traverse point.

The sampling is carried out generally for 5 to 10 minutes at each traverse point. In practice, for collecting a representative sample, the probe is marked for the position of various traverse points. After the sampling is over at first traverse point, the probe is moved further to the second traverse point, then third and so on for collection of a representative sample at one time only.

The results of particulate emissions are normally expressed at standard NTP conditions. For the detailed procedure and calculating the results, the reader is referred to EPA (1971) and NEERI (1981).

Gases and Vapours Determination

Maintenance of isokinetic conditions are not essential during the sampling of gaseous pollutants, as their concentration is more or less uniform across the stack. The sample is drawn from the centre point of the stack instead of various traverse points. It is sufficient to collect only grab samples, particularly when the process is uniform.

As the stack gas is a complex mixture of atmospheric gases and pollutants of various nature, some interfering substances may also be present for the determination of a particular gas. It is essential to remove these interferences prior to the collection of the actual pollutant in the impinger. For example, if any sulphuric acid mist is present, it has to be removed before collecting SO_2 gas.

The gaseous pollutants are collected in the impingers by absorption, adsorption or by freeze out/condensation techniques using suitable materials. The methodology for the estimation of some gaseous pollutants has been described in Chapter 15. Other details of the sampling procedures for gases and vapours are given in American Society for Testing and Materials (1971) and APHA (1977).

16.3 Pollution Indices in Air Monitoring

In most natural situations the effects of air pollution are as a result of the combined effects of various different pollutants rather than only a single pollutant. The magnitude of air pollution in such cases is difficult to be assessed on the basis of the concentration of individual pollutants alone, but the goal can be achieved by applying certain indices. The kind and number of pollutants for calculating the indices can be selected depending upon their predominance in the ambient air.

An air pollution index should indicate the gross level of pollution with reference to the standard limits of the individual pollutants. It should be easy to understand and should include the major air pollutants. If the use of indices is to be made on a national level, care has to be taken to include always same air pollutants to maintain the comparability.

Calculation of Air Pollution Indices

Several air pollution indices have been developed taking different pollutants into consideration. Almost all of these have arbitrary limits giving hardly any emphasis to the dose-response relationship. A detailed account of some important air pollution indices is given by Rao & Rao (1989). Calculation of some indices is given hereunder.

I. In one of the methods given here, the values of important individual pollutants are compared with their ambient air quality standards in percent terms and the air pollution index (API) is calculated by taking their average.

$$API = \frac{1}{n}\sum_{i=1}^{n} Ai$$

where,

$A_i = C_i/S_i \times 100$

C_i = Concentration of individual pollutant i

S_i = Ambient air quality standard for pollutant i

n = No. of air pollutants

II. In another method, ratios of three important air pollutants to their ambient air quality standards are first obtained and then the average of their sum is multiplied by 100.

$$API = \frac{1}{3}\left[\frac{I_{PM}}{S_{PM}} + \frac{I_{SO_2}}{S_{so_2}} + \frac{I_{CO}}{S_{CO}}\right] \times 100$$

Where. I_{PM}, I_{so_2} and I_{co} represent individual values of particulate matter, sulphur dioxide and carbon monoxide; and S_{PM}, S_{so_2} and S_{co}, their ambient air quality standards.

III. In this method, subindices (A_i) are first obtained for five air pollutants by giving them arbitrary numbers according to their range of ambient concentrations as indicated in Table 16.5. The air pollution index is then calculated as the sum of these subindices.

$$API = \Sigma A_i$$

Table 16.5 Sub-index value (Ai) of five important air pollution parmeters to calculate air pollution index (based on Rao 1989).

Air pollution paranleters	Sub Index values (Ai)					
	2	4	8	12	16	20
CO (ppm)	0-1	1-2	2-4	4-6	6-8	8-35
NO_2 (ppm)	0- 0.005	0.005-0.01	0.01-0.02	0.02-0.06	0.06-0.10	0.10-0.20
Oxidants (ppm)	0-0.5	0.5-1.0	1-2	2-3	3-4	4-5
Coefficient of haze						
Visibility (km)	12-24	8-12	6-8	4-6	2-4	0-2

IV. The air pollution index can also be calculated on the basis of a single parameter taking into consideration of only the dominant pollutant. For example, index for sulphur dioxide can be represented as follows.

$$API = \frac{I_{SO}}{S_{SO}} \times 100$$

Where I_{so} and S_{so} are ambient SO_2 concentration and its air quality standard respectively. Similarly, the example index can be calculated in the highly congested traffic areas. For industrial areas Index can also be calculated by taking two parameters into account, i.e., sulphur dioxide and particulate matter.

As all the above indices have been calculated on per cent basis, a common rating scale given below, can be used to indicate the air quality.

Index range	Quality of air
0 - 25	Clean air
26 - 50	Light air pollution
51 - 75	Moderate air pollution
76 - 100	Heavy air pollution
more than 100	Severe air pollution

The use of air pollution indices should be made with utmost care as they may, sometimes, give an entirely different picture of the air if calculated taking wrong air pollutants.

Proposed Design of Monitoring Network for India (Based on NEERI's Reports)

(a) Criteria for selection of monitoring stations ;

To start with, the areas for location of monitoring stations should be selected on the basis of following criteria.

1. Population and total areas
2. Level of industrialization and urbanization
3. Terrain, geographical location and physical features
4. Meteorological characteristics

Keeping the above in view, the areas for air quality monitoring in various parts of the country could be classified into three categories namely A, B and C. The definition of the categories are spelt out below.

(b) *Number of monitoring stations*

Class A areas

These include metropolitan cities with population above four millions. Also include in this category are industrial and other activities. For this category of areas, it is recommended to have five to eight monitoring stations.

Class B areas

This category includes the urban centres having population of 1-4 millions and the areas which are in the process of industrialization/urbanization. In each of these areas, three monitoring stations are recommended.

Class C area

These are areas relatively free from industrial and other polluting human activities. It is recommended to have only one station in each of these areas.

Background monitoring locations for class A and B areas

It is necessary to have a background monitoring station in each of the class A and B areas so as to obtain data on the background pollution level. Such a station should be located in the cleanest part of the area and it should be in the prevailing upwind direction away from the areas of sources of significant pollution.

While suggesting the number of sampling stations, the norms prescribed by WHO are taken into account. In each of the class A areas it will be necessary to identify industrial, commercial, residential and background monitoring sites. The other stations can be considered on the basis of prevailing activities and meteorological conditions. In class B areas, it will be necessary to select monitoring sites, one each at residential, commercial and industrial locations. In class C areas the monitoring sites should be selected in the locations having high population density.

(c) *Sampling design*

Sampling stations

While selecting the sampling stations, the following points need to be kept in view.

1. Accessibility to the site on a 24-h basis.
2. Availability of the site on a long term contract. The site should remain unchanged unless technical considerations and monitoring data dictate otherwise.
3. Site should have necessary security arrangements for instruments and equipments.
4. Elevation of the Neighborhood buildings or any other tall premises should not be within 120 degree angle of sight from the sampling level.

Selection of air quality parameters

The parameters which are to be monitored in the initial phase of programme are as follows.

1. Suspended particulate matter (total and respirable) and dust fall, volatile and soluble fractions.
2. Sulphur dioxide and sulphation rate
3. Oxides of nitrogen
4. Ozone and total oxidants
5. Pollens and aeropathogens
6. Total hydrocarbons (non-methane)
7. Coefficient of haze, smoke density, soiling indices

To begin with, it may not be possible to monitor all the parameters in all the areas. It is therefore suggested that the parameters to be monitored in various areas may be as follows.

Class A areas

1. Suspended particulate matter and dust fall
2. Sulphur dioxide and sulphation rate
3. Oxides of nitrogen
4. Ozone
5. Total hydrocarbons
6. Soke density and smog (optical measurements)

Class B areas

1. Suspended particulate matter and dust fall
2. Sulphur dioxide and sulphation rate
3. Oxides of nitrogen
4. Optical measurement of smog

Class C areas

1. Suspended particulate matter and dust fall
2. Sulphur dioxide
3. Pollens and aeropathogens

In addition to the air quality parameters as suggested above, all the monitoring stations would require to have facilities for measurement of meteorological characteristics, viz.

1. Wind direction
2. Wind speed
3. Temperature and humidity (including visual observation on fog/smog)
4. Precipitation

Sampling height

Various prescriptions are available in respect of heights at which samples for air quality monitoring for public and environmental health data are to be collected. These are:

1. Height at breathing level
2. Three meters above ground
3. Six meters above ground
4. 10-12 meters above ground

In case of meteorological measurements like wind speed and wind direction at ground level the practice is to collect the samples at 10 meters above ground. According to the guidelines issued by the Indian Standards Institution (now BIS), the samples for air quality monitoring should be collected at a height of 10 meters above ground. Considering the practical problems that may arise in adopting a rigid standard particularly in places having high rise structures and non-availability of required space in any area, it is recommended that the sampling height may range from 4-15 meters above ground which are to be suitably located by the monitoring organizations. However, for the purpose of comparing the data, it will be desirable to have samples collected at the same height in all the places at least in all the sampling stations located in a particular area. When the sampling is to be done for a specific reason at a different height other than the breathing level, the data should be correlated to the extent possible with that collected at a standard height.

Frequency and sampling period

Frequency and sampling periods depend on the nature of pollutants and the specific interest in monitoring. In class A areas, the Committee recommends collection of integrated 3-hourly samples continuously for 24 hours. Sampling is to be done on the above schedule twice a week every third day for 3 years, so as to obtain statistically reliable data on the concentration of pollutants in different periods. For B class areas, the programme should be essentially similar excepting that the samples can be collected every sixth day following the above schedule.

17 Biomonitoring of Atmospheric Pollutants

17.1 Introduction

Biomonitoring of pollution is using plants to detect the kind and level of pollution with or without measurement of air pollutants in that area. Biomonitoring has been found to be extremely useful in water pollution studies but its application to air pollution is also spreading worldwide and thousands of studies are available on this topic.

In the biomonitoring of air pollution we use presence/absence/abundance /distribution morphology and chemical characteristics of plants to arrive at a conclusion regarding air quality of that area. Since many plant species are sensitive to air pollution, it is possible to monitor the level of air pollution through proper quantification and standardization of plant responses of sensitive species.

There are several advantages in using plants as biomonitors of air pollution

1. Air quality monitoring based on equipments is very expensive and can not be undertaken at a very large scale and at frequent intervals.
2. The concentration of air pollutants in a particular area may not exactly indicate the potential effects of these pollutants to biota.
3. Air monitoring can be carried out relatively at much lower cost by using plants.

4. It is impossible to measure a very large number of pollutants present in a particular area, while the plants which stay in the polluted area integrate and present the sum total of effect of all pollutants.
5. They present internal and external symptoms which may be specific for certain pollutants.

Although some doubts have been raised regarding uniformity of plants response in all environmental conditions (temperature, humidity and wind), its overall usefulness has been found to be satisfactory and biological monitoring can be applied in predicting the impact of air pollutants (Posthumus 1983, 1985, Rao 1981).

The history of documentation on effects of air pollutants on plants is very old. Damages caused to the plants are reported from all parts of the world. It is reported that within the last century the flora of Holland lost 3.8% of its species of flowering plants, 15% of its terrestrial bryophytes, 13% of its epiphytic brophytes and 27% of its epiphytic lichens. In Amsterdam alone 23 species of bryophytes which occurred in the year 1900 are now extinct.

One of the earliest record of using plants for air pollution monitoring is of 1899 when plants in wooden boxes having uncontaminated soil were put in smoke filled areas to find out the impact of smoke on plants. Shantz (1911) is supposed to have: developed the concept of air monitoring. Clements (1920) is well known for his research on "plant indicators". Now a vast information is available on use of plants for monitoring air pollution (Beschel 1958, Barkman 1963, 1968, Desloover and Le Blanc 1968, Gilbert 1968 a,b, Rao & Le Blanc 1967, Le Blanc and Desloover 1970, Posthumus 1983, 1984, 1985, Le Blanc and Rao 1975, Floor and Posthumus 1977, Varshney 1985, Beg 1980, Yunus & Ahmad 1979, Agrawal 1985, Rao 1977, 1981, Chaphekar et al. 1985, Varshney 1992.

In India considerable work has been done on the effect of air pollution on plants which has been reviewed by Varshney and Garg (1979) and Chaphekar (1982).

It is very important to understand how the plants are used for biomonitoring. Some of the examples given below can provide an insight into these studies.

17.2 Floristic Studies and Vegetation Maps

Floristic composition of affected and non affected areas can be studied to detect the changes. Usual phytosociological studies can be employed here. For example, line or belt transects are laid from the source of the pollutants to different directions and frequency of various species is recorded. These data will reflect not only the sensitive and resistant species but will also delineate the affected area which can be supplemented with actual measurements of the pollution levels and represented in the form of a map delineating the boundaries by joining the points with similar readings. These maps, which show zones with different levels of atmospheric damage may be quite useful in demarkating the areas according to the sensitivity of air pollution (Fig. 17.1). The area of highest level of pollutants in this figure is represented as zone I characterized by the total absence of sensitive species. Zone 5 shows the normal structure of community with no effects of the air pollution.

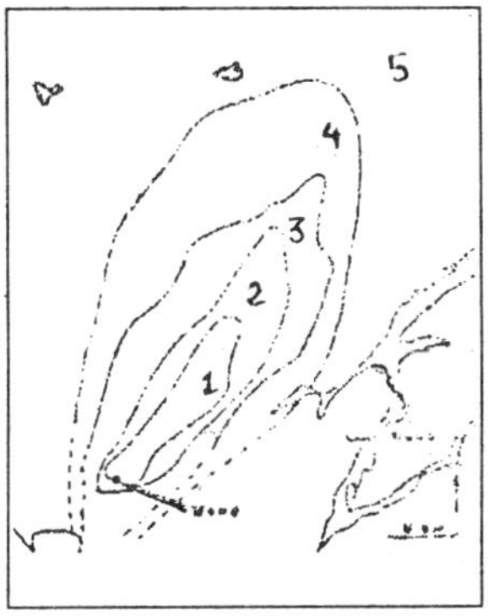

Fig. 17.1 Approximate boundaries of SO_2 pollution zones in the Wawa. Ontario. Canada area delineated on the basis of the number of epiphytic lichens and bryophytes and the concentration of soil sulphate. Note the elliptical shape of the zones influenced by the SW prevailing winds. zone 1:Sulphate concentration of the soil more than 1.4 mE/100g. Epiphytes absent. zone 2: sulphate concentration between 0.9 and 1.4 mE/100g. The epiphtic species range from 1-5 zone1: Sulphate concentration between 0.7 and 0.9 mE/100g. The number of epiphhytic species at any site ranges from 5-15. Zone 4: Sulphate concentration between 0.4 and 0.7 mE/100g. The number of epiphytic species range from 15-30. zone 5: Sulphate concentration less than 0.4 mE/100g.The number of epiphytic species at any site exceeds 30 (After LeBlanc & Rao 1974).

One can calculate an Index of Atmospheric Purity (IAP) based on this data as proposed by Le Blanc and De Sloover (1970).

$$IAP = L (Q \times F)$$

Where,

n = Total no of species present in the area studied

F = Frequency coverage score of each species

Q = The index of resistance factor of each species

The value of Q for a species is determined by adding the numbers of its companion species present at all investigated sites and then divided by the number of sites.

IAP is inversely proportional to the level of pollution indicating that an increase in pollution will be associated with decrease in the value of this index.

17.3 Eco-Physiological Studies

In these studies the healthy plants are put in the polluted environment and their different characteristics are studied over a period of time. Following are some of the important parameters used by different workers in these studies:

1. Visible injury
2. Estimation of chlorophyll and other pigments.

3. Growth rate as indicated by weight and length of root and shoot.
4. Leaf Area Indices
5. Anatomical features
6. Yield
7. Chemical composition of plant parts (e.g. sulphur content of leaves indicates the level of pollution in that area)
8. Seed germination
9. Pollen germination
10. Stomatal response with changes in foliar cuticle and epidermis
11. Plant metabolites, nucleic acids and enzymatic activity.

17.4 Lichens and Bryophytes as Plant Indicators

Lichens and Bryophytes have been found to be excellent indicator of air pollution. It was known by the middle of the nineteenth century that lichens are sensitive lo the city environment. Scientists used to observe poor growth of lichens in the city environment and attributed it to the higher level of smoke and gases in the city's environment. This property of lichens earned them a name 'Hygienometers'. Their usefulness was further confirmed by a study when regrowth of lichens was found in area after a particular factory generating air pollution was closed. It is established that no lichen can survive an average annual sulphur dioxide concentration of more than 30 ppb (Agrawal & Agrawal 1992).

The lichen thalli collected in the form of bark discs from nonpolluted regions are attached to trees growing in polluted areas. The dying rates changes with respect to injury, chlorophyll reduction, cellular plasmolysis, cell size reduction etc. are used as parameters for monitoring air pollution impact (Le Blanc et al. 1976).

According to De Wit (1983) ideal lichen indicators of air pollution are *Buellia punctata*, *Parmelia sulcata*. *Euernia prunasiri* and *Ramalina forinacea*.

Bryophytes derive their moisture and nutrients from the atmosphere and are thus severely affected by air pollution. Mishra (1985) has carried out some studies using mosses as indicators of air pollution in Bombay.

17.5 Higher Plants as Bioindicators

A number of higher plants have shown sensitivity to air pollution and specific symptoms as well as physiological and biochemical changes. A large number of studies are available on this aspect. Prominent studies on this aspect are presented below.

I. *Floristic composition*

1. Rao (1972) found *Mangifera indica* (mango) to be sensitive and thus an indicator of air pollution. Chaphekar (1972) also used the same plant in Bombay.

II. *Morphology*

1. Plants growing in the polluted environment show stunted growth (Fig.17.2) reduced leaf area

Fig. 17.2 Stunted growth of plants (right) grown in polluted area. The Plants at left show the growth in unpolluted area (Source:Science Today. September. 1980).

2. Chaphekar et al. (1980) carried out a study in Bombay to assess the level of dust pollution by simultaneous measurement of dustfall and exposing the plants in these localities. Four plants, *Commelina benghalensis*, *Crotalaria juncea*. Cyampsis tetra gonoloba and Helianthus anus were used. They found considerable reduction in shoot length and shoot dry weight in polluted areas.

3. Boralkar and Mukherjee (1983) have also carried out similar studies in Delhi by using alfalfa plant and based on growth responses of plants

4. Rao et al. (1987) have surveyed the air pollution status of Obra-Renukoot Singrauli area with respect to pollution load and changes in plant height and leaf area and number of alfalfa transplants kept at various distance from polluting source.

5. Leaf epidermal feature, size and frequency of epidermal cells, density and length of trichomes, stomatal density index and pore size etc. can be used to detect the level and kind of pollution (Yunus and Ahmad 1978, 1979, Garg and Varshney 1980, Ahmad 1982, Bhairavamurthy et al. 1983, Ahmad and Yunus 1985). Sharma and his coworkers used cuticular features as indicators of air pollution (Sharma and Butler 1973, 1975, Sharma and Tyree 1973, Sharma 1977, 1992). Their study on *Trifolium repens* indicated a decrease in stomatal frequency and all increase in length and frequency of trichomes in the polluted populations.

6. Pollen grains of some plants are extremely sensitive to air pollution. It has been reported that in vitro pollen germination can be successfully employed for onsite monitoring of atmospheric pollutants (Varshney 1985).

7. Relatively quick response of pollen grains to air pollutants is ideally suited for evolving a convenient short term bioassay of air pollution as revealed by the studies carried out by several workers (Dopp 1934).

III. *Physiology of the Plants*

1. Agrawal et al. (1985) observed transpirational measurement as a good plants indicator of stress conditions due to O_3 and SO_2 singly and in combination.

2. Chlorophyll has been traditionally used as a sensitive parameter for air pollution studies. Agrawal and Agrawal (1988) have reported a direct relationship between SO_2 and SPM concentration in air and decrease in chlorophyll content.

3. Nandi et al. (1980) have examined protein content of germinating seeds of *Phaseolus aureus* exposed to different pollutants and obtained reliable results. Banerjee et al. (1983) have also suggested it as a useful parameter.

4. Since the plants accumulate the pollutants present in the air are estimation of mineral content of various plant parts often gives reliable estimates of the level and kind of air pollution. Even prolonged small concentrations may be detected by this method. Varshney (1985) compared the sulphur content in leaves and bark of eleven common tree species growing around Indraprastha power station in New Delhi with sulphur contents of the plants at unpolluted sites and reported that sulphur content in tree bark varied widely with the species and quantum of pollution. Fluoride pollution can be monitored by measuring fluoride content of the leaf (Rao and Pal 1979, Rao et al., 1987). The traffic pollution has been quite successfully monitored by estimating lead content of the plants (Oliver et. al. 1974, Holland Harnpp 1975).

IV. **Biochemical changes**

1. Raza et al. (1985) have developed an index called" Air Pollution Tolerance Index" (APTI) for indicating the level of air pollution in an area.

$$\text{APTI} = \frac{A(T+P)+R}{10}$$

where

A = Ascorbic acid content of leaf in mg/g dry weight

T = Total chlorophyll of leaf in ffig/g dryweight

P = pH of the leaf extract

R = Relative water content of leaf extract (%)

The plants with higher index values are relatively more tolerant to air pollution in comparison to those having lower values.

2. Vora and Bhatnagar (1980) used the proline content of plants to monitor the dustfall level in Ahmedabad. The study revealed an accumulation of proline in leaves of certain plants like *Aelianthus excela*.

3. Varshney (1979) observed that the activity of the enzyme nitrate reductase was significantly reduced in fumigated pea seedlings. Varshney and Varshney (1983) have also found an increase in peroxidase activity of *Brassica nigra* and *Phaseolus radiatus* fumigated with 0.03, 0.05 and 0.1 ppm of SO_2 for 2 hrs daily for two weeks. The quick response of these enzymes to low levels of SO_2 is suggestive of their potential value as bioindicators of SO_2 pollution.

It will be essential to standardize the procedures developed so far preferably for different climatic conditions to develop suitable system for using plants as bioindicators of pollution.

18 Air Quality Management

The air quality management can be defined as the effort to abate the existing air pollution and to prevent its future rise. The air quality management programme should be administered as a complete programme that includes:

1. Identification and analysis of specific air pollution problems of an area (Air quality monitoring)
2. Preparation of source-emission inventory
3. Determination of air quality criteria
4. Formulation of desired air quality standards (both ambient and emission)
5. Promulgation of rules and regulations to ensure attainment of the air quality standards

18.1 Air Monitoring and Identification of Specific Problems

For any successful management programme, it is essential to know the type and sources of pollution in an area, which can be achieved by surveys and air monitoring systems. These monitoring systems should continuously monitor short and long term trends to evaluate the general air quality and its environmental effects. The data collected shall also be helpful later in attaining the air quality standards by reducing the source emissions to a desired level. The methodology of air sampling and monitoring has been discussed in Chapters 15 and 16.

Additional information can also be gathered on meteorological data and public reactions to the air pollution problems. Finally, all the gathered information should be converted into the meaningful information to be utilized later in preparation of inventories and achieving the air quality goals.

18.2 Source-Emission Inventory

There are two basic types of inventories of air pollution namely source and emission inventories. One of the important steps in air pollution management is to locate the sources of air pollution and their enumeration, tabulation and classification according to the quantity and quality of materials processed.

This kind of listing of pollution sources in an area is called a source inventory. The source inventory can be made on the basis of listing in the form of specific sources or multiple sources of air pollution. For example, in case of the specific sources, the listing is made of specific industries such as metal, textile, chemicals, mining, engineering, glass and so on together with the nature of activities therein and types of air pollution problems. For multiple source inventory, the process, producing the air pollutants, is given emphasis and the listing of the sources can be under the headings of combustion of fuels, odours production, incineration of wastes and evaporation of petroleum products and so on. Each process then lists the name of the industries and other sources that fall in this group. For example, under combustion of fuels the sources of air pollution can be listed as automobiles, railways, aircraft and ships as mobile sources; and homes, hospitals, power plants and industries, etc. as stationary sources.

After indentification of sources in a given area, full investigation is made to determine the quality and quantity of the air pollutants produced by each source. Listing is then made of the sources with the kinds of air pollutants and their emissions from them. Such kind of inventory is called emission inventory.

For preparation of emission inventory it is rather difficult to inspect each source for the quality and quantity of air pollutants emitted. The emission inventories are computed usually on the basis of the emission factors which can be defined as a statistical average of the mass of pollutants from each source of the pollution per unit quantity of material handled, processed or burned. This can be understood by studying the emission factors given previously for various industries in Chapter 4. From the emission factors, it is possible to calculate the total quantity of the various pollutants produced, if the quality and quantity of raw materials and fuels used by the each source are available.

As these two kinds of inventories relate closely to each other and involve almost a similar procedure, they are usually represented together, and called source-emission inventories. These inventories list the location and enumeration of pollution sources within an area along with kinds and quantities of air pollutants being released from each source. These inventories provide a vital data on air pollution of an area which can be used later for developing the control strategy and to prevent future air pollution.

18.3 Air Quality Criteria

Air quality criteria are descriptive documents reflecting the identifiable effects of air pollutants on health and human welfare. The air quality criteria serve as a basis for defining 'good' or 'bad' as well as 'clean' or 'dirty' air. They specify a certain pollutant level and the harmful effects that result if this level is exceeded. The air quality criteria are usually developed on the scientific facts using almost all our current knowledge relating to air pollution. Various types of scientific data can be employed to reach at certain conclusions. For evaluating the effects of air pollutants on humans and animals, both experimental and epidemiological studies might be quite useful. Under experimental conditions, the levels of various pollutants can be determined above which harm is caused to the individuals. Such kind of experiments have been frequently used for evaluating the effects of air pollutants on plants. The use of human volunteers and animals in such experiments has been discussed by Rjazanov (1965). Under epidemiological approach, the population or the selected groups of people like children, elderly or ill are usually studied. Such kind of approach has been very useful in evaluating the effects of certain pollutants on the workers in their work environment. However, the interpretation of data may be little difficult on account of the prevalence of certain factors other than pollution like socioeconomic status, infection, smoking and malnutrition, etc.

The relationship between time of exposure and the resultant effects is also an important factor which should be given due consideration. The effects of air pollution vary considerably with time of exposure. The ambient concentration of pollutants in a particular area is usually denoted as daily 24-h mean value, or annual mean of 24-h values. Air quality standards, developed on the basis of air quality criteria, should protect from both short as well as long term effects. If the effects are produced in 24-h or less, any control measure stipulating mean 24-h value should specify variations expected and number of days per year on which that specified concentration causing the effect reaches. Similarly, if any effect is caused in long term by 24-h annual mean, then daily 24-h value must vary only in that limit which would not increase the annual mean value.

In developing the air quality criteria the following points must be taken into account.

1. Chemical and physical characteristics of the pollutants.
2. Techniques for measuring air pollutants characteristics.
3. Susceptibility of receptors to ill effects.
4. Physical conditions of individuals and responses of receptors to ill effects.
5. Meteorological effects that influence dilution and dispersion of air pollutants.
6. Time of exposure to a specific pollutant and other considerations like relative humidity which influence the effects of air pollution associated with air quality criteria are the documents for controlling each air pollutant covered under the criteria.

18.4 Air Quality Standards

The information provided in the air quality criteria is used for the formulation of air quality standards. While the air quality criteria are descriptive in nature, air quality standards are prescriptive and specify the levels of the air pollutants at which the quality of air becomes harmful or unacceptable. The air pollution standards are not same everywhere, though they might have been developed on the same considerations, because of the differences in choosing air quality goals and providing different margins of safety.

According to the recommendations of a WHO expert Committee (WHO, 1972), for establishing air quality standards in addition to health effects, considerations should also be given to the impact on climate, vegetation, animal life, materials, as well as on the aesthetic quality of the environment. These effects have significant social, cultural and economic implications, and are, sometimes, more sensitive indicators of air quality than the effects on health.

In addition to stating the concentration limits for the pollutants, air quality standards should also specify the methods of measurement, the average time over which concentrations should be measured, and the frequency with which the limit may be exceeded.

The air quality standards are basically developed in two forms.

1. Ambient air quality standards
2. Emission standards (standards of performance)

Ambient Air Quality Standards

These specify the desired limit for specific pollutant levels in the surrounding air. The ambient standards usually incorporate annual average concentrations with highest 24-h concentrations in a year. Sometimes, a few short term values, such as based on the highest l-h average concentrations, can also be incorporated.

In USA, the ambient standards have been developed on two different criteria, and called primary and secondary air quality standards. The primary standards are those whose attainment and maintenance is required basically to safeguard the public health. In developing secondary standard the emphasis is laid down on protecting the whole environment necessary for public welfare. This includes the soils, water, climate, damage to property, hazards to transportation, as well as effects on economic values, and on personal comfort and well being, vegetation, animals and physical structures. The ambient air quality standards prevailing in India and in certain other countries are provided in Tables 18.1 and 18.2.

Table 18.1 Ambient air quality standards in India developed by Central Pollution Control Board

Area Category		Concentration μ g/m³			
		SPM	SO_2	CO	NO_x
A.	Industrial and mixed use	500	120	5000	120
B.	Residential and Rural	200	80	2000	80
C.	Sensitive area	100	30	1000	30

Table 18.2 National ambient air quality standards in the U.S.A. (Based on Public Law 91-604, Clean air act as amended in 1970).

Pollutant	Air quality standard μ/m³		Average times
	Primary	Secondary	
Sulphur oxides as SO_2	80	60	Annual arithmetic mean
	365	260	Max. 24-h concentration not to be exceeded more than ooce in a year
	-	1300	Max. 3-h concentration not to be exceeded more than once in a year
Particulates	75	60	Annual geometric mean
	260	150	Max. 24-h concentration not to be exceeded more than once in a year
Carbon monoxide (as mg/m³)	10	10	Max. 8-h concentration not to be exceeded more than ooce in a year
	40	40	Max. 1-h concenlration nol to be exceeded more than once in a year
Phtotochemlcal oxidants	160	160	Max. 1-h concentration not to be exceeded more than once in a year
Hydrocarbons	160	160	Max. 1-h concentration (6 a.m. to 9 a.m.) not to be exceeded more than once in a year
Nitrogen dioxide	100	100	Annual arithmetic mean

Emission Standards

The ambient air quality standards cannot be achieved unless a limit is put on the emissions of the air pollutants from the sources. For this purpose it is necessary to formulate the emission standards that specify the limits for maximum permissible emission levels for given pollutants at their source including both stationary and mobile sources. In USA, these standards are again of two kinds. The National standards which are applied to the new or modified sources and State standards those apply to already existing sources. The emission standards from certain stationary and mobile sources in India are given in Tables 18.3, 18.4 and 18.5.

Table 18.3 Limits for air emissions from certain industries.

Industry	SO_2	SO_3	Fluorine based gases	Particulates	NO_x and NO_2	Hydro-carbons (as CH_4)	Smoke
Phosphoric acid							
existing plants	-	-	1.5kg/t of P_2O_5	-	-	-	-
new plants	-	-	0.6kg/t of P_2O_5	-	-	-	
Single super phosphate,							
exiting plants	-	-	0.5kg/t of product	500mg/Nm^3	-	-	
new plants	-	-	0.1kg/t of product	500mg/Nm^3	-	-	
Triple super phosphate							
existing plants	-	-	0.3kg/t of product	4kg/t	-		
new plants	-	-	0.07kg/t of product	4kg/t	-		
Sulphurlc acid (100%)							
Existing plants							
1. <200t/day	16kg/t	5kg/t	-	-	-	-	
2. >200t/day	12kg/t	5kg/t	-	-	-	-	
Newplants							
1. <200t/day	12kg/t	5kg/t	-	-	-		
2. >200t/day	4kg/t	0.5kg/t	-	-	-		
Nitric acid and nitrogenous fertilizers							
existing plants	-	-	-	6kg/t product	24kg/t HNO_3	5kg/t of product	
new plants	-	-	-	0.5kg/t product	3kg/t of HNO_3	5kg/t of product,	

Table 18.3 *Contd.....*

Industry	SO_2	SO_3	Fluorine based gases	Particulates	NO_x and NO_2	Hydro-carbons (as CH_4)	Smoke
Petroleum refineries							
catalytic regenerating units	5.5kg/t	-	-	-	-		Other than white smoke not darker than No.2 of Ringlemann's Chart for more than 5 min in any consecutive 60 min and more than 6 h in any 10 day period
Other units	3kg/t	-	-	125mg/Nm^3	-	-	-do-
Cement plants							
1. <200t/d in the protected areas		-	-	250mg/Nm^3	-	-	-
in other area	-	-	-	400mg/Nm^3	-	-	-
2. >200t/d in protected areas	-	-	-	150mg/Nm^3	-	-	-
in other areas	-	-	-	250mg/Nm^3	-	-	-
Thermal power plants							
1. <200 MW in the proteced areas	-	-	-	150mg/Nm^3	-	-	-
in other areas	-	-	-	350mg/Nm^3	-	-	-
2. >200MW in protected areas	-	-	-	150mg/Nm^3	-	-	-
in other areas	-	-	-	150mg/Nm^3	-	-	-
Iron & Steel							
Sintering plant	-	-	-	150mg/Nm^3	-	-	-
during oxygen lancing	-	-	-	400mg/Nm^3	-	-	-
normal oprations (during steel making)	-	-	-	150mg/Nm^3	-	-	-

Table 18.3 *Contd.....*

Industry	SO_2	SO_3	Fluorine based gases	Particulates	NO_x and NO_2	Hydro-carbons (as CH_4)	Smoke
Calcium carbide							
Kiln	-	-	-	250mg/Nm^3	-	-	-
Arc furnace	-	-	-	150mg/Nm^3	-	-	-
Carbon black	-	-		150mg/Nm^3	-	-	-
Cu, Pb and Zn Smelting							
Concentrator	-	-		150mg/Nm^3	-	-	-
Smelter & converter	No release (all SO_2 + SO_3 should go for H_2SO_4 manufacture	-	-	-	-	-	-
Aluminium plants							
calcination	-	-		250mg/Nm^3	-	-	
Al smelting 250mg/Nm^3	-	-	1kg/t of Al	150mg/Nm^3	-	-	

Standards based on :

1. Sulphuric acid and phosphatic fertilizer Industries (IS : 8635-1977)
2. Nitric acid and nitrogenous fertilizers (IS : 9005-1978)
3. Petroleum Refineries (IS : 8636-1977)
4. All remaining industries (Central Pollution Control Board, Emission Regulations Part I 1984, & Part II 1985)

Nm^3 = per cubic metre under standard or normal conditions of air (temperature 25C°, Pressure 760 mm of Hg and moisture zero %)

Table 18.4 Indian emission standards for automobiles (Based on State of the art report on vehicle emissions, Deptt. of environment, Govt. of India, Jan., 1985).

Vehicle type	Vehicle category	Test procedure	Pemlisible limits			
			CO	HC	NO_x	Smoke
1. Passenger cars					-	-
A. New cars	All	Idle test	4.5%	-	-	-
	weight <1020 kg	Driving test	23.2g/km	1.83g/km	-	-
	1020-1250kg	-do-	26.4g/km	1.97g/km	-	-
	>1250kg	-do-	30.1g/km	2.12g/km	-	-
B. Cars in use	Pre-1986 cars	Idle test	6.0%	1200 ppm	-	-
	1986 or later	-do-	4.5%	1200 ppm	-	-
	Pre-1988 cars	-do-	4.5%	1200ppm	-	-
	1988 or later	-do-	3.5%	750ppm	-	-
2. Two and Three wheelers (2-stroke engines)						
A. New Vehicles	All	Idle test	2.5%	7800 ppm	-	-
	<100 CC engine	Driving test	12g/km	2g/km	-	-
	101-200CC	-do-	12g/km	3g/km	-	-
	> 200CC	-do-	12g/km	4g/km	-	-
B. Vehicles in use	All	Idle test	4.5%	7800 ppm	-	-
	Pre 1988 model	-do-	4.5%	7800ppm	-	-
	1988 o rlater	-do-	3.0%	7800ppm	-	-
3. Diesel Vehicles -						
A. New Vehicles	All	Free acceleration test	-	-	-	60 HSU or equivalent
B. Vehicles in use	Pre-1986 model	-do-	-	-	-	75 HSU
	1986 or later	-do-	-	-	-	60 HSU
	Pre-1988 model	-do-	-	-	-	60 HSU
	1988 or later	-do-	-	-	-	50 HSU

Table 18.5 Emission standards for automobile applicable from April 1, 1995 and April1, 2000 (Based on Central Pollution Control Board Report).

Vehicle type	Vehicle category	Test procedure	Max. pemisible limits		
			CO		NO_x + HC
1. Cars					
From 1-4-1995	weight < 1020kg	driving test	5g/km		2g/km
	1020-1250 kg	-do-	5.7g/km		2.2g/km
	1250-1470kg	-do-	6.4g/km		2.5g/km
	1470-1700 kg	-do-	7.0g/km		2.7g/km
	1700-1930 kg	-do-	7.7g/km		2.9g/km
	1930-2150kg	-do-	8.2g/km		3.5g/km
	>2150kg	-do-	9.0g/km		4.0g/km
From 1-4-2000	All cars	-do-	2.72g/km		0.97g/km
			CO		**HC**
2. Two wheelers					
From 1-4-1995	All	-do-	3.75g/km		2.4g/km
From 11-4-2000	All	-do-	2.0g/km		1.5g/km
3. Three wheelers					
From 1-4-1995	All	-do-	5.6g/km		3.6g/km
From 1-4-2000	All	-do-	4.0g/km		1.5g/km
			Carbon	**NO_x**	**HC**
4. Diesel vehicles					
From 11-4-1995	All		11.2g/KWH	14.4g/KWH	2.4g/KWH

KWH = Kilowatt hour equivalent burning of fuel

18.5 Promulgation of Air Pollution Control Regulations

After development of air pollution standards. Air pollution control regulations must be enacted to provide a legal basis for attaining the desired quality of air. Air pollution legislation in India and abroad has been dealt in detail in Chapter 19 in India the rules and regulations concerning air pollution are governed by Air (Prevention & Control) Act, 1981 and the modified Act, 1987. Under this Act the development of emission standards and their enforcement together with the regulation of use, design of equipment, and fuels and their consumption are important aspects to control air pollution. There is always a need for some agency to enforce the Acts. In India, Central Pollution Control Board and State Pollution Control Boards look after the air pollution problems and enforce the laws.

Legal aspects of air pollution control include apprehension, trial and penalty. The nature and magnitude of penalties in India have been clearly stated in the Air Pollution Acts. These penalties are in the form of fine and imprisonment.

18.6 Air Quality Management in India

Air pollution was not recognized as a major problem in India until 1974 when the hue and cry was made about possible adverse impact of Mathura refinery emissions on Taj Mahal. In India a comprehensive Act on air pollution control was passed as late as 1981. However, air pollution problem is acute in many parts of India. Many Indian cities like Kalkata, Delhi, Mumbai and Pune are ranked as one of the most polluted cities in world.

The problem is particularly serious in areas where industries have been erected near residential areas. A large number of highly polluting industries like petrochemicals, cement plants, refineries, fertilizers and thermal power plants have created havoc in many areas. Moreover, the growing number of automobiles in various parts of India, especially in big cities, has created visible air pollution problem and is being taken on priority in India.

Current Indian activities in the field of air pollution include :

1. Air quality monitoring by various agencies.
2. Emission inventory from selected industries.
3. Development of monitoring equipments.
4. Development of analytical techniques.
5. Research and development efforts on control systems.
6. Control of automobile exhaust and introduction of lead free petrol.

Traditionally, National Environmental Engineering Research Institute (NEERI) has been carrying out air monitoring studies at nine places in India where its Head Office and Regional Laboratories are located. These cities are Ahmedabad, Mumbai, Kalkata, Delhi, Hyderabad, Jaipur, Kanpur, Chennai and Nagpur.

Under National Air Quality Monitoring, baseline surveys for cities of Mumbai and Kalkata are being conducted since 1970, which have been sponsored by Brihan Mumbai Municipal Corporation (BMC) and Kalkata Metropolitan Development Authority.

In view of alerting the public and authorities about rising levels of air pollution, World Health Organization (WHO) in 1978 provided funding to some agencies including BMC for air pollution studies, particularly to monitor levels of air pollutants in highly polluted areas like metropolitan cities. Under this programme four parameters viz., sulphur dioxide, sulphation rate, SPM and dust-fall were given special attention coupled with the collection of meteorological information for data interpretation.

The Govt. of India enacted Air (Prevention and Control of Pollution) Act in 1981 and on 11 November, 1982, Central Pollution Control Board (CPCB) adopted air quality standards which were supposed to be applicable up to December, 1985.

On the basis of land use and other factors, the various areas were classified into three categories by concerning State Pollution Control Boards.

A. Industrial and mixed use areas

B. Residential and rural areas

C. Sensitive areas

The Central Pollution Control Board (CPCB) started National Ambient Air Quality Monitoring Programme (NAAQM) in 1984 lo monitor air quality in the above three areas which initially included 28 stations in 7 cities. Gradually the number of stations were increased, and by 1992 end the total stations were 290 covering 99 cities and industrial areas. The highest number of monitoring stations are in Uttar Pradesh (38) followed by Maharashtra (26), Madhya Pradesh (24), Gujarat (23) and Rajasthan (19). The monitoring of air quality is carried out at these stations by the respective State Pollution Control Boards mostly for SO_2, NO_2 and SPM. Heavy metals and secondary pollutants are not included in the routine monitoring at all the stations except for Delhi where occasional measurements are also made for cartain heavy metals. The monitoring is carried out for 24 hours on alternate days. At some places, like Delhi, automated monitoring has also been carried out continuously throughout the year also covering carbon monoxide. All the collected data are analysed statistically for interpretation and making averages. The air quality in India, based on the CPCB monitoring data, has been discussed in Chapter 1.

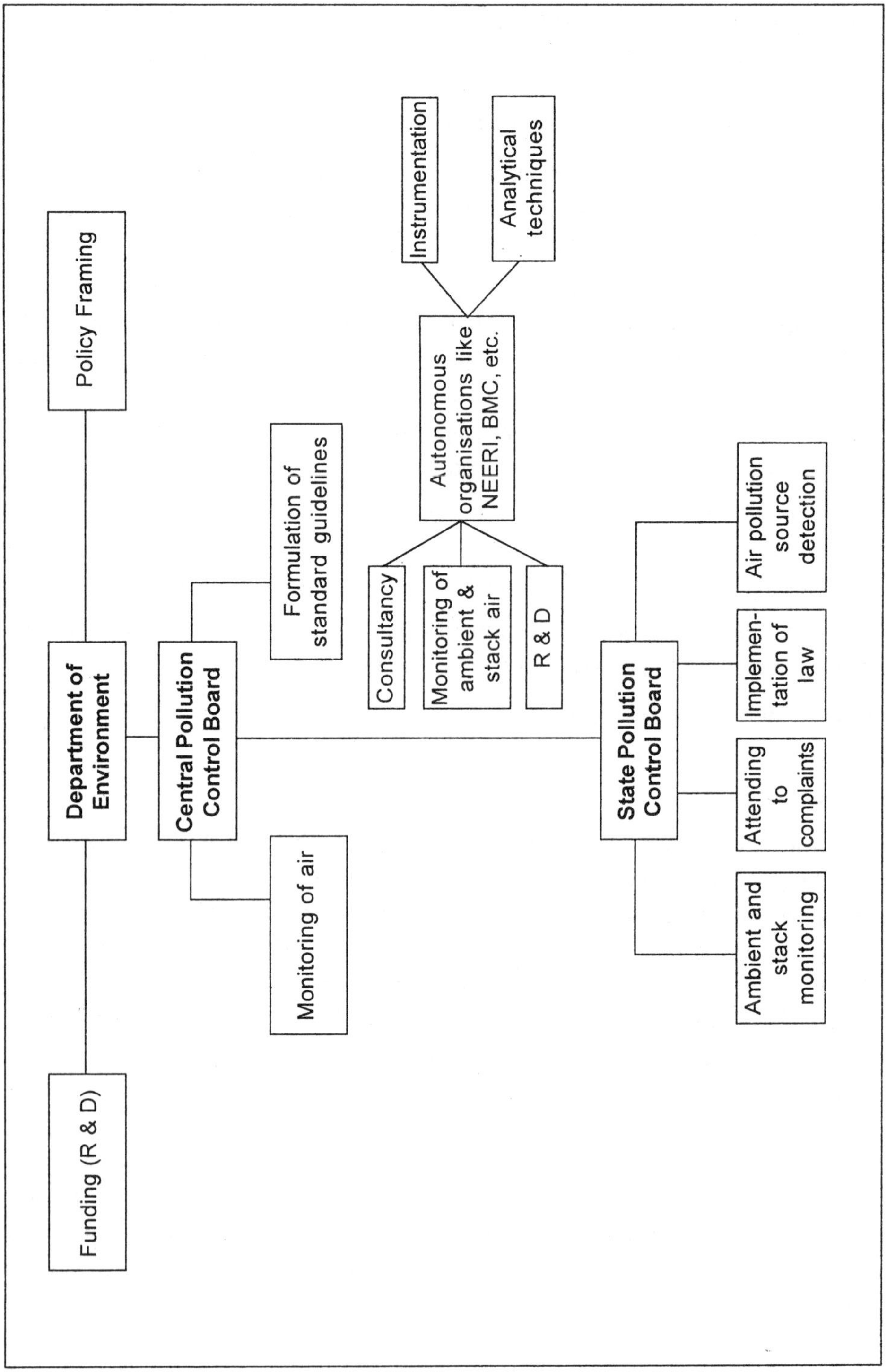

Fig. 18.1 System of air quality management prevailing in India.

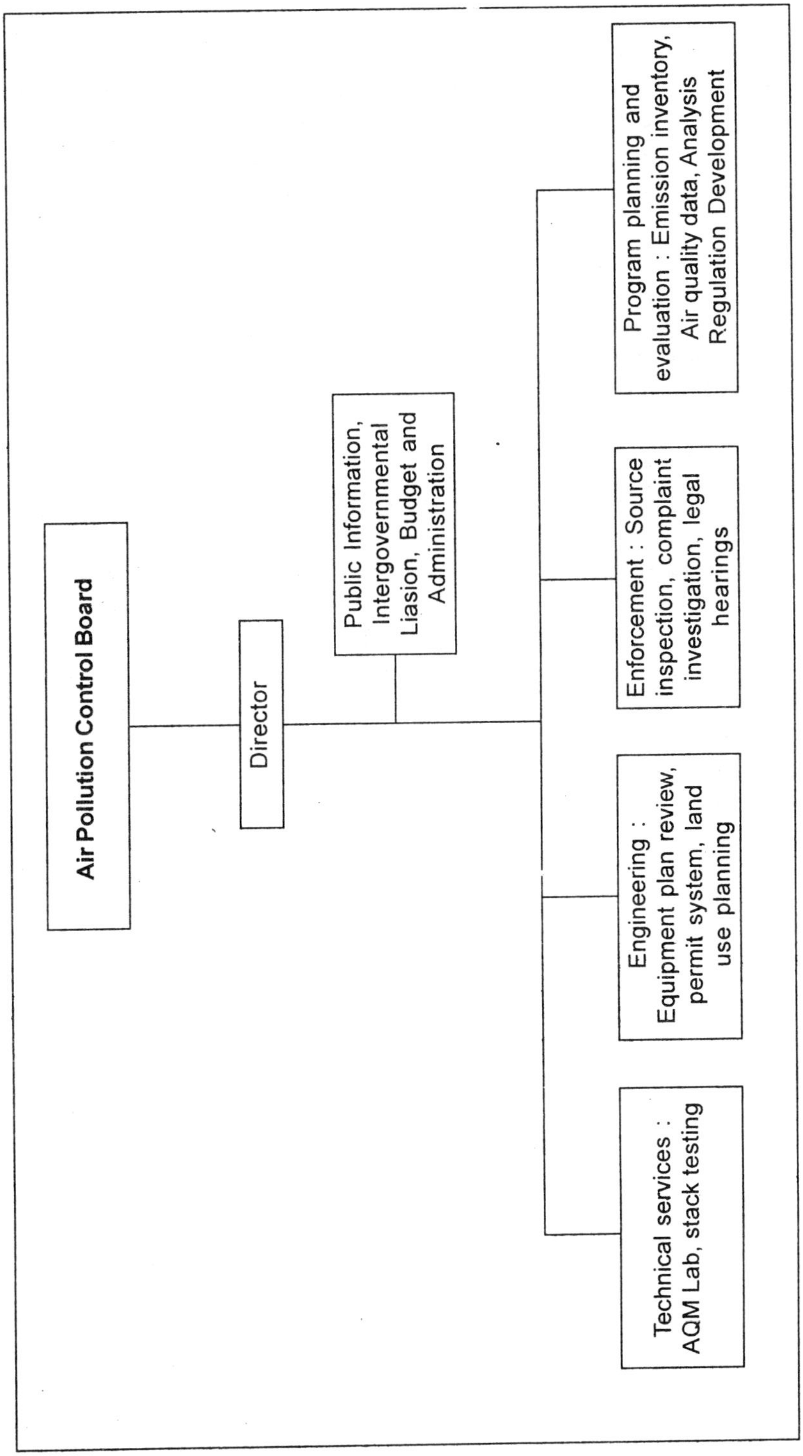

Fig. 18.2 A system of air quality management proposed by Dr. B.B. Sundaresan and A. Swaminathan.

Air quality management as a well defined programme has yet to emerge in India. Despite the collection of enormous air pollution data by various agencies and individual scientists, no effort has been made to construct proper air pollution inventories for most places. Fig. 18.1 gives a system of air quality management losely prevailing in India. All the aspects including the legal are looked after by Central and State Pollution Control Boards. The Central Pollution Control Board has formulated ambient and emission standards for air pollution, which have been adopted by State Boards with or without modifications depending upon the meteorology and local air quality achievement goals. The monitoring of vehicular pollution comes under the purview of Motor Vehicle Act and is looked after by Registration Authorities. State Boards carry out industrial monitoring for air emissions together with ambient air monitoring at selected places and are responsible for implementing the law. The data collected by other agencies like NEERI, Municipal Corporations, Research Organizations and individuals, though, may be of great academic significance, has no legal basis.

Dr. B.B. Sundaresan, former Director of NEERI, Nagpur and Dr. A. Swaminathan have proposed a system for air pollution management in India outlined in Fig. 18.2. However, in view of the constantly rising levels of air pollution and greatly increased industrial activity under liberalized economy, we need much more strengthened air quality management with continuous monitoring of air with automated equipment at all the required places. There is also an urgent need to study and analyse the data to make mathematical models to evaluate the long term trends so as to take proper preventive measures in advance before the situation becomes uncontrollable as happened earlier in many developed countries.

19 Air Pollution Legislation

19.1 Legislation in India

The constitution of India vide its Article 48-A provides for the pollution control and to protect and improve the environment in order to safeguard the human health, the forests and wildlife of the country. Though, the history of environmental enactments in India goes back to 1850s, a comprehensive legislation on air pollution covering the whole India appeared only recently with the coming in force of "The Air (Prevention and Control of Pollution) Act, 1981", from May 16, 1981. Under Article 253 of the Constitution of India, some of the provisions of the Act were subsequently modified in 1987, and the Act became II The Air (Prevention and Control of Pollution) Amendment Act, 1987. Besides, the Environment Protection Act, 1986 and the Motor Vehicle Act, 1988 also deal in part with the control of air pollution.

Following are the major legislations concerning Air Pollution in India.

1. Air (prevention and control of pollution) Act 1981.
2. Air (prevention and control of pollution) Rules 1981.
3. Noise pollution (Regulation and Control) Rules 2000.
4. Ozone depleting substances (Regulation and Control) Rules 2000.
5. The Environment Protection Act 1986.
6. Environment Protection Rules 1986.
7. The National Environment Tribunal Act 1995 (As related to Air Pollution).

8. The Air (Prevention and Control of Pollution) Amendment Act 1987.
9. Motor vehicles Act 1988.
10. Municipal solid wastes (Management and Handling) Rules 2000.
11. Air (Prevention and Control Pollution) Union Territories Rules 1983.

(Only the Air Prevention and Control Pollution Act 1981 alongwith the amendments is described here. For other acts Reader is referred to Trivedy, R.K. 2004).

Chapter-I : Preliminary (dealing with title, extent and definitions of terms) (Sections 1-2).

Chapter-II : Central and State Boards (Sections 3-15)

Chapter-III : Powers and Functions of Boards (Sections 16-18)

Chapter-IV : Prevention and Control of Air Pollution (Sections 19-31)

Chapter-V : Funds, Accounts and Audit (Sections 32-36)

Chapter-VI : Penalties and Procedure (Sections 37-46)

Chapter-VII : Miscellaneous (Sections 47-54)

Some of the important provisions of the above Act are as follows.

1. The Section 2 of the Act describes the definition of air pollutant as any solid liquid or gaseous substance present in the atmosphere injurious to human beings, living creatures or plant, property or environment. In the amended Act, the noise has also been included in the definition.
2. ***Applicability of the Act :*** The 1981 Act extends to whole of India and applies to only 20 air polluting industries, put under schedule of the Act, namely:
    - Asbestos and asbestos product industries
    - Cement and cement product industries
    - Ceramic and ceramic products industries
    - Chemical and allied industries
    - Coal and lignite based chemical industries
    - Engineering industries
    - Ferrous metallurgical industries
    - Fertilizer industries
    - Foundries
    - Food and agriculture products industries
    - Mining industries
    - Nonferrous metal metallurgical industries
    - Ores/mineral processing industries including benefication, pelletization, etc.
    - Power (coal, petroleum and their products) generating plants and boiler plants
    - Paper and pulp (including paper products industries)

- Textile processing industry (made wholly or in part of cotton)
- Petroleum refineries
- Petroleum products and petrochemical industries
- Plants for recovery from and disposal of wastes
- Incinerators

However, with the 1987 amendmend, the new amended Act applies to all the polluting industries instead of only these 20 industries.

3. ***Set-up of Central and State Pollution Control Boards :*** The Govt. under the Section 3 of the Water (Prevention and Control of Pollution) Act, 1974, constituted the Central and State Boards for prevention and control of water pollution. It was decided that no separate Board for Air Pollution Control shall be constituted, but the already existing Boards would exercise the powers and perform the functions of the Boards for the prevention and control of air pollution under the Air Pollution Act, 1981. These Boards are now called Central and State Pollution Control Boards according to the 1987 amendment.

Functions of Central Boards : The main functions of the Central Board are following.

- To improve the quality of air and to prevent, control or abate air pollution in the country.
- To advise the Central Govt. on any matter concerning the improvement of the quality of air and the prevention, control or abatement of air pollution.
- To plan and cause ,to be executed a nationwide programme for the prevention, control or abatement of air pollution.
- To coordinate the activities of the State Boards and resolve disputes among them.
- To provide technical assistance and guidance to the State Boards, carry out and sponsor investigations and research relating to problems of air pollution and prevention, control or abatement of air pollution.
- To plan and organize the training of persons engaged or to be engaged in programmes for the prevention, control or abatement of air pollution on such terms and conditions as the Central Board may specify.
- To organize through mass media comprehensive programme regarding the prevention, control or abatement of air pollution.
- To collect, compile and publish technical and statistical data relating to air pollution and the measures devised for its effective prevention, control or abatement, and prepare manuals, codes or guides relating to prevention, control or abatement of air pollution.
- To lay down standards for quality of air.
- Collect and disseminate information in respect of matters relating to air pollution.
- To establish or recognise laboratories.

Functions of State Boards : The important functions of the State Boards are outlined below.

- To plan a comprehensive programme for the prevention, control or abatement of air pollution and to secure its implementation.
- To advise the State Govt. on any matter concerning the prevention, control or abatement of air pollution.
- To collect and disseminate information relating to air pollution.
- To collaborate with the Central Board in organizing the programmes of training and mass education relating to abatement of air pollution.
- To inspect industrial plants, processes and control equipment and to give directions to such persons as may be necessary to take steps for controlling the air pollution.
- To inspect air pollution control areas for the air quality therein and take steps for the air pollution control.
- To lay down, in consultation with Central Board, the standards for emission of air pollutants into the atmosphere from industrial plants, automobiles or any outer source except ship and aircraft.
- To advise State Govt. with regard to the suitability of the location of industry.
- To establish and recognize laboratories for enabling it to perform its functions efficiently.

4. As per Section 38, a penalty for doing certain acts can be imposed in the form of a fine of Rs. 1000 or imprisonment upto 3 months or both. Some of the acts laid down in this section which attract this penalty are :

   - Destroying, pulling down, removing, injuring or defacing any pillar, post or stake fixed in the ground or any notice or other matter put up, inscribed or placed by or under the authority of the Board.
   - Obstructing any person acting under the orders or directions of the Board from exercising his powers and performing his functions.
   - Damaging any works or property belonging to the Board.
   - Failing to furnish to the Board or any offices or other employee of the Board any information required by the Board or such offices or other employee for the purpose of this Act.
   - Failling to intimate the occurrence of the emission of air pollutants into the atmosphere in excess of the standards laid down by the State Board or the apprehension of such occurrence to the State Board and other prescribed authorities or agencies.
   - Giving any information which a person is required to give under this Act, makes statement which is false in any material particular.
   - For the purpose of obtaining any consent under Section 21, makes a statement which is false in any material particular.

5. As per Section 39, whoever contravenes any of the provisions of this Act or any order on direction issued under, for which no penalty has been provided elsewhere in this Act, shall be punishable with imprisonment for a term which may extend to three months or with fine upto Rs. 10.000 or both. In case of continuing contravention, an additional fine upto Rs. 5000 can be imposed for every day during which such contravention continues after conviction for the first such contravention.
6. As per the amended Act, Central Govt. can direct Central Board to perform the function of State Board in case of State Pollution Control Boards default in complying with the directives of the Central Board and grave emergency arises due to such failure.
7. For controlling air pollution from automobiles, as per Section 20 of the Act, a State Govt. shall in consultation with the State Board, give instructions to the concerned authority in charge of registration under Motor Vehicles Act (1939) to ensure that the automobile emission standards prescribed by the State Board, are complied with.

19.2 Legislation in Other Countries

19.2.1 *U.S.A.*

The history of air pollution legislation in the U.S.A. is not old, which started with the promulgation of smoke control laws in the major cities by the local authorities in the beginning of this century.

In U.S.A. all the three local, State and Federal agencies are involved in the National programme of pollution control with framing of their own laws. The earlier laws in the history of the U.S. legislation were framed and promulagated by local authorities of several major cities to control the nuisance of smoke. By 1912, 23 cities out of 28 having population of more than 20,000 promulagted these smoke control laws which were found to be quite effective in eliminating or preventing serious smoke problems. The first State Law, specifically directed at air pollution control, was passed by the State of California in 1947 which developed out of the concern about the photochemical smog problem in Los Angeles basin. In the following years, several other states, taking the precedent from California, adopted specific air pollution control legislation.

The major federal role in controlling air pollution started in 1955 with the passing of "Air Pollution Control Research and Technical Assistance Act, 1955". The Act authorized Public Health Service of the Department of Health, Education and Welfare in cooperation with other agencies to recommend research programmes for controlling air pollution and providing technical assistance to the States. In the coming years, the federal role expanded considerably and several Acts, directed towards controlling air pollution, were passed. Some important federal Acts are given below.

- Air Pollution Control Research and Technical Assistance Act, 1955.
- Extension of 1955 Act, 1959.
- Clean Air Act, 1963.
- Motor Vehicle Air Pollution Control Act, 1969.
- Clean Air Act Amendments, 1966.
- Air Quality Act, 1967.
- National Environmental Policy Act, 1969.
- Environmental Quality Improvement Act, 1970.
- Clean Air Act Amendments, 1970.

The most important law defining the federal programme is the Clean Air Act, 1963 and its amendments of 1967 and 1970. The Act has three titles incorporating 52 Sections.

Title I : Air pollution prevention and control (18 Sections)

Title II : Emission Standards for moving sources

Part A : Motor vehicle emission and fuel standards (13 Sections)

Part B : Aircraft emission standards (4 Sections)

Title III : General (17 Sections)

19.2.2 *United Kingdom*

The oldest legislation in the history of air pollution control was provided as early as 1300 by King Edward-I in this country as described in Chapter 1. Later on several laws by different Kings and authorities were passed mainly to control the nuisance of smoke, but the comprehensive Act on air pollution was passed by the British Parliament only in 1956. called Clean Air Act. after the disastrous episode of London smog in 1952 which left more than 4000 people dead. The Act provides the declaration of certain areas as smoke control areas where only specific approved appliances and fuels can be used. The Act also deals with the specification of smoke emission standards, dust emissions and height of stacks. Under the British Motor Vehicles (Construction & Use) Regulations (1973), it is required that no motor vehicle should emit avoidable smoke or visible vapour.

20 Environmental Criteria for Siting of Industries and Green Belts

Industries cause the environmental effects by release of air pollutants, water pollutants and solid waste material. Besides, they may also affect the environment and neighbouring people by accidents such as leaks, explosions and fires. Bhopal gas leak and Chernobyl nuclear power plant are two well known examples of industrial accidents of recent past. The installation of control and safety equipment may not alone be helpful, but proper location of the industry is also necessary to prevent any significant damage to the surrounding environment and its ecological features! and urban population.

There are a number of industries which are potentially harmful in causing environmental degradation. Twenty industrial groups have been identified by Department of Industrial Development of India (Table 20.1). These are required to follow the specific guidelines with regard to their siting. Some of the areas with specific land uses, and some natural life-sustaining systems are extremely sensitive to pollution and require a safe distance from the pollution causing industry. Meteorological and micrometeorological considerations are also important for siting an industry as under certain weather conditions the air pollutants tend to accumulate in the atmosphere and are finally brought to the ground level.

Table 20.1 List of Polluting industries required to obtain environmental clearance for siting (After Department of Environment working group report 1986)

1.	Primary metallurgical producing industries viz. zinc. Lead, copper, aluminium and steel
2.	Paper, pulp and newsprint
3.	Pesticides/insecticides
4.	Refineries
5.	Fertilizers
6.	Paints
7.	Dyes
8.	Leather tanning
9.	Rayon
10.	Sodium/potassium cyanide
11.	Basic drugs
12.	Foundry
13.	Storage batteries (lead acid type)
14.	Acids/alkalies
15.	Elastics
16.	Rubrer-synthetic
17.	Cement
18.	Asbestos
19.	Fermentation industry
20.	Electroplating industry

(The list is now expanded to 30, please refer Trivedy, 2004).

20.1 Distance Considerations

The recommendations made by the National Symposium on Industrial Location, Urban Planning and the Environment organized by SOCLEEN (Society for Clean Environment, Bombay) in 1985, and the Department of Environment Working Group Report (1986) with regard to the distance between industry and surrounding areas are as follows.

1. There should be a distance of at least 25 km between pollution causing industry and the ecologically or otherwise sensitive areas. The areas indentified under this category are presented in Table 20.2.
2. The distance between industries and high-tide line of coastal areas should be at least 500 m.
3. Industry should be at least 500 m away from flood plain of the riverine system or modified flood plain affected by dam in the upstream or by flood control systems.
4. Industry should be at least 500 m away from the Highway and 2 km from the railway.
5. Various distances from 5 km to 50 km should be maintained between the population centres (population 3,00,000 or more) and the industry based on the toxicity of pollutants released from the industry. An exclusive zone of 1 km radius free from habitation and a "sterilized" zone of 5 km radius should be left.

Table 20.2 Ecological and otherwise sensitive areas to be protected from pollution (After Department of Environment working group report 1986)

1.	Religious and Historic places
2.	Archeological monuments
3.	Scenic areas
4.	Hill resorts
5.	Beach resorts
6.	Health resorts
7.	Coastal areas rich in corals. mangroves
8.	Estuaries rich in mangroves, breeding ground of specific species
9.	Gulf areas
10.	Biosphere reserves
11.	National parks and sanctuaries
12.	Natural lakes, swamps
13.	Seismic zones
14.	Tribal settlements
15.	Areas of scientific and geological interest
16.	Defence installations, specially those of security importance and sensitive to pollution a
17.	Border Areas (International)
18.	Air Ports

In the selected area for siting the industry, following criteria should also be observed.

1. For sustaining the industry no forest area should be converted into non-forest activity.
2. No prime agricultural land should be used for siting the industry.
3. In the selected site, industry should be at the lowest level so as to be away from the general sight.
4. Sufficient land should be acquired by the industry to accommodate sites for waste treatment plant. The treated water should be used for raising green belt, creating waterbody for aesthetics or aquaculture (if suitable). For the odorous industry, the thickness of the green belt should be atleast of 1 km.
5. Green belt should be provided between two adjacent industries.
6. Adequate space should be provided for storing solid wastes.
7. Industry lay out should be such that it should not affect the scenic features of the landscape.

   Associated township of the industry should have a physiographic barrier between it and the industry.

A tentative classification of industries (Table 20.3) in relation to air pollution and siting is provided by Maas (1976). It is based mainly on the basis of the severity of the effects of industry on the human population. Adequate buffer zones of various thickness are recommended for the different groups of the industry. These buffer zones are to be provided with green belts which are helpful in controlling the environment.

Table 20.3 Classification of industries with regard to their siting and thickness and type of green belts (After Maas, 1976).

Type	Industry	Examples	Situation & distance to town centre of housing areas	Nuisance produced			Buffer zone	
				Air pollution	Noise	Hazards	Type	Width
1.	Heavy Industry	Oil refineries chemical works, metal-lurgical & seaport indus-tries, Nuclear reactors	Outside the Urban area (>3200 m)	SO_2, H_2S, H_2SO_4, HF, NH_3	Moderate	Explosion and fire risk	forests to produce an economic yield, isolation greenary	> 2 km
2.	Heavy Industry	Machine manufacture, ship-building, Big-harbour-industries, power stations	Outside the Urban area (1600-3200 m)	CO, SO_2	May be considerable, includes traffic noise	Explosion and fire risk	As above but including parks and sport fields	1 km
3A.	Medium-heavy industry with much air pollution	Manufacture of straw-board, artifical fibres ceramics, cement works	Urban area (1600-3200 m)	Not very much (SO_2, HF, dust) but may include malodorous emissions	Considerable traffic noise	Fire risk	Screening parkland	500 m or more
3B.	Medium-heavy industry with little air pollution	Manufacture of cars, lamps, foods, textiles	Urban area (1600 m)	As in 3A	As in 3A	As in 3A	As in 3A	200 m or more

Table 20.3 *Contd.....*

Type	Industry	Examples	Situation & distance to town centre of housing areas	Nuisance produced			Buffer zone	
				Air pollution	Noise	Hazards	Type	Width
4.A	Light industry with small air pollution	Tannaries, textile and food industries	Near Town in fringe areas (400-1600 m)	not very much but may include malodorous emissions	Moderate	Fire risk	Screening plants (mainly for 4 m) trees of a decorative nature for screening parkland	50-100 m
4.B	Light industry with little air pollution	Manufacture of electronic apparatus and domestic machines	As in 4A	As in 4A	As in 4A	As in 4A	As in 4A	As in 4A
5.	Service Industry	Printing works bakeries, film laboraties	Near Town (< 800 m)	Little	Little	none	Decorative plants parkland	< 100 m
6.	Workshops handicrafts etc	Fashion studios, photo-printing shops, potteries	Near Town (<400 m)	None	Little	none	Decorative plants	< 50 m

20.2 Meteorological Considerations

Meteorological conditions are very important in regulating the transport, dispersion and fate of air pollutants in the atmosphere. The stable atmospheric layers with frequent inversions are the meteorological conditions which help accumulation of pollutants in a localized area. On the other hand, atmospheric instability and turbulence promote greater dispersal of pollutants, thus keeping the air clean.

Based on the meteorology, Ashar (1985) divided the whole India into various pollutability zones as shown in Fig. 20.1. The figure indicates that the northern part of India has relatively stable layers of the atmosphere for several days during major part of the year. On the other hand, the zones in south India have considerably low frequency of stable layers. The central India and other parts have variable frequency of stable layers. For highly polluting industries, a site in the zones of frequent unstable layers shall be most appropriate for preventing the accumulation of air pollutants in atmosphere.

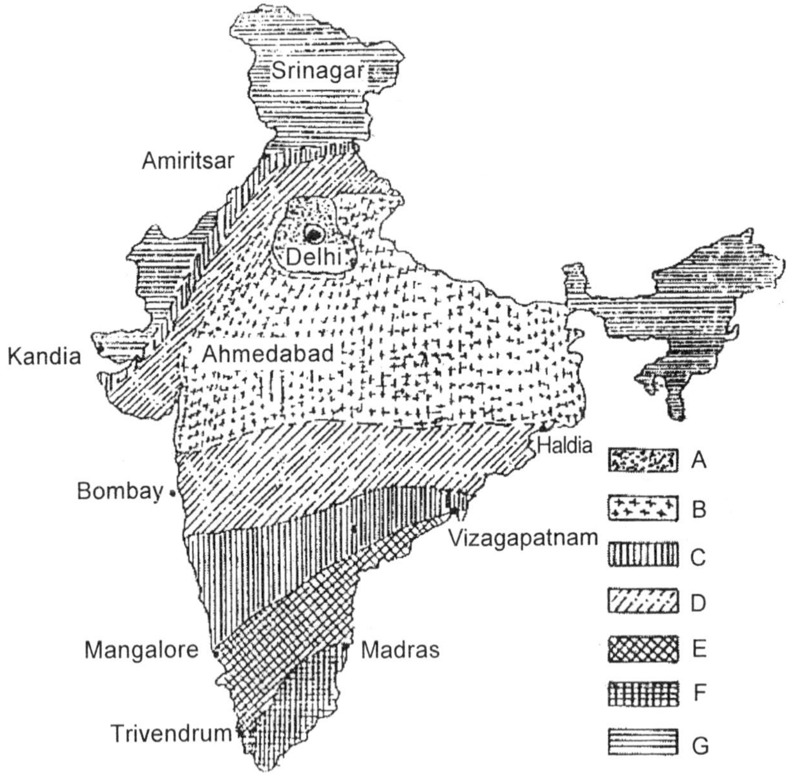

Fig. 20.1 Pollutability zones in India based on air stagnation periods. (A) Stable layer persisting beyond 24 hrs except for monsoon, (B) Stable layer persisting beyond 24 hrs primarily during winter, (D) Area of Moderate stability, (E) Continuous air change at least once a day, (F) Frequency of stable layers is very low, (G) Not adequate data is available and terrain is uneven.

However, an industry cannot be located alone on the consideration of macro-climatic data as the micrometeorological features may be more influential in deciding the fate of pollutants in a particular area. For example, the direction and velocity of the local winds and topography may be more important factors in deciding whether the air pollutants shall accumulate in the atmosphere near the ground level or shall be dispersed away. Residential areas should not be allowed to develop downwind of the industries to avoid a direct transport of pollutants to the population.

20.3 Green Belts

The green areas or the parks in urban areas not only determine the structure and provide aesthetic value, but are also important in controlling the atmospheric pollution. The plants absorb the gaseous pollutants such as oxides of sulphur and nitrogen besides many others, directly from the air. The trees provide roughness to the surface, which promote turbulence in air. The increased turbulence prevents accumulation of pollutants in atmosphere by allowing greater dispersal and dilution. The green areas also stimulate the sedimentation of aerosols and dust present in the air.

Green areas also reduce the noise from industries as they interrupt the sound and shock waves. Accidental fires and explosives can also be isolated by the green belts. Plants are also useful in providing oxygen and water vapours to the atmosphere.

Microclimate is greatly influenced by the presence of green areas. Green areas and parks are normally cooler than the surrounding areas. If the green belts are arranged radially in an urban area, it will promote the flow of cooler fresh air from the surrounding countryside along the green belts, with the rise of urban air due to the heat island effect. This will result in the presence of fresh, cleaner and cooler air in the green areas. The green areas, thus, are different from the other areas with regard to temperature, moisture and wind. The effect of green areas increases with the increase in width and variability in its components. For example, a green area my be more effective in controlling the environment, if it consists of a variety of plants in different layers (such as trees of various heights and shrubs), clumps of trees, open spaces and small water ponds etc. Green areas if provided in buffer zones between industries and residential areas, may be very useful in controlling atmospheric pollution and protecting the health of people. These areas can also be developed in the form of parks of recreational value.

Hill (1977) has reported about considerable uptake of sulphur dioxide and nitrogen dioxide by alfalfa plant: It has been estimated that a continuous cover of assimilating alfalfa canopy under certain conditions could remove more than 1/4 ton of NO_2 or SO_2 per square mile per day from air containing an average NO_2 concentration of 6pphm or to the mean SO_2 concentration measured over a 200 square mile area of 1-3 pphm (Thakre 1994). Das (1981) and Das et al. (1981) have carried out dust collection efficiencies of various trees. They found that evergreen trees with simple leaves having rough and hairy surface, are relatively better dust collectors as compared to deciduous trees. *Ficus, Mangifera, Tectona* and *Polyanthia* have been reported to be efficient dust collectors (Varshney 1992). Many authors have reported *Solanum melongena* and *Cyamopsis tetragonoloba* to be efficient remover of SO_2.

According to Thakre (1994) HF, SO_2, NO_2, O_3 and Cl_2 can be effectively absorbed by the vegetation. PAN is absorbed to a lesser extent while CO and NO are not effectively absorbed.

The establishment of green belt helps in attenuation of air and noise pollution. It comes to the immediate rescue during accidental release/explosion minimizing the risk to considerable extent. Green belts can also serve as soil protection measure and are well known as 'shelter belts' in abating soil erosion. Green enhance aesthetic value of the area and can take-up waste water for its growth, thus, solving the problem of water pollution to some extent.

According to Thakre (1992) prime consideration for recommending GB plantation schemes are;

1. Nature of pollutant
2. Emission level height and source strength
3. Maximum impact zone
4. Selection of appropriate plant species. The plants should be fast growing with thick canopy cover perennial and evergreen and having large Leaf Area Index (LAI) as well as resistant to the pollutants.

Some general guidelines provided by Thakre (1994) for green belts are:

1. Tall trees with height more than 10 meters should be planted around the source.
2. Planting of trees should be in appropriate encircling rows, each row alternating the previous one to prevent further fanning and horizontal pollution dispersion.
3. Since tree trunks are normally devoid of foliage, it would be appropriate to have small shrubs in front and in between the tree species.

Netherlands has been a prime country in this field. Following is the green belt criteria followed in Netherlands.

Class	Industry	Width of GB (m)
I	Heavy industry with high potential of air pollution	> 500
II	Heavy industry with low potential of air pollution	200 to 500
III	A. Medium heavy industry with high potential of air pollution	100 to 200
	B. Medium heavy industry with low potential of air pollution	100 to 200
IV	A. Light industry with high potential of air pollution	50 to 100
	B. Light industry with low potential of air pollution 50 to 100	
V	Service industry	10 to 50
VI	Workshops, handicrafts, etc.	< 10

Appendixes

I. National Ambient Air Quality Standards (NAAQS) for India (in µg/m^3).

	K – Concentration in ambient air			
Pollutant and time-weighted average	**Industrial area**	**Residential, rural, and other areas**	**Sensitive area**	**Methods of measurement**
Sulphur dioxide				Improved West and
Annual average	80.00	60.00	15.00	Gaeke method
24 hours	120.00	80.00	30.00	Ultraviolet fluorescence
Oxides of nitrogen				Jacob and Hochheiser
Annual average	80.00	60.00	15.00	modified (Na-Arsenite) method
24 hours	120.00	80.00	30.00	Gas-phase chemiluminescene
Suspended particulate matter				
Annual average	360.00	140.00	70.00	High-volume sampling (average flow rate not less
24 hours	500.00	200.00	100.00	than 1.1 m^3 per minute)

I. *Contd...*

(in $\mu g/m^3$)

Pollutant and time-weighted average	K – Concentration in ambient air: Industrial area	Residential, rural, and other areas	Sensitive area	Methods of measurement
Respirable particulate matter (size less than 10 µgm)				
Annual average	120.00	60.00	50.00	Respirable particulate matter sampler
24 hours	150.00	100.00	75.00	
Lead				
Annual average	1.00	0.75	0.50	Atomic absorption spectrometr after sampling using
24 hours	1.50	1.00	0.75	EPM 2000 or an equivalent filter paper
Carbon monoxide				Non-dispersive infrared spectroscopy
8 hours	5.0[a]	2.00[a]	1.00[a]	
1 hour	10.0[a]	4.00[a]	2.00[a]	
Ammonia				
Annual average	-	400.00[a]	-	-
24 hours	-	100.00[a]	-	-

Notes :

1. Annual average is annual arithmetic mean of minimum 104 measurement in a year taken twice a week at 24-hourly intervals.
2. 24-hourly and 8-hourly values should be met 98 per cent of the time in a year. However, 2 per cent of the time, it may exceed but not on two consecutive days.
3. NMQS, the levels of air quality necessary with an adequate margin of safety to protect public health, vegetation, and property.
4. Whenever and wherever two consecutive values exceed the limit specified above for the respective category, it would be considered adequate reason to institute regular/continuous monitoring and further investigations.
5. The state government/state board shall notify the sensitive and other areas in the respective states within a peroid of six months from the date of notification of NAAQS.
6. Standard for ammonia specified vide notification dated 14" October 1998. It does not mention the type of areas for its applicability nor the method of measurement is being specified.
7. $\mu g/m^3$

Sources :

1. Central Pollution Control Board, Ministry of Environment and Forests
2. CII. 1999. *Environmental Legislation in India.* A Guide for Industry and Business New Delhi : Environment Managetnent Division, Confederation of Indian Industry.

II Maximum permissible limits ($\mu g/m^3$) of pollutants in the air set by the WHO

Pollutant	Time-weighted average	Averaging time
Sulphur dioxide (WHO:1979,1987)	500	10 minutes
	350	1 hour
	100 to 150[a]	24 hours
	40 to 60[a]	1 year
Carbon monoxide	30	1 hour
	10	8 hours
Nitrogen dioxide (WHO 1987, 1977)	400	1 hour
	150	24 hours
Ozone (WHO 1987, 1978)	150 to 200	1 hour
	100 to 120	8 hours
Total SPM (Suspended Particulate Matter)	**150 to 230[a]**	24 hours
	60 to 90[a]	1 hour

Note : [a] guideline values for combined exposure to sulphur dioxide and SPM (they may not apply to situations where only one of the components is present).

Source : 'WHO/UNEP, 1992. *Urban Air Pollution in Megacities of the World. Washington, DC : World Health Organisation and United Nations Environment Programme*

III Emission norms for petrol-driven vehicles, with reference to catalytic converters

(In g/km)

Pollutant	Emmission standards for petro-driven four wheelers	
	Without catalytic converter	With catalytic converter
Carbon monoxide	8.68-12.40	4.36-6.20
Hydrocarbons + oxides of nitrogen	3.00-4.36	1.50-2.18
Total (carbon monoxide + hydrocarbon + oxides of nitrogen)	**11.68-16.7**	**5.84-8.38**

Source : *MoEF (1998)*

IV Emission limits for petrol-driven vehicles (Idling Condition)

(In per cent)

Parameter	Type of vehicle	Limit (by volume)
Carbon monoxide	Four-wheelers	3.0
	Two and three-wheelers	4.5

Source : *CPCB 1998. Pollution Control Acts, Rules, and Notifications issued hereunder. Volume I. p. 314*
New Delhi : *Chennai Pollution Control Board, Ministry of Environment and Forests. 501 pp*

V Mass emission standards for petrol-driven vehicles

(in g/km)

	1 April 1991	1 April 1996		1 April 2000	1 April 2005
		Without catalytic converter	With catalytic converter	Euro I Norm	Euro I Norm
Four-wheelers-passenger vehicle					
Carbon monoxide	14.3-27.1	8.68-12.40	4.34-6.20	2.72	2.2
Hydrocarbon	2.0-2.9	-	-	-	-
Hydrocarbon and oxides of nitrogen	-	3.00-4.36	1.50-2.18	0.97	0.5
	1 April 1991	1 April 1996 Indian driving cycle with warm start	1 April 1998 Indian driving cycle with cold start	1 April 2000 Indian driving cycle with cold start	
Two-wheelers					
Carbon monoxide	12.0-30.0	4.5	4.5	2.0	
Hydrocarbon	8.0-12.0	-	-	-	
Hydrocarbon and oxides of nitrogen		3.6	3.6	2.0	
	1 April 1991	1 April 1996 Indian driving cycle with warm start	1 April 1998 Indian driving cycle with cold start	1 April 2000 Indian driving cycle with cold start	
Three-wheelers					
Carbon monoxide	12.0-30.0	6.75	6.75	4.0	
Hydrocarbon	8.0-12.0	-	-	-	
Hydrocarbon and oxides of nitrogen	-	5.40	5.40	2.0	

Source : *AIAM. 1999. Fuel and Vehicular Technology, New Delhi :*

VI Emission limits for diesel vehicles

Method of test	Light absorption coefficient (millilitre)	Maximum smoke density	
		Bosch units	Hartridge units
Full load at a speed of 60-70 per cent of maximum engine-rated speed specified by the manufacturer	3.1	5.2	75.0
Free acceleration	2.3	-	65.0

Source : CPCB 1998. *Pollution Control Acts, Rules, and Notifications issued thereunder.* Volume I.p.314. *New Delhi :* Chennai Pollution Control Board, Ministry of Environment and Forests. 501 pp.

VII Mass emission standards for diesel-driven vehicles (In g/kWh)

	1 April 1992	1 April 1996	1 April 2000	Euro II	Euro III
Gross vehicle weight > 3.5 tonnes					
Carbon monoxide	14.00	11.20	4.50	4.00	2.00
Hydrocarbon	3.50	2.40	1.10	1.10	0.60
Oxides of nitrogen	18.00	14.40	8.00	7.00	5.00
Particulate matter for > 85 kW	0.00	0.00	0.36	0.15	0.10
Particulate matter for < 85 kW	0.00	0.00	0.61	0.15	0.10

	1 April 1992 (g/kWh)	1 April 1996 (g/km)	1 April 2000 (g/km)
Gross vehicle weight < 3.5 tonnes			
Carbon monoxide	14.00	5.0-9.0	2.72-6.90
Hydrocarbon	3.50	-	-
Oxides of nitrogen	18.00	2.4-4.0	0.97-1.70
Particulate matter	0.00	-	0.14-0.25

Source : AIAM 1999. *Fuel and Vehicular Technology,* New Delhi: Association of Indian Automobile Manufacturers

VIII Emission factors from cooking stoves for various fuel-stove combinations

(In g/kg)

Fuel a pollutant	Conventional metal	Improved metal	Improved mud
Total suspended particulates			
Fuel wood	1.3-2.7	1.1-3.8	1.8-2.1
Crop residues	2.1-5.0	2.1-2.0	3.5
Dung cakes	4.1-5.3	4.2-7.8	7.4
Carbon monoxide			
Fuelwood	13.0-22.0	25.0-62.0	32.0-48.0
Crop residues	20.0-39.0	23.0-114.0	48.0
Dung cakes	11.0-16.0	34.0-67.0	46.0

Source: Ahuja D R .et al. 1987. *Environmental performance of cookstoves in regard to thermal efficiency and emissions from combustion.* Submitted to the Ministry of Enviroment and Forests, New Delhi : Tata Energy Research Institute. 131pp.

IX Maximum permissible limits for emissions of particulate matter from thermal power stations

(In mg/m^3)

Boiler size	Maximum permissible limits: Protected areas	Maximum permissible limits: Other areas
Less than 210 MW	150.00	350.00
210 MW or more	150.00	150.00

Source : CPCB 1998. *Pollution Acts, Rules, and Notifications issued thereunder.* Ministry of Environment and Forests. 501 pp.

X Maximum permissible limits for emissions from integrated iron and steel plants

(In mg/m^3)

Pollutant and sources	Emission limit
Particulate matter	
Sintering plant	150.00
Coke oven	50.00
Steel making	-
During normal operation	150.00
During oxygen lancing	400.00
Carbon monoxide	
Coke oven (kg per ton of coke produced)	3.00

Source: CPCB 1998. *Pollution Acts, Rules, and Notifications issued thereunder.* Volume l. p.279. Ministry of Environment and Forests, 501 pp.

XI Maximum permissible limits for emissions of particulate matter from cement plants

(In mg/m^3)

Capacity	Maximum permissible limits	
	Protected areas	Other areas
200 TPD	250	400
Greater than 200 TPD	150	250

Note TPD -tons per day.

Source: CPCB 1998. *Pollution Acts, Rules, and Notifications issued thereunder.* Volume l. p.280. Ministry of Environment and Forests. 501 pp.

XII Maximum permissible limits for emissions from fertiliser plants

(In mg/m^3)

Product	Pollutant	Emission limit
Urea		
Pricing tower	Particulates	50.00
Phosphatic fertiliser		
Acidification of rock phosphate	Fluorides	25.00
Granulation, mixing and grinding of rock phosphate	Particulates	150.00

Source : CPCB *Pollution Acts, Rules, and Notifications issued thereunder,* Volume I. p. 278. Ministry of Environment and Forests. 501 pp.

XIII Maximum permissible limits for emissions of sulphur dioxide from oil refineries

(In kg per feed[a])

Process	Emission limit
Atmospheric and vacuum distillation	0.25
Catalytic cracker	2.50
Sulphur recovery unit	120.00 ,

Note: Indicates the feed for the specific part of the process under consideration.

Source: CPCB 1998. P*ollution Acts. Rules, and Notifications issued thereunder.* Volume I.p.284, Ministry of Environment and Forests. 501 pp.

XIV Maximum permissible limits for emissions of particulate matter from calcium carbide plants (In mg/m^3)

Source	Emission limit
Kiln	250.00
Arc furnace	150.00

Source : CPCB 1998. *Pollution Acts, Rules, and Notifications issued thereunder.* Volume I.p.278., Ministry of Environment and Forests. 501 pp.

XV Maximum permissible limits emissions from copper, lead, and zinc smelting units

(In mg/m^3)

Pollutant	Source	Emission limit
Particulate matter	Concentrator	150 mg/m^3
Oxides is sulphur	Smelter and converter	4 kg per ton of concentrated (100 per cent) acid produced

Note : Off-gases must be utilised fur sulphuric acid manufacturing.

Source : CPCB 1998. *Pollution Acts, Rulcs, and Notifications issued thereunder.* Volume 1.p.279., Ministry of Environment and Forests. 501 pp.

XVI Maximum permissible limits for emissions of particulates from carbon black industry

(In mg/m^3)

Pollutant	Emission limit
Particulate matter	150.00

Source : CPCB 1998. *Pollution Acts, Rules, and Notifications issued thereunder.* Volume I.p.279. New Delhi : Central Pollution Control Board, Ministry of Emvironment and Forests. 501 pp.

XVII Maximum permiss le limits for emissions of particulates matter from Aluminium Industry

(In mg/m^3)

Process	Emission limit
Calcination	250.00
Smelting	150.00

Source : CPCB 1998. *Polltion Acts, Rules and Notifications issued thereunder.* Volume I.p. 278., Ministry of Environment and Forests. 501 pp.

XVIII Guidelines for minimum stack heights (In meters).

Power generation capacity		**Stack height**
Less than 200/210 MW		– a
200/210 and above to less than 500 MW		220.00
500 MW and above		275.00
Steam-generating capacities of boilers (tons per hour)		
less than	2	– b
more than	2 to 5	12.00
	5 to 10	15.00
more than	10	18.00
	15 to 20	21.00
	20 to 25	24.00
	25 to 30	27.00
more than	30	– a

Note : (a) using formula $H = 14\ Q^{0.8}$, whichever is more, where Q is the emission rate of sulphur dioxide in kg/h and H is the stack height.

(b) 2.5 times the height of the neighbouring building or 9 m whichever is more.

Source : CPCB 1998. *Pollution Acts, Rules, and Notifications issued thereunder.* Volume I.p.283., Ministry of Environment and Forests. 501 pp.

XIX Ambient air quality levels in highly polluted cities : 1997

(In $\mu g/m^3$)

State/Union territory	Sulphur dioxide		Oxides of nitrogen		Suspended particulate matter	
	Industrial	Residential	Industrial	Residential	Industrial	Residential
Andhra Pradesh						
Hyderabad	53.8	44.8	97.7	86.5	459.0	405.0
Vishakhapatnam	26.4	67.3	40.3	136.3	159.0	592.0
Bihar						
Dhanbad	-	37.3	-	47.5	-	181.0
Jharia	45.0	-	57.0	-	408.0	-
Patna	-	41.9	-	49.3	-	832.0
Sindri	41.0	-	54.4	-	212.0	-
Delhi	90.8	56.3	172.4	134.0	1689.0	1399.0
Gujarat						
Ahmedabad	7.6	52.9	13.3	66.5	219.0	722.0
Ankleshwar	27.2	35.7	17.9	27.9	169.0	976.0
Surat	-	54.9	-	17.5	-	412.0
Vadodara	36.3	80.3	9.0	26.5	285.0	595.0
Vapi	-	32.4	-	40.0	-	321.0
Goa						
Ponda	-	11.2	-	20.5	-	123.0
Vasco	9.7	-	18.1	-	94.0	-
Himachal Pradesh						
Damtal	-	6.3	-	10.4	-	100.0
Parwanoo	6.1	6.8	13.8	14.2	132.0	118.0
Shimla	-	6.4	-	17.9	-	97.0

XIX *Contd....*

State/Union territory	Sulphur dioxide		Oxides of nitrogen		Suspended particulate matter	
	Industrial	Residential	Industrial	Residential	Industrial	Residential
Haryana						
Faridabad	37.8	-	14.6	-	405.0	-
Yamuna Nagar	27.8	-	17.9	-	143.0	-
Karnataka						
Bangalore	53.4	30.3	37.3	22.1	304.0	222.0
Mysore	64.7	-	59.7	-	212.0	-
Kerala						
Kochi	31.5	14.6	41.4	35.6	340.0	225.0
Thiruvananthapuram	25.5	24.8	23.1	45.1	180.0	269.0
Kottayam	6.2	6.1	28.8	19.1	95.0	44.0
Kozhikode	-	12.6	-	17.1	-	152.0
Maharashtra						
Mumbai	36.0	39.2	35.9	67.1	240.0	653.0
Nagpur	20.7	30.9	38.5	71.3	254.0	611.0
Pune	111.8	50.3	126.1	60.4	698.0	204.0
Madhya Pradesh						
Bhilai	33.1	31.1	37.4	68.4	223.0	276.0
Bhopal	17.3	31.7	28.9	49.7	300.0	467.0
Indore	7.3	14.4	10.2	19.9	232.0	408.0
Jabalpur	-	6.0	-	11.9	-	77.0
Korba	-	30.2	-	40.8	-	279.0
Nagda	81.8	116.3	26.4	86.8	109.0	285.0
Raipur	9.1	8.4	27.4	24.4	183.0	156.0
Satna	14.6	11.9	16.5	13.3	205.0	146.0

XIX *Contd....*

State/Union territory	Sulphur dioxide		Oxides of nitrogen		Suspended particulate matter	
	Industrial	Residential	Industrial	Residential	Industrial	Residential
Orissa						
Angul	12.7	20.9	9.8	21.4	97.0	106.0
Rourkela	54.0	-	45.3	-	314.0	-
Punjab						
Jalandhar	-	46.0	-	77.4	-	399.0
Ludhiana	40.5	18.4	92.6	42.8	651.0	245.0
Rajasthan						
Alwar	13.6	26.8	78.7	155.7	418.0	595.0
Jaipur	10.6	14.8	20.9	23.8	251.0	405.0
Kota	16.4	16.9	48.1	48.6	164.0	151.0
Tamil Nadu						
Coimbatore	9.5	15.2	14.3	24.6	141.0	189.0
Chennai	61.3	18.4	41.8	23.4	332.0	201.0
Tuticorin	-	43.6	-	53.4	-	193.0

XX Suspended particulate matter in some Indian Cities

(In µg/cum)

City concentration	Annual mean concentration	Annual maximum
Indian standard	140.0	200.0
Surat	412.0	712.0
Patna	408.6	1,229.0
Jharia	408.0	892.0
Faridabad	405.0	548.0
Kanpur	392.4	1,385.0
Agra	391.9	1,222.0
Ankleshwar	384.2	1,198.0
Delhi	339.3	1,055.0
Alwar	338.5	1,237.0
Howrah	325.3	886.0
Vapi	321.0	523.0
Guwahati	303.0	523.0
Gobindgarh	286.5	338.0
Anpara	274.5	520.0
Dehra Dun	271.0	691.0
Chandigarh	266.8	1,254.0
Gajraula	62.7	486.0
Jodhpur	260.3	518.0
Bhopal	259.0	399.0
Ghaziabad	257.6	746.0
Ahmedabad	238.5	675.0
Indore	213.3	709.0
Haldia	210.0	591.0
Jaipur	208.9	583.0

References

Agarwal, Madhoolika, 1985. Plant factors as indicators of SO_2 and O_3 pollutants. *In : Biological Monitoring of the State of the Environment (Bioindicators)*. Indian National Science Academy, New Delhi. pp. 225-231.

Agarwal, M. and Agarwal, S.B. 1992. Use of plants in air pollution monitoring. *In : Environmental Issues and Programmes in India*

Agarwal, S.B. and Agarwal, M. 1988. Relative susceptibility of certain tree plants to gaseous ammonia. *Poll. Res.*, 7(1-2): 1-7.

Ahmad, K.J. 1982. Survey of Indian flora in relation to atmospheric pollution. AICCP 7-3C Report.

Ahmad, K.J. and Yunus, M. 1985. Leaf surface characteristics as indicators of air pollution. Symp. Biomoni. State Environ. 254- 257.

Akland, G.G., de Koing, H., Mage, D.T. and Ozolins, G.1992. In: (Dunnette, D.A., O.Brien R.J., eds.). The Science of Global Change: The impact of human activities on the environment. Washington D.C., American Chemical Society (ACS Symposium Series No.483) 162-184.

American Society for Testing and Materials, 1962. ASTM Standards on Methods of Atmospheric Sampling Analysis. Philadelphia, Pa. APHA, 1977. Methods of Air Sampling and Analysis. American Public Health Association, Washington DC.

Ashar, N.G. 1985. Air pollution control Act and its impact on Indian chemical industry in the eighties. Chemical Age of India , 36(2): 1992-210.

Ashenden, T. W .and Mansfield, T .A. 1977. Influence of wind speed on the sensitivity of ryegrass to SO_2 *J. Exp. Bot.*, 281: 729-735.

ASTM. 1971. Standards of Methods for the Sampling and Analysis of Atmospheres. Part 23. American Society for Testing and Materials.

Ayazloo, M., Bell, J.N .B. and Read, S.C. 1980. Modification of chronic sulphur dioxide injury to *Lolium perenne* L. by different sulphur and nitrogen nutrient treatments. *Environ. Pollut.* 22: 295-307.

Babich. H. and Stotzky, G. 1978. Air Pollution and Microbial Ecology. CRC Crit Rev. Environmental Control. 4: 353-421.

Banerjee, A.K., Boralkar, D.B. and Chaphekar, S.B. 1980. A closed chamber for exposing plants to air pollutants. *Indian J. Air Pollution Control.* 3(1): 23-26.

Banerjee, A., Sarkar, P.K. and Mukherjee, S. 1983. Reduction in soluble protein and chlorophyll contents in a few plants as indicators of automobile exhaust pollution. *Int. Jr. of Environ. Studies.* 20: 239-243.

Barkman, J.J. 1963. De epifytenflora en-vegetate van mideen-Limburg (Belgie) *Verh. Kon. Wed.. A Kad. WetenschAft. Natunrk, Tweede Sect.,* 54: 1-46.

Barkman, J.J. 1968. The influence of air pollution on bryophytes and lichens. In: *Air Pollution,* Proc. 1st European Congress on the influence of air pollution on plants and animals, Wageninger, April 22-27.

Beg, M. W. 1980. Vegetation and environmental monitoring. *Ind. J. Air Pollution Control.* 3:31-40.

Bennett, J.H. and Hill, A.C. 1973. Inhibition of apparent photosynthesis by air pollutants. *J. Environ. Qual.* 2: 526-530.

Beschel, R. 1958. Flechtenvriene der stadte standflachten und irh washtum Ber Naturwiss. *Med Ver Innusbruck.,* 52: 1-158.

Bhiravamurthy, P.V. and Kumar. P.V. ·1983. Air pollution and epidermal traits of *Calotropis gigantea* (L.) R.Br., *Indian J. Air Pollut. Control.* I : 23-26.

Bhiravemurthy, P. V. Kumar, P. V. Rethy, P. and Anuradha, Y. V., 1985. Foliar traits as indicators of air pollution in *Cassia tora* L. and *Pergularia daemia* (Forsk.) Balatt & McC. In : *Biological Monitoring of the State of the Enviromnent (Bioindicators).* Indian National Science Academy, New Delhi, p.p. 249-253.

Bidwell, R.R.S;. and Fraser, D.E. 1972. *Can. J. Bot.* 50: 1435- 1439.

Billings, C.E. 1974. Technological sources of air pollution. In: (N. lrving Sax, ed.) *Industrial Pollution*, Van Nostrand Reinhold Company, New York.

Boralkar, D.B. and Chaphekar, S.B. 1980. Nature of sensitivity of plant species to sulphur dioxide. (Personal Communication).

Boralkar, D.B. and Mukherjee, V. 1983. Use of Alfalfa plants for the ambient air quality monitoring in the city of Delhi (Meiographed, unpublished).

Bose, A.K., Sinha, I.K. and Singh, B. 1985. Coal utilization and environmental pollulion studies in Jharia coal fields. National Seminar on pollution control and environment management. NEERI, Nagpur.

Bressan, R.A., Lecureux, L., Wilson, L.C. and Filner, P. 1979. Emission of ethelene and ethane by leaf tissue exposed to injurious concentrations of sulfur dioxide or bisulphite ion. *Plant Physiol.* 63: 924-930.

Chaphekar, S.B. 1972. Effects of atmospheric pollutants on plants in Bombay. *J. Bioi. Sci.*, 15: 1-6.

Chaphekar, S.B. 1982. Air pollution and plants. *Indian Rev. Life Sciences.* 2 : 41-46.

Chaphekar, S.B., Boralkar, D.B. and Shetye, R.P. 1980. Plants for air monitoring in industrial areas. *Trop. Ecol. Develop.* 669-675.

Chaphekar, S.B., Boralkar, D.B. and Shetey, R.P. 1980. Effects of industrial pollution on plants. Final report of UGC sponsored project.

Chaphekar, S.B., Ratna Kumar, M. and Bhavani Shankar, V. 1985. Biomonitoring of industrial air pollution with plants. In: *Biological Monitoring of the State of the Enviromnent (Bioindicators)*. Indian National Science Academy, New Delhi. pp.258-263.

Choudhary, C.S. and Rao. D.N. 1977. Study of some factors in plants controlling their sucsceptibility to SO_2 pollution. Proc. Nat. Sc. Acad. 46B: 236-241.

Clements, F.E. 1920. Planl indicators. Carnegie Inst. Washington. Dancer, W.S., Paterson, L.A. and Chesters, G. 1973. Soil Sci. Soc. America Proc., 67p.

Das T .M. 1981. Plants and pollution, Presidential address in section of agricultural sciences. Indian Sc. Cong. Assoc. Meeting, B.H.U., Varanasi.

Das, T.M., Bhaumic, A., Ghosh, A., and Chakraborty, A. 1981. Trees as dust filters. *Science Today*. 19: 19-21.

DeSloover, J. and LeBlanc, F. 1968. Mapping of atmospheric pollution on the basis of lichen sensitivity In: (Mishra, R. and Gopal, B., ed.) *Proc. Symp. Rec. Adv. Trop. Ecol. Int. Soc. Trop. Ecol.*'Varanasi, pp. 42-56.

Dewit, T. 1983. Lichens as indicators for air quality. *Environ. Monit. & Asses.* 3:273-282.

DOE Working Group Report. 1986. Envirorunental guidelines for siting of industry. *Encology*, 1(7): 12-17.

Dopp. W. 1934. Uber die wirkung der schwefligen sure auf Blutenorgane, Ber Deut. *Bot. Ges.*, 49: 173-221.

Dubey, P.S. and Shevade, A. 1982. SO_2 stress and germination of fungal spores. *Sci. & Cult.* 48(12) : 443-444.

Dubey, P.S. 1983. Additive toxicity of SO_2 and herbicides, a new air pollution problem. In: *Proceedings of the symposium on air pollution control.* New Delhi, Indian Assoc. for Air Pollution Control.

Dugger, W.M., Koukol, J. and Palmer, R.L. 1966. *J. Air Pollut. Control Assoc.*, 16: 467-471.

Dugger, W.M. Jr., Taylor,O.C., Thompson, C.R. and Cardiff, E. 1963. The effect of light on predisposing plants to ozone and plant damage. *J. Air Pollut. Contr. Assoc.* 13: 423-428.

Duprey, R.L. 1968. *Compilation of Air Pollutant Emission Factors*. US.P.H.S. Publ. No.999 AP-42, NCAPC, Durham, North Carolina.

EPA. 1971. Standards of performance for new stationary sources, Notice of proposed rule making. *Federal Register*. Vol. 36: No. 159, pp. 15704-15722.

Feder, W.A. 1968. *Science*. 160: 1122.

Floor, H. and Posthumus, A.C. 1977. Bilogische Erfassurg Von oon and PAN imissionen in den Niederlanden. 1973, 1974 and J975. VDT-Berichte. 270 : 183-190.

Gajendragadkar, S.K. 1982. Personal Communication.

Garg, K.K. and Varshney, C.K. 1980. Effect of air pollution on leaf epidermis at the submicroscopic level. *Experientia*. 36:1364-1366.

Gilbert, O.L. 1968a. *Biological Indicators of Air Pollution*. Ph.D. Thesis, Univ. of Newcastle-upon-Tyne.

Gilbert, O.L. 1968b. Bryophytes as indicators of air pollution in Tyne Valley. *New Phytol.*, 67 : 15.

Guderian, R. 1977. Air Pollution: Phytotoxicity of acidic gases and its significance in air pollution control. *Ecological Studies*, Vol.22. Springer-Verlag, Berlin. pp. 122.

Halbwachs, G. 1984. Organismal responses of higher plants to atmospheric pollutants: Sulphur dioxide and fluroide In: (Treshow, M., ed.) *Air Pollution* and *Plant Life*. JohnWiley & Sons Ltd. pp.175-214.

Hansen, G.P. and Stewart, W.S. 1970. *Science*, 168: 1223-1224.

Heck, W.W. 1968. Effects of oxidant air pollutants. *J. Occupational Med.* 10 : 485-499.

Hill, A.C. 1971. Vegetation: A sink for atmospheric pollutants. *Journal of the Air Pollution Control Association.*, 21: 341-346.

Holl, W. and Hampp, R. 1975. *Lead and Plants Residue Reviews*. 54- 79.

Horsman, D.C. and Wellburn,A.R. 1975. Synergistic effect of SO_2 and NO_2 pclluted air upon ezyme activity in pea seedlings. *Environ. Pollut.* (Ser.A.) 8 : 123-133.

Houston, D.B. and Dochinger, L.S. 1977. Effects of ambient air pollution on cone, seed and pollen characteristics in eastern white and red pine. *Environ. Pollut.* 12: 1-5.

Hutchinson, G.L., Millington, R.J. and Peters, D.B. 1972. *Science*, 175: 771.

Jacobs, M.B. 1967. *The Analytical Toxicology of Industrial Inorganic Poisons*. John Wiley, New York & London.

Jafri, S., Srivastava, K. and Ahmed, K.J. 1979. Environmental pollution and epidermal structure in *Syzygium cuminii* (L.). Skeel., *Indian J. Air Pollut. Control*, 2 : 74-77.

Jager, H.J. Pahlich, E. and Steubing, L. 1972. Effect of sulphur dioxide on amino acid and protein content of pea seedlings. *Angew. Bot.*, 46: 199-211.

Kandler, U. and Ullrich, H. 1964. *Natuwissenschaften*, 51: 518.

Karnosky, D.F. and Stairs, G.R. 1974. The effect of SO_2 on *in vitro* forest tree pollen germination and tube elongation. *J. Environ. Qual.*, 3: 406-409.

Katz, M. 1969. *Measurements of Air Pollutants-Guide to the Selection of Methods*. World Health Organization, Geneva.

Kenline, P.A. and Hales, J.M. 1964. *Air Pollution in the Kraft Pupling Industry*. US P.H.S. Publ. No. 999-AP-4, NCAPC Cincinnati, Ohio.

Koukol, J. and Dugger, W.M. Jr. 1967. Anthocyanin formation as a response to ozone and smog treatment in *Rumex crispus*, L. *Plant Physiol.*, 42: 1023-1024.

Kulkarni V.S., Kaul, S.N. and R.K. Trivedy. 2002. A Handbook of Environment Impact Assessment. Scientific Publishers, Jodhpur.

Kulshreshtha, K., Yunus, M., Dwivedi, A.K. and Ahmad, K.J. 1980. Effect of air pollution on the epidermal traits of *Jasminum sambac*. *New Botanist*, 7: 193-197.

Kumar, S. 1982. Indian Coals-Resources, deposits, production, properties and utilization. *Chemical Age of India*, 33(12):683-694.

Kumar, S. 1984. Atmospheric emission from Coal-fired power plants in India. *Indian J. Environ. Protec.*, Vol. 4.

Kumar, Naresh and Singh, V. 1987. Effects of SO_2 and NO_2 pollution on flowering yield and carbonhydrate contents of *Vigna radiata* C. V. PS-16., *Poll. Res.* 6(3-4): 123-125.

Le Blanc, F. and DeSloover. J. 1970. Relation between industrialization and the distribution and growth of air pollutants on lichens and mosses in Montreal. *Can J. Bot.* 48: 1485-1496.

Le Blanc. F. and Rao.. D.N. 1975. Effects of air pollutants on lichens and bryophytes. In: J.B. Mudd & T.T.K. Kozlowski (ed.) *Response of plants to air pollution*. Academic Press. New York.

Le Blanc. F., Robitaille, G. and Rao. D.N. 1976. Ecophysiological response on lichens transplants to air pollution in the Murdochville Gaspe coper mine area. *Quebec Jour. Haltori. Bot. Lab.* 40 : 27-40.

Liptak. B.C. 1974. *Environmental Engineers, Hand Book: Vol. II - Air Pollution*. Chilton Book Company, Radnor, Pennsylvania.

Little, P. 1973. *Environ. Pollut.* 5: 159.

Little, P. and Martin. M.H. 1974. *Environ. Pollut.* 6: 1.

Lynn, D.A. 1976. *Air Pollution-Threat and Response*. Addison-Wesley Publishing Company, Inc.

Ma T.H. and Khan. S.H. 1976. Pollen mitosis and pollen tube growth inhibtion by SO_2 in cultured pollen tubes of *Tradescantia, Environ. Res.* 12: 144-149.

Maas. F.M. 1976. Town and country planning. In : *Manual on Urban Air Quality Management*. WHO Regional office for Europe. Copenhangen.

Malhotra. S.S. 1977. Effects of aqueous sulphur dioxide on chlorophyll destruction in *Pinus contorta, New Phytol.* 78: 101-109.

Manning. W.J. and Feder, W.A.1976. Effects of ozone on economic plants. In: (Mansfield. T.A.. ed.) *Effects of Air Pollutants on Plants*. Cambridge Univ. Press. Cambridge.

Mansfield. T.A. 1976. *Effects of Air Pollutants on Plants*. Cambridge Univ. Press.. Cambridge.

Mansfield. T.A. and Feder-Smith. P.H. 1981. Effects of urban air pollution on plant growth. *Bioi. Rev.*, 56: 343-368.

Matsumoto, H.. Wakiuchi. N. and Takahashi. E. 1971. *Physiol. Plant.*, 25 : 353-357.

Meenakshi. V.. Mahadevan, T.N. and Zutshi, P.K. 1981. *Environ. Sci.* Technol.. 15: 358.

Mell. C. 1956. *Paint Technol.* 20: 135.

Miller, J.E. Koeppe. D.E. and Miller. R.J. 1975. Effects of anion on swelling. respiration and phosphorylation of isolated com mitochondria. *Physiol. Plant*, 34 : 153-156.

Miller, G.T. Jr. 2004. *Environmental Science*, Thomson Learning Inc., U.S.A.

Mudd. J.B. and Dugger. W.M. 1963. *Arch. Bioclzem. Biophys.* 102: 52-58.

Mudd. J.B., Leavitt. R., Ongun. A. and McManus. T.T. 1969. Reaction of ozone with amino acid and protein. *Atmos. Environ.* 3: 283-288.

Naegele. J.A. 1974. In: Sax N.(ed.) *Industrial Pollution*. Litton Educational Publishing Inc. 1974.

Nandi. P.K., Singh. M. and Rao. D.N. 1980. Effect of ozone, sulphur dioxide and their mixture on organization of *Phaseolus aureus* seeds. *Ind. J. Air Pollu. Contr.* 3: 50-55.

Nandi, P.K. Singh. M. and Rao, D.N. 1981. Potassium ascorbate as an antidote to SO_2 phytotoxicity. *Beitr. Biol. Pflamerns.* 55: 405-407.

NEERI. 1981. *Air Quality Monitoring- A Course Manual*, National Environmental Engineering Research Institute, Nagpur.

NEERI.1992. Annual Report. NEERI, Nagpur.

Nieboer. E., Richardson, D.H.S., Puckett, K.J. and Tomassini, F.D. 1976. The phytotoxicity of sulphur dioxide in relation to measurable responses in lichens. In: (Mansfield, T.A., ed.) *Effects of Air Polultants on Plants*. Cambridge Univ. Press, Cambridge.

Oblisami. G., Padmanabhan, G. and Padhmanabhan, C. 1978. Effect of particulate pollutants from cement kilns on cotton plants. J. Air Pollut. Control. 1: 91-94.

Oden Swante, 1971. Nederbordens forsurning-ett generellt hot mot ekosystemem. In: (Mysterud, I., ed.) *Forurensning Og Biologisk Miljovern*, Oslo Universitets forlaget.

Oliver, B.G., Milne, J.B. and Labbare, N. 1974. *J. Water Poll. Control Fed.* 46: 766.

Ordin, L. and Hall, M.A. 1967. *Plant Physiol.*, 42: 205-212.

Ordin, L. and Skoe, B.P. 1964. *Plant Physiol.*, 39: 751-755.

Pahlich, E. 1975. Effects of SO_2 poltution on cellular regulation. A general concept of the mode of action of gaseous air contamination. *Atmos. Environ.* 9: 261-263.

Painter, D.E. 1974. *Air Polllition Technology*. Reston Publishing Company, Inc. Reston, Virginia.

Patri Manorama and Naik, B.N. 1994. Effects of air pollution on Man and property. In: R.K. Trivedy (ed.) *Encyclopedia of Environmental Pollution and Control*, Enviro Media, Karad.

Pawar, K. and Dubey, P.S. 1985. Changes in soil microflora due to gaseous pollutants from a rayon industry. *Geobios*. J2:218-220.

Pierre, M. and Queiroz, 0.1981. Enzymic and metabolic changes in bean leaves during continuous pollution by subnecrotic levels of SO_2. *Environ. Pollut.*, 25 : 41-51.

Pippen, E.L., Potter, A.L. Randall, V.G., Ng. K.G., Rutter, F.W., Margan, A.C. and Oshima, R.J. 1975. Effect of ozone fumigation on crop composition. *J. Food. Sci.*, 40 : 672-676.

Porter, L.K.. Viets, F.G. and Hutchinson., G.L. 1972. *Science*, 175: 759-761.

Posthumus, A.C. 1963. Higher plants as indicators, accumulators of gaseous air pollution. *Environ. Monitor. & Assers.* 3:263-272.

Posthumus, A.C. 1984. Monitoring levels and effects of air pollutants. In: M. Treshow (ed.) *Air Pollution & Plant Life*. John Wiley & Sons Ltd. pp. 73-95.

Posthumus, A.C. 1985. Plants as bioindicators for atmospheric pollution. In: H.W. Numberg (ed.) *Pollutants and their ecotoxicological significance*. John Wiley & Sons Ltd. pp. 55-65.

Rao, D.N. 1972. *Mangifera indica* a bioindicator of pollution in the tropics. Proc. 22nd Int. Geog. Congo Montreal, p.272.

Rao. D.N. and Pal, A.D. 1975. A plant growth chamber for air pollution studies. *Indian J. Environ Hlth.* 17(2): 105-110.

Rao, D.N. 1977. Use of plants as indicators and monitors of SO_2 pollution. *Chemical Age Indica.* 28: 555-571.

Raȯ, D.N. and Pal, D.1979. The effects of fluoride pollution on cattle. pp. 281-290. In: Symposium Volume on Environmental Pollution & Toxicology. Today & Tomorrow, New Delhi.

Rao, D.N., 1981. Phytomonitoring of air pollution. Proc. of the Workshop on Biological Indicators and Indices of Environmental Pollution, Osmania Univ. Hyderabad.

Rao, D.N. 1985. Biomonitoring of air quality. In : *Biological Monitoring of the State of the Environment (Bioindicators)*. Indian National Science Academy, New Delhi pp. 262-263.

Rao, D.N., Nandi, P.K. and Agarwal, M. 1985. Responses of plants to sulphur dioxide air pollution. In : (Trivedy, R.K. and Goel, P.K., eds.) *Current Pollution Researches in India.*, Environmental Publications, Karad, pp. 15-37.

Rao, D.N. and LeBlanc, F. 1966. Effects of SO_2 on the lichen alga with special reference to chlorophyll. *Bryologist*, 69: 69-75.

Rao, D.N. and LeBlanc, F. 1967. Influence of an iron-snitering plant corticolour epiphytes in Wawa, Ontario. *Bryologist*, 70: 141-157.

Rao, D.N. Agarwal, M., Deo Narayan, Singh, J., Khanam, N. and Misra, S. 1987. Industrial air pollutants and their effects on ecosystem structure and function. pp. 14-39. 2nd Tech. Report of DOEn. Sponsored res. Project NO DOen/14/256/MAB/RE.

Rao, D.N., Agarwal, M., Jha, P.C. and Singh, J. 1987. Study of pollution sink efficiency, growth response and productivity patterns of plants with flyash and SO_2 .pp 1-78. 2nd Tech. Report of DOEn Sponsored Research Project No.DOen/14/256/MAB/RE.

Rao, M.N. and Rao, H. V .N. 1989. *Air Pollution*. Tata McGraw Hill Publishing Co. Ltd., New Delhi.

Raviprakash and Naik, B.N. 1988. Effects of emerging precipitation on biological materials at Talchar, Orissa: A case study for developing country. *Poll. Res.*, 7 (1-2): 29-36.

Raza, S.H., Vijaya Kumari, N., Murthy, M.S.R. and Ahmed Adeel. 1985. Air Pollution Tolerance Index of certain plants of Hyderabad. In : *Biological Monitoring of the State of the Environment (Bioindicators)*. Indian National Science Academy, New Delhi. pp.243-245.

Riazanov, U.A. 1965. *Bulletin of the World Health Organisation*, 32: 389.

Saranathan, T.R. 1987. Automobile Pollution-Sources, laws and implementation. *Encology*, 1(12): 32-35.

Saxe, H. 198-3. Long-term effects of low levels of SO_2 on bean plants (*Phaseolus vulgaris*) II. emmission-response effects on biomass production : quantity and quality. *Physiol Plant.* 57: 108-113.

Shantz, H.L. 1911. Natural vegetation as indicator of the capabilities of land for crop production in Greater Plains Are, USDA Bur Pl. Indust. Bull. p. 201.

Shapiro, R., Servis, R.E. and Welcher, M. 1970. Reactions of uracil and cytosine bisulfite. A specific deamination method. *J. Amer. Chem. Soc.*, 92: 422-424.

Sharma, G.K. 1977. Cuticular studies as indicators of environmental pollution. *Water and Soil Polut.*, 8: 15-19.

Sharma, G.K. 1992. *Bougainvillea glabra* L. cuticular response to environmental pollution. *Geobios*, 19: 239-242.

Sharma, G.K. and Butler, J. 1973. Leaf cuticular variations in *Trifolium repens* L. as indicators of environmental pollution. *Environ. Pollut.*, 5: 287-293.

Sharma, G.K. and Butler, J. 1975. Environmental Pollution: leaf cuticular patterns in *Trifolium pratense* L. *Ann. Bot.*, 39: 1087-1090.

Sharma, M.C. and Srivastava, B.N. 1992. Ultraviolet radiation received in Antartica in comparison with the Indian region. *Atmospheric Environment.* 26A (4): 731-734.

Sharma, G.K. and Tyree, J. 1973. Geographic leaf cuticular and gross morphological variations in *Liquidamber styraciflua* L. and their possible relationship to environmental pollution. *Bot. Gaz.*, 134 : 179-184.

Shimazaki, K. and Sugahara, K. 1979. Specific inhibition of photosystem II activity in chloroplasts by fumigation of spinach leaves with SO_2. Plant Cell Physiol., 20: 947-955.

Shimazaki, K., Sakaki, T., Kondo, N. and Sugahara, K. 1980. Active oxygen participation in chlorophyll destruction and lipid peroxidation in SO_2 exposed leaves of spinach. *Plant Cell Physiol.*, 21(7): 1193-1204.

Singh, S.N. and Rao., D.N. 1978. Possibilities of using chlorophyll and potassium contents in plants to detect cement dust pollution. J.I.P.H.E., India 1 : 10-13.

Singh, M. and Rao, D.N. 1982. The influence of ozone and sulphur dioxide on *Cicer arietinum* L. *J. Ind. Bot. Soc.*, 16: 51-58.

Spedding, D.J. 1969. *Nature*, 224: 1229.

Spedding, D.J. 1978. The interaction of gaseous pollutants with materials at the surface of the earth. In: (Bokris, J.OM., ed.) *Environmental Chemistry*. Plenum Press. New York.

Strauss, W. 1977. Formation and Control of Air Pollutants. In : (Bokris, J.O.M., ed.) *Environmental Chemistry*, Plenum Press, New york.

Swain, R.E. 1923. Atmospheric pollulion by industrial wastes. *Ind. Eng.Chem.*, 15: 296-301.

Swaminathan. R. and Sundareshan, B.B. 1980. Auto exhaust emissions in India. WHO/ UNEP BI-Regional Workshop.

Taylor, O.C. and Eaton, F .M. 1966. Suppression of plant growth by nitrogen dioxide. *Plant Physiol.*, 41: 132-135.

Thakre, Rekha. 1994. Green belts for pollution abatement. In: R.K. Trivedy (ed.) *Encyclopedia of Environmental Pollution and Control.* Enviro Media, Karad.

Thomposon, C.R.. Hensel, E.G. and Kats, G. 1973. *J. Air Polutt. Contr. Assn.*, 23: 881.

Ting, I.P. and Mukherji, S.K. 1971. Leaf ontogeny as a factor in susceptibility of ozone : Amino acid and carbohydrale changes during expansion. *Am. J. Bot.*, 58: 497-504.

Tingey, D.T., Files, R.C. and Wickliff, C. 1973. Ozone alteration of nitrate reduclion in soybean. *Plan. Physiol.*, 29: 33-38.

Trivedy, R.K. 1989. Pollution Management in Industries. Environmental Publication, Karad.

Trivedy, R.K. 1984. Encyclopedia of Environmental Pollution and Control. Vol-1&2. Envivo Media, Karad.

Trivedy, R.K. and Raman, N.S. 2002. Industrial Pollution & Environmental Management, Scientific Publishers, Jodhpur.

Trivedy, R.J. 2004. *Handbook of Environmental laws, rules, acts, guidelines, compliances and standards* Vol-1&2. Second revised and updated edition. B.S. Publications, Hyderabad, A.P.

Turner, N.C., Waggoner, P.E. and Rich, S. 1974. *Nature*, 250: 486.

UNEP 1982. Ozonation-a quarterly publication of the organization exclusively dealing on ozone layer protection and dedicated to implementation of the Montreal Prolocol-Various Issues of 1991 & 1992.

Varshney, C.K. 1979. Plant responses to sulphur dioxide poilution. CRC Critical Reviews in Environmental Control, 9: 27-49.

Vershney, S.R.K. and Varshney, C.K. 1981. Effect of sulphur dioxide on pollen germination and pollen tube growth. *Environ. Poll.* Ser A, 24 : 87-92.

Varshney,C.K. 1985. Pollen bioassay of air quality monitoring. In: *Biological Monitoring of the State of the Environment (Bioindicators)*. Indian National Science Academy, New Delhi pp. 246-248.

Varshney, S.R.K. and Varshney, C.K. 1981. Effect of sulphur dioxide on pollen germination and pollen tube growth. *Environ. Pollut.* (Ser.A), 24: 87-92.

Varshney, S.R.K. and Varshney,C.K. 1984. Effect of SO_2 on ascorbic acid of crop plants. *Environ, Pollution*. 35: 285-291.

Varshney, C.K. 1992. Role of plants in indicating, monitoring and mitigating air pollution. pp. 383-400. In: Wahi et al. (ed.) *Environment Management in Petroleum Industry*. Wiley Eastern, New Delhi.

Vannesland, B. and Jetschmann, C. 1971. *Arch. Biochem. Biophys.*, 144 : 248-253.

Vora, A.B. and Bhatnagar, A.R. 1986. Comparative study of dust fall on the leaves in high pollution and low pollution areas of Ahmedabad. IV-Altered proline contents of leaves. *Poll. Res.*, 5(3 -4): 153-157.

Wakiuchi, N., Matsumoto, H. and Takahashi, E. 1971. *Physiol. Plant.*, 24 : 248-253.

Webstr, C.C. 1967. *The effects of air pollution on plant and soil.* Agricultural Research Council, London.

Wilson, M.J.G. 1968. *Proc. Roy. Soc.* A., 300; 215.

Yocom, J.E., Clink, W.L. and Cote, A. 1971. *.J. Air Pollutt Contr. Ass.*, 21: 251.

Yunus, M. and Ahmad, K. J. 1978. Effects of air pollution on some plants. Proc.of International Symposium on Envirorunental Agents and their biological effects, Dept. of Genetics, Osmania Univ., Hyderabad. pp.96-102.

Yunus, M. and Ahmad, K.J. 1979. Use of epidermal traits of plants in pollution monitoring. Proc. of National Seminar on Environmental Pollution and its control. A status review. National Productivity Council, Bombay.

Yunus, M. and Ahmad, K.J. 1980. Effect of air pollution on *Psiduim guajava* L. *Indian J. Air Pollution Control*, 3: 62-66.

Yunus, M., Ahmad, K.J. and Gole, R. 1979. Air Pollutants and epidermal traits in *Ricinus communis* L. *Environ. Pollut.*, 20: 189-198.

Yusuf, M. and Vyas, L.N. 1982. Effect of cement dust pollution on some selected plant species growing around Udaipur Cement Works, Bajaj Nagar, Udaipur. Presented at All India Seminar on Air Pollution, April 1982, Indore.

Zeevaart, A.J. 1976. Some effects of fumigating plants for short periods with NO_2. *Environ. Pollut.* (Ser. A). 11 : 97-108.

Zelitch, I. 1957. a-Hydroxysulfonates as inhibitors of enzymatic oxidation of glycolic and lactic acids. *J. Biol. Chem..* 224: 251-260.

Ziegler, I. and Happm, R. 1977. Control of $^{35}SO_4^{-2}$ and $^{35}SO_3^{-2}$ incorporation in spinach chloroplasts during photosynthetic CO_2 fixation. *Planta,* 137: 303-307.

Zutshi, P.K. and Mahadevan, T.N. 1975. *J. Air Pollut. Control Assoc.* 25: 856.

Index

A

B

C

D

E

F

G

H

M

O

P

R

S